ASSER International Sports Law Series

More information about this series at http://www.springer.com/series/8858

Katarina Pijetlovic

EU Sports Law and Breakaway Leagues in Football

ASSER PRESS

Springer

Katarina Pijetlovic
Helsinki
Finland

ISSN 1874-6926 ISSN 2215-003X (electronic)
ASSER International Sports Law Series
ISBN 978-94-6265-047-3 ISBN 978-94-6265-048-0 (eBook)
DOI 10.1007/978-94-6265-048-0

Library of Congress Control Number: 2014955793

Published by T.M.C. ASSER PRESS, The Hague, The Netherlands www.asserpress.nl
Produced and distributed for T.M.C. ASSER PRESS by Springer-Verlag Berlin Heidelberg

Printed on acid-free paper

Springer Science+Business Media B.V. Dordrecht is part of Springer Science+Business Media
(www.springer.com)

Series Information

Books in the *ASSER International Sports Law Series* comprehensibly chart and analyse legal and policy developments in the emerging field of European and international sports law. Within scholarly publishing, the series is the most cited in its area and uniquely features contributions from the leading sports law scholars. It is a valuable resource for practitioners, academics, sports officials, and anyone interested in or impacted by sports and the law.

The Series is developed, edited and published by the ASSER International Sports Law Centre in The Hague. The Centre's mission is to provide a centre of excellence in particular by providing high-quality research, services and products to the sporting world at large (sports ministries, international—intergovernmental—organisations and federations, the professional sports industry, etc.) on both a national and an international basis. As a pioneer in the field of European and international sports law, the Centre has established a worldwide network of academics and practitioners and co-operation agreements with various sports law institutes and centres in Europe and beyond.

Apart from the Series, the Centre edits and publishes *The International Sports Law Journal.*

Series editors

Dr. David McArdle
e-mail: d.a.mcardle@stir.ac.uk

Prof. Dr. Ben Van Rompuy
e-mail: b.van.rompuy@asser.nl

Marco A. van der Harst, LL.M.
e-mail: m.van.der.harst@asser.nl

Editorial Office

ASSER International Sports Law Centre
T.M.C. Asser Instituut
P.O. Box 30461
2500 GL, The Hague
The Netherlands
www.sportslaw.nl

international sports law centre

For Mum

Preface

I am delighted to be able to contribute the first English-language book on the topic of the treatment of breakaway leagues under EU sports law. The book has been in preparation over a period of several years and there were some longer breaks in the research and in the writing. It was finally completed during this summer and reflects the law as it stood in August 2014.

Each chapter of this book addresses different but connected topics. As the reader moves through the chapters 'the story' progresses and incorporates increasingly complex legal analysis. The first two chapters introduce the subjects of sports law, EU sports law and policy, and the sporting industry with its specificities; the third chapter highlights the tensions and governance issues in European football amid breakaway threats by elite clubs; Chaps. 4 and 5 are the core of EU sports law and include a detailed analysis of the EU internal market and competition law as applied to legal issues in the sporting industry; Chap. 6 categorises sporting exceptions through the prism of convergence between the internal market and competition law and is the most significant contribution of this book to general EU law; and Chap. 7 analyses the legality of UEFA restrictive clauses and the behaviour of elite clubs under EU law. Whereas the first two chapters are suitable for anyone interested in the subject of sports law, the third chapter is of interest to sports lawyers, managers and journalists, and Chaps. 4–7 strongly focus on the legal technical aspects of the case law and are therefore aimed at sports law academics and practitioners.

My intention at all stages was to provide alternative viewpoints and novel perspectives in relation to what has already been said and written. Thus, the readers will find, for example, unique comments on the home-grown rule in the light of the 3 + 2 rule from the *Bosman* case, an original approach to categorising sporting exceptions through converging EU internal market and competition law analytical frameworks, proposals on the treatment of special responsibility of superdominant undertakings under Article 102 TFEU, and details of the 1998 Media Partners proposals which have not been published previously.

I am enormously grateful to those people who have supported and encouraged me during this project—thanks are due to David McArdle, Samuli Miettinen, Geoff Pearson, Ryan Gauthier and, most of all, to Daniel Lovric, who spent many days on a linguistic review of this book without asking a cent in return. Many thanks (hvala!) to my Serbian friend Mateja Sponza for his technical assistance in creating the illustrations that appear in Chaps. 5 and 6.

New York, August 2014 Katarina Pijetlovic

Contents

1 Introduction 1
1.1 The Multidimensional Nature of Sport 2
1.2 Commercialisation and Juridification of the Sports Sector 3
1.2.1 Commercialisation 3
1.2.2 Juridification 5
1.3 Sports Law 5
1.3.1 Definition of Sport and Objectives of Sports Legislation 6
1.3.2 Lex Sportiva 7
1.3.3 Legal Status and Autonomy of the Global Governing Bodies 9
1.3.4 EU Sports Law and Policy 12
1.3.5 Boundaries of Legal Intervention 22
1.4 The Subject Matter of the Volume 24
1.4.1 The Arrangements in European Football Giving Rise to Legal Problem Posed by Breakaway Structures 24
1.4.2 Description of Chapters 1–7 26
References 29

2 The Sporting Industry 31
2.1 Specificities/Special Characteristics of the Sporting Industry 31
2.1.1 Preliminary Remark on Phraseology 31
2.1.2 The Concept of Specificity of Sport in EU Law and Policy 32
2.1.3 Special Characteristics of Sport 34
2.2 Structural Models of Sport 36
2.2.1 Classic European Model of Sport 36
2.2.2 US Model of Sport 38
2.2.3 Changing Characteristics of European Football 40

2.3 Financing of Sport . . . 42
2.3.1 Macroeconomic Aspects. . . . 42
2.3.2 Microeconomic Aspects . . . 43
References . . . 45

3 Breakaway Leagues and Governance Issues in European Football . . . 47
3.1 Introduction . . . 48
3.1.1 Concept of Breakaway/Alternative League . . . 48
3.2 European Structural Ideals . . . 49
3.2.1 Rhetoric in the EU Policy Instruments. . . . 49
3.2.2 Sports Associations and Other Stakeholders in Football . . . 52
3.3 Breakaway Threats and UEFA/FIFA Concessions. . . . 53
3.3.1 Rules on Alternative Competitions in the UEFA Statutes . . . 54
3.3.2 Media Partners Proposal: European Football League . . . 55
3.3.3 UEFA Concessions in the 1998 Media Partners Case . . . 59
3.3.4 Formation of the G14 Alliance. . . . 61
3.3.5 Plans for 'European Golden Cup' in 2003? . . . 62
3.3.6 UEFA Concessions on Compulsory Player Release Rule, the *Oulmers* Case and Formal Dissolution of G14 . . . 62
3.3.7 July 2011: New Breakaway Threats, Old Strategies of Old Allies . . . 68
3.3.8 Alternative Leagues in European Football. . . . 70
3.4 New Trends in the Governance of European Football . . . 74
3.4.1 Stakeholder Theory . . . 74
3.4.2 UEFA Mandate. . . . 76
3.4.3 European Club Association: A New Face of G14 . . . 77
3.4.4 Professional Football Strategy Council . . . 79
3.4.5 The UEFA Club Competitions Committee . . . 81
3.4.6 Social Dialogue and Collective Agreements in Professional Football . . . 81
3.4.7 UEFA Club Licensing and Financial Fair Play Regulations. . . . 88
3.5 Risks in the Commercial and Legal Environment . . . 92
3.6 Is the UEFA Champions League an Open Competition?. . . . 94
3.7 Conclusion . . . 96
References. . . . 97

4 EU Internal Market Law and Sport . . . 99
4.1 Introduction to the General Principles and Analytical Framework . . . 101
4.2 Case 36/74 *Walrave* and *Koch* [1974] . . . 102
4.3 Case 13/76 *Donà* [1976]. . . . 103

4.4 Case C-415/93 *Bosman* [1995]. 104
4.4.1 Factual Background 104
4.4.2 The Judgment of the Court. 105
4.4.3 Comment 108
4.5 Joined Cases C-51/96 and C-191/97 *Deliège* [2000]. 118
4.6 Case C-176/96 *Lehtonen* [2000]. 120
4.7 Case C-438/00 *Kolpak* [2003], Case C-265/03 *Simutenkov* [2005], and Case C-152/08 *Kahveci* [2008] 121
4.8 Case C-325/08 *Bernard* [2010] 123
4.8.1 Facts of the Case. 123
4.8.2 Analytical Overview of the Judgment 124
4.9 Cases T-385/07, T-55/08 and T-68/08 *FIFA and UEFA v Commission* [2011] 134
4.10 Joined Cases C-403/08 and C-429/08 *Murphy* [2011]. 136
4.10.1 Facts of the Case 136
4.10.2 Analytical Overview of the Judgment 137
References. 147

5 EU Competition Law and Sport 149
5.1 Article 101 TFEU. 150
5.1.1 Prohibition Provision: Article 101(1) TFEU 150
5.1.2 Exemption Provision: Article 101(3) TFEU. 154
5.1.3 Nullity Provision: Article 101(2) 157
5.1.4 Commercialisation Agreements 157
5.2 Article 102 TFEU. 158
5.2.1 Definition of Relevant Market 158
5.2.2 Establishing Dominance. 159
5.2.3 Abuse of Dominant Position 160
5.2.4 Objective Justification and the Efficiency Defence 161
5.3 Oligopolistic Market Structures and the Concept of Collective Dominance 162
5.3.1 The Oligopoly Problem 162
5.3.2 Collective Dominance 163
5.4 Simultaneous Application of Articles 101 and 102 TFEU. 167
5.5 Articles 101 and 102 TFEU in the Sporting Context. 168
5.5.1 Basic Elements. 168
5.5.2 Relevant Market. 170
5.5.3 Collective Dominance 172
5.5.4 Analytical Framework for Commercial Rules in Sport 173
5.5.5 Analytical Framework for Regulatory Rules: C-519/04 *Meca-Medina* [2006] 179
5.6 Blocking Competing Organisations. 187
5.6.1 C-49/07 *MOTOE* [2008]. 187
5.6.2 Commission Investigation in *FIA/Formula One* Case 196
5.6.3 Case C-250/92 *DLG* [1994]. 199

5.7 Superdominance and Special Responsibility 202
5.7.1 The Concept of Superdominance 203
5.7.2 Special Responsibility of Dominant Undertakings: The Sliding Scale Approach 206
5.7.3 The Content of Special Responsibility of Superdominant Sports Undertakings 208
5.8 Conclusion 211
References 212

6 A Quest for Convergence in the Application of EU Internal Market and Competition Law to Sport 215
6.1 Introduction 215
6.2 Addressees 216
6.3 Prohibition Level Convergence—Categories I, II and III of Sporting Exception. 217
6.3.1 Sporting Rules That Do not Produce Any Economic Effect 218
6.3.2 'Purely Sporting' Rules 218
6.3.3 Inherent Rules. 224
6.4 Justification Level Convergence—Category IV Sporting Exception 228
6.5 Burden of Proof 233
References 235

7 Treatment of UEFA Restrictions on Breakaway Leagues in Football Under EU Law 237
7.1 Introduction 237
7.2 The Conflict 239
7.3 Defining the Relevant Market. 240
7.3.1 The Market for Organisational Services for Transnational Club Football in Europe. 241
7.3.2 Connected Downstream Market: Exploitation Market. 244
7.3.3 Connected Upstream Market: The Market for Clubs' Services 246
7.3.4 Relevant Geographic Market 247
7.4 Classification of the Parties and the Restraints 248
7.4.1 Undertaking or Association of Undertakings/Agreement or Decision? 248
7.4.2 Market Power of UEFA on the Relevant Market 253
7.4.3 Article 49 of the UEFA Statutes: Restrictive Effects 259
7.5 Applicable Justification Framework. 267
7.6 The Existence of Elements of Justification 268
7.6.1 The Overall Context: Legitimate Aims in Public Interest . . . 269
7.6.2 Suitability of the Article 49 Rule: Effectiveness Test. 272

7.6.3 Inherency Requirement ... 278
7.6.4 Proportionality ... 281
7.7 Effect on Intra-Union Trade ... 301
7.8 The Conditions of Article 101(3) TEFU ... 302
7.9 Collective Dominance and Collusion by Elite Clubs ... 303
7.10 Concluding Remarks ... 308
References ... 309

Table of Cases ... 311

Table of Legislative Acts ... 319

Index ... 325

Abbreviations and Acronyms

AVMS	Audio Visual Media Services
BSkyB	British Sky Broadcasting
CAD	Conditional Access Directive
CAS	Court of Arbitration for Sport
CCC	UEFA Club Competitions Committee
CJEU	Court of Justice of the European Union
CLFFP	Club Licensing and Financial Fair Play Regulations
CSR	Corporate Social Responsibility
DG	Directorate General
ECA	European Club Association
ECF	European Club Forum
EFL	European Football League
ENIC	English National Investment Company
EPFL	European Professional Football Leagues Association
FAPL	Football Association Premier League
FC	Football Club
FFP	Financial Fair Play
FIA	Fédération Internationale d'Automobile
FIBA	International Basketball Federation
FIFA	Fédération Internationale de Football Association
FIFPro	Federation Internationale Des Associations De Footballeurs Professionnels
FIGC	Federazione Italiana Giuoco Calcio (Italian Football Federation)
G14	Group of 18 Wealthiest Football Clubs in Europe
IOC	International Olympic Committee
MLB	Major League Baseball
MPI	Media Partners International Ltd.
NBA	National Basketball Association
NFL	National Football League
NHL	National Hockey League

PFSC	Professional Football Strategy Council
SSNIP	Small but Significant Non-transitory Increase in Price
TEU	Treaty on European Union
TFEU	The Treaty on the Functioning of the European Union
UEFA	Union des Associations Européennes de Football

Chapter 1
Introduction

In this year 1894 and in this city of Paris, whose joys and anxieties the world shares so closely that it has been linked to the world's nerve centre, we were able to bring together the representatives of international athletics, who voted unanimously (so little controversial is the principle concerned) for the restoration of a two-thousand-year-old idea which today as in the past still quickens the human heart for it satisfies one of the most vital, and whatever may have been said on the subject, one of its most noble instincts. In the temple of science these delegates heard echo in their ears a melody also 2000 years old, reconstituted by an eminent archaeologist through the successive labours of several generations. And in the evening electricity transmitted everywhere the news that Hellenic Olympism has re-entered the world after an eclipse of several centuries.

Contents

1.1 The Multidimensional Nature of Sport 2
1.2 Commercialisation and Juridification of the Sports Sector 3
1.2.1 Commercialisation 3
1.2.2 Juridification 5
1.3 Sports Law 5
1.3.1 Definition of Sport and Objectives of Sports Legislation 6
1.3.2 Lex Sportiva 7
1.3.3 Legal Status and Autonomy of the Global Governing Bodies 9
1.3.4 EU Sports Law and Policy 12
1.3.5 Boundaries of Legal Intervention 22

Speech by Pierre de Frédy, Baron de Coubertin at Paris Congress held at the Sorbonne on 16–23 June 1894, when International Olympic Committee was established.

K. Pijetlovic, *EU Sports Law and Breakaway Leagues in Football*,
ASSER International Sports Law Series, DOI 10.1007/978-94-6265-048-0_1

1.4 The Subject Matter of the Volume 24
1.4.1 The Arrangements in European Football Giving Rise to Legal Problem Posed by Breakaway Structures 24
1.4.2 Description of Chapters 1–7 26
References 29

1.1 The Multidimensional Nature of Sport

Sport is a global phenomenon that performs many important functions in contemporary society. It is most often mentioned in its positive role as a tool contributing towards education of children and young adults, a means of social integration and overcoming cultural differences, a major source of employment in modern society, and a vehicle towards better mental and physical health. In addition, in its socio-cultural dimension, sport is a part of the popular culture that entertains billions of people worldwide. Many people identify with their local or national team, follow their games 'religiously' and derive a sense of pride if their team wins. This effect that sport has on masses and its immense cultural importance has made it a most valuable content for broadcasters, as well as a target for political propaganda.[1]

Sporting activity crosses a wide range of legal subjects such as contract law, tort law, intellectual property law, competition law, constitutional law, labour law, internal market law and fundamental rights. It involves everyone (people of all ages, genders, races, etc.) at all levels (beginners, recreationists, amateurs, semi-professionals and professionals) and in all capacities (spectators and television viewers, players, coaches, medical doctors, psychologists, agents, etc.). There are more than 800,000 sport clubs with more than 70 million members, while as many as 271 million people engage in some form of sport activity in the European Union. Football alone has 23 million registered male and female players, in addition to 350,000 referees, with many more millions playing informally.[2] Tennis involves 75 million participants worldwide,[3] 24 million of whom are registered in

[1] See Halgreen 2004, pp. 19–23. The decision of the International Olympic Committee to award the 2008 Olympic Games to China was not well-received in the world and some saw it as an opportunity for China to cover up its poor human rights record and maintain a totalitarian regime. Throughout history, there have been boycotts of the Olympics because of the country in which it was held, and also exclusion from participation by national teams from countries that were under international sanctions. Some authors note that using sport as a political tool was vital in the fight against apartheid in South Africa. Gardiner and Felix 1995, pp. 189–220.

[2] Independent European Sport Review (2006) hereinafter referred to as 'Arnaut Report'.

[3] Pluim et al. 2007, pp. 703–704.

Europe[4] making it the most popular individual sport on the continent. The cumulative audience of the 64 matches of the 2010 *Fédération Internationale de Football Association* (FIFA) World Cup was expected to be in excess of 26 billion (i.e., around four times the world's population) and was subsequently reported to reach those figures by the news networks.[5] These figures emphasise the scale and the social importance of sports.

Many amateur clubs survive only thanks to the sponsorship from local businesses, while many sports clubs and governing bodies are, both in essence and in legal form, not much more than commercial entities.

1.2 Commercialisation and Juridification of the Sports Sector

1.2.1 Commercialisation

Much like in terms of the described socio-cultural impact, professional sport has become equally comprehensive in its scope on a commercial level. In the 1990s, changes in the structure of the demand for sports broadcasting took place resulting in the transformation of the sports industry. Namely, the broadcasting sector used to be characterised by the presence of only a few players on the market. In the 1980s there were only four commercial TV operators in all of Europe.[6] The de-cartelisation of the broadcasting sector and the emergence of an increasing number of operators, coupled with advancements in mass media technology, have brought about fierce competition for the broadcasting rights of sports events, which caused their value to skyrocket.[7]

For example, when the live transmission of English football league matches began in 1983 the BBC and ITV duopoly acted collusively in order to purchase the rights to two seasons at a deflated value of £5.3 million.[8] In comparison, the UK domestic auction for the 2007–2010 broadcasting rights for the matches of the English Premier League is valued at £1.7 billion, £1.3 billion of which were paid by British Sky Broadcasting (BskyB) for its four packages of games,[9] whereas the 2013–2016 seasons cost domestic broadcasters a total of over £3 billion. In the 2013–2016 seasons, as compared to 2010–2013, overseas markets have seen an increase in value of 12,400 % in Burma, 432 % in Thailand and 273 % in the USA, helping the Premier League to earn a record £2 billion on overseas

---

4 See Advantage by Tennis Europe at http://www.tenniseurope.org/file_download.aspx?id=28613.

5 '26 Billion People Watching the World Cup. True?' by Pamela Falk, CBS News, June 14 2010.

6 Collins 1994, p. 146.

7 For more about broadcasting see Sect. 5.5.4.

8 Massey 2007, p. 88.

9 'Premiership in New £625 m TV Deal' BBC News, 18 January 2008.

broadcasting deals.[10] Similarly, the acquisition of rights to the 1990, 1994 and 1998 Football World Cup cost the European Broadcasting Union cartel US$240 million. The contract for the same event for 2002, 2006 and 2010 saw a 900 % increase in the value of the rights, which were purchased at a cost of US$2.36 billion by the Kirch Group.[11]

The more exposure the sport events had in the media, the more interest and value it also had for the sponsors. Sports sponsorship and endorsement contracts with star players are seen as a prestigious and effective means of advertisement for products and services. According to the European Sponsoring Association (ESA), 91 % of all the sponsorship deals in 2005 went into sports. The value of world sponsorship rights rose by US$25 billion between 1990 and 2000. In Formula One motor racing this means that the 1.9 billion-person cumulative worldwide audience that follows the 17 or 18 annual Formula One (F1) races will be exposed to 100 sponsorship logos.[12] Sponsorship brought EUR 664 million to 11 F1 teams in 2006 and big car manufacturers invested over a billion euros into their six teams.[13] In 2004, sport generated EUR 407 billion accounting for 3.7 % of EU GDP, and employed about 15 million people, or 5.4 % of the labour force.[14] Consumer spending has significantly increased, and millions of new jobs in the European Union (EU) have been created directly or indirectly by the sports industry.[15]

Players have also been major beneficiaries in this changing landscape of the sports business. According to Forbes, Tiger Woods has earned US$1 billion in prize money during his career so far, making him the richest player in the history of sports, while Michael Jordan and Michael Schumacher earned US$800 million and US$700 million during their careers respectively.[16] Many football players in the English Premier League earn wages of £100,000 per week (and some earn even more), with similar salaries paid to their continental counterparts.[17]

There are many other actors whose business includes strong ties with sporting industry, such as travel agencies that profit from packet arrangements for certain sporting events (notably, the Olympics and FIFA World Cup), while newspapers and magazines often sell on the basis of their sport content and exclusive interviews with sportspeople.

[10] See '£5.5bn: The Staggering Sum TV Companies Around the World Will Pay to Screen Premier League' by Nick Harris, Daily Mail, 24 November 2012.

[11] Hoehn and Lancefield 2003, p. 555.

[12] Cygan 2007, p. 75.

[13] Ibid.

[14] European Commission White Paper on Sport, COM (2007) 391 final, Chap. 3.

[15] Mario Monti, European Commissioner for Competition. 'Sport and Competition' Speech/00/152 at a conference organised by the European Commission, Brussels 17 April 2000.

[16] Source: 'Report: Tiger Richest Athlete in History', ESPN, 2 October 2009.

[17] Contrast this with a narration in a film based on true events about football in 1930s: 'Football was still young. Back then, it was not the rich people running on the pitch while the poor people were watching—it was the other way around'. *Montevideo* at 07:13.

1.2.2 Juridification

The described increase in commercialization of the sports industry was followed by *juridification*. With regard to traditional sport as an autonomous social field, this term is used to describe the process by which sport leaves the safe zone of internal self-regulation and becomes a subject of legal control. Under such a process 'what were intrinsically social relationships between humans within a "social field" become imbued with legal values and are understood as constituting legal relationships—thus social norms become legal norms.'[18] Foster saw this concept as merely reproducing the traditional idea of private and public realms, with private areas increasingly becoming subject to public or judicial control.[19] Indeed, the process of juridification took place in many other social fields (notably, labour law) and the concept has been in use for decades. Depending on the field regulated and degree of legal control, it is possible to attach a negative meaning to it such as excessive control of social relationships, overregulation, 'legal pollution',[20] or a positive meaning embodying the benefits and beneficiaries of legal control within the regulated field. In its neutral form it connotes the simple idea of legal control of self-regulation.

In the EU, the rules of sporting organisations regulating, for example, players' contracts and transfers, training compensation fees, the profession of coaches and agents, or eligibility for participation in certain matches and competitions, may fall under the scrutiny of internal market and competition laws. The most extreme example is the examination of the International Olympic Committee (IOC) anti-doping rules under the provisions of EU competition law before the EU Courts.[21] The sport sector caught the attention of the EU legal regulators, *inter alia*, by the ability of the industry to profoundly affect the competition in and structure of the downstream markets (for example the broadcasting market and ticketing market), and to affect the commercial interests of clubs and professional careers of athletes, and ultimately, the welfare of consumers. Hence, regulation and governance of sport, which in the past exclusively belonged to the sport governing bodies' sphere of competence, have become judiciable.

1.3 Sports Law

There is no other area of law that is as diverse as sports law. The nature of this activity requires a corresponding, all-comprehensive but well-balanced regulatory approach covering amateurs and professionals, health and safety, doping and ethics,

---

[18] For more detailed explanation of the concept see Gardiner et al. 2007, pp. 84–88.

[19] Foster 1993, p. 108.

[20] See Teubner and Bremen 1987, pp. 3–6.

[21] Case T-313/02 *David Meca-Medina and Igor Majcen v Commission* [2004] ECR II-3291 and Case C-519/04 *David Meca-Medina and Igor Majcen v Commission* [2006] ECR I-6991.

broadcasters and spectators, licencing, and financial accountability, to mention a few topics. This section will discuss the bodies, the legal and quasi-legal instruments regulating these issues, and the very sensitive and crucial issue of 'distribution of competences' between international sporting organisations and the European institutions. But first it is important to look at some basic concepts and the ideas behind them.

1.3.1 Definition of Sport and Objectives of Sports Legislation

Everyone knows what sport is. But defining sport presents an analogous predicament to the one Hart described when, in his attempts to explain difficulty in defining the concept of law, he said: 'I can recognize an *elephant* when I see one but I cannot define it'.[22] As observed by Soek there is no homogeneous approach to the concept of sport whatsoever and there are only definitions determined by the objective of sport, the capacity in which sport is played, or the social function of sport.[23]

Indeed, various jurisdictions, organisations and academics provide very diverse definitions.

The European Sports Charter of the Council of Europe defines sport as follows: 'Sport means all forms of physical activity which, through casual or organised participation, aim at expressing or improving physical fitness and mental well-being, forming social relationships or obtaining results in competition at all levels.'[24]

Quite a different take is provided by a North American commentator, Malloy, who considered that 'despite the many sub-sectors of sport that are diverse and often mutually exclusive, the common link with each is that sport is a vehicle toward something (e.g., profit, friends, health).'[25]

The 1998 version of the Estonian Sport Act contained a definition of sport[26] as '[…] playing activity of a predominantly competitive and physical nature, or a corresponding educational activity.' The Estonian Sport Act of 2005, as amended,[27] no longer contains this definition and instead focuses on the objectives of the Act. The 2005 Act

> …provides for the general organisational and legal bases of the organisation of sport, the rights and obligations of sportsmen, sportswomen and coaches, the bases for application for and grant of state support for winners of the Olympic Games, the bases for the

---

[22] Hart 1961.

[23] Soek 2006, p. 28.

[24] Article 2(1) of the Recommendation No. R (92) 13 Rev. of the Council of Europe's Committee of Ministers to Member States on the Revised European Sports Law Charter (the European Sports Law Charter).

[25] Malloy 2003, p. 59. Available at http://www.cces.ca/files/pdfs/CCES-PAPER-Malloy-E.pdf.

[26] *Spordiseadus* (Sports Act) passed on 15.6.1998 (RT I 1998, 61, 982), Chap. 1, General Provisions, § 2.

[27] *Spordiseadus* (Sports Act) passed on 6.4.2005 (RT I, 2005, 22, 148), as last amended on 29.12.2011.

> financing of sport, the requirements for the organisation of sports events and liability for violation of the requirements.[28]

So it is the organisational purpose of sport that underlies the adoption of this particular act.

In the UK, there is no formal definition of sport and the state has a more non-interventionist approach to sports governance than many other countries.[29]

The Finnish Sports Act of 1998 also does not contain a definition of sports. However, Chap. 1, Sect. 1 (second sentence) states that the purpose of the Act is 'to promote equality and tolerance, cultural diversity and the sustainable development of the environment through sports'.[30] This indicates that the general goals of sports policy in Finland are related to ethical values. The preamble of the Nicaraguan Sports Act has an ideological *ratio legis* and states as follows:

> The People's Sandinista Revolution has as its historical purpose to contribute to the development of a new mankind which is necessary to guarantee the physical and mental well-being of the population. Sport promotes the integration of man in society and helps strengthen the ties of brotherhood between the nations in an atmosphere of peace and mutual respect.[31]

Health is often a part of the sports legislation objectives. For instance, Canada's Physical Activity and Sports Act of 2003, Article 3 states that:

> The objectives of the Government of Canada's policy regarding physical activity are (*a*) to promote physical activity as a fundamental element of health and well-being; (*b*) to encourage all Canadians to improve their health by integrating physical activity into their daily lives; and (*c*) to assist in reducing barriers faced by all Canadians that prevent them from being active.[32]

Moreover, international participation, national prestige, recreation and entertainment are a part of the legislative and policy goals of some countries.[33] The European Sports Charter aims include making the activity of sport accessible to everyone ('sports for all').[34]

Still, despite their diversity, all these definitions and objectives put together do not do justice to the proper explanation of the activity of sport.

1.3.2 Lex Sportiva

The term *lex sportiva* refers to the conditionally autonomous legal order in which the body of norms that binds its subjects is created and enforced by national or

---

[28] Ibid. § 1(1).

[29] James 2010, p. 3.

[30] *Liikuntalaki* (Sports Law) 18.12.1998/1054, as amended.

[31] Soek 2006, p. 31.

[32] Physical Activity and Sport Act, passed on 19.3.2003, S.C. 2003, c.2, as last amended on 17.10.2011.

[33] Soek 2006, p. 33.

[34] Article 1 of the European Sports Charter.

international sports federations including, in particular, the jurisprudence of the Court of Arbitration for Sport (CAS). 'Global sports law'[35] and 'domestic sports law'[36] are two parts of *lex sportiva* and, within this concept, form an inseparable whole, in particular in those sports where the organisational structure confers strict hierarchy of authority (the pyramid structure). The former pertains to the rules created and applied by private global bodes that govern international sport, and the latter to rules created and applied by the national sports governing bodies that govern their respective sports on domestic level. The chief characteristics of global sports law, according to Foster, are 'first that it is a contractual order, with its binding force coming from agreements to submit to the authority and jurisdiction of international sporting federations, and second that it is not governed by national legal systems'.[37]

Sports governing bodies have their regulatory and organisational rules spelled out in their statutes, charters, regulations, codes and other rulebooks and constitutions, as the case may be. The impact that these regulations have on sportspersons is no different than the impact of formal laws passed by the states. In addition, they are far reaching in their scope as, when passed by the international federations, they apply globally to all the athletes and regulate in a collective manner every aspect of their professional lives and often some aspects of their private lives. For the administration of the whole body of rules and regulations issued by sports organisations and the decisions of their dispute settlement bodies, the Olympic Movement established the Court of Arbitration for Sport in 1984. CAS has sole jurisdiction to rule on the commercial issues in disputes related to sport, and it acts as an appellate body of the last instance in disciplinary cases, most of which concern disputes involving employment contracts and breach of anti-doping regulations by athletes. In the first instance disciplinary cases are usually dealt with at the level of the competent authorities of the sport in question by their quasi-judicial dispute settlement mechanisms.[38] Hence, CAS jurisprudence itself has become one of the main sources of *lex sportiva*.[39]

As juridification of the sector took place, more sophisticated and accountable mechanisms of sporting justice were developed within the sporting community. The restrictions on the scope of the autonomy of the governing bodies coming from *lex sportiva* itself have become stricter. This is the consequence of the increasing pressure of juridification, emerging unionisation of players, an increase

[35] According to nuances made by Foster, 'international sports law' is a different concept and deals with relations between nation states. Foster 2003, pp. 1–3.

[36] As termed and defined in James 2010 , p. 6.

[37] Foster 2003, p. 2.

[38] For more information on the Court of Arbitration for Sport see, e.g., Blackshaw 2009, pp. 45–99.

[39] In as far as the dispute concerns a matter within the scope of the EU law, a party that loses a case before the CAS may turn to the EU Commission to examine the sporting rule in question (and not to contest the CAS decision), and appeal the Commission decision to the Court of Justice of the European Union. In fact, there is no requirement in EU law to exhaust remedies available in the sporting justice system in order to be able to turn to the Commission.

in representation, as well as recognition that if sport can provide for fair rules and proper dispute settlement mechanisms the necessity for interference by non-sporting entities (such as EU institutions) and ordinary laws is going to be reduced to a minimum.[40] Elias uses the term 'sportisation' to describe a process in the course of which the framework of rules applying to sport becomes stricter, implying more differentiated and just rules and more efficient supervision.[41]

1.3.3 Legal Status and Autonomy of the Global Governing Bodies

The *Fédération Internationale de Football Association* (FIFA) and the *Union des Associations Européennes de Football* (UEFA) are international sports associations registered in the commercial register in accordance with the Swiss Civil Code, with headquarters in Switzerland. Formally, therefore, they are private bodies. However, in terms of their powers, and regardless of their formal classification, the true legal status of these sport governing bodies can be found on the equilibrium between private and public authorities.[42] They rely on commercial sponsorship and sales of broadcasting rights to sporting events rather than state funding and thus have a high degree of financial autonomy. Furthermore, there is perhaps no other economic sector in which private bodies have the same scope of regulatory latitude as in the sports sector,[43] within which they have constructed a virtually autonomous social field. Attesting to this status is the fact that FIFA has direct contacts with many heads of State[44] and is a powerful participant in global affairs, whereas the International Olympic Committee has been granted observer status at the United Nations, enabling it to participate in the work and sessions of the United Nations General Assembly.[45] These private bodies take decisions that have profound economic effects on many different actors in the world of sport and outside of it, and they can affect the functioning of the internal market and the trade between Member States within the meaning of the TFEU. Because sport federations possess state-like competences whose regulatory effect is equivalent to those of state action, the question of accountability for violations of law is a pressing one.[46]

---

[40] Casini explains that creation of CAS was attributable to this necessity. See Casini 2010, available at http://papers.ssrn.com/sol3/papers.cfm?abstract_id=1621335.

[41] Elias and Dunning 1986.

[42] Pijetlovic 2013.

[43] Paragraph 3.7 of the Arnaut Report.

[44] Gardiner and Felix 1995, p. 189.

[45] Resolution adopted by the UN General Assembly [on the report of Sixth Committee (A/64/458)], 22 October 2009.

[46] Brems and Lavrysen 2012, p. 227.

During most of the twentieth century, the majority of European states allowed sport organisations to function as bodies fully independent of the public authorities. In 1975 the Council of Europe adopted the Sport for All Charter, which was replaced by the European Sport Charter in 1992 and so became the first European intergovernmental organisation to take an interest in this sector. Although the Court of Justice of the European Union ('CJEU' or 'the Court') had passed its first judgment in the area of sport in 1974,[47] it was not until the mid-90s and the judgment in *Bosman* that the EU begun more active involvement in sport.[48] The judgment in *Bosman* forced global changes in UEFA regulations which profoundly affected the way that football clubs do their business. Eleven years later in *Meca-Medina*, the Court made it clear that *any* sporting rule that has an economic effect, even an ethical rule of an anti-doping policy, may become subject to scrutiny under EU law. This holding clashed with the understanding of the scope of autonomy to which sporting federations thought they were entitled. Through the process of juridification, sport became a *semi*-autonomous social field within which it may govern itself internally but, according to Moore,

> it is also vulnerable to rules and decisions and other forces emanating from the larger world by which it is surrounded. The semi-autonomous social field has rule-making capacity, and the means to induce or coerce compliance; but it is simultaneously set in a larger social matrix which can, and does, affect and invade it.[49]

Article 7 of the UEFA Statues (2012) imposes an obligation on its member associations to manage their affairs independently with no influence from third parties, and to provide in their statutes for a procedure guaranteeing the completely independent and free election and appointment of their executive and other bodies. In the event of the non-fulfilment of this obligation, UEFA shall not recognise such bodies, and may sanction that member association (for example, suspend and exclude their national team from participation in competitions). Article 7 of the UEFA Statutes is presumably an obligation on national associations to be free from interference of their national governments. Article 60 of the UEFA Statutes further obliges member associations to refer disputes of a national dimension in the last instance to an independent and impartial court of arbitration, to the exclusion of any ordinary court, subject to their national legislation. Disputes of a European dimension[50] fall under the exclusive jurisdiction of the Court of Arbitration for Sport, to the exclusion of any ordinary court or any other court of arbitration, unless they belong to the competence of a UEFA organ.[51] A claim and desire for

---

[47] Case 36/74 *Walrave and Koch v. Union Cycliste Internationale and others* [1974] ECR 1405.

[48] See Parrish 2003.

[49] Moore 1973, p. 719.

[50] Such as disputes between UEFA and associations, leagues, clubs, players or officials; or disputes of a European dimension between associations, leagues, clubs, players or officials. See Article 61 of the UEFA Statutes (2012 edition), available at http://www.uefa.com/MultimediaFiles/Download/EuroExperience/uefaorg/WhatUEFAis/01/80/54/03/1805403_DOWNLOAD.pdf.

[51] Article 61 of the UEFA Statutes (2012 edition).

autonomy is apparent from these articles but the transformed commercial landscape and scrutiny by the Court and the Commission (i.e., juridification of the sector), especially since *Bosman*, has downsized these aspirations for complete autonomy to attempts to bring as many issues as possible into the realm of the so-called 'sporting exception'. The precise contours and content of this concept, which relies on the 'specificity of sport', have never been set in absolute terms and its application is always assessed on a case-by-case basis. However, after the *Meca-Medina* judgement eroded the perception that the 'sporting exception' sheltered many rules from examination, sport governing bodies are gradually shifting the focus away from relying *ex ante* on the sporting exception to creating a complaint-proof internal system. Such a system implies, for example, representation of all the stakeholders in decision-making, as rules that are commonly agreed by all the concerned parties are unlikely to be challenged; a priori consultations with the EU Commission; and creating reliable dispute settlement mechanisms that fully respect the principles of natural justice, such as *nemo judex in casua sua* and *audi alteram partem*. In short, it implies adhering to the principles of good governance.

1.3.3.1 Issues of Good Governance in the Light of Autonomy

Due to the high degree of discretion held by the sporting authorities in performance of their central roles, it is necessary that 'various stakeholders must be properly represented at both national and European levels because this is a precondition for ensuring that these authorities are best equipped to speak on behalf of all with interests in the game'.[52] In its White Paper on Sport, the Commission considered that 'most challenges can be addressed through self-regulation *respectful of good governance principles, provided that EU law is respected*',[53] and that it is ready to play a facilitating role or take action if necessary. The Commission also acknowledged the autonomy of sporting organisations and representative structures. Similarly, the 2000 Nice Declaration, adopted after the meeting of the EU Heads of States and Governments, provided that:

> The European Council stresses its support for the independence of sports organisations and their right to organise themselves through appropriate associative structures. It recognises that, *with due regard for national and [EU] legislation and on the basis of a democratic and transparent method of operation*, it is the task of sporting organisations to organise and promote their particular sports, particularly as regards the specifically sporting rules applicable and the make-up of national teams, in the way which they think best reflects their objectives [emphasis added].[54]

---

[52] Paragraph 3.6 of the Arnaut Report.

[53] White Paper on Sport, para 4 [emphasis added].

[54] Declaration on the specific characteristics of sport and its social function in Europe, of which account should be taken in implementing common policies 13948/00, Annex to the Presidency Conclusions, Nice ('Nice Declaration').

The Commission Communication on Developing the European Dimension in Sport[55] states in clear terms that '*good governance in sport is a condition for the autonomy and self-regulation of sport organisations*.'[56] In European policy (as well as in application of EU law) the right to self-govern for the sporting organisations is therefore subjected to certain conditions and sets of principles for good governance in decision-making, such as transparency, democracy, accountability and representation of stakeholders (associations, federations, players, clubs, leagues, supporters, etc.). The sport governing bodies would derive their own benefits if they were to provide for truly representative and democratic forums in their decision-making, as this would be an effective mechanism to reduce litigation.

1.3.4 EU Sports Law and Policy

Unlike the set of rules developed by sporting community, 'EU sports law' is 'the law created by the EU institutions, in particular the European Court of Justice, that affects the regulation or governance of sport or which has been developed to resolve sports disputes'.[57] 'EU sports policy' is the term that reflects the ideological and political goals of the EU institutions in the area of sport. It is contained in non-binding policy documents, some of which have been cited by the Court in its sporting judgements.[58]

1.3.4.1 Theoretical Foundations and Emergence of EU Sports Law and Policy

Sport was historically viewed as a self-regulating activity in which there was not much scope for legal intervention. Legal and academic commentaries in this area were virtually non-existent in Europe as recently as the early 1990s. Late in the 1990s, policy discussions sparked by the 1995 judgement of the Court in the *Bosman* case and a number of policy documents tended to focus on the topic of 'sport and the law' rather than 'sports law'. With the exception of the United

[55] Communication from the Commission to the European Parliament, the Council, the European Economic and Social Committee, and the Committee of the Regions 'Developing the European Dimension in Sport' COM(2011) 12 final, 18. 1. 2011.

[56] Ibid. para 4.1.

[57] 'National sports law' is the law created by national parliaments, courts and enforcement agencies. It may directly affect the regulation, organisation, and governance of sport within a national territory. See James 2010, p. 3.

[58] For example, the Treaty of Amsterdam declaration on sport (declaration nr. 29) has been cited in Joined Cases C-51/96 and C-191/97 *Christelle Deliège v. Ligue francophone de judo et disciplines associées ASBL, Ligue belge de judo ASBL, Union européenne de judo and François Pacquée* [2000] ECR I-2549, para 42.

States, which already earlier had a comparatively developed system, similar trends of gradual legal intervention were taking place globally. There is no official recognition procedure to identify, constitute and name areas of law, and that procedure is mostly effected through the gradual recognition by academics and practitioners of the growing application of law to a new area of social life.[59] Opie noted that

> there seems to have always been court cases concerning sport but these were isolated and are insignificant comparing with the variety and the volume of court proceedings that are to be observed today. [...] the courts pursued a policy of non-intervention by holding that sport disputes were private matters which did not raise any justiciable issues. Any informed observer will realise that the position is vastly different today.[60]

Beloff et al. recognised that '[...] the law is now beginning to treat sporting activity, sporting bodies and the resolution of disputes in sport, differently from other activities or bodies. Discrete doctrines are gradually taking shape in the sporting field.'[61] It has to be acknowledged that *at the present time* academic discussions on whether [EU] sports law has established itself as a discrete area of law are somewhat outdated as it should be clear that there is indeed such a legal discipline. Support for this proposition is presented by the inclusion of Article 165 TFEU (the so-called 'sports article'), the newly obtained EU sports competence, a solid body of CJEU case law and Commission decisional practice, and the huge amount of institutional action in the area that has taken place in the past 3 years. These debates in any case, as Lewis and Taylor put it, bring out 'an issue of academic rather than practical interest'.[62] The content of EU sports law, on the other hand, remains somewhat of a puzzle.

When the Court handed down its judgment in the *Bosman* case in 1995, it provoked many different reactions. Critics of the ruling have seen it as an unacceptable intrusion of EU law into the dominion of the football governing body and an extension of Union competence into areas not intended to be regulated by the EU and its treaties. Others have welcomed the judgement as a necessary corollary of freedoms guaranteed by EU internal market provisions. Lobbying inside the European institutions and outside of them by the two rival opinion groups became the norm behind the search for clearer sports policy. The birth of EU sports law has been perceived by Parrish as attributable to post-*Bosman* dynamics of political discussions that were at the heart of this process.[63] His dissertation on 'Sports Law and Policy in the European Union' is the most significant contribution to the theoretical discourse on the subject to date and deserves a closer look.

---

[59] See Gardiner et al. 2007, p. 91. The emergence of any new field of law is normally preceded by similar debates and its acceptance as a distinct area of law has undergone a similar process (e.g. labour law). Cyber-law is an example of an area that has only recently in history achieved such recognition.

[60] Opie 1996, pp. 74–94.

[61] Beloff et al. 1999, p. 3.

[62] Lewis and Taylor 2003, preface.

[63] Parrish 2003, p. 17.

Parrish recognized that both EU sports law and EU sports policy developed without the engine of legislation, as the Union did not have relevant competence to adopt legally binding acts.[64] EU sports law has thus emerged as an activity-led, as opposed to rule-led discipline. According to the theory, within the EU there are a number of policy-specific subsystems, the sports policy subsystem being one of them. Two rival advocacy coalitions operating within this subsystem attempting to steer the policy in the direction consistent with their belief system are the socio-cultural coalition and the Single Market coalition.

Belonging to the socio-cultural coalition are the European Parliament and the Education and Culture Directorate within the European Commission, whose mandate closely aligns them to the people's Europe project, Member States in the European Council and the Council Presidency (which are in general opposed to the idea of the expansion of Union competence), as well as sport bodies, Olympic Committees, and the Council of Europe (who see sport as a social and cultural pursuit rather than an economic activity). Deep core beliefs, not shared by all the members of the coalition, encompass a concern for the promotion of positive integration. Core policy beliefs are related to the acknowledgment that sport is not above the law but they emphasize the social and cultural characteristics which require soft application of law. Within secondary beliefs there exist considerable differences which suggest that the socio-cultural coalition is a coalition of convenience. Namely, maximalists such as the Education and Culture DG and most of the EU governments preferred a Treaty basis for sports which would clearly define the application of EU law in the area and would give a base for the EU budget to support sporting activities. Moderates, such as sports governing bodies, did not want to see further expansion of the Union's influence in sports but who did want to see a clarification of the legal environment. Minimalists, who cling to the concept of subsidiarity did not favour granting sports a treaty base and believe that the EU has no competence to regulate sports. For instance, the British, Danish and Swedish governments belong to this category.[65]

Members of the Single Market advocacy coalition, on the other hand, seek to ensure that the legal foundations of the single market are protected and view sport rules as a significant economic activity which should comply with EU law. This advocacy coalition is primarily composed of the Competition Policy Directorate in the European Commission and the CJEU. Secondary members, whose affiliation is fluid, enter the coalition depending on the topic under consideration and whether and in which way it affects their legal and commercial interests. Thus, Parliament can shift on specific issues from the socio-cultural coalition to the Single Market coalition and it has done so in relation to, for example, lifting the restrictions on players' mobility in European sports. Sports federations also align themselves with one or another coalition depending on the issue involved. Regardless of the fluidity of membership, the author identifies certain common features of the belief system

64 Ibid. p. 2.

65 Ibid. pp. 68–71.

belonging to the Single Market advocacy coalition. Their deep core beliefs include the belief in negative integration and the protection of the four fundamental freedoms under the Treaty. Their policy core belief system goes no further than emphasizing that sport is subject to EU law in as far as it constitutes economic activity and that there cannot be any general exemption for the whole of the industry. Secondary aspects of the coalition's beliefs provide flexibility by acknowledging the socio-cultural dimension of sport which should be taken into account in the application of law.[66] Given that both advocacy coalitions have relatively equal access to institutional resources, each one is able to influence policy in a manner which has the potential to undermine the fundamental beliefs of the rival coalition.

A compromise is possible and coalitions would be willing to negotiate within secondary aspects of their beliefs in order to protect the core beliefs. From this process of mediation the *separate territories approach*—i.e., the definition of territories for sporting autonomy and for legal intervention[67]—emerged, which in turn meant that a particular legal approach to sports has been developed, establishing a discrete body of sports law within the EU.[68]

In a different theory, a few Nordic scholars have discerned the scope of sports law by dividing the law into two different areas: a *core* and a *surrounding area*. In their view, the core consists of the rules and regulations of sports organisations based on their autonomous rulemaking (such as the UEFA Statutes or the IOC Charter), and the surrounding area consists of 'ordinary laws' in society. The only way that these ordinary laws could interfere with the autonomy and influence of sports organisations is in the case of a conflict of laws.[69]

Halgreen questioned both of these theories because they do not provide clearer answers to what should be understood as sports law. Further, he correctly pointed out that there is no hard evidence to support the idea that there is a core that is untouched by traditional legal principles applied in the 'real world', as there seems to be a constant risk of conflicts of law on every corner. Halgreen then proposed that if sports law is to be recognised as a genuine legal discipline the solutions posed by the disputes in the sporting community should *sometimes* be different than solutions provided in the 'real world', or in his words, the 'considerations specific to the sporting community would lead to a result that would otherwise not likely be achieved outside the sporting community'[70] when ordinary laws are applied to sports disputes.

---

[66] Ibid. pp. 65–68.

[67] However, see also Weatherill 2007, pp. 48–73. Therein, Weatherill considered that the legal order established by the Treaty and the legal order that governs sports (a set of legal rules established by sports federations) overlap to a large extent. This is because of the economic dimension of sport. The area of overlap is nourished by the appreciation that in some respects sport is special. See p. 49.

[68] Parrish 2003, p. 79.

[69] Halgreen 2004, p. 26.

[70] Ibid. p. 27 (emphasis added).

In general, there are two kinds of sports law in Europe: one made by sport federations and specialised tribunals for resolving sports disputes, such as CAS, and the other by national and European legislators and courts. It is clear that the first category, *lex sportiva*, can be properly called sports law. This is not just because it is adopted by sports bodies and organs for the regulation and organisation of sport, but because it is adopted by sports bodies and organs that were recognised by constitutions or legislation of the Member States, as well as by European policy documents, as having autonomy to do so in relation to their sporting discipline. Their autonomy is therefore based on its express or implied acceptance of national and European regulators. Although this autonomy was initially self-proclaimed, subsequently it became a matter not unlike the delegation of competence by public to private bodies to regulate themselves within the confines of the law. In the EU, it is clear that sport has this kind of 'conditional autonomy' as confirmed and reiterated by numerous policy documents.

The second kind of sports law is composed of various national and European legislative acts and decisions by public authorities including the judiciary. In determining whether a case can be put into the 'EU sports law box', one of the important questions to ask is whether a dispute entails (implicitly or explicitly) considerations of the specificity of sport? If so, then it is sports law that is being applied to resolve the dispute, even though it is also EU competition law or freedom of movement law being applied. This is due to the specificities of the sports sector that must, as a matter of constitutional requirement, be taken into account in the application of EU laws, and in this process the ordinary law is transformed into its specific version that can be referred to as EU sports law. The specificity of sport that brought about 'sporting exceptions' of various kinds[71] is the very feature that justifies the 'EU sports law' label but it is also one of the features that justifies the autonomy of the sport governing bodies. Limiting the scope of that autonomy (i.e. conditioning it), influencing those bodies' considerations in decision-making and confirming or remoulding their rules via judicial or administrative review is clearly going to be a part of sports law. In fact, a different question could be asked to approach the issue from another end of the process and enquire if any organisational or regulatory sports rule or practice has been amended/disposed of/confirmed as a result of an administrative or judicial decision at the EU level? If so, then the law applied should be taken as forming a part of sports law.

Finally, many rules that are adopted or not adopted by sporting bodies outside the process of any dispute are influenced by the need to pay due regard to the ordinary laws, in particular, EU competition and internal market principles. In *Murphy* Advocate General Kokott said that Articles 6(e) and 165 TFEU '*require* account to be taken of the specific nature of sport and its structures based on voluntary activity' which has been interpreted to 'imply horizontal reach of Article 165 into other Treaty competences'[72] and this is true as regards the application of EU law.

---

[71] See Chap. 6 on convergence and sporting exceptions.

[72] Parrish 2012, p. 732. However, there is no need to take Article 165 TFEU into consideration in any of the EU legislative procedures, as it is not a horizontal provision.

By taking due considerations of one another's requirements, the first and the second kind of sports law formed an inseparable unit in which discussion and consultation have gradually replaced conflicts and confusions. This is very much reflected in the modern practice of consultation between UEFA and the EU Commission on issues of common interest, such as the implementation of the UEFA Club Licensing and Financial Fair Play Regulations and legal certainty for sport, support and cooperation in matters related to match-fixing, and issuing of common statements by the Commission and UEFA.[73] Compared to 15 years ago, EU sports law is certainly developing in a different and more stable environment.

1.3.4.2 Relevant Institutional Actors

The Education and Culture Directorate-General of the European Commission includes the Sport Unit which is responsible for cooperation within the Commission and with other EU institutions on sport-related issues, and for cooperation and meetings with national and international sports institutions, organisations and federations.

Prior to the entry into force of the Lisbon Treaty, EU Sport Directors and Ministers had been meeting regularly in an informal setting, outside the formal structures of the EU Council of Ministers in order to address sport-related matters of common concern, exchange good practice, and give political guidance to the Commission. Following the entry into force of the Lisbon Treaty, the Ministers responsible for sport of the 28 EU Member States can now meet in the formal setting of the Council.[74] However, the informal meetings will continue also after the entry into force of the Treaty provisions for sport as they can be useful to exchange views on matters of common concern and to prepare the ground for work in the Council, where the formal decisions are taken. Six EU working groups have been set up in recent years to co-operate more closely, at technical level, on specific topics. Each working group includes representatives of at least ten Member States and is chaired by the Commission.[75] On 16 September 2010, the European Council changed the name of the Council in charge of Education, Youth and Culture. Officially the Council is now called the Education, Youth, Culture—including Audiovisual Affairs—and Sport Council. Sport was discussed for the first time by the Education, Youth and Culture Council, meeting in Brussels on 10–11 May 2010.

---

[73] Joint Statement of UEFA and the EU Commission of 21 March 2012 is available at http://www.uefa.com/MultimediaFiles/Download/uefaorg/EuropeanUnion/01/77/21/58/1772158_DOWNLOAD.pdf.

[74] For e.g., meeting of EU Sports Directors in Genval 16–17 September 2010.

[75] The following Working Groups were established: in 2005—Working Group 'Sport & Health', in 2006—Working Group 'Sport & Economics', in 2007—Working Group 'Non-Profit Sport Organisations'; in 2008—Working Group 'Anti-Doping'; in 2009—Working Group 'Education and Training in Sport'; in 2010—Working Group 'Social Inclusion and Equal Opportunities in Sport'.

In addition to the structures within the Commission, the Council and the European Council, it is important to mention the European Parliament's standing committee on culture and education, whose tasks include development of a sports and leisure policy. Finally, in its role as interpreter of EU law, the CJEU played a central role in interpretation of the existing economic provisions in the sporting context. In the absence of binding legislation specifically enacted to govern aspects of sport, these cases have for a long time provided a track for EU sports law to develop, in so far as they involved the practice which constituted economic activity.

The European Commission, an institution known as 'the guardian of the Treaty', may inquire about, and if necessary may open up formal proceedings against, suspected cases of infringement. It may also receive complaints from third parties. Commission decisions may be appealed to the CJEU under Article 263 TFEU. The case may also reach the CJEU via the preliminary reference procedure under Article 267 TFEU. Until the entry into force of the Lisbon Treaty amendments, the Commission played a reactive role to the legal issues posed by sport. The paragraphs that follow will illustrate the effects of these amendments in practice and it will become clear that the Commission and other institutions involved in the legislative process have assumed a more pro-active role in accordance with their newly acquired mandate under Articles 2(5), 6(e) and 165 TFEU.

1.3.4.3 Applicable Legislation and Existing Policy Instruments

Until the entry into force of the Lisbon Treaty on 1 December 2009, the EU did not have direct legislative competence to regulate sports. The traditional instruments were (and still are) therefore essential to protecting the core objectives of the Union when the rules and activities of sporting bodies obstruct the functioning of internal market and distort competition. The primary articles in the TFEU involved are the rules on competition in Articles 101 and 102, freedom of movement for workers (Article 45–48), freedom of movement for self-employed (Article 49–55) and freedom to provide services (Articles 56–62). Moreover, all other Treaty provisions, such as those relating to EU citizenship and equal treatment, also apply to sport. The Charter of Fundamental Rights of the EU ought to be applicable to the rules and practices of the sport governing bodies due to their state-like competences, as well as the scope and impact of their regulatory latitude. However, it is only in the context of Union's competence over sport in as far as it constitutes economic activity that the Charter may be utilized to supplement athletes' legal arguments—for example, in the judicial test for regulatory rules in sport devised by the Court in *Meca-Medina* and the equivalent internal market objective justification framework. As such, it may provide a counterbalance to the Article 165(1) TFEU concept of the 'specificity of sport' that sporting federations rely on to justify their restrictive measures.[76]

[76] As argued in Pijetlovic 2013.

Relevant secondary EU legislation includes the Audio-Visual Media Services Directive,[77] the Directive on the Legal Protection of Databases,[78] the Citizens Rights Directive[79] and the Environmental Impact Assessment Directive,[80] as well as some general procedural instruments such as Regulation 1/2003[81]—utilised when a competition case is investigated by the Commission's Directorate General IV. The first piece of legislation mentioned is primarily adopted to regulate sports broadcasting and allow Member States to designate the list of national and non-national events of great importance to their society to be provided on free-to-air television.[82] None of the other instruments has played much role in practice so far.

There is a growing number of non-binding policy instruments on sport adopted to articulate the position of the individual EU institutions on sporting issues and set out an approach to EU regulation of the sport sector in general.[83] They provide an impetus for development of legal principles guiding the enforcement and interpretation of traditional rules in this regulatory environment. The 2007 White Paper on Sport, accompanied by the Commission Staff Working Document,[84] is the most comprehensive and high profile initiative adopted by the Commission, issued after 2 years of consultation with relevant stakeholders, each expressing different observations and expectations. The White Paper includes all aspects of the EU *acquis* that have an impact on sport, enhances visibility of sport in EU policy and

[77] Directive 2010/13/EU of the European Parliament and of the Council of 10 March 2010 on the coordination of certain provisions laid down by law, regulation or administrative action in Member States concerning the provision of audiovisual media services (Audiovisual Media Services Directive), OJ L 95, 15/4/2010, pp. 1–24.

[78] Directive 96/9/EC of 11 March 1996 on the legal protection of databases OJ L 077, 27/3/1996.

[79] Directive 2004/38/EC of the European Parliament and of the Council of 24 April 2004 on the right of citizens of the Union and their family members to move and reside freely within the territory of the Member States amending Regulation (EEC) No 1612/68 and repealing Directives 64/221/EEC, 68/360/EEC, 72/194/EEC, 73/148/EEC, 75/34/EEC, 75/35/EEC, 90/364/EEC, 90/365/EEC and 93/96/EEC, OJ L 158, 30/4/2004, pp. 77–128.

[80] Council Directive of 27 June 1985 on the assessment of the effects of certain public and private projects on the environment 85/337/EEC OJ L 175, 05/07/1985, pp. 40–48, as amended.

[81] Council Regulation (EC) No 1/2003 of 16 December 2002 on the implementation of the rules on competition laid down in Articles 81 and 82 of the Treaty OJ L 1, 04.01.2003, pp. 1–25.

[82] For cases interpreting this rule see Sect. 4.9

[83] Such as: Declaration on the specific characteristics of sport and its social function in Europe, of which account should be taken in implementing common policies 13948/00, Annex to the Presidency Conclusions, Nice (Nice Declaration); Declaration No. 29 in Amsterdam Treaty (Amsterdam Declaration); Report from the Commission to the European Council with a view to safeguarding current sports structures and maintaining the social function of sport within the Community framework ('The Helsinki Report on Sport') Brussels, 10 December 1999 COM(1999) 644 final; and most notably, Commission White Paper on Sport, Brussels 11 July 2007 COM(2007) 391 final.

[84] Ibid. See also Commission Staff Working Document, The EU and Sport: Background and Context, Accompanying Document to the White Paper on Sport, COM (2007) 391 final.

actions, acknowledges the specificities of the industry, and improves transparency of the application of EU law to sport for all actors concerned.[85]

Four years later, in 2011, the Commission took another important step in defining sports policy by adopting the Communication on Developing European Dimension in Sport.[86] The Communication credits the White Paper on Sport for greatly enhancing EU-level cooperation and dialogue in the area. Similarly, a European Parliament Resolution[87] welcomed and, in general, supported the approach of the White Paper on Sport. The EU Parliament called on the Commission to propose an EU sport programme as well as preparatory actions in the field of sport from 2009. From December 2008 onwards, the Parliament approved an annual budget for such preparatory actions, and the Commission, by means of decision, adopted an Annual Work Programme on grants and contracts for the preparatory actions. The main objective is to implement the sport provisions in Article 165 TFEU by providing policy support for the identification of future policy actions in the area of sport through studies, conferences, seminars and surveys; testing the establishment and functioning of suitable networks and good practices through calls for proposals; and promoting greater European visibility at sport events.[88]

Furthermore, the Parliament asked the Commission to 'have due respect for the specificity of sports, by *not* taking a case-by-case approach and to provide more legal certainty by creating clear guidelines on the applicability of European law to sports in Europe [...]'.[89] This is in contrast to the view on the White Paper on Sport expressed by the study group on the Lisbon Treaty and the European Union sports policy that considered it unnecessary for the Commission to issue any additional guidelines,[90] and it is also in contrast to the Commission's case-by-case approach outlined in the accompanying documents to the White Paper on Sport.[91] The third EU Sport Forum took place in Budapest on 21–22 February 2011. This is an annual event and the key platform for dialogue on sport at EU level (as foreseen in the White Paper), which gathers EU Sport Ministers, and all the main stakeholders in sport including UEFA, FIFA and the European Olympic Committees. Themes included reflections on the Commission Communication 'Developing European Dimension in Sport', developments in sport at the EU level since the last EU sport forum in Madrid 2010, and the presentation of results of 18

[85] See Velázquez Hernández 2008, pp. 78–79.

[86] COM (2011) 12 final, 18. 1. 2011.

[87] European Parliament resolution of 8 May 2008 on the White Paper on Sport (2007/2261 (INI)).

[88] See http://ec.europa.eu/sport/preparatory_actions/studies-surveys-conferences-and-seminars_en.htm.

[89] Ibid. para 4, (emphasis added).

[90] See the European Parliament, Directorate-General for Internal Policies, study on the Lisbon Treaty and EU Sports Policy (2010), p. 12.

[91] Commission Staff Working Document, para 4.1.

projects in the field of sport supported through Preparatory Action 2009. In 2009–2010 the Commission provided more than €6 million to support around 40 sport projects, and in 2011 launched 12 new projects.[92]

1.3.4.4 TFEU: EU Competence in Sport and Article 165

On 1 December 2009, the Lisbon Treaty entered into force. The inclusion of sport in Article 165 under Title XII on Education, Vocational Training Youth and Sport has sparked many debates as to its precise effects on the powers of EU institutions in the field, and ultimately its effects on sport. Article 165(1) states that 'The Union shall contribute to the promotion of European sporting issues, while taking account of the *specific nature of sport*, its structures based on voluntary activity and its *social and educational function*' [emphasis added]. According to Article 165(2) 'Union action shall be aimed at: [...] developing the European dimension in sport, by promoting *fairness and openness in sporting competitions* and cooperation between bodies responsible for sports, and by protecting the physical and moral integrity of sportsmen and sportswomen, especially the youngest sportsmen and sportswomen'.

A study on the Lisbon Treaty and European Union Sports Policy that was recently commissioned by the European Parliament reveals that, in general, Article 165 will have a limited impact on the EU's legal powers over sport.[93] Unlike the Treaty provisions on environmental protection and public health, Article 165 TFEU does not contain a horizontal clause requiring EU institutions to take sporting issues into account in the exercise of other powers and when making policies in other areas, such as free movement and competition law, although they may choose do so. There is no constitutional requirement to take into account the specificity of sports in either legislative or administrative action and therefore Article 165 TFEU should not alter the existing sports-related jurisprudence of the Court and the decision making practice of the Commission.[94]

Two sport-related cases decided after the entry into force of the Lisbon Treaty in which the Court made reference to the new article are the judgments in *Bernard* and *Murphy*. The study on the Lisbon Treaty and European Union Sports Policy concludes that reference to the 'specific nature of sport' in *Bernard* merely reinforces already existing judicial possibilities and that Article 165(1) TFEU will add little further protection for contested sports rules beyond those already provided by the Court and the Commission because the two institutions have already been highly receptive to the 'specific nature of sport' concept.[95] However, the study also

---

92 See the Commission Press Release IP/11/43 'Commission Strengthens European Dimension of Sport' 18 January 2011. Details of the budget are in the Final Report on evaluation of preparatory actions and special events in the field of sport that has become publicly available on 29 July 2011.

93 The Lisbon Treaty and EU Sports Policy 2010, p. 10.

94 Ibid.

95 Ibid. p. 11.

finds that whereas *Bernard* has not opened any new previously undiscovered avenues of appeal, the Court's treatment of Article 165 TFEU in that case supports the view that '*the new sports competence may have given further weight to sports-related arguments*'. On a different basis, namely, the treatment of certain sport-specific issues in the 2010 *Bernard* case as compared to the 1995 *Bosman* judgement, it is argued in Chap. 4 that the new 'sports article' has indeed given an additional weight to the sports related arguments.[96] This was later confirmed by the Court's approach in *Murphy*, also discussed in detail in Sect. 4.10.

Articles 2(5) in combination with Article 6 of the Treaty gives the Union the competence to carry out actions that support, coordinate or supplement the actions of the Member States in the area of sport and that do not entail harmonisation of the Member States' laws or regulations. Article 165(4) states that EU institutions shall, in accordance with the ordinary legislative procedure, adopt incentive measures excluding any harmonisation of the laws and regulations of the Member States, and the Council shall adopt recommendations on a proposal from the Commission. However, the study group's examination of the equivalent past prohibitions of harmonisation and their treatment by the Court[97] suggests that harmonising measures can be taken so long as they are nominally based on another Treaty competence and convergence can be achieved in practice by using another legal basis to pass the harmonising legislation. Importantly, the new sports competence allows the EU to allocate part of the budget to sport directly without the need to justify this by reference to other Treaty competencies, as has been the practice so far.[98]

1.3.5 Boundaries of Legal Intervention

Thus far, the traditional starting point for all discussions on the delimitation of regulatory competences in sports has been the autonomy of sporting bodies followed by an assessment of the appropriate level of intervention into that autonomy. However, the categories of rules that do not produce economic effects (i.e. 'rules of the game') may be mentioned subsequently, as an exception, to the dominant fact that sporting rules and practices are subject to EU law. The White Paper on Sport simply states: 'Sport activity is subject to the application of EU law.'[99] Only then it does it go on to discuss specificity and nowhere does it mention that there might be a sporting rule that is a priori not subject to the application of EU law. Instead, Annex I to the Commission Staff Working Document accompanying the White Paper on Sport talks about the rules that are 'unlikely to infringe' against

[96] See also Pijetlovic 2010, pp. 858–869.

[97] Such as in the fields of social policy, education, vocational training, culture, and public health.

[98] See The Lisbon Treaty and EU Sports Policy Study 2010, p. 11.

[99] Paragraph 4.1.

competition provisions, emphasising that there can be no general exemption for any of the sporting rules and recognising that 'each sport may require different rules and each rule will have to be looked at individually'. This case-by-case approach is all-inclusive and leaves a broad scope to challenge virtually any of the sporting rules.

Furthermore, sports law cannot be understood in purely national terms at any level and the debates on regulatory competences should be placed within the wider European and international context.[100] International sports federations are the best-placed authorities to set the rules of the game, establish specialised dispute resolution bodies, design codes of conduct on and off the playing field, and decide on other matters that concern organisational and regulatory aspects of their respective disciplines. European policy instruments recognise this independent nature of sport governing bodies and the need to support and protect their central role in ensuring cohesion and financial solidarity. While it is true that the EU does not have competence to interfere into sporting autonomy via legislative action, any sphere of sporting activity and any sporting rule that produces cross-border economic effects may become subject to scrutiny under EU law, the provisions on non-discrimination, competition and free movement being the most relevant. These provisions dictate what private and public authorities, including sporting bodies, may *not* do. As such, EU law will interfere into sporting authority inasmuch as their rules and practices are in breach of negative Treaty provisions.[101]

What the EU policy documents have in common is their mission to reconcile the interests of different stakeholders, in other words, to preserve the traditional values of sport and the autonomy of sport governing bodies on the one hand, and on the other hand to have sporting rules and practices comply with the EU law. Accordingly, sport bodies enjoy a form of autonomy that allows them to organise and regulate their respective sport conditionally upon compliance with these economic provisions, whereas the Union has an equivalent duty to take into account the specificity of the sector (including social, educational and cultural functions inherent in it) in the implementation of common policies.

Furthermore, it is often emphasised that the practice of sport is subject to Union law only in so far as it constitutes economic activity, and that 'purely sporting rules' do not constitute such economic activity.[102] In Weatherill's theory, there is an unavoidable overlap between the EU economic laws which regulate the sport from the 'outside' and the network of governance which represents 'internal' sports law. The area of overlap is nourished by appreciation that in some way 'sport is special' (the concept which is referred to as 'specificity of sport'[103]). It is commonly thought that after the Court's decision in *Meca-Medina* it is clear that

---

[101] Weatherill 2009, p. 79.

[102] See Sects. 4.1.2 and 4.1.3 for cases establishing the rules. See also Chap. 6 for detailed discussion on different categorises of sporting exceptions.

[103] The concept is discussed below in Sect. 2.1.

[100] Gardiner et al. 2007, p. 92.

only a very small category of rules may be referred to as 'purely sporting rules' devoid of any economic effect.[104] These conclusions came as a result of the Court's statement in paragraph 27 of the judgment that 'the mere fact that a rule is purely sporting in nature does not have the effect of removing from the scope of the Treaty the person engaging in the activity governed by that rule or the body which has laid it down'. Most sporting rules will actually belong to the area of overlap, and the scope for unfettered autonomy virtually does not exist. However, it is hard to imagine some rules being challenged in legal action, such as most of the rules of the game, or nationality discrimination when selecting, say, football players for World Cup or EURO to represent their countries. This will de facto leave out some rules from the area of overlap.

As a final point, it is important to emphasise that the fact that the sporting rule or practice falls under the scope of EU law, or that it is being challenged in a legal action before the Commission or the CJEU, does not automatically render that rule or practice in breach of any legal provision. In fact, at least half of the sporting rules that have so far been examined by these EU institutions have been confirmed as being in compliance with EU law.

1.4 The Subject Matter of the Volume

1.4.1 The Arrangements in European Football Giving Rise to Legal Problem Posed by Breakaway Structures

In general, sports federations are responsible for creating rules that regulate all important aspects of their respective disciplines. Decisions on the structure of the sport, and regulatory and organisational matters are usually within their exclusive competence. At the same time, sporting federations are also commercial actors with economic interests in the sport they regulate. This intermingling of regulatory and commercial functions in a single body often leads to a conflict of interests, to the detriment of any actual or potential competitor on the relevant market. In Europe, sport has traditionally been organised in a 'pyramid' structure with one governing federation per sport. The EU sports policy led by the Commission, European Council and the European Parliament expressed support for the preservation of such traditional organisational structures. However, the factor of incremental commercialisation, coupled with the application of the internal market and competition provisions of the Treaty in the area of sport, have made this political and ideological goal increasingly difficult to maintain in practice.

Namely, European sports are characterised by a high degree of financial solidarity (or so the theory goes) between amateur and professional leagues, as well as between clubs playing in the same league. Football is very representative of this

[104] See, for e.g., Weatherill 2006, pp. 645–657.

arrangement. Many football clubs are content with the terms of this arrangement but the same cannot be said of the commercially most powerful clubs who share a part of their proceeds with their less well-off competitors and with grassroots football. Not surprisingly, financial solidarity is not self-imposed: UEFA, in its capacity as the governing body mandated with organising and regulating European football, conditions participation of the clubs in European competitions upon the transfer of commercial rights to UEFA. UEFA then sells the rights collectively on behalf of participants in the league and distributes the profits in accordance with the principle of solidarity. The discontent of the top football clubs with the distributional as well as other rules affecting their commercial interests (such as compulsory and uncompensated player release for international matches of national representative teams) has in the recent past resulted in threats of the elite group of top-earning clubs to break away from their current organisational structures and form their own closed private league on a pan-European level. Apart from the standard commercial risks brought about by the market itself, another problem that the actualisation of such a project faces is contained in the rules of Article 49 of the UEFA Statutes (2012) that subjects the participation of the clubs in alternative competitions to prior authorisation. Any deviation from these rules would result in disciplinary and financial penalties. The other side of the story is that financial solidarity is a fundamental mechanism enabling the governing body to fulfil its mandate and promote its discipline at all levels. Without such solidarity, the traditional European football structure would have to be substantially re-organised. UEFA also provides organising services to the clubs participating in the pan-European competitions and manages all practicalities involved in such organisation.

Sporting rules that produce economic effects, even if only indirect and potential, may come under the administrative and judicial scrutiny of EU institutions. The TFEU competition rules in the Court's sporting judgments treat the sporting bodies and clubs as undertakings or an association of undertakings for the purposes of bringing them under the scope of legal control. Rules of the sporting bodies such as the one under Article 49 of the UEFA Statutes (2012) making participation in alternative championships subject to prior authorisation (which would probably not be given to the elite rival league) can therefore constitute a breach of Articles 101 and 102 TFEU. Although the legal analysis should focus on the application of competition law, the restrictive rule under examination produces effects also in the area of the internal market, in particular regarding freedom to provide services in Article 56 TEFU. A specific set of legal principles forming the core of EU sports law was created by the Court in the interpretation of these Treaty articles and their application to sporting rules and regulations. European policy endeavours that are focused on maintenance of the traditional structures will have to take into consideration a high degree of commercialisation of professional sports and their relationship with the Treaty, and might therefore require adjustment and reformulation to conform to the prevailing legal and commercial realities. Hence, it will also be interesting to consider what kind of role, if any, the EU policy goals in non-binding and declaratory instruments that expressed support for preservation of traditional European sporting structures would play in the application of the principles of open market economy outlined in the Treaty as interpreted by the CJEU.

This volume will: 1. set out the problems and highlight the power struggles in European football governance in the light of the context of the topic of this book; 2. provide progressive interpretation of the applicable EU sports law; 3. set out a novel theory of convergence between TFEU provisions on competition and the internal market in the light of sporting exceptions and; 4. explore the legality of the Article 49 rule in UEFA statutes and the case for formation of alternative structures in European football under the EU sports law.

Should the clubs be free to 'take the ball and go home' and under which conditions, if any? Conversely, are the UEFA Statutes making the formation of alternative leagues subject to approval, which is in practice never given, in accordance with the requirements of EU law? This legal problem has been looming since the late 1990s but apart from a few shorter papers there exists no comprehensive legal research in English on this topic to date. Football has been chosen as the focus of this volume because it is the most important sport in Europe in terms of its commercial impact, the most powerful sport in terms of its social impact, and more than half of the cases before EU institutions were focused on football. This volume touches upon and interconnects many areas of EU law and policy including different areas of competition law, internal market law, constitutional law, theories of sports law and policy, and the discussion on corporate social responsibility in this context.

1.4.2 Description of Chapters 1–7

The current chapter began by offering some guidance on the definitions and terminology used, while highlighting the differences in the way that the legislation of individual countries and international organisations view the primary functions that sport ought to perform. Sport's internal self-regulation and the sources of the autonomy of that self-regulation from the point of view of the statutes of the governing bodies were then looked at. It was shown that claims for self-regulation have been replaced by the aspirations towards a more expansive interpretation of the concept of sporting exception developed in the Court's jurisprudence. Self-regulation was also looked at from the point of view of the European institutions as expressed in their policy instruments. Respect for the principles of good governance was seen as instrumental for the conditional autonomy offered to sports governing bodies. The chapter further discussed what it later identifies as two amalgamated types of sports law: first, sources of *lex sportiva* including CAS decisions, and different documents spelling out regulatory and organisational rules, and second, European sports law and policy. The latter was considered in more detail, including theories on the historical development and acceptance of sports law as an independent area of law, EU institutional actors and their relevant functions and activities, and applicable EU policy and legislative instruments (in particular Article 165 TFEU, the so-called the sports article, added by the Lisbon Treaty amendments).

The basic features of the sporting industry in Europe are outlined next in Chap. 2, with emphasis on the concept of 'specificity of sport' in EU law and policy as the key rationale behind the 'sporting exception' in EU law. As the structural set-up of sport is essential for understanding the application of the law, a section is dedicated to a comparative overview of the European and American models of sport, each with their own characteristics.

The underlying theme of Chap. 3 is rooted in the recognition of apparent conflict between, on the one hand, the EU policy goals to preserve the traditional European sporting structures, and on the other hand, the neo-realities regarding commercial aspects and governance of European football. Beneath the EU policy goals and sporting organisations' endeavours to maintain the structural status quo in Europe, creeps the factor of incremental commercialisation with all its corollaries, which, in the view advanced by this book, renders the current organisational structure prone to breakaway challenges and power struggles resulting in compromises at the expense of other stakeholders. Chapter 3 reveals the details of the 1998 Media Partners proposal which offered an attractive package of financial benefits to elite football clubs to form an alternative breakaway league outside the European pyramid structure. In order to keep the clubs under its roof, UEFA reacted by establishing an expanded Champions League with more matches and more money for the teams, and with several places in the Champions League guaranteed for the clubs coming from the 'big five' leagues. Consequently, the Media Partners proposal never reached an implementation stage, but the economic interest grouping known as the G14 was formed by some of the main proponents of the proposal who apparently discovered how to gain an upper hand in the power struggle. Due to the dissatisfaction of the G14 with the FIFA rules on compulsory and uncompensated player release for international representative matches of national teams, another threat of a breakaway took place in 2006. By January 2008, the world governing body entered into a peace deal with the G14 that resulted in the creation of a compensation pool for the clubs that release players and in changes to the governance structure, in return for withdrawal of, *inter alia*, the *Oulmers* case, and the dissolution of the G14. It is submitted that this compromise by FIFA was not necessary as regards the outcome in the *Oulmers* case—the deal was driven in big part by the fear of formation of an alternative closed league led by the G14. The responses of FIFA and UEFA when presented with the prospect of breakaway by elite clubs illustrate the influence that the group had on the decisions of the governing bodies. That influence is used to change the rules governing football every time important financial interests of the most powerful clubs are at stake. Furthermore, Chap. 3 presents the relevant dynamics behind the governance of European football. It portrays the threat of a breakaway competition as an ongoing latent disease of the pyramid structure. In particular, it is argued that notwithstanding the formal disbandment of the G14, the group and its allies continue to present a powerful lobby with special commercial interests not possessed by any other competitors in their league. At the conclusion of the January 2008 deal with FIFA that resulted in formal disbandment of the G14, their role has not ended de facto; it has just been deinstitutionalised, re-institutionalised, and legitimised in the form of the European Club Association. The dominant representation of the elite clubs on the Executive Board of the European Club Association coupled with the changing economic reality of the sports sector has contributed toward a gradual shift and *unwelcome form* of decentralization of the governance of the European football. This body also represents European clubs on the Professional Football Strategy Council (PFSC)—three out of four members are former G14 clubs. Central decision making without proper representation of all the affected stakeholders might be a sign of bad governance, but decentralised decision making to the advantage of big clubs as stakeholders and the disadvantage of football as a whole, is potentially even worse. Although the PFSC appears to be a step in the right direction, as long as the ECA remains 'elitist' and as long as European Professional Football Leagues represent only the top leagues, democratic representation in the governance of European football will remain a privilege of the rich. Finally, it is stated that the legal and commercial environment for the sports industry is in the process of changing, doubling the market risks involved in any potential breakaway.

The purpose of Chaps. 4 and 5 is to set out and discern the principles underlying the application of EU freedom of movement and competition law to legal disputes in the sports sector. These chapters present alternative views on several sports judgments and contribute original ideas on the general framework relevant to the enforcement of Treaty provisions in sporting disputes. Chapter 4 briefly introduces the main analytical framework and legal principles in the field of free movement of persons. Thereafter, all the important sports judgments of the Court are analysed in chronological order, from *Walrave* decided in 1974 to *Murphy* in 2011. The analysis of the seminal *Bosman* decision offers a fresh perspective on the '3+2' rule and its implications for the current UEFA home grown rule. Judgment in the *Bernard* case is considered in detail as it is the first sporting judgment of the Court after the Lisbon Treaty amendments. The issues considered in Chap. 5 are custom-tailored to the extent possible to correspond to the title and the purpose of this book. In the subheading on 'Blocking competing organisations', three cases that are factually most relevant to the breakaway leagues are analysed: *MOTOE*, *FIA/Formula One* and *DLG*. Moreover, contrary to suggestions from the Arnaut Report, Article 106(2) TFEU is described as superfluous and undesirable in terms of its applicability to sport. Finally, the subheading on 'Superdominance and special responsibility' makes certain parallels between the expanded concept of special responsibility of superdominant undertakings and corporate social responsibility. It suggests that the content of the legitimate aim relied on by superdominant undertakings (such as sports governing bodies) to avoid application of competition law by fulfilling the *Meca-Medina/Wouters* test, could be made binding by the Commission, via the procedure similar to commitment decisions under Article 9 of Regulation 1/2003.

Chapter 6 sketches a novel way of looking at the different categories of sporting exceptions through the prism of convergence between EU free movement law and competition law. It connects back to the Sect. 5.5.5.5 discussion on para 31 of the *Meca-Medina* case. The text is supported by graphic illustrations wherever deemed useful. This is probably the most significant theoretical contribution of this work to the study of EU sports law in general.

Chapter 7 is the most significant contribution to the topic of breakaway structures in the English language. It starts from the determination of the relevant market, the position of the parties on the relevant market and the designation of the restraints under EU competition and internal market law. The *qualitative* analysis of the existence of UEFA dominance on the market, as supported by established legal principles and the Court's case law, lead to the unexpected result that it would be a challenging task to demonstrate that such dominance indeed exists. On the other hand, demonstrating market foreclosure is easier task despite the fact that the specific traditional competition law doctrines have proven particularly awkward to apply to the organisational rules in question. The core of the outcome of the analysis in this chapter lies in the elements of justification framework that are transposable and shared between competition and internal market provisions. The proportionality of the rules on breakaway leagues is the culminating point of these analyses.

References

Beloff MJ, Kerr T, Demetriou M (1999) Sports law. Hart, Oxford

Brems E, Lavrysen L (2012) Human rights and international legal discourse. Human rights and sport—special issue, pp 226–228

Blackshaw I (2009) Sport, mediation and arbitration. T.M.C. Asser Press, The Hague

Casini L (2010) The Making of a Lex Sportiva (draft paper for the Max Planck Institute International Conference 'Beyond Dispute: International Judicial Institutions as Law-makers') Heidelberg, 14–15 June. http://papers.ssrn.com/sol3/papers.cfm?abstract_id=1621335

Collins R (1994) Broadcasting and audiovisual policy in the European single market. John Libby, London

Cygan A (2007) Competition and free movement issues in the regulation of formula one races. In: Bogusz B, Cygan A, Szyszczak E (eds) The regulation of sport in the European Union. Edward Elgar, UK, pp 74–94

Elias N, Dunning E (1986) Quest for excitement: sport and leisure in the civilising process. Blackwell, Oxford

Foster K (1993) Developments in sporting law. In: Allison L (ed) The changing politics of sport. Manchester University Press, Manchester, pp 105–124

Foster K (2003) Is there a global sports law. Entertain Law 2:1–18. http://www2.warwick.ac.uk/fac/soc/law/elj/eslj/issues/volume2/number1/foster.pdf

Gardiner S, Felix A (1995) Juridification of the football field: strategies for giving law the elbow. Marquette Sports Law Rev 5:189–220

Gardiner et al (2007) Sports law, 3rd edn. Routlege, London

Halgreen L (2004) European sports law: a comparative analysis of the European and American models of sport. Forlaget Thomson, Copenhagen

Hart HLA (1961) The concept of law. Clarendon Press, Oxford

Hoehn T, Lancefield D (2003) Broadcasting and sport. Oxford Rev Econ Policy 19:552–568

James M (2010) Sports law. Palgrave Macmillan, London

Lewis A, Taylor J (eds) (2003) Sport: law and practice. Butterworths, London
Malloy DC (2003) Understanding the nature of ethics, and purposes of business health care and law. The sport we want: essays on current issues in community sport in Canada, Canadian centre for ethics in sport, pp 59–79. http://www.cces.ca/files/pdfs/CCES-PAPER-Malloy-E.pdf
Massey P (2007) Are sports cartels different? An analysis of EU commission decisions concerning collective selling arrangements for football broadcasting rights. World Compet 30:87–106
Moore SF (1973) Law and social change: the semi-autonomous filed as an appropriate field of study. Law Soc Rev 7:719–746
Opie H (1996) Sports associations and their legal environment. In: McGregor-Lowndes M, Fletcher K, Sievers S (eds) Legal issues for non-profit associations. LBC, Sydney, pp 74–94
Parrish R (2003) Sports law and policy in the European Union. Manchester Unuiversity Press, Manchester
Parrish R (2012) Lex Sportiva and the European Union sports law. Eur Law Rev 37:716–733
Pijetlovic K (2010) Another classic of EU sports jurisprudence: legal implications of Olympique Lyonnais SASP v. Olivier Bernard and Newcastle UFC (C-325/08). Eur Law Rev 35:858–869
Pijetlovic K (2013) Fundamental rights of athletes in the EU post-Lisbon. In: Kerikmäe T (ed) Protecting human rights in the EU: controversies and challenges of the Charter of Fundamental Rights. Springer
Pluim B et al (2007) Sports science and medicine in tennis. Br J Sports Med 41:703–704
Soek J (2006) Sport in national sports acts and constitutions: definition, ratio legis and objectives. Int Sports Law J 3–4:28–34
Teubner G, Bremen F (1987) Juridification—concepts, aspects, limits, solutions. In: Teubner G (ed) Juridification of social spheres: a comparative analysis in the areas of labor, corporate, antitrust, and social welfare law. European University Institute/de Gruyter, Berlin, pp 3–6
Velázquez Hernández P (2008) The European Commission's White Paper on Sport. In: Blanpain R, Hendrickx F, Colucci M (eds) Future of sports law in the European Union: beyond the EU Reform Treaty and White Paper. Kluwer Law International, The Netherlands, pp 77–86
Weatherill S (2006) Anti-doping revisited—the demise of the rule of 'purely sporting' interest? Eur Compet Law Rev 27:645–657
Weatherill S (2007) Overlapping legal orders: what is the 'purely sporting' rule. In: Bogusz B, Cygan A, Szyszczak E (eds) The regulation of sport in the European Union. Edward Elgar, Cheltenham, UK, pp 48–73
Weatherill S (2009) The influence of EU law on sports governance. In: Gardiner S, Parrish R, and Siekmann RCR (eds), EU, sport, law and policy: regulation, re-regulation and representation, T.M.C Asser Press, The Hague, pp 79–100

Chapter 2
The Sporting Industry

Contents

2.1 Specificities/Special Characteristics of the Sporting Industry 31
2.1.1 Preliminary Remark on Phraseology 31
2.1.2 The Concept of Specificity of Sport in EU Law and Policy 32
2.1.3 Special Characteristics of Sport 34
2.2 Structural Models of Sport 36
2.2.1 Classic European Model of Sport 36
2.2.2 US Model of Sport 38
2.2.3 Changing Characteristics of European Football 40
2.3 Financing of Sport 42
2.3.1 Macroeconomic Aspects 42
2.3.2 Microeconomic Aspects 43
References 45

2.1 Specificities/Special Characteristics of the Sporting Industry

2.1.1 Preliminary Remark on Phraseology

A lot of academic discussions thus far have focused on the question of 'is sport special?' in EU law and policy.[1] The objection to this is not related to the debate itself but to the phrasing of the theme of the debate. Regarding the general approach under freedom of movement provisions, sport is in principle not treated much differently than any other industry. The European Commission and the Court of Justice of the European Union ('CJEU' or 'the Court') always take into

[1] See, for e.g. Szyszczak 2007, pp. 3–32; and Siekmann 2008, pp. 37–49.

K. Pijetlovic, *EU Sports Law and Breakaway Leagues in Football*,
ASSER International Sports Law Series, DOI 10.1007/978-94-6265-048-0_2

consideration the specificities of each industry and special circumstances of each case when enforcing and interpreting the provisions of the Treaty, and certain industries are in fact separately regulated due to their own specific requirements. In this sense, while it has its peculiar characteristics (specificities or special nature) which have to be taken into account in the application and interpretation of EU law as a matter of constitutional requirement under Article 165(1) TFEU, as well as a matter of judicial and administrative practice so far, sport is not special. The Nice Declaration on Sport states that 'the Community must, in its action under the various Treaty provisions, take account of the social, educational and cultural functions inherent in sport and making it special'. This is not to say that sport is special under EU law but that, as many other industries, it has its own specificities which distinguish it from other sectors. By the same token, agriculture, fisheries, transport and the financial sector each have their own specificities which make them special in the sense that no other industry has that particular characteristic. Not once in the Court's jurisprudence or the Commission's practice was there an indication that sport is 'special' or that such an interpretation might hold to justify the wording in which the question is asked. In *Walrave* the Court made an exception for rules on direct discrimination of workers/service providers in the sporting sector in the matters that pertain to the selection of athletes for national representative teams. However, this is not incomparable to the exception for directly discriminatory measures regarding employment in the public service under Article 45(4) TFEU. In *Meca-Medina* the Court adopted a special approach under Article 101(1) for regulatory rules in sport. But this approach was borrowed from *Wouters* and its predecessor *DLG*, in which regulatory rules in a non-sporting context were examined and in both of which the Court applied the same test prior to *Meca-Medina*. Therefore, the discussion should be reconceptualised and the question refocused on the specificities of the industry that distinguish it from other 'ordinary' industries and merit consideration, the significance those specificities possess in EU law, and the degree to which they [should] matter when applying EU law to the specific sporting issues.[2] The answers to these enquiries are very context-sensitive and would have to be considered on a case-by-case basis. It is time to dispose of the question 'is sport special?' in academic writing on the topic.

2.1.2 The Concept of Specificity of Sport in EU Law and Policy

The legal concept of the specific nature of sport has been established, recognised and taken into account in the jurisprudence of the Court and in the Commission's practice. In freedom of movement cases when the case does not fit into any of the

[2] The only use of the idea and the word of sport being 'special' can be found in European policy documents which represent political and ideological goals and should therefore not be taken as conveying authoritative legal expressions. See, for instance, Nice Declaration.

sporting exceptions that apply at the level of restriction analysis (that themselves take into consideration the specificity of sport), the specific nature of sport was taken into consideration on the level of objective justification and proportionality analysis.[3] Similar analysis, which adopted the *Wouters* approach, was also conducted in the sports cases falling under EU competition law.[4] The European Commission explained that in order to assess the compatibility of sporting rules with any EU law, it considers the legitimacy of the objectives pursued by the rules, whether any restrictive effects of those rules are inherent in the pursuit of the objectives and whether they are proportionate to them.[5] Some examples of the objectives specific to the sporting community accepted as legitimate so far have been ensuring regularity of competitions,[6] maintaining the balance between clubs by preserving a certain degree of equality and uncertainty as to results, encouraging the recruitment and training of young players,[7] and combating doping in order for competitive sport to be conducted fairly including the need to safeguard equal chances for athletes, athletes' health, the integrity and objectivity of competitive sport and ethical values in sport.[8] However, 'each sport has its specificities and deserves to be treated differently according to these objectives. The EU will thus not impose general rules applicable to all European sports'.[9] This approach is something that sport federations agree on with the Commission.[10]

The White Paper on Sport addressed some of the general aspects of, and divided the approach to, the concept of specificity of sport into *the specificity of the sport structure* (notably including the autonomy and diversity of sport organisations, a pyramid structure of competitions from grassroots to the elite level, organised solidarity mechanisms between the different levels and operators, the organisation of sport on a national basis, and the principle of a single international federation per sport), and *the specificity of sporting activities and of sporting rules* (such as separate competitions for men and women, limitations on the number of participants in competitions, and the need to ensure uncertainty of outcomes and preserve a competitive balance between clubs taking part in the same competitions).[11] The Commission Staff Working Document on Sport and Free Movement

---

[3] See, for e.g. Case C-325/08 *Olympique Lyonnais SASP v. Olivier Bernard and Newcastle United FC* judgment of Grand Chamber of the Court delivered on 16 March 2010.

[4] Case C-519/04 *David Meca-Medina and Igor Majcen v. Commission* [2006] ECR I-6991 discussed in detail in Sect. 5.5.5.

[5] Commission Communication on Developing European Dimension in Sport (2011), para 4.2.

[6] Case C-176/96 *Lehtonen and Castors Braine* [2000] ECR I-2681.

[7] Case C-415/93 *Union Royale Belge Sociétés de Football Association and others v. Bosman and others* [1995] ECR I-4921, and Case C-325/08 *Bernard*, judgment delivered on 16 March 2010.

[8] Case 519/04 *Meca-Medina*.

[9] Paragraph 4.1 of the Commission Staff Working Document.

[10] See White Paper Consultation by Commissioner Figel with European Sport Federations, Sport Governance in Europe, Brussels 20/09/2006. More than 30 European sports federations took part in the meeting.

[11] White Paper on Sport, para 4.1.

of January 2011 states that 'the specificity of sport cannot be used as an excuse for making a general exception to the application of free movement rules to sports activities. Exceptions from the EU's fundamental principles must be limited and based on specific circumstances'.[12]

Finally, the concept of specificity of sport has been included in the Article 165 of the Treaty. Whereas the general approach to sports cases and the analytical structure have not been changed by this inclusion, there is an indication that after the Lisbon Treaty amendments entered into force, the concept might have gained some additional weight within the framework of the familiar analysis.[13] The study group on the Lisbon Treaty and EU sports policy recommended to the sports movement to take a lead in defining the contested term, rather than passively relying on the reference to the 'specific nature of sport' contained in Article 165 to seek to repel the influence of EU law in sport. They further recommended that the 'definition should be built into the relevant sports regulations following an open and transparent method of operation facilitated by the governing bodies but involving affected stakeholders. The definition should be thoroughly reasoned and backed with robust data'.[14] Presumably, therefore, if the regulations and rules are drafted in this way, they are likely to comply with the requirements of EU law. Compliance with EU law is also the reason why after the *Meca-Medina* judgment and the White Paper on Sport, governing bodies have been much concerned with enhancing their adherence to the principles of good governance.

In case of doubt, the sport stakeholders are free to turn to the Commission for guidance on the relation between EU law and sporting rules in professional and amateur sport as well as ask about appropriate interpretation of the concept of the specific nature of sport. Regarding the application of EU competition law, the procedure in Regulation 1/2003 will continue to apply.[15]

2.1.3 Special Characteristics of Sport

The typical list of general characteristics peculiar to the sporting industry includes the following: First, *mutual interdependence* between the clubs fostered by the need to preserve uncertainty of the result is a truly distinctive feature not possessed by any other industry. It is not the purpose of clubs in their role as undertakings to eliminate their competitors from the market because without competitors there would be no purpose to running a club. The product of a certain sports league is the game, and the game must be interesting and integrated into a structured competition in order to attract an audience. Accordingly, the more equal the competitors,

---

[12] At p. 7.

[13] See Sect. 1.3.4.4 above on Article 165 TFEU and Sect. 4.8 below on the *Bernard* case.

[14] The Lisbon Treaty and EU Sports Policy Study (2010), pp. 11–12.

[15] Commission Communication on Developing European Dimension in Sport (2011), para 4.2.

the more uncertain the result, and the more interesting the game—i.e. the product, becomes more marketable.[16]

Second, the need to maintain *competitive balance* is a driving force behind *financial solidarity* mechanisms that exist in many sports.[17] The most common ones are vertical and horizontal solidarity in the same discipline. For example, a football club's participation in a league is often conditioned upon the transfer of the broadcasting rights to the league, which after collectively selling the rights thus acquired, distributes the profits to all the participating clubs with a view to improving competitive balance between them. Sometimes a part of this profit goes to the lower leagues consisting of clubs that are, at least theoretically, potential future competitors. In no other industry would the companies share a part of their profits with their less well-off competitors, i.e. engage in horizontal solidarity.[18] Vertical solidarity implies channelling part of the finances from the most profitable leagues to the grassroots. Vertical investments and support for social causes, however, can find its parallels in other industries, albeit on a voluntary basis related to social responsibility rather than as a matter of a compulsory rule of the association or organisation to which they are affiliated.

Third, sports have a *transient nature*: individual sportsperson's careers are short and prone to many interruptions or abrupt endings due to injuries; sports broadcasting must take place as the event occurs; sports betting is a time-restricted game of chance and skill; commercial exploitation of, for example, certain sports merchandise, is limited to a short period in which the theme affixed to the item is popular; live attendance at the stadiums is a once-in-a-lifetime event and so on. It is essential that the personal or commercial assets are used in timely fashion—otherwise the possibility of their exploitation is lost.

Fourth, as recognised by the Court in its case law,[19] sport performs an important *social, cultural and educational function*. This function is confirmed by the inclusion of sports into the framework of the Treaty, as well as by numerous policy documents. Apart from the obvious, it includes issues such as social inclusion, the health of the population, the fight against doping, and prevention of violence and racial intolerance. It is mostly this aspect of sports that has formed the basis of objective justifications accepted as such thus far in the Court's jurisprudence. In addition, the Association of European Team Sports (ETS) has drawn attention to the importance of volunteering which is 'deeply entrenched in the community and

[16] Simmons 2009, p. 79. Scientific evidence on the correlation between uncertainty and popularity varies as some researchers suggest that the game is to be more visited when the home team has two times more chances of winning.

[17] There are vertical and horizontal solidarity mechanisms: the former implies financial solidarity between professional and amateur leagues and clubs, financing of various social causes, infrastructure, etc. The latter implies financial solidarity between the clubs participating in the same league.

[18] This is not to say that the commercially most successful clubs are happy with the distributional solidarity system. See Chap. 3.

[19] See, for e.g. Case C-415/93 *Union Royale Belge Sociétés de Football Association and others v. Bosman and others* [1995] ECR I-4921.

volunteer movements' whose 'selfless commitment underpins grassroots activities, the development of the federations' respective sports and the promotion of sporting values'.[20]

Finally, specificities inbuilt in certain aspects of sport confer upon it a certain degree of *exemption from application of ordinary laws*. This is most obvious in the application of criminal laws. For example, hitting and injuring another person is allowed in combat sports within the agreed-upon rules (such as boxing) and might win a match rather than time in prison,[21] and use of illegal drugs will subject sportspersons to sporting sanctions such as prohibitions on competing for a certain period of time rather than being subject to criminal proceedings. Similarly, normal labour laws do not apply to players in their capacity as 'workers' in the sporting industry. Their employment is still regulated differently from employment in the ordinary private sector.[22] A number of other regulatory and disciplinary aspects are left entirely in the hands of sporting authorities but can be challenged before the ordinary administrative and/or judicial authorities in addition to sport's own internal dispute settlement mechanisms.

These are some of the most distinctive features of the sector. While it is easy to list them and recognise that no other industry possess quite the same characteristics, it is much more difficult to develop specific guidelines as to the scope and mode of application of the term 'specificity of sport' in legal disputes. This is because the analysis is conducted on a case-by-case basis and the scope and mode of application therefore depend on many different factors surrounding the dispute. The White Paper on Sport provides a sufficient legal compass for assessment of the sporting rules for their compatibility with the EU law.

2.2 Structural Models of Sport

2.2.1 Classic European Model of Sport

Sport in Europe is typically (but not necessarily and not in all sports) organised in a pyramid structure. At the bottom of the pyramid are the amateur, semi-professional and professional clubs that play in various leagues according to their sporting achievements. They are all members of the national federations for their particular sport. The purpose of amateur clubs is largely recreation and the development of young players, while the more professional clubs operate as commercial undertakings with the main goal of maximising profits. National federations organise competition and regulate the sport in question at the national level, and

[20] The Position of the ETS on Article 165 of the Lisbon Treaty, p. 2.

[21] See, however, Blackshaw 2008, pp. 106–107.

[22] For instance, rules on transfer of players between clubs, contractual ties, as well as the 'home grown rule' on fielding the players are a part of the debates on this topic. A related topic is the application of internal market rules to the rules of sport bodies governing the players' contracts.

represent their branch at the European and international level.[23] European and global governing bodies are at the apex of the structure. Only one federation per country can be a member of the European or global governing body.[24] European and other regional confederations (usually organised roughly by continent) support and share the organisation of sport with the world federation. Nafziger saw the facilitation of an equitable distribution of revenue among the constituent sports clubs with the purpose of encouraging mass participation and competitive balance among clubs as the primary function of the pyramid structure.[25]

The described 'one-federation-per-sport' structure reveals the apparent monopolistic position of the governing bodies that regulate everything from professional to amateur and youth sports. They are able to pass the rules and regulations which affect the way in which clubs buy and sell players, dispose of their commercial rights, conduct themselves on the stock market, impose disciplinary sanctions which in turn affect the clubs' profits, and so on.

For example, in football, a club such as FC Milan is affiliated with the Federazione Italiana Giuoco Calcio (Italian football federation—FIGC). The FIGC, the national federation, governs the game of football in Italy from all levels of clubs as well as the national team and is affiliated with *Union des Associations Européennes de Football* (UEFA). UEFA has 53 such member national associations. In addition to playing games in its Italian-based league, FC Milan, is (at the moment) one of the top four teams in the Italian Serie A (the highest Italian league) and is thus eligible to play in the UEFA-organised Champions League.[26] The world governing body for football is the *Fédération Internationale de Football Association* (FIFA). FIFA regulates matters and organises football events that have worldwide importance, such as the men's and women's World Cups. FIFA is comprised of six continental federations and 208 national federations. Many other sports in Europe have similar basic organizational arrangements (such as basketball), while others do not (such as boxing).

However, as the European Commission points out, in view of the diversity and complexities of European sport structures, it is unrealistic to try and define a unified model of organisation.[27]

> [...]it must be recognised that any attempt at precisely defining the 'European Sport Model' quickly reaches its limits. Some of the features often presented as 'characteristic', such as the system of open competitions based on promotion and relegation, are actually

---

[23] Most of the European countries also have a pan-federation of national federations acting as an umbrella organisation for all national federations.

[24] European Commission, The European Model of Sport, Consultation Document of DG X (September 2008).

[25] Nafziger 2009, p. 37.

[26] The best performing football clubs in the highest national leagues are qualified to play in the UEFA Champions League, the most prestigious pan-European league. Every European country has a space for at least one club. The number of places in the competition depends on the national association's rank in the UEFA coefficients table. Accordingly, countries such as Spain, England and Italy have 4 places reserved for their best teams in the Champions League, whereas, for instance, Finland, Sweden and Estonia have only one place.

[27] White Paper on Sport, para 4.

limited to a certain category of sport (team sport in this specific case). As a matter of fact, even for team sports the system of open competitions is somewhat mitigated by a licensing system that introduces financial criteria for participation in competitions.

Other sports present in Europe have adopted a totally or partially closed system for participation in professional sport competitions, such as motor-sports or cycling. The relevance of the pyramid structure for the organisation of competitions (and of the sport itself) is thus greatly reduced. It should be noted that the organisation of competitions also largely diverges from the pyramid structure in other sports, such as golf or tennis.[28]

European sports leagues are open and operate on the basis of a system of promotion and relegation. Clubs are able to move up and down through the leagues depending on their on-pitch performance. If a club is successful in its league during a season, as measured by the number of points won, it can pass to compete in the higher league as of next season (promotion), and conversely, if a club constantly underperforms it can fall out into the lower league at the end of season (relegation). While there are different schemes for this system, depending on the rules of the respective national associations, it is common that the three best teams from the lower league pass into the higher league and are replaced by the three worst performing team from that league. For example, in the English Football League Championship, the two best performing teams are automatically promoted into the Premier League while the next four teams compete for the third place in the Premier League through play-offs.[29] In practice, however, rich clubs are almost never relegated as their financial resources ensure the acquisition of the star players helping them to win matches. Conversely, small clubs playing in the third or fourth national division and depending on different model of financing[30] are likely to never make it to the first league. This performance-based ranking in an 'open league' structure is not incomparable to the competitive 'ordinary markets' in which undertakings operate, notwithstanding the lack of a formal league structure.

2.2.2 US Model of Sport

The European model of sport must be contrasted with the American model. What follows is the orthodox (i.e. slightly exaggerated and often misjudged) European description of the distinctive features of the American model. Following the description, it will be shown that there is more similarity between the two than commonly described, and that the convergence is likely to grow in the years to come when the European model of sport formally (by formation of breakaway structures) or *de facto* (through concessions granted by the federations to the most powerful clubs, which is already happening in European football) begins to crumble.

The United States model of sport is characterised by the clear separation of amateur and professional sports. Professional sport leagues in the US are honest

[28] Commission Staff Working Paper, para 4.1.

[29] For more examples, see Szymanski 2009, p. 685.

[30] For different models of financing see Sect. 2.3.2.

and unambiguous about profit maximising being their most important goal. The four most popular professional team sports are organised in major leagues, each currently with 30–32 teams: Major League Baseball (MLB), National Hockey League (NHL), National Basketball Association (NBA) and National Football League (NFL). Participating teams adopt a constitution similar to business corporations, and elect a Commissioner in charge of administration, interpretation and enforcement of the rules and the discipline of the sport and the league. Commercially the leagues operate as associations of franchises, but also as joint ventures among the constituent teams. Each franchise is usually owned by either very wealthy individuals or large corporations.[31]

Furthermore, in US sports the leagues consist of a collection of franchises and do not operate the system of promotion and relegation. The leagues are closed for their members and clubs cannot fall out of the league, nor is there is a possibility for new clubs to enter the league, unless a super-majority of the participating members decide to expand and admit new members or expel existing ones. Entry is usually subject to substantial fees which are then divided between the existing members. In this sense, the leagues are 'hermetic'. But they are also 'closed' because teams belonging to different leagues in the same discipline do not compete with each other, and play only within their own league.[32] Their players normally do not participate in the World Cups to represent their country. However, NBA 'dream teams' participate at the Olympic Games, MLB players have participated in the 'World Baseball Classic', and NHL players regularly participate in the World Hockey Championships. The latter is qualified because the Championships run during the same time as the NHL playoffs, so only those players who are not in the playoffs, or who are eliminated in the first round show up. But, unlike in European football, where the rules requiring national service are mandated by FIFA, the NHL is not under the umbrella of the world governing body for ice hockey, so even if there were such rules the NHL would not be bound by them. Solidarity mechanisms that are designed to maintain the internal equilibrium in competitions of US professional leagues include collective sales of media rights (like in Europe), and the salary caps and draft system (unlike in Europe).

The lower level in the professional hierarchy is represented by the minor leagues that compete at levels below that of major leagues. There can be many geographically distributed minor leagues. In baseball, all of the minor leagues are run as independent businesses, and many are members of Minor League Baseball, an umbrella organization for leagues that have agreements to operate as affiliates of MLB. Each league affiliated with Minor League Baseball comprises teams that are independently owned and operated but always directly affiliated with, and occasionally named after, one major league team, enforced through the so-called Player Development Contracts with that team. These are beneficial for the minor-league

[31] Two exceptions to the rule are the NFL's Green Bay Packers, who are owned by members of the local community, and teams that end up under league stewardship, such as the NHL's Phoenix Coyotes, or the NBA's New Orleans Hornets.

[32] Halgreen 2004, p. 77.

teams as they get borderline major-league talent, and usually funding/staff, etc. from their major-league teams. This is why the lower levels of the professional sports are sometimes referred to as 'farm systems'. Independent leagues do not have any links to MLB, and thus are not members of 'organized baseball'.

Amateur sports in the US are separated from the professional structures.[33] The extent to which high-school and college sport is associated with education is remarkable. Students often receive scholarships to universities and colleges in recognition of their sporting potential and some of the universities are more known and respected for their sport teams than academic quality. These amateur sports are seen as the incubators for talent from which professional leagues' clubs often draft top student athletes to sign professional contracts once they have completed their education. European sporting organisations, by contrast, are traditionally unconcerned with the education of young athletes alongside their sporting career.

2.2.3 Changing Characteristics of European Football

It has already been noted that the European description of the US model is exaggerated and that many features are not as extreme as commonly depicted by European commentators. Grassroots involvement as well as the strong social role of non-professional competition in North American sports culture is often ignored; even though the American model is closed and horizontally integrated, there is a subtle pyramid structure (albeit not formally organised as it is in Europe) which is also ignored; the slow and gradual process of promotion and relegation mechanisms do exist in a form with the possibility for teams to be relocated from big to small cities (i.e. from big to small markets) when they fail to produce satisfactory commercial revenues (from, for e.g. ticket sales) due to their poor competitive standing such as Seattle to Oklahoma (in NBA); Atlanta to Winnipeg (in NHL); LA to St. Louis and to Oakland (in NFL). Conversely, there are many examples of clubs from small markets moving to big markets, such as Montreal to Washington (in MLB); Winnipeg to Phoenix and Quebec to Denver (in NHL); Cleveland to Baltimore (in NFL); and Charlotte to New Orleans (in NBA).[34]

On the other side of Atlantic, the changes in the club licensing system in football have eroded the strict system of promotion and relegation. They were introduced at the beginning of the 2004/2005 season and were modelled on the French practice of replacing the competitive merit-based approach to the clubs' standing with more comprehensive criteria. A series of defined quality standards, which

---

[33] Amateur sports—essentially competitions involving unpaid athletes—are governed by several layers of authority: community leagues, school athletic associations, state and national regulatory boards, the National Collegiate Athletic Association (NCAA) and other supervisory organisations at the non-professional level, the Amateur Sport Act, and the rules and processes of the Olympic movement. See Nafziger 2008, p. 102.

[34] Thanks are due to Ryan Gauthier for interview, 2 May 2011.

now must be fulfilled in order for a club to be admitted to any of the UEFA club competitions cover matters including youth football development, medical care, experience of club staff, coaching standards, stadium and training facilities, legal declarations, audited accounts, settlement of debts, additional financial disclosures and financial budgets with supporting assumptions among the 34 specific criteria.[35] The result of the changed licensing rule is apt to be a semi-closed tournament system similar to the North American model.[36] Apparently, the criteria will be easier to fulfil for the clubs already in good financial standing than for those that struggle with budgetary problems. Contrary to the goals related to preserving competitive balance that UEFA relies on to defend some of its restrictive rules, this is a way to solidify the imbalance that already exists in European football.[37]

Globalisation of the world's economies, the technological revolution within the broadcasting and telecommunication industries, and the subsequent explosion in media revenues are seen as factors that have brought the European and American sports industries closer to one another.[38] The European Parliament Report on the future of professional football in Europe recognises that the current trend of clubs going to the stock market is one step closer to the US model. It can be questioned whether the two goals (winning the game and maximising the shareholders' profits) can be combined within the traditional open European model.[39] Furthermore, both models of sport have certain shared ends such as the quest to find balance between cooperation and competition, and to enhance competitive balance between the clubs based on two principles of competition: equality of teams and uncertainty of outcome. It is the means by which they achieve these ends that differ. In the US, rules on annual players' drafts, hard and soft salary caps, sharing of broadcasting revenues, as well as the strong role of the players' unions are intended to reinforce the competitive balance. In European football 'a traditional reluctance' to adopt such restraints has led to competitive imbalances with the result that well-established elite clubs dominate the sport and reinforce those imbalances.[40] It seems, however, that despite the restraint mechanisms, the US sports are plagued with the same disease of imbalance in competitive strengths of the teams. ESPN reported that '[m]oney allows the NBA to ignore the fact that a third of its teams exist in an underclass. Despite more than half of the league (16 of 30 teams) qualifying for the

---

[35] UEFA Club Licensing and Financial Fair Play Regulations.

[36] Nafziger 2008, p. 101.

[37] Manchester United has won the Premier League (in which 20 teams compete) 10 times since its creation in 1992, Arsenal 3 times and Chelsea 2 times. C.F. Real Madrid has won 9 times in the European Cup/Champion League, 31 times in the Spanish League, and 17 times in the Spanish Cup. C.F. Real Madrid, AC Milan, Manchester United, FC Bayern Munich, and Liverpool F.C have between themselves won 28 European Cups/Champions Leagues since the creation of this competition in 1956.

[38] Halgreen 2004, p. 42.

[39] European Parliament Report on the future of professional football in Europe (2006/2130(INI)), Committee on Culture and Education, final A6-0036/2007, p. 14.

[40] Nafziger 2008, p. 104. See also Camatsos 2005, pp. 155–180.

playoffs every year, 11 teams have either won no playoff series or gotten past the first round just once in the last 10 years. The Washington Wizards have made it past the first round exactly once in the last 30 years'.[41] This leads to the conclusion that the mechanisms aimed at enhancing competitive balance between the teams in the league do not work if they are not accompanied by efficient financial solidarity mechanisms, and conversely, financial solidarity (especially if insufficient) will not contribute in any perceptible way towards competitive balance if unaccompanied by effective restraints on competition.

2.3 Financing of Sport

2.3.1 Macroeconomic Aspects

On a macroeconomic level, European sport is directly financed from four major sources. They are: (1) households (purchasing of sporting goods and services, sports betting); (2) the central government; (3) the local government, and; (4) enterprises (e.g. sponsorship, TV and media rights).[42] Partial tax exemption is available in most European countries as an indirect source of finance for sport organisations supplying public utility sporting activities, or for private persons who bring funds into sport.

Households are by far the most significant private sector contributor in all European countries, whereas local and regional governments account for most of the contributions in the public sector. Available data from 1990 that included 11 European countries attributed an average of 64 % of overall sport financing to households, 9.5 % to enterprises, 20 % to local governments, and only 6.5 % to central governments. Information dating back to 2000 showed a trend of increase in household, and decrease in public (both local and central government) share of sport finance.[43] Unfortunately, a much-needed report of a newer date is lacking, which prevents any conclusions on the current trends based on macroeconomic indicators. Currently, the Commission is preparing a study to assess the sport sector's contribution to the Europe 2020 strategy, with particular emphasis on contribution to economic growth and employment in the EU.

A study taken during the French presidency of the EU distinguished between three categories of sports participation (amateur sport contests, leisure and health sports practice, and high level sport) and demonstrated that each source of finance is predominantly allocated to one of those three categories. Households are geared toward leisure and health sport practice and then to high level sport; enterprises prioritise high level sport with high media exposure in a limited number of sport

[41] ESPN 'The Sports Bubble' by Howard Bryant, 7 March 2013.

[42] Andreff 2009a, p. 271.

[43] Ibid. p. 272.

disciplines; local authorities allocate their sport budgets mostly to amateur sport contests, and central government to high level sport.[44] Several economists have observed such allocation of central government contributions, accompanied by a tendency for private finance to flow into media-exposed high level sport, is threatening to break down the European pyramidal structure at its foundations due to the lack of financing.[45] Taking into consideration the organisation of sport in Europe, they suggest that averting this threat will require adoption of a series of measures: strong solidarity mechanisms at the Member State level; favouring private financing of mass sport (sport governance matters here and it should be designed so as to avoid a takeover of sport by purely financial concerns); supporting voluntary work, which is the pillar of the European model, and; a more pro-active role for the local authorities in defining sports public policy. Furthermore, betting and gambling revenue paybacks to sport must be maintained as they can make up to three quarters of a sports minister's budget (as was the case in Greece) and one quarter of overall public sport financing.[46] What this proposal actually entails is the concerted effort of different stakeholders in sport necessary to bring about a series of measures to consolidate the foundations of the pyramid structure, if such a structure is to be maintained.

2.3.2 Microeconomic Aspects

On a microeconomic level, it is important to distinguish between financing of amateur and professional clubs. Economic viability of the former is primarily dependent on subscriptions, private cash donations, subsidies and, in cases of more advanced amateur clubs with a certain fan base, gate receipts and sponsorship. All the sources of finances for amateur clubs are local.[47]

Regarding professional clubs, it is important to emphasise the differences between traditional and contemporary models of financing. The traditional model that prevailed in the 1960s until the 1990s relied on gate receipts, subsidies and corporate sponsorship. TV revenues as sources of income appeared only in the 1980s but were not an important contributor to the overall budget. In fact, in 1967, the English Football Premier League turned down a £1 million offer from the BBC for the live broadcasting of championship matches because it was afraid that acceptance of such a contract would lead to losses from declining gate receipts.[48] As no other broadcasting companies existed at the time, there was no competition for the

---

[44] Cabinet Amnyos, 'Etude du financement public et privé du sport', Etude réalisée dans le cadre de la présidence française de l'Union européenne, Ministère de la Santé, de la Jeunesse, des Sports et de la Vie Associative et du Secrétariat d'Etat aux Sports, Paris (October 2008) cited in Andreff and Szymanski 2009.

[45] Andreff et al. 2009.

[46] Ibid.

[47] Andreff and Staudohar 2000, pp. 257–276.

[48] Andreff 2009b, p. 690.

TV rights and the offers remained confined to that of monopsony, usually held in each country by one public channel. This situation, which prevailed until the early 1990s, changed dramatically. The emergence of private broadcasters and increase in number of public broadcasters coupled with tremendous technological progress in the audiovisual industry started a new era in football financing: TV rights became the biggest part of the professional football club revenue. Broadcasting companies were competing to make the best offer and the leagues or clubs were negotiating the best possible deal for their rights.[49] Sponsorship deals consequently became far more lucrative due to television exposure. Merchandise was marketed more professionally and their sales made up a significant portion of the budget in some better-known clubs. These changes led to the decline of the traditional model of financing.[50] The contemporary model is based on professional management in the club administration, ownership by corporate giants including broadcasters, entry into capital markets, and a sole concern for profit maximising and growth to gain the competitive edge over other clubs' financial performance (i.e. a strategy focused on enhancing the main factor that determines the outcome of the matches).

The essence of successful on-pitch performance is the acquisition of star players through the liberalised player transfer market, a rare commodity. Excess demand has inflated the salaries of the star players to a level that often placed clubs into financial trouble. Deloitte's Annual Review of Football Finance 2012 notes that 'control of player wages, in order to deliver robust and sustainable businesses, continues to be football's greatest commercial challenge'. The sustainability of the contemporary model of financing for professional clubs therefore heavily depends on a dynamic equilibrium between a club's spending on wages and its media revenues.[51] Due to a trend of ownership by wealthy tycoons some clubs are able to spend far more than they earn. Seeking to attain a better balance between revenue and costs and reduce the burden of ongoing funding required from owners or other sources, the new UEFA Financial Fair Play Regulations require the clubs to at least break even and to be able to operate on the basis of their own revenues.

More recent business strategies of the most successful leagues and clubs involve expanding to new markets such as Asia and North America. The Premier League has been particularly effective in creating and exploiting these new markets. Only a few big clubs and leagues are able to engage in a profitable business outside of Europe while for the rest of the clubs and leagues expanding to other geographical markets would be an unrealistic goal.

The main shortcoming of the contemporary model of finance and governance in European football is the dominance by rich clubs and the consequences associated with such dominance. This is the undertone of the theme of breakaway leagues, to which we turn in Chap. 3.

---

[49] See Sect. 1.2.

[50] This has been acknowledged by the Discussion Paper at the First European Conference on Sport 'Relations between Sport and Television', Olympia, 21 and 22 May 1999, p. 2.

[51] Andreff 2009b, p. 695.

References

Andreff W (2009a) Sport and financing. In: Andreff W, Szymanski S (eds) Handbook on the economics of sport. Edward Elgar, UK, pp 271–281

Andreff W (2009b) Team sports and finance. In: Andreff W, Szymanski S (eds) Handbook on the economics of sport. Edward Elgar, UK, pp 689–699

Andreff W, Staudohar P (2000) The evolving European model of professional sports finance. J Sports Econ 1:257–276

Andreff W, Szymanski S (eds) (2009) Handbook on the economics of sport. Edward Elgar, Cheltenham

Andreff W, Dutoya J, Montel J (2009) A European model of sports financing: under threat? Revue Juridique et Economique du Sport 90:75–85. http://www.playthegame.org/index.php?id=14&type=123&tx_ttnews%5Btt_news%5D=4364&cHash=6670707d68&filename=News%20Article.pdf

Blackshaw I (2008) Jail players who commit dangerous tackles. Int Sports Law J 1–2:106–107

Camatsos S (2005) European sports, the transfer system and competition law: will they ever find a competitive balance? Sports Law J 12:155–180

Halgreen L (2004) European sports law—a comparative analyses of the European and American models of sport. Forlaget Thomson, Copenhagen

Nafziger JAR (2008) A comparison of the European and North American models of sports organisation. Int Sports Law J 3–4:100–108

Nafziger JAR (2009) A comparison of the European and North American models of sports organisation. In: Gardiner S, Parrish R, Siekmann CR (eds) EU, sport, law and policy: regulation, re-regulation and representation. T.M.C Asser Press, The Hague, pp 35–55

Siekmann R (2008) Is sport 'special' in EU law and policy. In: Blanpain R, Hendrickx F, Colucci M (eds) Future of sports law in the European Union: beyond the EU Reform Treaty and White Paper. Kluwer Law International, The Netherlands, pp 37–49

Simmons R (2009) The demand for spectator sports. In: Andreff W, Szymanski S (eds) Handbook on the economics of sport. Edward Elgar, UK, pp 77–89

Szymanski S (2009) The promotion and relegation system. In: Andreff W, Szymanski S (eds) Handbook on the economics of sport. Edward Elgar, UK, pp 685–688

Szyszczak E (2007) Is sport special? In: Bogusz B, Cygan A, Szyszczak E (eds) The regulation of sport in the European Union. Edward Elgar, UK, pp 3–32

Chapter 3
Breakaway Leagues and Governance Issues in European Football

Contents

3.1 Introduction ... 48
  3.1.1 Concept of Breakaway/Alternative League ... 48
3.2 European Structural Ideals ... 49
  3.2.1 Rhetoric in the EU Policy Instruments ... 49
  3.2.2 Sports Associations and Other Stakeholders in Football ... 52
3.3 Breakaway Threats and UEFA/FIFA Concessions ... 53
  3.3.1 Rules on Alternative Competitions in the UEFA Statutes ... 54
  3.3.2 Media Partners Proposal: European Football League ... 55
  3.3.3 UEFA Concessions in the 1998 Media Partners Case ... 59
  3.3.4 Formation of the G14 Alliance ... 61
  3.3.5 Plans for 'European Golden Cup' in 2003? ... 62
  3.3.6 UEFA Concessions on Compulsory Player Release Rule, the *Oulmers* Case and Formal Dissolution of G14 ... 62
  3.3.7 July 2011: New Breakaway Threats, Old Strategies of Old Allies ... 68
  3.3.8 Alternative Leagues in European Football ... 70
3.4 New Trends in the Governance of European Football ... 74
  3.4.1 Stakeholder Theory ... 74
  3.4.2 UEFA Mandate ... 76
  3.4.3 European Club Association: A New Face of G14 ... 77
  3.4.4 Professional Football Strategy Council ... 79
  3.4.5 The UEFA Club Competitions Committee ... 81
  3.4.6 Social Dialogue and Collective Agreements in Professional Football ... 81
  3.4.7 UEFA Club Licensing and Financial Fair Play Regulations ... 88
3.5 Risks in the Commercial and Legal Environment ... 92
3.6 Is the UEFA Champions League an Open Competition? ... 94
3.7 Conclusion ... 96
References ... 97

K. Pijetlovic, *EU Sports Law and Breakaway Leagues in Football*,
ASSER International Sports Law Series, DOI 10.1007/978-94-6265-048-0_3

3.1 Introduction

3.1.1 Concept of Breakaway/Alternative League

Breakaway leagues and alternative leagues are used as synonyms in this volume. Breakaway or alternative structures can be generally defined as closed or partly open private leagues created by a group of clubs that are joined by some common commercial interest. Thorp and Shah defined a breakaway league (in cricket) as 'a league that has been set up without the sanction of the "official" national or supra-national governing body for that sport'.[1] Breakaway leagues are often established without consent of a governing body and as such lack the recognition of a governing body. This would automatically remove such a league from the central regulatory and organisational control. At the same time, clubs participating in such a league would miss out on the advantages offered by a governing body to its members. A breakaway league can be based on a closed model as opposed to being integrated into a system of promotion and relegation with the other leagues in a given sport. The member clubs in alternative leagues are usually of comparable competitive and financial standing and are often connected by geographic proximity and/or their elite status. The clubs' decision to set up their own competition and break away from their previous structural affiliations is triggered by what is perceived as unused financial prospects existing outside the confines of that affiliation. If the clubs belonging to a breakaway group are economically the most powerful and participate in the most prestigious national and pan-European leagues, they are also capable of producing the highest quality product with a correspondingly high market value for their broadcasting rights, merchandise, tickets, etc. They are the golden goose for their discipline in a system where solidarity plays a big part in financing of the rest of the sport, and their governing bodies do not want to lose them. It is exactly this feature in European football which gives elite clubs the *supreme bargaining power* that enables them to influence the decisions of the governing bodies.

So far, all the breakaway threats by elite clubs in pan-European football have been successfully averted. However, while the pyramidal structure remains largely unchanged in its external shape, changes within the pyramid have contributed towards substantial decentralisation of the European football governance, but not necessarily in a good way, and not according to standards compatible with good governance and fair representation of all the stakeholders. The elite clubs represent a separate group of stakeholders that has been able to exert pressure on *Union des Associations Européennes de Football* (UEFA) and they have done so each time their commercial interests have been adversely affected, as described below in this chapter.

The underlying theme of this chapter is rooted in the recognition of apparent conflict between, on the one hand, the EU policy goals to preserve the traditional

---

[1] Thorp and Shah 2008, p. 6.

European sporting structures, and on the other hand, the neo-realities regarding commercial aspects and governance of European football. The endeavours of the governing bodies and most of the stakeholders in football are naturally aligned with the goals of policy-makers on the issue of structural changes. The prospects for creation of a pan-European breakaway league can be analysed from the point of view of football governance, the commercial environment and the legal environment.

3.2 European Structural Ideals

3.2.1 Rhetoric in the EU Policy Instruments

A political consensus regarding the need to preserve the structures of sport in Europe was emphasised by a number of EU policy documents, notably in the Commission Helsinki Report, with a view to safeguarding the current sports structures.[2] In this Report 'the temptation for certain sporting operators and certain large clubs to leave the federations in order to derive the maximum benefit from the economic potential of sport for themselves alone' was considered symptomatic of several phenomena: the rise in popularity and internationalisation of sport, and the unprecedented development in the economic dimension of sport.[3] The Amsterdam Declaration on Sport[4] and the Nice Declaration[5] both centred on the social significance of sport. The Nice Declaration notes the developments in the world of sport, but considers that federations must continue to be the key feature of a form of organisation providing a guarantee of sporting cohesion and participatory democracy, and that ties of solidarity binding the practice of sport at every level must be preserved.[6] These policy statements are based on the desire to preserve fundamental values such as the societal role of 'sport for all', self-regulation and solidarity between professional and amateur levels, as well as the highly beneficial effects that sports have on youth, health and social inclusion policies.[7]

The 2007 Parliament Report on the future of professional football in Europe (Committee on Culture and Education) noted in a similar spirit that 'European

---

[2] Report from the Commission to the European Council with a view to safeguarding the current sports structures and maintaining the social function of sport within the Community framework ('The Helsinki Report on Sport') COM (1999) 644 final.

[3] Ibid. section 2.

[4] Declaration on sport in Amsterdam Treaty, Declaration no. 29 ('Amsterdam Declaration').

[5] Declaration on the specific characteristics of sport and its social function in Europe, of which account should be taken in implementing common policies 13948/00, Annex to the Presidency Conclusions, Nice ('Nice Declaration').

[6] Ibid.

[7] Halgreen 2004, p. 64.

sport, and football in particular, is an inalienable part of the European identity, European culture and citizenship, and the European Football Model, characterised by open sports competitions within a pyramid structure in which several hundred thousand amateur clubs and millions of volunteers and players form the base for the top professional clubs […]' and identified the growing concentration of economic wealth and sports power as a threat to the future of professional football in Europe. It stressed 'its attachment to the European Football Model, with its symbiotic relationship between amateur and professional football'.[8]

In 1998, the Commission published 'The European Model of Sport' that says: 'There is a European model of sport with its own characteristics. This model has been exported to almost all other continents and countries, with the exception of North America. Sport in Europe has a unique structure. *For the future development of sport in Europe these special features should be taken into account*'.[9] This document rejected the free market model for the future of European sport, resisting the pressures of 'Americanisation' which is seen as the ultimate evil of excessive commercialism (leading to destruction of European sporting values, the only true sporting values). This is a prime example of one of the exaggerated European depictions of the American model. As noted by Halgreen, 'one should always remember that globalisation and commercialisation are not just American inventions'.[10] In the Opinion given by the Committee of Regions on 'The European Model of Sport', the American model is centred too much on a business and market-oriented approach to sport making a clear distinction between professional and amateur sport and giving them totally separate structures. The Committee of Regions retained its faith in, and asserted its preference for, the European sociocultural model. It further emphasised the special characteristics of the European model and said that the inclusion of an economic factor should not be allowed to jeopardise traditional values.[11] There are many more policy documents with an identical take on the issue of organisational structure.

Nevertheless, there are some indications of the Commission's readiness to introduce some flexibility in the European policy regarding sporting structures. The first hint of it was given in the 2001 speech by Mario Monti, addressing the question of a single federation per sport. He acknowledged that '[w]hile the existence of a single federation overseeing both the regulatory and organisational aspects of a sport is common in Europe […] other scenarios exist or can be envisaged'.[12] In the Commission's White Paper on Sport there is a small move in the

[8] See Motion for the Parliament Resolution in the European Parliament Report on the future of professional football in Europe (2006/2130(INI)), Committee on Culture and Education, final A6-0036/2007.

[9] European Commission, The European Model of Sports, Consultation Document of DG X (September 2008) para 1.3, emphasis added.

[10] Halgreen 2004, p. 64.

[11] Opinion of the Committee of the Regions on 'The European Model of Sport' 1999/C 374/14.

[12] Mario Monti, European Commissioner for Competition. 'Competition and Sport Rules of the Game' Speech/01/84. Conference on 'Governance in Sport', Brussels 26 February 2001.

articulation of sports policy away from the prevalent socio-cultural approach towards a more economic-based approach. The Commission first repeated the previous policy statements on the pyramid structure and labelled it as worthy of support. But it went on to recognise that there is no unified description of a 'European Sports Model', as there exist partially or totally closed leagues in some sports such as motorsports and cycling, and that organisation of competitions largely diverges from the pyramid structure in other sports, such as tennis or golf. It further acknowledged that:

> *[n]ew tendencies are challenging the traditional vision of a unified "European Sport Model"*. Economic and social developments that are common to the majority of the Member States (increasing commercialisation and stagnation of public spending on the one hand, and an increase in the number of participants together with stagnation in the number of voluntary workers on the other) have resulted in new challenges for the organisation of sport in Europe. The emergence of new stakeholders (participants outside the organised disciplines, professional sports clubs etc.) and the increasing recourse to litigation are posing new questions as regards governance, democracy and representation of interests within the sports movement. [...] The Commission considers that each sport has its specificities and deserves to be treated differently according to these. The EU will not impose general rules applicable to all European sports. However, EU law will continue to apply to sport, particularly as far as competition, freedom of movement and non-discrimination rules are concerned.[13]

The Commission Communication on Developing European Dimension in Sport that came after the Lisbon Treaty amendments, however, interprets the 'specificity of sport' referred to in Article 165 TFEU as the concept encompassing 'all the characteristics that make sport special, such as for instance the interdependence between competing adversaries or the pyramid structure of open competitions'.[14]

There is no doubt that Article 49(1) and (3) of the UEFA Statutes[15] on sanctioning alternative competitions and a pyramid structure find a firm support in European sports policy. But this policy should be taken within its own limits as having no binding force[16] and within its own wording as not being absolute but rather dependant on a rule in question which is to be examined against the requirements of EU law. On a careful reading, all that the Commission emphasised is the need to take the pyramid structure with open leagues into account in the application of EU economic provisions, as it falls under the concept of 'specificity of sport' in Article 165 TFEU. It is the word of the Court, the original creator of the concept, in the exercise of the functions conferred to it under the Treaty that can ultimately decide the matter. The reasoning that the Court is likely to apply to the UEFA rules on sanctioning of alternative leagues, if challenged, is explored in Chap. 7 in detail.

---

[13] Whiter Paper on Sport, para 4.1 [emphasis added].

[14] Paragraph 4.2 of the Communication, COM (2011) 12 final, 18. 1. 2011.

[15] Cited below in Sect. 3.3.1.

[16] According to Article 288 TFEU.

3.2.2 Sports Associations and Other Stakeholders in Football

The Memorandum of Understanding 2007 between UEFA and the Fédération Internationale des Associations des Footballeurs Professionnels (FIFPro)[17] confirms the commitment of these bodies to key values and recognition of: solidarity, equitable distribution of wealth, collective rather than individual exploitation of resources, the need for a correct balance between labour legislation and the specific characteristics of football as a sport (which might also be achieved through collective bargaining agreements), the continuing participation of all players and clubs in the main national leagues and UEFA club competitions as essential to supporting the existence of a large and healthy professional football sector in Europe, the specificity of the career of a professional footballer, the specificity of sport, the autonomy of federations and the fact that football is best-served by the existing football family structures (although the balance of representativeness of key stakeholders within those structures can be developed further).[18] According to this memorandum, FIFPro and UEFA are opposed to the idea of breakaway involving elite football clubs. The FIFPro statement, in particular, is significant. It is the body which represents the interests of the potential employees of the breakaway structure in football, for example in the process of European social dialogue.

The Association of European Team Sports (ETS),[19] of which UEFA is a member, has expressed their commitment to principles such as: the public interest role of sports federations and their ability to regulate their respective sports; the principles of promotion and relegation and sporting merit; the financial solidarity of elite competitions with amateur sport due to the centralised sale of media rights; the fundamental importance of youth player development and the central role of the federations in this area, as well as the importance of fair compensation for clubs training players. This support is not surprising, as the core mission of the ETS is to strive for recognition of the European sports model and its constituent parts, namely the specificity of sport and the autonomy and central role of the sports federations. The ETS also supported the Commission Communication: 'The European Commission gives its backing to several aspects of the European sports model by endorsing the pyramidal governance structure, the autonomy of sports associations and open competitions based on sporting merit and the principles of promotion and relegation. The Communication also promotes financial solidarity between amateur and professional sport, and welcomes UEFA's Financial Fair Play Regulations'.[20]

The Professional Football Strategy Council within UEFA where players, leagues and clubs are represented in equal numbers is said to ensure that football

[17] Association of Professional Football Players.

[18] Memorandum of Understanding between UEFA and FIFPro, 11 October 2007.

[19] The ETS is an association of European team sports federations. It was created on 8 December 2009 and, to date, groups together the following federations: CEV (volleyball), EHF (handball), FIBA Europe (basketball), FIRA-AER (rugby), IIHF (ice hockey) and UEFA (football).

[20] News item by European Handball Federation 'ETS Supports European Commission Communication on Sport' 25 January 2011.

stays together as one family, with professional and amateur football living together within the single sports structures of the pyramidal system.[21] These bodies are committed to preserving the essential values underpinning the current European pyramid structure in sport. The fans, as stakeholders in football, are very much on UEFA's side on this issue.[22]

One of UEFA's 11 values concerns the European sports model and the specificity of sport. UEFA declares its total commitment to the European model of sport and its defining characteristics which, in its opinion, is what sport, and especially football, is all about. Protecting this model is important 'because sport is not simply a business like any other and [UEFA] cannot allow it to be treated as such'. Therefore, it is convinced that its arguments will prevail for the good of football. Another one of the 11 UEFA values concerns the pyramid structure and subsidiarity. The pyramid at the international and European level is seen as reflecting the autonomy of football, while the respect for the principle of subsidiarity in its work with the *Fédération Internationale de Football Association* (FIFA) and national associations allows UEFA to defend the interests of football in the best possible way.[23]

Beneath the EU policy goals and endeavours of numerous football bodies to maintain the structural status quo in Europe creeps the pressing factor of commercialisation and clubs' quest for new sources of profits, the corollaries of which, in the view advanced by this volume, render the pyramidal organisational structure with current style of governance damaging to the interests of European football as a whole.

3.3 Breakaway Threats and UEFA/FIFA Concessions

The formation of alternative private leagues is seen as the number one structural threat to the classic pyramidal model of football. Dissatisfaction of the elite clubs with FIFA/UEFA so far mostly related to the long-standing football rules, which further confirms the shift in power in the governance of European football. Elite clubs, as any other business undertaking, are interested in profit alone and it cannot be excluded that one day a rich Qatar corporation or an Asian tycoon will make an attractive offer that they cannot refuse.[24] According to their corporate commitments, the management of the clubs is responsible to their shareholders and not to the promotion of sport, fans or society and its causes. Their main task is to maximise returns for the owners.

---

[21] See http://www.uefa.com/uefa/stakeholders/professionalfootballstrategycouncil/index.html.

[22] See, for example, Supporters Direct 2008, pp. 2–3.

[23] UEFA—Eleven values: http://www.uefa.com/uefa/elevenvalues/index.html.

[24] Just recently French *Le Cahiers du Football* published 'Qatar Launches Dream Football League', a report on a breakaway group of 24 elite clubs that was later admitted to have been falsified. This story was reported by many news networks, occupying several pages in The Times. See 'Dream League or the Fantasy Football—Has 'The Times' Scored an Own Goal?' by John Lichfield, The Independent, 17 March 2013.

3.3.1 Rules on Alternative Competitions in the UEFA Statutes

With a different agenda and a different mandate to fulfil, UEFA fiercely opposes the formation of any such breakaway league by the elite clubs. Their rules are designed to impose severe financial and sporting penalties on the teams participating in alternative competitions without their prior approval. Article 49(1) and (3) of the UEFA Statutes provide that:

> UEFA shall have the sole jurisdiction to organize or abolish international competitions in Europe in which Member Associations and/or their clubs participate. […] International matches, competitions or tournaments which are not organized by the UEFA but are played on UEFA territory shall require the prior approval of FIFA and/or UEFA and/or the relevant Member Associations in accordance with the FIFA Regulations Governing International Matches and any additional implementing rules adopted by the UEFA Executive Committee.[25]

Although existing as a possibility, the approval is highly unlikely to be given to any alternative establishment by the elite clubs due to its terminal effect on the crown jewels of UEFA's respective dominion. In a UEFA press release that was published after the Media Partners International threat was averted, as discussed in Sects. 3.3.2 and 3.3.3, UEFA was opposed to 'any concept susceptible of having a negative influence on the existing domestic and European competitions and of endangering the future of national teams'.[26] In addition, Article 51(1) of the UEFA Statutes prohibits

> combinations or alliances between UEFA Member Associations or between leagues or clubs affiliated, directly or indirectly, to different UEFA Member Associations [to] be formed without the permission of UEFA.

Forming alliances between the participating clubs is the first step to the successful establishment of any alternative league. Thus, Article 51(1) of the UEFA Statutes may be seen as an additional hindrance for the formation of a breakaway structure.

Under the 2010 edition of the UEFA Statutes, Article 49(3), the prior approval for unsanctioned cross-broader tournaments and competitions was entirely up to UEFA and its Executive Committee. On 3 March 2011, FIFA Regulations Governing International Matches were adopted by the FIFA Executive Committee and entered into force in August the same year. The FIFA Regulations Governing International Matches set forth the procedure for notification, authorisation and other requirements for organising international matches that are relevant, *inter alia*, in the context of breakaway leagues, and were included in Article 49(3) of the UEFA Statutes (2012 edition).

The European Club Association expressly agreed to these rules via Memorandum of Understanding 2012 that governs the relationship between the clubs and UEFA.

25 UEFA Statutes, edition 2012.

26 UEFA news item 'European Club Football—National Associations, their leagues and clubs want UEFA to remain in charge', 30 July 1998.

According to paras D.1, D.3 and D.4, clubs undertake 'to recognise UEFA as the governing body of football at European level in accordance with its Statutes [...]; to ensure that none of its member clubs participate in any competition that is not organised or recognised by UEFA/FIFA' and 'to ensure that its member clubs are not members of any other association or grouping involving clubs from more than one country [...]'.[27]

Over the years UEFA has demonstrated a willingness to compromise in order to keep the pyramid structure together with itself at the apex, which brings into question the actual effect of the rule in Article 49 of the UEFA Statutes. This strategy has altered the power balance inside the pyramid and has decentralised the governance of the European football from within. This is best illustrated by considering first, the history of breakaway attempts and UEFA's responses, and second, the current governance of European football.

3.3.2 Media Partners Proposal: European Football League

It was the 1998 Media Partners proposal for the establishment of an alternative structure—which would have in all likelihood brought about the commercial death of the Champions League—that set the ball rolling. The proposal detailed all the aspects of the plan for the new pan-European football league, including finances, in a document around 200 pages long. A concise summary of that document is set out in the following paragraphs.

3.3.2.1 Notification to the Commission

The briefing paper that was presented to the Commission's Directorate General for Competition in 1998 set out the detailed plan to launch a new European Football League (EFL) outside the FIFA/UEFA structures.[28] The brief came at an advanced stage of preparation and after substantial work and resources had been invested in the project over many years. The architects of the project were the international partnership Media Partners International Ltd. (MPI). A leading international financial institution had been chosen to act as an adviser to the project. The project leaders recognised that the proposal to establish the EFL involved substantial financial risks to MPI and other potential investors. For that reason they were willing to take such risks only if a core group of clubs committed to playing in the EFL competitions (SuperLeague and the Pro Cup) on an exclusive basis for a minimum period

---

[27] Memorandum of Understanding between UEFA and ECA (2012).

[28] A series of agreements called 'Project Gandalf' on the establishment of the European Football League was notified to the Commission in Case IV/37/400—'Project Gandalf' [1999] OJ 13, C 70/5.

of 6 years, and all commercial rights to EFL competitions for the period of 6 years would belong to the EFL. These conditions are restrictions that clearly raise an issue of EU competition law, specifically, of Article 101 TFEU and therefore the notification under the (now repealed) Regulation 17[29] was deemed necessary.

3.3.2.2 Ownership and Selection Criteria

The EFL was to be 100 % owned by the 52 Founder[30] and Candidate Clubs[31] who contractually agreed to take part in the EFL for a minimum of six seasons. These clubs were given rights to decide on the rules and conduct of the competitions. Clubs offered ownership were to be selected on an objective basis according to their success in national and international competitions. The selection criteria for Founder and Candidate Clubs used a weighted average of the following components: success in European and domestic competitions over the last 10 years (45 %); commercial value of their national premier league (20 %), UEFA 1996 country ranking (10 %); average attendance at home games (10 %); stadium capacity (5 %); turnover (5 %); and number of supporters (5 %).

The EFL would have owned all of the intellectual property rights that related to the competition itself including brand name, TV rights, merchandising rights, sponsorship, advertising, licensing and multimedia rights. The marketing of media/sponsor/advertising contracts under these rights were to be managed by FootballCo, which would receive 5 % of the marketing fee. This entity was owned by MPI (up to 100 %) and other potential investors and financial institutions. The plan for FootballCo was to have a management contract with the EFL with a place on the EFL board for an initial term of 6 years.

The EFL membership was to remain fluid, as the league took account of clubs' performances. Shareholders were to be able to grant new franchises if they so decided, and to promote Candidate clubs into Founder clubs, and other clubs into Candidate clubs. Each Founder club was to have the same shareholder rights regardless of market value.

---

[29] Regulation 17/62 (EEC), the first regulation implementing Articles 85 and 86 of the Treaty, OJ 013, 21.2.1962, pp. 204–211. The system of prior notification was abolished by Council Regulation (EC) No 1/2003 of 16 December 2002 on the implementation of the rules on competition laid down in Articles 81 and 82 of the Treaty OJ L 1, 04/01/2003, pp. 1–25, in force as of 1 May 2004.

[30] Manchester United, Liverpool, Arsenal, Paris Saint-Germain, Olympique Marseille, Bayern Munich, Borussia Dortmund, Panathinaikos, Juventus, AC Milan, Inter Milan, Benfica, Real Madrid, Barcelona, Ajax and Galatasaray.

[31] Rapid Wien, Anderlecht, Club Bruges, Broendby, Aston Villa, Chelsea, Newcastle United, Blackburn Rovers, HJK Helsinki, Monaco, Bordeaux, Auxerre, Nantes, Kaiserslautern, Stuttgart, Bayern Leverkusen, Werder Bremen, Hamburg, AEK Athens, Roma, Lazio, Napoli, Parma, Rosenborg, Porto, Sporting Lisbon, Atletico Madrid, Valencia, Deportivo La Coruña, Atletico Bilbao, Glasgow Rangers, Göteborg, Grasshopper Zürich, PSV Eindhoven, Feyenoord and Fenerbahçe.

3.3.2.3 Competitions

The proposal planned two competitions to be operated by the EFL as of 2000/2001 season: the SuperLeague and the Pro Cup. The SuperLeague would consist of 32 top European Clubs (16 Franchise Clubs that automatically qualified for the SuperLeague and 16 Candidate/Invited clubs) who would compete in a league-style competition, whereas the Pro Cup would be a two-leg knockout competition between another 55 European clubs (Candidates/Invited). The winners of these two competitions would automatically qualify for the SuperLeague the following year. Additionally, the plan included a number of competitions called the Shootouts: the 3 winners of the Shootouts would qualify for the SuperLeague and the 9 losers for the Pro Cup. Invited clubs (clubs invited to participate in EFL on the basis of their performance in the national leagues in the preceding season) from certain countries would automatically qualify for the SuperLeague while others would play in the Shootouts.[32] These clubs would be free to choose on an annual basis whether to play in EFL- or UEFA-organised competitions.

The EFL was intended to have its competitions compatible with national competitions since the winners of national competitions would be entitled to participate in the EFL. It was apparent from the proposal that only the other pan-European competitions were considered competitors to EFL and not the national leagues.

Individual players would be eligible to represent their respective countries in international matches organised under the auspices of FIFA and UEFA, unless these governing bodies and the affiliated European national associations decided to penalise them for participating in the EFL organised competitions by excluding them from playing for their country.

As such, the EFL was intended to be a combination of the American franchise system and the European merit-based system.

3.3.2.4 Benefits and Financial Aspects of the EFL

In the EFL, more high-quality games would be guaranteed for the top European clubs. The SuperLeague undertook to ensure a minimum of 15 matches against other top European clubs. In comparison, in the 1996–1997 season Bayern Munich played only 2 European games (one home and one away match with the same opponent) and Real Madrid did not play at all. In the EFL they would both be guaranteed at least 15 European games per season, each against a different club. Under the UEFA system at the time, even the most successful clubs that

---

[32] Shootout was intended to be a competition divided into three draws of four teams. The three shootouts were made up of Nordic Shootout (Sweden, Norway, Finland and Denmark), Latin Shootout (Portugal, Italy, France and Spain) and Central Shootout (Austria, Switzerland, Netherlands and Germany). The Shootout teams were the second highest placed non-Franchise clubs in the previous season's national leagues in each of the countries mentioned. The highest placed non-Franchise clubs were automatically qualified for the SuperLeague.

reach the finals of a UEFA competition typically play a maximum of 11 matches. In addition, more games would mean more gate receipts. Significantly, more live matches would be shown on both free and pay-TV in each country due to a greater number of match nights, and more use of pay-TV. There would be 91 matches in the EFL format as against 40 in UEFA's three competitions at the time. There would be greater predictability for clubs, fans, viewers and broadcasters in terms of the number of matches between the most popular clubs in Europe.

As a result of an increased number of matches, greater predictability and better management of competitions, the EFL was expected to generate revenues of around US$ 1–2 billion per season, an amount which at the time had far greater value than it has today. UEFA competitions generated, according to MPI estimates, around US$ 500 million per season excluding gate receipts, and the clubs competing in the Champions League only received approximately 55 % of the gross revenues generated by the competition. Clubs participating in EFL would substantially increase their revenues as compared to their income earned from UEFA competitions at the time. All participating clubs would have guaranteed incomes for competing in the EFL together with the prize money according to their performance in the EFL.

FootballCo was to arrange for US$ 3.23 billion to be available over 3 years to ensure the availability of funds for the guaranteed payments to clubs.[33] Therefore, under the terms of the proposal FootballCo was entitled to 10 % of the EFL net income as a return for the cost and risk involved in setting up the EFL, including putting in place the financial structure to be able to guarantee club payments. The guaranteed payments in the SuperLeague were to be divided between the clubs in relation to their market value, with clubs like Juventus, Milan, Real Madrid, Barcelona, Manchester United and Bayern Munich being at the top of this list with 7 % of the market value each. Additional incentives in the first EFL season were offered to Founder Clubs that signed the Founders' Club Agreement.

3.3.2.5 Support for Football in Europe

A surprising feature of the proposal is that it included plans for the distribution of resources for the benefit of the game, amateur football and the national leagues. According to the UEFA's latest publicly available accounts at the time, in the 1994–1995 season only US$ 14 million was paid out to the national associations every season and approximately US$ 2.64 million was spent on development of youth football. These amounts were paid from UEFA's overall resources and not just from revenues generated by the three main inter-club competitions organised by UEFA every year. In contrast, the EFL planned to establish the 'Special Fund' to which 5 % of the EFL net annual revenues would be paid amounting to US$ 50–100 million per year. These amounts would be channelled into development

[33] J.P. Morgan was to launch the formal bank syndication process aimed at putting in place a bank facility in this amount.

of football in Europe through the existing institutions involved in administration of football. The effect of this would be creation of job opportunities by setting up youth football programmes with money received from the 'Special Fund'.

3.3.2.6 Relationship with FIFA and UEFA

UEFA was expected to continue organising both inter-club competitions and international competitions between national representative teams. However, if most of the European top clubs were to join the EFL, UEFA would have to alter the format of its inter-club competitions or even withdraw from that market entirely. The drafters of the proposal believed that the major inter-club competitions in Europe should be run on a professional basis and owned by the clubs themselves, similar to models adopted in, for example the United Kingdom and in the Netherlands.

The EFL was to have a professional staff of approximately 150 who would run a number of technical and advisory committees such as a Rules Committee, a Disciplinary Committee, a Stadia and Security Committee and a Medical Committee. The proposal intended to offer representations on these Committees to FIFA and UEFA.

Some of the principles expressed in the Founders' Club Agreement include honouring the administrative functions of the existing global and European football authorities of FIFA and UEFA and participating in the EFL within valid and enforceable FIFA rules and regulations. By signing that agreement, the Founder Clubs would have been under an obligation to ensure that all players participating in the EFL were eligible to play in the international competitions organised by UEFA and FIFA, and to support UEFA in organising club competitions for territories outside the European Union but within the UEFA umbrella and which were not included in the proposal at the outset but were to be included in the future seasons, presumably after the first 6 years of the EFL and provided it proved successful as planned.

3.3.3 UEFA Concessions in the 1998 Media Partners Case

Participation in the Champions League is conditioned upon the transfer of broadcasting rights to Champions League matches to UEFA, which then collectively sells them to the highest bidders in each territory (broadcasting is still very national in character). Nearly 30 % of the proceeds from these collective sales are not distributed back to the participating teams but are a part of the contributions to European football in accordance with the principle of financial solidarity.[34] So when Media Partners made a proposal to elite football clubs to form a new European Football League, UEFA reacted by establishing an expanded Champions

[34] See UEFA Financial Report for 2009/2010 season.

League with more matches and more money for the teams, and with several places in the Champions League for the clubs coming from the 'big five' leagues (Spanish, English, Italian, German and French).[35] The qualification system has been restructured so that the national champions from lower ranked countries have to take part in one or more qualifying rounds before the group stages, while runners-up from higher ranked countries enter in later rounds. The competition as adjusted therefore included the features of both the system of promotion and relegation, and a closed league. In 2000, UEFA issued a statement on club football which included 10 principles for European club football:

1. Domestic club football is the lifeblood of the professional game and must be protected.
2. UEFA's club competitions should be in juxtaposition to the domestic programmes—a stimulant, not a dominant or damaging influence.
3. Club traditions should be recognised, respected and maintained.
4. The demands made of the players must always be considered.
5. Competitions must be authentic and based on sporting criteria.
6. Fan attendance must be the key objective—the safety and comfort of the supporters in the stadia must be a priority.
7. A balance must be maintained between commercial interests and football as a sport.
8. Solidarity must be maintained.
9. The UEFA Champions League should be the benchmark for international club football.
10. There can only be one governing body for European Association football (UEFA) and transnational competitions in Europe.[36]

Today's format of the UEFA Champions League was designed to fend off a threat of formation of a semi-closed private league outside the UEFA structure. It worked. Parrish and Miettinen note that:

> serious consequences have flown from the creation of the Champions League which amounts to a UEFA Super-league. Teams entering this competition are able to invest significantly more in squads than those not qualifying. This has implications for competitive balance in national competitions as the richer Champions League teams continue to compete with the poorer teams who do not qualify. This leads to a concentration of teams regularly qualifying for the Champions League and a progressive diminution of domestic competitive balance.[37]

It remains only to be speculated whether the Media Partners proposal would have succeeded commercially had the clubs addressed decided to accept it. But it is a fact that concessions from UEFA certainly made the choice easier for the clubs.

---

[35] See 'UEFA to Review Superleague' BBC, 21 August 1998, and 'UEFA Finalises Bid to Head off European Super League' Sports Illustrated, 28 August 1998.

[36] UEFA Statement on club football, 15 December 2000. Available at http://kassiesa.home.xs4all.nl/bert/uefa/news/001215.html.

[37] Parrish and Miettinen 2008, pp. 212–213.

As a rule of thumb, changing the status quo will only happen if the new venture offers a good degree of certainty and more than just theoretical advantages. The description of the project necessary for the clubs to take up an offer include clear practical gains demonstrable from the terms of a proposal in a mature contractual and implementation-ready stage that follows a thorough market feasibility test and contains an acceptable degree of commercial risk for the clubs.

3.3.4 Formation of the G14 Alliance

The Media Partners case was quite instructive for those it addressed. In September 2000, 14 elite European football clubs formed the G14, an alliance intended to ensure its members a unified voice in negotiations with UEFA and FIFA. The founding members were Manchester United, Liverpool, Bayern Munich, Borussia Dortmund, Juventus, Internazionale Milano, A.C. Milan, Ajax, PSV Eindhoven, Porto, Marseille, Paris Saint-Germain, Real Madrid and Barcelona. Their geographical spread included seven different EU Member States. In 2002 Arsenal, Olympique Lyonnais, Valencia and Bayer Leverkusen joined the G14 alliance. The membership, which then stood at 18, was opened invitation only. The member clubs were the top clubs in their own countries winning ca. 250 national league titles between them, but also top European clubs winning UEFA Champions League titles 41 times out of 51 seasons.[38] Unambiguous in their profit maximising goals, 'elitist' in nature,[39] richer and therefore superior in their on-field competitive and off-field commercial performance, these clubs were, and still are, in the hands of the owners who are generally unconcerned with the European sports model and the financial solidarity underlying its structures. The G14 and its subsequent allies can be classified as a European Economic Interest Grouping under EU law.[40]

The official face that the G14 initially presented was that of a group concerned for the good of the game. The main objectives as they are specified in the G14 foundation agreement are: 'to promote the cooperation, amicable relations and unity of the member clubs; to promote and improve professional football in all its aspects and safeguard the general interests of the member clubs; to promote cooperation and good relations between G14 and FIFA, UEFA and any other sporting institutions and/or professional football clubs, paying special attention to negotiating the format, administration and operation of the club competitions in which the member clubs are involved'. It seems that nobody, including fans and the media,

[38] Prior to 1992 the UEFA Champions League was officially called the European Champion Clubs' Cup.

[39] See 'Platini calls for disbandment of elitist G14' ESPN, 28 May 2007.

[40] Council Regulation (EEC) No 2137/85 of 25 July 1985 on the European Economic Interest Grouping (EEIG) OJ L 199, 31.7.1985.

bought this ruse as suspicion of the real motives grew. The suspicions were confirmed in March 2006 when a G14 classified internal document entitled 'G14 Vision Europe' was leaked to The Guardian. The document laid out the plan of the G14 to hijack the Champions League tournament from UEFA by asserting its right to financial and regulatory independence.[41]

3.3.5 Plans for 'European Golden Cup' in 2003?

Earlier, in 2003, The Guardian reported on the G14's consideration to establish the Super League in the 2006–2007 season as a response to UEFA's move to cut the second phase of the Champions League from that season—a move that would reduce each club's number of potential European matches by four.[42] Allegedly, a group of Spanish businessmen said that they were aiming to establish a 16-team competition called the 'European Golden Cup' as a rival to the UEFA Champions League. Andreff and Bourg said that 110 million Euros was envisaged for the winner of the European Golden Cup.[43] No aspect of this plan was confirmed by the G14. However, the organisation has never made secret its distrust of UEFA.[44] By forming the G14, its members created a powerful lobby group to counterweight and influence the rules and decisions of UEFA and FIFA to their advantage. Formally, the group has been disbanded by the FIFA-G14 deal in the beginning of 2008, but its activity continues. The relations of the former G14 with UEFA are currently ordered through a Memorandum of Understanding (2012) between UEFA and the European Club Association. The first version of this memorandum was signed in January 2008 after the *Oulmers* affair.

3.3.6 UEFA Concessions on Compulsory Player Release Rule, the Oulmers *Case and Formal Dissolution of G14*

Article 1, Annex 1 of the FIFA Regulation on the Status and Transfer of Players lays down an obligation on clubs to 'release their registered players to the representative teams of the country for which the player is eligible to play on the basis of his nationality if they are called up by the association concerned. Any

[41] See 'Takeover Bid Could Change the Face of Football' by Matt Scott, The Guardian, 18 March 2006.

[42] See 'G-14 Considering Super League' The Guardian, 4 February 2003.

[43] Andreff and Bourg 2006, p. 63, note 2.

[44] See 'Cash Windfall for Clubs as G14 Disbands' by Mihir Bose, BBC, 18 January 2008.

agreement between a player and a club to the contrary is prohibited'.[45] There are no serious objections that can be raised against this rule as it stands unqualified. It is an honour (and possibly a right) for any athlete to represent his or her country if called upon by national associations but also an opportunity for national associations to field their finest talent against that of other countries. International competitions have special appeal to fans and promote a sense of national identity which is *inter alia* a cultural aspect and value of sport that Europe is aspiring to protect. Continental championships (EURO in Europe), the World Cup, as well as qualifying matches for international tournaments are examples belonging to the category of competitions for which compulsory release is required. In addition, these championships provide an exposure for the clubs' players and increase their value on the player transfer market.

However, matters become more complicated when reading the rule in its proper context, in conjunction with Article 2 of the Annex 1 which emphasises the responsibility for financial and insurance matters:

> Clubs releasing a player in accordance with the provisions of this annexe are not entitled to financial compensation.[...] The club with which the player concerned is registered shall be responsible for his insurance cover against illness and accident during the entire period of his release. This cover must also extend to any injuries sustained by the player during the international match(es) for which he was released.

Furthermore, disciplinary sanctions for failure to comply with Article 1 are laid down in Article 6 of the Annex 1:

> If a club refuses to release a player or neglects to do so despite the provisions of this annexe, the FIFA Players' Status Committee shall furthermore request the association to which the club belongs to declare any match(es) in which the player took part to have been lost by the club concerned. Any points thus gained by the club in question shall be forfeited. Any match contested according to the cup system shall be regarded as having been won by the opposing team, irrespective of the score.

These rules on compulsory and uncompensated release of players for international matches of their national representative teams have attracted a lot of attention since 2006 when the *Oulmers* case[46] was brought before the CJEU. Apart from giving up the player for the duration of the competition for which he was released, the main problem is that players might get injured while playing for their country. In that situation there is no possibility for the clubs to obtain financial compensation *vis-à-vis* the damages sustained. During the time their player is released, clubs are responsible for his insurance against illness and accident, and have to continue paying his salary.

---

[45] FIFA Regulation on Status and Transfer on Players, edition 2010. The 2005 edition applicable at the relevant time set out the same rule in identical terms.

[46] Reference for a preliminary ruling from the Tribunal de commerce de Charleroi lodged on 30 May 2006, Case C-243/06 *SA Sporting du Pays de Charleroi, G14 Groupment des clubs de football européens v. Fédération internationale de football association (FIFA)*. The case was removed from the Court register by order of the President of the Court of 25 November 2008.

The pressure on FIFA to change these rules exerted by the G14 culminated in the *Oulmers* case in 2006.[47] The escalation of the conflicting priorities resulted in the G14 threatening to break away from the rest of the football structure.[48] It began with the Belgian club Charleroi challenging the Annex 1 rules before a Belgian national court when their player, Moroccan midfielder Abdelmajid Oulmers, returned injured after being released to play for his national team in an international friendly against Burkino Faso in November 2004. Charleroi claimed that their chance to succeed in the national league had been damaged by his 8-month long absence. The G14 joined the action stating that:

> G14's objective in bringing this case is to avoid professional clubs being forced to incur damages when they release their players for national team duty. G14 wants a situation in which a fair percentage of the revenues of tournaments, notably the World Cup, are redistributed among those clubs who release their players.[49]

On a preliminary reference, the Belgian national court in Charleroi asked the CJEU to consider the compatibility with Articles 101 and 102 TFEU of the rule on compulsory player release to national federations without compensation and the unilateral and binding determination of the coordinated international match calendar by the football governing bodies.[50]

While the case was pending, the G14 invited a further 22 teams to join it in 2007, which would more than double its membership and further increase its influence and geographic spread.[51] Amid mounting tension, FIFA and the G14 entered into a peace deal in January 2008, resulting in the creation of a monetary pool compensating for player release, and in changes to the governance structure. In return, the G14 had to formally disband as a group (it then reorganised in the form of the European Club Association) and withdraw the *Oulmers* case and other lawsuits, but its executive said that its goals had already been met by these financial concessions. Unfortunately for those that looked forward to the clarification on release for international duty by the Court, the *Oulmers* case was settled shortly before the judgment was due and it was withdrawn from the Court's register as a part of the broader deal struck between the G14 and FIFA.[52]

The amendments related to compensation for compulsory player release illustrate the power the group of elite football clubs in Europe has on the decisions

---

[47] Ibid.

[48] 'Europe's top football teams in plot to go it alone' by Glen Moore, The Guardian, 18 March 2006.

[49] 'G14 clubs Demand the Share of the World Cup Gate Receipts' by John Nisbet, The Independent, 23 March 2006.

[50] Case C-243/06 *SA Sporting du Pays de Charleroi, G14 Groupment des clubs de football européens v. Fédération internationale de football association (FIFA)*. A factually similar case involved French club Olympique Lyon and a player Eric Abidal who broke a metatarsal bone during a friendly match with Costa Rica.

[51] See 'Cells get slot but Gers snubbed' Evening Times Reporter, 31 October 2007.

[52] See, for example 'G14 to Disband as Deal is Struck' by Paul Kelso, The Guardian, 16 January 2008.

of the world governing body. FIFA created a compensation pool for every player released under Article 1 of the Annex 1. Sport Business International reported that:

> the money will be drawn from a central pool financed by UEFA and FIFA from the commercial money raised from the sale of TV rights and tournament sponsorships. Although the exact amounts remain undecided, it is understood that each club will receive the same amount for every player they provide - irrespective of the players' club salaries.[53]

The idea of a compensation pool soon materialised and the amounts became known before the start of the 2010 FIFA World Cup. The total prize money was US$ 420 million (as compared to US$ 261 million in the FIFA 2006 World Cup) of which US$ 40 million (ca. EUR 30 million) was provided by FIFA via the member associations to the clubs whose players took part in the 2010 FIFA World Cup as a contribution for their participation in the competition.[54] The FIFA Secretary General confirmed that the individual contributions to clubs amounted to US$ 1,600 (EUR 1,208) per player per day of his commitment to the national team, running from 2 weeks before the start of the World Cup until the team's elimination. It is expected that the fund in the player release compensation pool will increase to US$ 70 m for the FIFA 2014 World Cup in Brazil.[55] Barcelona received EUR 654,237 (for its 13 players), Bayern Munich EUR 587,755, followed by Chelsea, Liverpool, Real Madrid and other former G14 members, many of which were also beneficiaries receiving similar sums. Given that the total commitment in the compensation pool was ca. EUR 30 million (US$ 40 million) encompassing ca. 400 clubs worldwide, this means that the system almost exclusively contributes to the budget of the richest clubs. These sums were given even if a player was not injured, even though the fixtures are set not to conflict with the UEFA or national championships, and even if the World Cup provides an additional exposure and value to the player on the transfer market when later sold by his club.

Similar arrangements were agreed between UEFA and the European Club Association (the new institutional face of the G14) under the terms of the Memorandum of Understanding from 2008 (and were reiterated in its 2012 version). UEFA allocated EUR 100 million for the clubs participating in the quadrennial EURO competition. From this amount, EUR 40 million was meant to be distributed equally on the 'per player, per (qualifying) match' basis to the clubs that released their players for the *qualifying* games of UEFA EURO 2012. The remaining EUR 60 million was distributed to those clubs that released their player(s) for the UEFA EURO 2012 *final* tournament. This amount was broken down into a fixed amount per player per day and weighted in accordance with a

[53] 'G14 Group to Disband after FIFA/UEFA Agree Compensation Deal' Sports Business International, 16 January 2008.

[54] FIFA news item 'FIFA Executive Committee Holds a Historic Meeting at Robben Island' 3 December 2009. Available at http://www.fifa.com/aboutfifa/organisation/news/newsid=1143269/index.html.

[55] 'Prize money increased by 61 % for 2010 World Cup' by Owen Gibson, The Guardian, 3 December 2009.

club categorisation.[56] It will come as no surprise that richer clubs are categorised higher. For UEFA EURO 2016 the compensation pool will increase to EUR 150 million.[57] According to Memorandum of Understanding between UEFA and European Club Association,[58] the latter undertakes to:

> ensure that its member clubs and itself [...] comply with the FIFA Regulations on release of players as stipulated in articles E.4 and E.5 [...] and make no further claims (a) in relation to the cost of insurance of players against UEFA and/or any National Association or (b) in relation to any other matter relating to the release or participation of players to European national teams in general against UEFA and/or any European National Associations for all matches foreseen in the International Match Calendar.[59]

The reason that FIFA signed off on the deal was fear of the formation of an alternative league by the G14. When only Charleroi was involved in the case, the president of FIFA Sepp Blatter refused an offer by the president of Charleroi to settle the case for EUR 615,000. The alarms were set off in FIFA and national associations when the G14 joined the lawsuit and demanded their own compensation in the amount of EUR 869 million. This is what ultimately brought the parties to the negotiating table. FIFA finally yielded to pressures even though there would not be much support in EU law for the legal action taken against its Annex 1 rules under the *Meca-Medina* analytical framework. However, FIFA was one move away from checkmate: winning *Oulmers* would possibly mean losing the clubs. Losing the *Oulmers* litigation would mean a loss of up to EUR 869 million and all the subsequent compensation payments for player release. Therefore, from the point of view of FIFA, compromise was the safest option. It kept the clubs within the structure and at the same time formally disbanded the group. For the time being, the pyramid survived once again.

In the following subsection it will be argued that had the *Oulmers* case been litigated, it would have been won by FIFA.

3.3.6.1 The Compulsory and Uncompensated Player Release Rule Is Compatible with EU Law

The power of the G14 on the world stage is best demonstrated by the fact that in the 2006 FIFA World Cup it provided a stunning 22 % of participating players for the national teams. While it is true that the richest clubs are the ones that have in their squads, more so than the others, a lot of high-quality foreign players and that the release for international matches will therefore affect their composition more profoundly, certain factors are capable of countering any financial damage to the clubs. For example, the exposure that the players get during their participation in

---

[56] UEFA news item 'Clubs to benefit from UEFA EURO 2012' 30 June 2012.

[57] Memorandum of Understanding between UEFA and ECA, para C.5.

[58] See Sect. 3.4.3.

[59] Paragraph D.6.

the national representative teams can be invaluable in terms of raising the player's value on the transfer market.[60] The big national team competitions that require several weeks of player absence are staged in between seasons. The potential damage that clubs might suffer could be considered a part of financial solidarity and a mechanism of ensuring competitive balance between clubs that has been chronically lacking from European football for long time. In this context, it is submitted that even if the player release rule would be considered as affecting the club's commercial interests, it represents one of the mechanisms for maintenance of competitive balance between league participants in Europe, an objective recognised as legitimate by the Court.[61] Also UEFA envisioned the rule with this purpose in mind; in its internal document entitled UEFA Vision Europe it stated that: 'clubs releasing players to national teams is a form of solidarity that has existed since the creation of football—this is UEFA's main source of funding for grass roots football in Europe and must be protected'.[62] The (uncompensated) player release rule might counterweight the fact that G14 clubs have better purchasing power and can afford the contracts with the best players than many other less well-off clubs.[63] The risk of the released player getting injured is a part of sport, it is the same upon everyone, the richest clubs more than others due to their high-profile composition, and the clubs take this into account when buying players on the international football transfer market. It should be taken as an intrinsic characteristic of the industry and of their business when operating on the supply market: the clubs buy players in full knowledge that they are subject to the scheduled release and this fact comes attached to the player himself. Usually, more expensive players affordable only by the richer clubs are the ones being called upon by their national association. Clubs in poor financial and competitive standing cannot afford any high-quality players and will rarely have to release anyone from their squad for international **duty**. The player release rule is therefore perfectly fit for the exemption in EU law as it adds to the overall solidarity and competitive balance between the clubs, while creating compensation pools is in fact working against those objectives. These arguments could provide a support to the compulsory player release rule in the application of the analytical framework provided for in the *Meca-Medina* judgment discussed below in Sect. 5.5.5.[64]

In addition, EU competition law primarily exists to protect consumer welfare. It is hard to argue against the compulsory release of players rule in this context. What consumers want to see is their national representative teams composed of

---

[60] See Weatherill 2009, p. 94.

[61] In Case C-425/93 *Bosman* discussed in Sect. 4.4.

[62] At p. 11. Available at http://www.uefa.com/newsfiles/374875.pdf.

[63] The turnover of Real Madrid in the 2004–2005 financial year was EURO 275.7 million.

[64] In the view of the authors of the 2006 Arnaut Report the 'player release rule is (1) motivated by purely sporting considerations; (2) necessary to protect the regularity and proper function of international competitions; and (3) a key component of the overall system of financial solidarity of European football'. This rule can be seen as a prime example of a 'sports rule' which should fall outside of the scope of Union law. See para 3.47.

their best players, and at the same time they need an interesting product of the league matches which can best result from the league in which clubs are in relative competitive balance.

The motivation of the G14 to deal away with the rule is purely commercial and directed at their wealth maximisation at the expense of smaller clubs and the public interest, which might not be a popular argument before the Court in the absence of overwhelming efficiency gains, especially when presented by the collectively dominant group of undertakings.[65] Creating the compensation pool of the kind described above went too far—if the clubs were to be compensated at all, the compensation should have covered only the actual damages, i.e. the damages for injured players. The system as it is actually pays the richest European clubs for the release of players, the poorer European clubs not having many, if any, players that were called upon by their national association. It will be argued in Sect. 7.9 that this kind of strategy of exerting influence over the regulatory bodies to adjust the system according to commercial interests of the elite can amount to abuse of a collective dominant position under Article 102 TFEU, and a concerted practice under Article 101 TFEU.

The compulsory player release rule also seems to have been proportionate to achieve the objectives of competitive balance and proper functioning of international competitions. *Any* system that provides compensation to the well-off clubs further contributes towards competitive imbalance in European football and further reduces the effectiveness of solidarity mechanisms.

The compromise made to accommodate the requests of the G14 reflects the influence that the group is capable of exerting and contributes towards the shift in the balance of power in football governance. Whereas before the decisions were made from the centre and many objections related to the lack of representation, a recognisable decentralisation has now taken place, still without proper representation of most of the clubs. Such decentralisation is therefore not a positive development because the central body, unlike the elitist clubs, has a clear mandate to act in the interest of all the stakeholders and represent 'sport for all'. True, some of the battles fought and won by G14 have incidentally been won for all clubs, not just for the group itself, but nevertheless, G14 was the biggest beneficiary of the compromises made by FIFA and UEFA and often the sole beneficiary. This in turn rendered the gap between the clubs in European football even wider.

3.3.7 July 2011: New Breakaway Threats, Old Strategies of Old Allies

On July 27, 2011, The Guardian reported a new breakaway threat by the elite clubs and said that: 'European clubs will break away from FIFA and UEFA and

[65] It is argued in Sects. 7.4.2.2 and 7.9 that the elite clubs are collectively dominant undertakings.

create their own super league unless the world governing body urgently addresses their growing concerns over international fixtures and finances'.[66]

Only a month before, the same newspapers reported (and FIFA denied[67]), that it announced plans to expand international fixtures by five more games in international friendlies raising the number to 17.[68] The greatest net beneficiaries were assumed to be the federations of smaller European nations. The ECA alleges UEFA has pulled back from its commitment to provide insurance for players who are called up for international duty.[69] The ECA also complained that this was driven through UEFA's political structures without consultation with the clubs.[70] The breakaway was set to happen after 31 July 2014 when the first term of the Memorandum of Understanding between UEFA and the ECA expires. The chairman of the ECA, Karl-Heinz Rummenigge, made comments about a 'revolution' for football in the form of a European Super League that would see the clubs seize control of their own affairs from the regulators. Furthermore, a board member is reported to have said that after 31 July 2014 'we can no longer be forced to respect FIFA statutes or UEFA regulations. And we won't be obliged to compete in their competitions'.[71] Media reports suggested that the richest European clubs using the institutional resources of the ECA managed to easily score a point in negotiations with UEFA concerning international fixtures and insurance for players on international duty.[72] The deal involves cutting down the number of international matches a year from 12 to 9 and it is yet to be approved by FIFA.[73]

This threat might have been deliberately timed to coincide with the corruption scandal that was at the time shaking the world football governing body. The bizarre election process and re-election of Sepp Blatter in June 2011 as FIFA's president did not help FIFA's legitimacy.[74]

---

[66] 'Top European Clubs Threaten to Break Away from FIFA and UEFA' by Matt Scott, The Guardian, 27 July 2011.

[67] See FIFA Statement on international matches, 17 June 2011, available at http://www.fifa.com/aboutfifa/organisation/administration/news/newsid=1454155/index.html.

[68] 'FIFA Risks War with European Clubs Over International Friendlies', by Matt Scott, The Guardian, 14 June 2011.

[69] The Guardian, 27 July 2011.

[70] The Guardian, 14 June 2011.

[71] The Guardian, 27 July 2011.

[72] 'European Clubs Clinch Deal with UEFA to Cut International Matches' by Owen Gibson, The Guardian, 28 February 2012.

[73] Ibid.

[74] For more on these topics see Andrew Jennings' webpage at http://www.transparencyinsport.org/.

3.3.8 Alternative Leagues in European Football

3.3.8.1 Atlantic League in 2000 and 2001

In 2000 and 2001 there was an attempt by the leading football clubs in smaller countries[75] to establish the Atlantic League. The clubs would play each other on weekends and would no longer play in their national leagues. The commercial motives such as revenues generated by increasing the target TV audience to 40 million and an estimated 30,000 average stadium attendance would make the Atlantic League among the biggest leagues in Europe. The result would be more lucrative broadcasting contracts and attracting more quality players. The idea behind this proposal was to create a league that can pair with the most successful national leagues in Europe and give a fair chance to the top clubs from smaller markets to prevail over the top clubs coming from the 'big five' (Italy, Spain, England, France and Germany). With the dominant clubs leaving, national leagues would then become more competitive but also probably less profitable in terms of TV rights. The ties through promotion and relegation would still remain with national leagues and with European-wide leagues: the best clubs in the Atlantic League would qualify for Europe-wide competitions such as the Champions League and the UEFA Cup, and the worst performing clubs would be relegated back to their top national leagues and replaced by the champions in those leagues.

However, UEFA and the six affected national leagues had rejected the idea of the Atlantic League as envisaged by the clubs. The clubs were told they would not be able to play in UEFA competitions any longer and the national associations similarly said they would sever all ties with the would-be Atlantic League clubs. To head off the threat of breakaway, UEFA promised an expanded and changed format of UEFA Cup and the inclusion of a group phase in the tournament. The clubs said they would still be committed to their own tournament if an expanded UEFA Cup did not meet their needs. The group stages were introduced for the 2004–2005 season. Following the merger with the UEFA Intertoto Cup, the UEFA Cup was rebranded into the UEFA Europa League in 2009.[76]

The Atlantic League should not be confused with the Atlantic Cup played between the champions of the Icelandic Premier League and the Faroe Island Premier League between 2002 and 2008.[77]

---

[75] Celtic and Rangers (Scotland); Ajax, PSV and Feyenoord (the Netherlands); Benfica and Sporting Lisbon (Portugal); Anderlecht and Club Bruges (Belgium); Gothenburg and AIK Stockholm (Sweden); Brondby and FC Copenhagen (Denmark).

[76] Sources: 'Celtic Back Atlantic Breakaway'. BBC Sport, 16 January 2000; 'Clubs step up pressure for Atlantic League' by Martyn Ziegler, The Independent, 1 February 2001; 'Bold plan for Europe' by Gabriele Marcotti, The Times, 20 November 2006; 'UEFA moves to head off Atlantic League' by Mark Tallentire, The Guardian, 8 February 2001: 'UEFA warn clubs over Atlantic League', [http://www.sportbusiness.com] 27 September 2001.

[77] For more on history of the cup see http://www.soccerandequipment.com/soccer-atlantic-cup.html.

3.3.8.2 Royal League in 2004

A 'successful' establishment of a closed football league was accomplished with different actors in April 2004 when an agreement was reached between UEFA, football clubs, and federations in Denmark, Sweden and Norway. It was the short lived Royal League whose members were the four best teams from each of these Scandinavian countries. The 12 member clubs had among their aims to develop football in Scandinavia in general, create a sporting and attractive offer to the top clubs, improve the conditions for the Scandinavian clubs in order to compete against the greatest in Europe (for instance by extending the season in order to maintain player's physical fitness by playing in the Royal League), and to strengthen the development of talents in the Scandinavian countries.[78]

The Royal League staged championships in the 2004–2005, 2005–2006 and 2006–2007 seasons, which took place during the 3-month winter break and did not interfere with the respective national tournaments in the relevant countries (with the exception of Denmark). The profits were distributed among other Scandinavian clubs that did not qualify for the league and there were talks of the expansion of membership to include Finland and Iceland.[79] Technically, the Royal League still exists but it has not staged championships since the 2006–2007 season for financial reasons and an inability to sell TV rights.

3.3.8.3 Commonwealth of Independent States Cup (as of 1994) and Channel One Cup 2006–2008

The Commonwealth of Independent States Cup (CIS Cup) is played between the clubs from all of the former Soviet Union states, with occasional participation from Serbian and Finnish clubs. It has organised contests in the second part of January each year (which sometimes included also the beginning of February) as of the 1994 season. Although it sounded attractive to arrange the competition during the summer months to be played on natural grass, the window in the calendar during the summer months was too short for many clubs and the CIS Cup remained a winter tournament. The decision to stage this alternative competition was enthusiastically adopted in June 1993 at a general meeting of the Executive Committee of Football Association of CIS countries. The original idea behind the CIS Cup was to preserve football ties throughout the countries of the former Soviet Union. Naturally, the financial and sporting benefits for all the participants were the main reason for keeping the competition alive until today. There are also many examples of players from small peripheral clubs in the participating states who were able to pursue a worthwhile career in a much stronger championship than that offered on a domestic level.[80]

---

[78] http://www.royalleague.com.

[79] Halgreen 2004, p. 81.

[80] Official website of the CIS Cup: http://www.ciscup.ru/2008_XVI/index.htm.

In 2006–2008, the Russian TV Channel One and Roman Abramovich's foundation, the National Football Academy, organised the Channel One Cup that involved champions and runners-up of Russian, Ukrainian, and later also the champions of Israeli and Serbian premier leagues. As it was organised at the end of January each year, it temporarily affected the CIS Cup with teams from Russia and Ukraine participating in the Channel One Cup instead. Therefore, the idea of uniting the two cups was briefly considered in 2007, but it never materialised. The global economic crisis negatively affected the Channel One Cup and 2009 competition was cancelled for financial reasons. It was never staged again.

3.3.8.4 Other European Cross-Border Leagues

The Baltic League is played between 16 teams from Latvia, Lithuania, and Estonia as of 2007.[81] The Setanta Cup features teams from the Republic of Ireland and Northern Ireland. It has staged competitions since 2005.[82] On his visit to Montenegro on 13 November 2010, the president of UEFA Michel Platini stated that he would, in principle, not be opposed to a regional league between the countries from former Yugoslavia,[83] but the president of the Football Association of Montenegro was sceptical that such a Balkan league would ultimately get a green light from UEFA.[84] However, some unconfirmed media reports suggest that a Balkan Super League involving countries from former Yugoslavia has been eventually approved by UEFA and is set to start in 2015.[85] Finally, in 2012, UEFA sanctioned a cross-border league in women's football involving clubs from Belgium and the Netherlands, the so-called BeNe league.[86]

3.3.8.5 Criteria for Successful Establishment of a Breakaway League

A common thread that connects all of the breakaway leagues in football that have taken place so far concerns

- *limited geographical area*, geographical connection and proximity between the clubs involved;
- *use of vacant space* in the international match calendar;
- *short time frame* of the competitions;
- participation of *smaller European clubs*.

---

[81] http://www.balticleague.com.

[82] http://www.setanta.com/ie/News/Football/Setanta-Sports-Cup.

[83] 'Platini Nije Protiv Regionalne Lige' (Platini is not Against Regional League), B92, 13 November 2010.

[84] 'Savicevic o Regionalnoj Ligi' (Savicevic on Regional League), Sportal, 14 November 2010.

[85] 'Balkan Super League Possibly on Tap for 2015', SB Nation, 10 October 2012.

[86] UEFA news item 'Best of Belgian and Dutch Unite in the BeNe League' 23 January 2013.

Such competitions did not overlap with any of the UEFA-organised pan-European events in which the clubs were engaged. Therefore, they did not affect the UEFA competitions and financial balance sheets in any way. Resources that are at the disposal of even the most successful clubs in such breakaway leagues were far below that of their counterparts in the Western European countries, the 'big five' in particular. The Atlantic League that got a red light from both UEFA and the concerned national associations did not fit these criteria. No breakaway league so far has been expressly approved, but none has been a subject of the disciplinary measures either.

Normally, committing to any form of participation in international club competitions not organised or not approved by the concerned governing bodies will entail disciplinary measures as specified in the codes implementing FIFA Regulations Governing International Matches and disciplinary codes of national associations (Article 19 of the FIFA Regulations Governing International Matches (2012), Article 12 of the FIFA Disciplinary Code (2011), Article 53 of the UEFA Statutes (2012), and Article 6 of the UEFA Disciplinary Regulations (2013)). The sanctions that may be imposed by UEFA provide that any club in breach of the UEFA Statutes may become subject to a withdrawal of their license, full or partial stadium closure, disqualification from competitions in progress and/or exclusion from future competitions, and fines in an amount of no more than EUR 1 million.[87]

In recent years, UEFA's general attitude to the idea of cross-border leagues became more moderate. After the meeting of the UEFA Management with UEFA Member Association General Secretaries which was held on 26–27 October 2005 in Nyon, UEFA considers that a cross-border competition is conceivable, but only if the proposal for such project a priori satisfies the following criteria:

> 1. The cross-border competition must be approved by the respective UEFA member associations; 2. The cross-border competition must be organised by the respective UEFA member associations; 3. All clubs planning to participate in the cross-border competition must be affiliated to a UEFA member association (or to a league/regional football association subordinated to such association); 4. Geographical aspects should be taken into consideration when a cross-border competition is being assessed; 5. All clubs planning to participate in the cross-border competition must recognise, as a condition of participation, that the ownership of the competition and its core commercial rights belong centrally to the competition organiser - in this case the associations (not the league, clubs, etc.) - not to the individual clubs (same model as the UEFA Champions League); 6. Minimum standards should be fixed with regards to the levels of solidarity distributions from the commercial rights revenues (core commercial rights commercialised centrally), for example: i. Minimum 10 % of commercial rights revenues must be distributed to amateur football in the countries concerned, via the associations involved; ii. Minimum 10 % of commercial rights revenues must be distributed to professional football clubs of the associations concerned but only clubs who are not participating in the cross-border competition concerned (providing that they fulfil, as a minimum, the sporting criteria of the UEFA Club Licensing System); iii. Of the remaining revenues divided amongst the participating clubs, a minimum of 25 % (ideally a minimum of 50 %) must be distributed equally, with the

[87] Similarly, the most severe sanction under Article 12 of the FIFA Disciplinary Code involves expulsion from competitions and a fine of no more than CHF 1 million.

> remainder based on on-field performance. 7. The competition regulations must be in compliance with the UEFA statutes/regulations and need to be approved by UEFA; 8. Participating clubs must be licensed in accordance with the UEFA Club Licensing System; 9. The competition regulations must include, among other things, provisions concerning, for example: i. Refereeing; ii. Disciplinary matters; iii. Independence of clubs (integrity of competition); iv. Anti-doping. 10. The cross-border competition must not conflict with the international match calendar; 11. The matches of the cross-border competition may not be played on the same day as UEFA club competitions; 12.. The cross-border competition must not replace the national championships and must be arranged around the calendar of the national championship; 13. Approval of FIFA.[88]

The criteria are particularly onerous: they do not allow a direct access to the exploitation market,[89] the proposed league has to be confined to a specific geographical area and organised so as not to conflict with the international or national match calendar, the matches in the proposed league cannot be played on the same day as UEFA club competitions, both vertical and horizontal solidarity contribution is required, regulatory competence remains mostly with UEFA including club licensing, clubs presumably have to remain as participants in their national championships, and the approval of national associations, UEFA and FIFA is required, which in all probability depends on the fulfilment of all the other conditions. UEFA perceives these rules as a natural and legitimate part of their mandate and a necessary means of the proper organisation and financing of football. In particular, it is seen as a means of ensuring financial solidarity and a system of promotion and relegation throughout the European pyramid. Conversely, clubs may claim that the Article 49 rule presents a restriction upon their commercial freedom in breach of TFEU competition provisions and free movement rules on services and establishment. The Article 49 rule in the UEFA Statutes is not likely to be challenged in abstract by the clubs, but only when the conflict materialises, i.e. only if the authorisation by the relevant governing body or bodies has not been obtained and/or the clause is used as a basis to impose sanctions on the clubs participating in the unsanctioned breakaway league.

3.4 New Trends in the Governance of European Football

3.4.1 Stakeholder Theory

When deciding on their business strategies, including corporate social responsibility (CSR),[90] corporations should take into account the interests of all of the stakeholders. Freeman broadly defines stakeholders as any group of individuals who can

[88] Cited in Master Thesis by Jaka Lucu, Mico Petcovic, Mihai C. Tudoran and Victor Vasiliev, 'Central European Football League: Dream or Reality' (International Centre for Sports Studies (CIES), Neuchatel, 2007), pp. 42–43.

[89] For detailed analysis of relevant market from the point of view of competition law see Sect. 7.3.

[90] For definition of this term see Dahlsrud 2006, published online in Wiley InterScience at http://www.mcxindia.com/csr/newsarticle/pdf/csr_news45.pdf.

affect, or is affected by, the performance of an organisation.[91] The current and future strategies of one organisation are affected by (1) external pressures (the marketplace including competitors, buyers and suppliers; shareholders; pressure groups; and government), (2) internal pressures (existing commitments, managers, employees and their trade unions), and; (3) personal ethical and moral perspectives of senior managers.[92] Shareholders, managers, employees, consumers, distributors, suppliers, financiers, government and society in general were identified in a non-exhaustive list as interested parties whose relative power will be a key variable, and the organisations will on occasion 'trade-off' one against the other, establishing a hierarchy of relative importance. Because their interests are different, these various stakeholders are not affected in the same way by every strategic decision and consequently their relative influence will vary from decision to decision.[93] Thompson gives an example of a company's investment into new technology which can improve the quality of the product and bring an increase in profits. This will satisfy the customers and shareholders but may lead to the loss of jobs for employees and some managers.[94] Shareholders, employees (including managers), and customers are seen as three key stakeholders that an undertaking must satisfy, but in a competitive environment, if they fail with any group long term invariably they will place the undertaking in jeopardy through a spiral of decline.[95]

The Arnaut report identified five different types of stakeholders in European football: the leagues as represented by the European Professional Football Leagues (EPFL), the clubs as represented the European Club Forum (ECF),[96] the G14 as an Economic Interest Group operating in parallel with the ECF, the players represented by FIFPro, and supporters (not organised in any pan-European representative body) as key stakeholders in football.[97] After the G14 deal with FIFA, the ECF and G14 have been merged into one body, the ECA. According to stakeholder theories, this list can be expanded to include television broadcasters and other media operators, football equipment suppliers and manufacturers, sponsors, amateur and grassroots levels, trainers and all other employees of clubs and leagues, etc. However, when it comes to strategic decisions and considering the interests of all the stakeholders in European football, the Arnaut Report observes that:

> The elite professional clubs and the biggest leagues (coming from the largest national TV markets) consider themselves to be more important and, correspondingly, to be deserving of greater involvement in the decision-making process, both at national and European

---

91 Freeman 1984.

92 Newbould and Luffman 1979.

93 Thompson 2001, p. 87.

94 Following the same logic, the *Bosman* case created a liberalised market for player services whilst also playing into the hands of those clubs with the greatest disposable income and resources to spend on players, widening the gulf between amateurs and professionals and between the top and the bottom of sport in Europe. See para 4.20 of the Arnaut Report.

95 Thompson 2001, pp. 89–90.

96 ECF has been replaced with European Club Association after disbandment of G14.

97 Paragraph 4.32 of the Report.

> level. If the football authorities fail to take account of their views, there was a risk of secession ('breakaway' leagues) and this fact also required the football authorities to adapt.[98]

The elite clubs consider themselves at the top of the hierarchy of stakeholders and threaten secession if the consideration of their interests falls below a high level of importance in UEFA decision-making. The effect is the creation of new rules that are often to the prejudice of all other stakeholders in football.

3.4.2 UEFA Mandate

The UEFA Mission Statement provides that 'UEFA's core mission is to promote, protect and develop European football at every level of the game, to promote the principles of unity and solidarity, and to deal with all questions relating to European football.' It further emphasises the principles of democracy, solidarity, fairness, transparency, accountability, entrepreneurship, professionalism, pride, and respect for the different stakeholders within European football in pursuing its wide range of aims that include:

> organisation of competitions for professional, youth, women's and amateur football; increase in access and participation; supporting growth in the grassroots of the game; achieving commercial success and sound finances without distorting the sporting qualities of our competitions; using UEFA's revenues to support re-investment and redistribution in the game in accordance with the principle of solidarity between all levels and areas of sport; targeting specific aid and assistance to help member associations with the greatest need; promoting positive sporting values (such as fair play, anti-racism, and safe and secure match environment); running an anti-doping programme aiming at preserving the ethics of sport, safeguarding the players' health and ensuring equal chances for all competitors; and ensuring that the needs of the different stakeholders are properly reflected in UEFA's thinking.[99]

When it comes to some aspects of CSR, UEFA is unlike ordinary commercial undertakings because its mandate includes representing interests of all levels of football equally, so support for certain social causes is a part of their *compulsory* activities. The pressures of secession and endless compromises to accommodate the elite clubs create a wider and wider gulf of competitive imbalances in European football and are making it harder for UEFA to fulfil its main regulatory and organisational functions related to other stakeholders, especially those weakest in the bargaining process.

The internal UEFA document entitled 'Vision Europe' sets out the strategy for development of European football over the period of 10 years starting from 2005 and poetically describes the ideal football world as the one in which there exists, among other things: a stronger than ever football pyramid with a strong base as the

---

98 Ibid. para 4.21.

99 See UEFA Vision Europe 2005, p. 7.

only way to ensure a strong apex; a football world where UEFA deals with all questions relating to European football, where it is the governing body of European football and speaks for the whole of European football; UEFA shaping and driving the debates and setting the agenda at European level based on football priorities; solidarity at all levels and distribution mechanisms which guarantee an equitable distribution of wealth.[100] Furthermore, Vision Europe document also foresaw the future with a UEFA that 'has a unique position with regards to being the exclusive organiser of the official European football club competitions' because 'this was always the case historically and it is only by virtue of this fact that UEFA can effectively regulate European football'.[101] Some of these ideals are realities while others are not. Without a doubt, many of the statements in Vision Europe insinuate that the breakaway structures would be profoundly damaging for the interest of European football, and that pressures UEFA experiences from the elite clubs and compromises it makes is taking an unwelcomed precedence over the priorities of the football as a whole. Similarly, under Article 2 of the UEFA Statutes (2012) the objectives of UEFA include preventing all methods or practices which might jeopardise the regularity of matches or competitions or give rise to the abuse of football; ensuring that sporting values always prevail over commercial interests; and ensuring that the needs of the different stakeholders in European football (leagues, clubs, players, supporters) are properly taken into account.

Under the terms of Articles 60 et seq. of the Swiss Civil Code, UEFA is a private non-profit-making association that formally does not have a public mandate, although functionally it resembles some of the characteristics of a private body with a public mandate. At the time of its creation in 1955 its main goal was the organisation of pan-European national and club competitions. FIFA approved of such club competitions but only if 'directly organised' by UEFA. Thus, the creation of the European Club Forum in 2002 that preceded the European Club Association was seen as 'a natural evolution in the relationship between UEFA and the clubs playing in UEFA competitions'.[102]

3.4.3 European Club Association: A New Face of G14

The influence of the former G14 clubs is reflected in the neo-governance of football in Europe. UEFA has developed structures to give an institutional voice to all the stakeholders: leagues, clubs, and players in particular. Clubs are currently represented in the European Club Association that was formed from the former G14 members and a more representative European Club Forum after the January 2008 peace deal between the G14 and FIFA. The ECA consists of club

[100] Ibid. pp. 8–14.

[101] Ibid. p. 12.

[102] Ibid. p. 15.

representatives of all 53 European associations, totalling 207 clubs, 103 of which are ordinary members and 104 are associated members. The number of ordinary members from each member association is distributed according to the UEFA association ranking coefficients. Thus, the three highest ranking associations each have five clubs; the next three, four clubs; the associations ranked from 7 to 15 will each have three clubs; associations ranked from 16 to 26 each have two clubs; and associations ranked 27–53 will have one club each. The association ranking is directly related to the performance of their clubs at the European championships, which is directly related to the amount of money that the clubs have to spend on their players and coaches. Therefore, the membership in the ECA is closely related to clubs' financial standing.

The ECA is chaired by Karl-Heinz Rummenigge of Bayern Munich, a former G14 member. Two out of three vice-presidents are also former G14 members. The ECA elects an Executive Board consisting of 11 members. Six out of the eleven of the board members were included in the Media Partners proposal for the European Football League. Three out of four board members who represent the ECA on the Professional Football Strategy Council (PFSC) also used to belong to the G14.[103] Under the Memorandum of Understanding signed with UEFA, the ECA is recognised as the sole body representing the interests of clubs in Europe.[104] The voice of the clubs is therefore the voice of former G14 members, as well as other elite clubs included in the Media Partners proposal. These clubs have special commercial interests not shared with other member clubs of ECA, which is confirmed by their former membership in the closed G14 interest group.

At a conference in The Hague in 2009, Michael Gerlinger, the Director of Legal Affairs for FC Bayern Munich, spoke about the ECA. In his answer to a comment concerning the undemocratic structure of the ECA and the fact that power is in the hands of the former G14 members and other elite clubs, he said that the ECA Executive Board is 'trying to take into consideration also the needs of the small clubs when making decisions'.[105] Illustrative as it is, this statement confirms that the elite clubs are in total control and that small clubs can only hope their needs are 'taken into consideration'. What is supposed to be a truly representative body with the mandate to speak on behalf of all the member European clubs has become another undemocratic forum, further contributing to the imbalance in European football.

Therefore, it is possible to draw a rather firm conclusion that notwithstanding its formal disbandment, the G14 and its allies will continue to present a powerful lobby group with special commercial interests not possessed by any other

[103] They are David Gill (Manchester United), Florentino Pérez (Real Madrid), Umberto Gandini (AC Milan) and Maarten Fontein (Alkmaar).

[104] See paras A.1 and D.10 of the Memorandum.

[105] Michael Gerlinger, lawyer from Bayern Munich FC. 'The European Club Association (ECA): background, mission, composition, activities'. Speech at The Hague 19 February 2009, VIII Asser-Clingendael Sports Lecture on 'Current Topics in the Governance in Sport: ECA and MOTOE'.

competitors in their league. On the conclusion of the January 2008 deal with FIFA, their role has not ended *de facto*; it has just been deinstitutionalised, re-institutionalised and legitimised by the broad membership of the ECA. The broad membership is just a smoke screen to provide legitimacy to the ECA decisions and portray them as decisions of an all representative body. The ECA is used as a platform to represent the interests of the elite when their common commercial interests are affected. So long as there is football and financial interests involved in it, the prospect of the formation of breakaway structures will be alive and well. This is confirmed by an article in The Guardian citing the statement of the AC Milan director and the first vice-president of the ECA Executive Board, Umberto Gandini: 'I still believe a European league will be an unavoidable step, though it may take more time than expected.' It further says that 'the dissolution of the G14 pressure group of clubs and the institution of the European Club Association as a UEFA talking shop was described as a 'historic moment' for football. However, it is clear that despite its disappearance, the ambitions promoted by the G14 have not been diluted and ambitions for more control remain.'[106] Commenting on the latest breakaway threat, the article in The Guardian notes:

> [a]lthough the ECA has a broad constituency, representing [207] European clubs, it is the interests of nine in particular that will drive this agenda. They are Real Madrid, Milan, Liverpool, Internazionale, Manchester United, Barcelona, Arsenal, Chelsea and Rummenigge's Bayern. When the Guardian contacted the four English clubs for their views on the matter, all declined to comment. However, a director at one of the clubs said: '[Financially] there is a lot of unfulfilled potential in football as it stands.'[107]

Whereas it is not disputed that UEFA's power to govern the game has to be subject to effective control and accountability, the decentralisation of the kind described is probably the worst kind of decentralisation that could happen to European football in terms of enhancing competitive balance between clubs, or strengthening solidarity mechanisms. On the top of this, a recent trend included the emergence of new stakeholders outside of organised sports structures, such as, for example, local communities. Central decision-making without proper representation of all the affected stakeholders might be a sign of bad governance, but decentralised decision-making to the advantage of big clubs as stakeholders and the disadvantage of football as a whole, is potentially even worse.

3.4.4 Professional Football Strategy Council

The creation of the Professional Football Strategy Council (PFSC) in June 2007 was a response to the 2006–2008 breakaway threat and the G14 demands for more

---

[106] 'Big Clubs Restate the Claim for European League' by Matt Scott, The Guardian, 24 February 2009.

[107] The Guardian, 27 July 2011.

representation in the governance of European football. This move also happened to correspond to the European policy demands for democratic stakeholder representation within the UEFA structures.[108] Article 11(4) of the UEFA Organisational Regulations (2011) provides that 'the purpose of the PFSC as a consultative body is to make recommendations to the Executive Committee', while considering the interests of all stakeholders in European football recognised by UEFA. With this purpose in mind the PFSC:

> a) identifies solutions for improving collaboration between the various stakeholders in European football, in particular by exploring the possibility of establishing a European Professional Football Charter; b) deals with issues pertaining to the social dialogue in European professional football matters; c) works with the existing professional football consultative bodies on all relevant issues; d) ensures that football stays together as one family, with professional and amateur football living together within the existing sports structures and the pyramidal system; e) discusses the views of the clubs, leagues, players and UEFA's member associations and informs the Executive Committee accordingly.[109]

Members of the PFSC decide on the topics that can be brought to the discussion table and that may include: '(a) UEFA club competitions and their calendars; (b) the position of professional clubs within the international football environment; (c) financial and commercial aspects of European football, and; (d) issues related to the European Union.'[110]

The PFSC is composed of 16 members: four UEFA vice-presidents, and the same number of EPFL representatives, FIFPro representatives and ECA representatives.[111] The four bodies represented in the PFSC are also partners in the social dialogue process at the European level. Their role and the part the PFSC plays in that process will be discussed in Sect. 3.4.6.

---

[108] See, for e.g., Nice Declaration on Sport (2000), point 10. See also Commission Communication on Developing European Dimension in Sport (2011), para 4.1 for the most recent policy document.

[109] UEFA Organisational Regulations, edition 2011, Article 11(1).

[110] Ibid. Article 11(2).

[111] Ibid. Article 10. The EPFL representatives in the PFSC for the term 2011–2013 are Frédéric Thiriez (Deputy Chairman of the EPFL and President of the French LFP), José Luis Astiazarán (President of the Spanish Professional Football League and Member of the EPFL Board), Frank Rutten (CEO of the Dutch Eredivisie and Member of the EPFL Board), and Holger Hieronymus (COO of the DFL Bundesliga and Member of the EPFL Board). On behalf of FIFPro Division Europe, the representatives appointed to attend the meetings of the PFSC are Philippe Piat (president of FIFPro Division Europe, president of UNFP, France), Theo van Seggelen (secretary general of FIFPro Division Europe), Bobby Barnes (board member FIFPro Division Europe, deputy chief executive PFA, England), and Luis Rubiales (president AFE, Spain). On 13 July 2011, the ECA Executive Board appointed the four members representing ECA on the PFSC for the two upcoming seasons (2011–2013). They are Umberto Gandini (AC Milan), David Gill (Manchester United FC), Maarten Fontein (AZ Alkmaar), and Florentino Pérez (Real Madrid CF), in other words, three former G14 members out of four representatives.

3.4.5 *The UEFA Club Competitions Committee*

The UEFA Club Competitions Committee (CCC) exchanges views on the current UEFA club competitions, draws up modifications to the existing competitions and their regulations, assists in the process for selecting final venues, proposes models for the distribution of revenues, and monitors the competitions while they are in progress. The recommendations made by the CCC always receive close attention from the UEFA Executive Committee, especially with regard to the revamping of the club competitions in recent times through changes to the access list in the UEFA Champions League and the launching of the UEFA Europa League. The Committee is composed of a chairman, a deputy chairman, a first, second and third vice-chairman (two vice-chairmen are elected by the ECA), as well as nine ordinary members (five of whom are elected by the ECA). The CCC is chaired by UEFA Executive Committee member Michael van Praag. On 13 July 2011 the ECA appointed seven members to represent it on the CCC. Five of these seven representatives are former G14 members.[112]

3.4.6 *Social Dialogue and Collective Agreements in Professional Football*

3.4.6.1 EU Legislation

Articles 153–155 of the TFEU make the Commission responsible for promoting and supporting the European social dialogue. Ideally, social dialogue results in collective agreements entered into by representatives of both sides of the industry and plays a significant role in shaping employment relations and working conditions. Article 154 obliges the Commission to consult management and labour on the content of legislative proposal in the social policy field before they are formally submitted. According to Article 155, an agreement between the two sides of the industry concluded at the Union level, depending on its content, may be implemented in accordance with procedures and practices of the Member States or by a Council decision on a proposal from the Commission at the joint request of the signatories. The European Parliament is left out of this legislative procedure.

In order to participate in social dialogue at European level, the social partner organisations must apply jointly to the European Commission. When submitting the joint application, those organisations must meet the cumulative criteria set forth in Article 1 of the Commission Decision 98/500 of 1998 on the

---

[112] Diogo P. Brandão (FC Porto), Umberto Gandini (AC Milan), David Gill (Manchester United FC), Karl Hopfner (FC Bayern München), Sandro Rosell (FC Barcelona), John McClelland (Rangers FC), Damir Vrbanovic (NK Dinamo Zagreb).

establishment of Sectoral Dialogue Committees promoting the dialogue between the social partners at European level. It provides that:

1. Sectoral Dialogue Committees [...] are hereby established in those sectors where the social partners make a joint request to take part in a dialogue at European level, and where the organisations representing both sides of industry fulfil the following criteria:
   (a) they shall relate to specific sectors or categories and be organised at European level;
   (b) they shall consist of organisations which are themselves an integral and recognized part of Member States' social partner structures and have the capacity to negotiate agreements, and which are representative of several Member States;
   (c) they shall have adequate structures to ensure their effective participation in the work of the Committees.[113]

The phrasing of the criterion of representativeness under Article 1(b) of the 1998 Decision and the words '[...]which are representative of several Member States' have been subsequently rephrased to read 'which are representative of all Member States, as far as possible.'[114]

In terms of the application of EU competition law, the collective bargaining agreements would normally fall outside of the ambit of competition law articles on the basis of the well-established exemption in the *Albany, Brentjens* and *Drijvende Bokken* line of case law.[115] EU free movement law would remain applicable.

3.4.6.2 FIFPro, Social Partners and Developments So Far

In Europe, unlike in the US,[116] the social dialogue and collective bargaining agreements in sports are still in their infancy. Since 2001, the Commission has been supporting projects for the consolidation of social dialogue in the sport sector globally as well as specifically in the football sector.[117] Studies were conducted to identify the social partners[118] and the labour-related themes and issues suitable to be dealt by means of

---

[113] Commission Decision of 20 May 1998 (98/500/EC) on the establishment of Sectoral Dialogue Committees promoting the dialogue between the social partners at European level, OJ L 225, 12.8.1998, p. 27.

[114] See, for instance, Report on the Representativeness of European Social Partner Organisations (1999).

[115] Case C-67/96 *Albany International BV v. Stichting Bedrijfspensioenfonds Textielindustrie* [1999] ECR I-5751, Cases C-115, 116 and 117/97 *Brentjens' Handelsonderneming BV v Stichting Bedrijfspensioenfonds voor de Handel in Bouwmaterialen* [1999] ECR I-6025 and Case C-219/97 *Drijvende Bokken* [1999] ECR I-6121.

[116] For the US see Halgreen 2004, p. 209.

[117] See list of projects in fn. 6, Sect. 5.3 in Commission Staff Working Document, The EU and Sport: Background and Context, Accompanying Document to the White Paper on Sport, COM (2007) 391 final.

[118] See Promoting Social Dialogue in European Professional Football (Candidate EU Member States), Report for the European Commission (November 2004) and; Study on the Representativeness of the Social Partner Organisations in the Professional Football Player Sector, Report for the European Commission, Project No VC/2004/0547 (2006).

social dialogue in professional football,[119] but also in some other professional sports.[120] Social partner organisations on the European level in professional football whose representative nature was confirmed by those studies are the International Federation of Professional Footballers' Associations (FIFPro) Division Europe on the side of employees and the EPFL complemented by the ECA on the side on employers.

The EPFL members are only from the top leagues in Europe, representing 16 out of 27 EU Member States, and 7 out of 26 non-EU countries. It was argued that EPFL is not an independent organisation: its member professional leagues are affiliated and subordinated to their respective national football associations while EPFL itself is 'directly and very closely linked to UEFA and FIFA'.[121] Further, because it represents only top leagues, it was thought that the role of EPFL 'may assume added importance as a potential vehicle for a breakaway super-league in which the question of employer representativeness would be assured'.[122] Nevertheless the EPFL was deemed to fulfil the sub-condition of representativeness under Article 1(b) of the Commission Decision 98/500.[123] In addition, not all of the EPFL members are 'themselves an integral and recognized part of Member States' social partner structures' and have 'the capacity to negotiate agreements' within the meaning of Article 1(b), first requirement.[124]

The ECA, as described above in Sect. 3.4.3, is dominated by the top European clubs and may be used as a tool to pursue their common commercial interests whenever necessary. The Memorandum of Understanding between UEFA and the ECA recognises a 'need to find the right balance between labour legislation and the specific characteristics of football, for example through the vehicle of social dialogue and/or collective bargaining agreements.'[125] Adequately representing only the interests of its top members (regardless of its much wider constituency) makes the ECA, much like EFPL, a tool used by the elite in the European social dialogue process. On 13 July 2011, the ECA Executive Board appointed five individuals to represent the ECA on EU Social Dialogue Committee.[126] Four of them were affiliated with the clubs of the former G14.

---

119 See Study into the Identification of Themes and Issues which can be Dealt with in a Social Dialogue in the European Professional Football Sector, Report for the European Commission (May 2008). See also the press release in 2008 The International Sports Law Review 1–2, p. 109.

120 Such as cycling. See Study into the Identification of Themes and Issues to be Dealt with in a Social Dialogue in the European Professional Cycling Sector, report for the European Commission (2009).

121 Siekmann 2006, p. 77.

122 Parrish and Miettinen 2008, p. 48.

123 Siekmann 2006, p. 79. See Report for the European Commission, Project No VC/2004/0547 (2006).

124 Such as for instance the Finnish *Jalkapalloliiga* or the English FA Premier League.

125 Paragraph A4, fifth indent, of the Memorandum.

126 Pedro Lopez Jimenez (Real Madrid CF), Jean-Michel Aulas (Olympique Lyonnais), Raúl Sanllehí (FC Barcelona), Michael Gerlinger (FC Bayern München), and Michele Centenaro (ECA General Secretary).

FIFPro represents professional players all over the world and its membership currently exceeds 50,000. The Board of FIFPro consists of eleven persons: five representatives, from each of: the United Kingdom, France, The Netherlands, Italy, and Spain, in their capacity of permanent representatives; two representatives from each of the American Division and the European Division; and one representative from each of the African Division and Asian Division.[127] The FIFPro Division Europe consists of 24 professional football players' member associations.[128]

Responding to a joint request made by the EPFL and the FIFPro Division Europe in December 2007, the Commission acknowledged the existence of conditions for the creation of the EU sectorial Social Dialogue Committee in the professional football sector (the Committee).[129] The Committee was formally established by the Commission decision of 20 May 1998—98/500/EC. The public ceremony establishing this Committee and adopting its rules of procedure took place in Paris on July 1, 2008. By this time the ECA was also considered a party to the social dialogue representing the employers.[130] Furthermore, the EPFL and FIFPro agreed to engage UEFA in this process as an associated partner. According to the rules of procedure the Committee shall 'work in harmony with the Professional Football Strategy Council and submit any item for discussion in the Committee to the Strategy Council for agreement' before being formally placed on the Committee agenda.[131] The social partners agreed to invite the UEFA President to chair the Committee.[132] Via these rules of procedure UEFA became involved in the social dialogue in which it previously did not have any formal role, as it does not represent employers or employees and thus cannot be considered a social partner.

Governing bodies should not have access to the social dialogue legislative process[133] of the type which UEFA has now obtained. The consequences of its involvement may be that certain terms of collective bargaining agreements might be considered ineligible for the competition law exemption if challenged before the Court. It was argued that 'although independence is not an official, explicit criterion for admissibility to European Social Dialogue, on the basis of the fundamental consideration that in a democratic society social partner organisations

---

127 Article 10 of the FIFPro Articles of Association.

128 The Division board is led by president Philippe Piat, a former French professional player, the other members of the board are Bobby Barnes a former English professional player, Joachim Evangelista, a former German professional player, and three other members.

129 In its communication of March 13, 2008.

130 See the Commission Press Release IP/08/1064 'Footballers and Employers Launch New EU Forum on Social Dialogue' 1 July 2008.

131 Article 2 of the Rules of Procedure for the European Sectoral Social Dialogue Committee in the Professional Football Sector. See also European Sectoral Social Dialogue Committee in the Professional Football Sector Work Programme 2008–2009.

132 Ibid. Rules of Procedure, Article 4.

133 Parrish and Miettinen 2008, p. 48.

should be independent from national governments […] similar conclusion would in principle apply to the issue of independence at European level.'[134] The role of UEFA as associate partner, and the crucial consensus of the PFSC, a body within the UEFA structure, for the work of the Social Dialogue Committee, jeopardise the independence of the social partners and the legitimacy of the entire process that is supposed to be free from interference by the government or regulatory governing bodies such as UEFA. The utility of placing items before the PFSC which consists of the same members as the Social Dialogue Committee is questionable. The differences are the influence of the UEFA which is higher in the PFSC than in the social dialogue, and the fact that the ECA and the EPFL are basically sharing one voice in the Social Dialogue Committee, whereas in the PFSC they have two separate voices.

The main goal of the Work Programme of the Committee for the years 2008–2009 was to discuss and disseminate the concept of Minimum Requirements on Professional Football Player Contract throughout the EU Member States and promote studies, conferences, workshops and round tables in the new Member States or Candidate Members.[135] Two working groups were set up: the first concerning the Implementation of the Minimum Requirements of Professional Football Player Contract and the second on The Transformation of the Minimum Requirements into a Collective Agreement at the European level. In March 2011, FIFPro expressed its 'bitter disappointment' with the reluctance of the other three parties to sign the agreement on minimum requirements for standard player contracts. According to it, the Commission set the date of 5 April 2011 for the official signing ceremony which it then had to cancel.[136] On 8 August 2011 FIFPro appeared far more optimistic and hoped to sign the agreement during the meeting of the PFSC to be held on 26 August 2011.[137] The minimum requirements for professional football players' contracts in Europe were finally agreed between the social partners and UEFA in April 2012. The first collective bargaining agreement in European football includes *inter alia* provisions on dispute resolution and applicable law; defines the basic rights and obligations of club and players (for example, it specifies the matters which must be included in the contract, such as salary, health insurance, social security, paid leave, etc. and provides that players must play matches to the best of their abilities, maintain a healthy lifestyle and high level of fitness, behave in a sporting manner, not bring their club into disrepute, etc.); and contains provisions on exploitation of image rights.[138] The substance of the terms remains a matter for negotiation between the parties to the contracts, until and unless new collective agreements regulating substantive aspects are

---

[134] Siekmann 2008, p. 95.

[135] Ibid. Work Programme 2008–2010.

[136] FIFPro news item 'Only FIFPro is Ready to Sign Minimum Requirements' 1 March 2011.

[137] For details see Carvalho 2010, pp. 48–51.

[138] Agreement regarding the minimum requirements for standard player contracts in the professional football sector in the European Union and in the rest of the UEFA territory, available at http://ec.europa.eu/sport/news/documents/agreement_football_contracts_en.pdf.

concluded between the social partners. In January 2013, the study on transfer of players commissioned by the European Commission recommended that FIFA should be invited to participate in the social dialogue as it is the competent body in the field of international transfers and sets minimum rules in case of contractual disputes.[139] The study proposed that the European social dialogue take up and issue and regulate the use of 'buyout clauses' in order to prevent abuse and excessive payments, so that retrospectively the power of control exercised by judges may be a useful complement to Article 17 of the FIFA Regulations. It also suggested that the Committee should consider the following points: protection of minors; excessive transfer fees; solidarity; fair and balanced competition; and rules on non-EU players.[140]

Whereas the minimal formal contractual requirements are supposed to be easy to implement by all clubs, certain substantive requirements might prove too difficult to implement by the clubs operating in small markets. The good news for these clubs is that less than 2 % of the texts adopted by European social partners are binding agreements, while the rest are soft measures such as declarations and recommendations.[141] This quantitative measure, however, does not imply that non-binding agreements are not effective.[142] Some substantive items stipulating minimum requirements are therefore more suitable to be dealt by national-level social partners (if such partners exist in a given European state) due to the homogenous economic conditions prevailing on the statewide markets. Salary caps, on the other hand, might become a subject of discussion on a pan-European level before the Committee. In order to counter the negative effects on competitive balance (such as the effects of player market liberalisation and increasing foreign ownership with all its financial consequences), in addition to the adoption of Financial Fair Play Regulations, UEFA's President suggested the introduction of salary caps. Although this particular item is thought to be difficult to implement in an open league system,[143] it is not impossible and might be necessary to design a working method of implementation in view of growing competitive imbalance that has plagued European football since the mid-1990s. In this sense, as long as the threat of breakaway is not used to force compromises in the social dialogue process, having UEFA participate in the social dialogue appears to be beneficial for interests of least well-off stakeholders and the game of football as a whole. In a pyramid model in which there would be a democratic stakeholder representation with

[139] Study on the Economic and Legal Aspects of Transfers of Players (2013), p. 255. Available at http://ec.europa.eu/sport/library/documents/f-studies/cons-study-transfers-final-rpt.pdf.

[140] Ibid. p. 258.

[141] Pochet (2007) European Social Dialogue Between Hard and Soft Law. European Union Studies Association (EUSA) Tenth Biennial International Conference, Montreal, 17–19 May, cited in Parrish 2011, p. 224.

[142] Parrish 2011, p. 245.

[143] See Martins 2009, p. 397.

democratic composition of the Executive Boards of the representative bodies, UEFA's presence would not be necessary. However, the changes in the state of affairs in the governance of European football makes their presence necessary because '[t]he [...] social partners are not so concerned with improving the working conditions of an already cosseted category of worker, but are motivated by a desire to exercise greater influence within football in order to control the wealth generated from it'.[144] Both the players and the clubs view the social dialogue as a tool for pressuring FIFA and UEFA to improve their position within the football governance structures.[145]

3.4.6.3 Comments

Participation as a partner in European social dialogue has given a valuable resource to FIFPro outside of the UEFA structure, and the power to influence the affairs and protect the interests of its members. Similarly, representation on the PFSC within the UEFA structure has also given FIFPro a voice in football governance. In fact, the social partners involved in social dialogue and the bodies represented in the PFSC are exactly the same parties. The worrying trend in European football is that players, clubs and leagues from non-EU countries—save for Switzerland where UEFA and FIFA have their headquarters—and other European football nations that are not in the top 5–9 on the UEFA coefficient rankings have no proper representation in any of the social partner bodies regardless of their membership. It should be remembered that country ranking is directly related to the performance of their clubs in European competitions, while competitive performance is directly correlated to the amount of money that clubs have to spend. Even though they will not be in any of the EPFL leagues, or on the ECA Executive Board, and their players will not get to decide on any of the FIFPro affairs, the collective bargaining agreements will apply to them. In this sense, it is absolutely necessary to have proper representation on the ECA, FIFPro and the EPFL of those belonging to the non-elite end of professional football. There are at least two different stakeholders within each of these bodies (the best-off and the worst-off) and their presence and difference of interests, to the extent it exists on specific issues, should be acknowledged formally by giving them equal voice in decision-making. Therefore, even though a form of stakeholder representation is taking place, it is the rich that ultimately make the decisions in European football due to the structure of the boards and the representatives of ECA, EPFL and FIFPro in the social dialogue process and on the PFSC. It is exactly because of these inequalities that the pyramid structure survives.

---

[144] Parrish and Miettinen 2008, p. 49.

[145] Parrish 2011, p. 225.

3.4.7 UEFA Club Licensing and Financial Fair Play Regulations

The changes that have taken place since 2004 in regards to the club licensing system have led to yet another departure from promotion and relegation, the defining feature of the European football model. Changes to the club licensing system are largely viewed as a positive development contributing towards good governance in sports, and are based on key principles of transparency, integrity, credibility and capability. Article 2 of UEFA Club Licensing and Financial Fair Play Regulations, edition 2012, (CLFFP Regulations) sets out as its objectives, *inter alia*, to promote and improve the standard of all aspects of football in Europe, and specifically to: ensure an adequate level of management and organisation; to adapt clubs' sporting infrastructure to provide players, spectators and media representatives with suitable, well-equipped and safe facilities; to allow the development of benchmarking for clubs in financial, sporting, legal, personnel and administrative, and infrastructure-related criteria throughout Europe; and to encourage responsible spending for the long-term benefit of football. Each club that wishes to compete in UEFA-organised competitions must fulfil a series of defined quality standards annually to obtain a license and thus gain admittance to those competitions. Licenses are granted by the national associations and confirm that a quality level required by the CLFFP Regulations is achieved. There are 36 specific criteria of the licensing system that can be broken down into five principal categories: sporting criteria (Articles 17–23 of CLFFP Regulations), infrastructure criteria (Articles 24–26 of CLFFP Regulations), personnel and administrative criteria (Articles 27–42 of CLFFP Regulations), legal criteria (Articles 43–46 of CLFFP Regulations), and financial criteria (Article 46bis-52 of CLFFP Regulations).

The club licensing system has been seen as a 'good instrument to help improve the financial stability of the clubs, to increase transparency and business credibility of club operation and thus deliver the short and long-term benefits for clubs and football as a whole'.[146] Ensuring that clubs remain solvent throughout the competition and that they do not drop out or play with a depleted squad because they cannot pay their players also acts to protect the interests of players and the public.[147] A Commission Staff Working Document mentions ensuring of financial stability of sport clubs/teams as one of the objective justifications as it relates to the organisation and proper conduct of competitive sport.[148] Whereas the introduction of these rules seems like a positive step forward for European football as a whole, the downside of it is that the criteria are easier to fulfil for the wealthier clubs in good competitive standing which is another factor on the list contributing towards the diminishing of the principle of promotion and relegation, and widening the

146 Arnaut Report, para 3.53.

147 Ibid. para 3.52.

148 Annex I, para 2.1.5.

gulf between the best and the rest.[149] There are 730 clubs playing in the top divisions of the 53 national associations. Of these 730, only 608 applied for the license for 2009/2010 season. Of the 608 clubs that applied, 110 were refused a license for their inability to fulfil various criteria listed in CLFFP Regulations. Between 2005 and 2009, 49 clubs that directly qualified for one of the UEFA clubs competitions on sporting merit, were refused a license for their inability to meet some of the licensing criteria. All of them came from some of the poorest European countries.[150] Refusal to license them directly denied them the access to, and the benefits of participation in, the UEFA competitions, further worsening their financial situation. Benefiting from the system of promotion and relegation is no longer a matter of sporting merit alone—it is a privilege that must be paid for by those who can afford it. In addition to a refusal to be licensed, the clubs also may suffer sanctions ranging from warning to fines, and may be a subject to disciplinary proceedings on a national level.

The concept in the second part of CLFFP Regulations (FFP) was added in 2009 and regulates the score on the clubs' balance sheets. In essence, the licensed clubs are required to (at least) break even in a given monitoring period,[151] and comply with other designated criteria.[152] The introduction of FFP into European football was prompted by the increasing trend for the clubs to spend more than they earn. In some cases such practice was enabled by the wealthy owners whose investments would set-off any financial losses,[153] whereas in other cases it led clubs to insolvency.[154] It is to be remembered that the sustainability of the contemporary model of financing for professional clubs depends on a dynamic equilibrium between a club's spending on wages and its media revenues.[155] As discussed in Sect. 1.2, the value of media rights has steadily increased over the past 15 years or so. However, the player wages and their value on the transfer market increased at a rate beyond that of revenues from the sales of media rights. Clubs were overspending on inflated player wages to remain competitive in the sporting sense, which left many of them in financial trouble. Clubs accounts are being monitored under FFP since the beginning of 2011/2012 season and the first assessment will take place in the 2013/2014 season.

In May 2013, a legal challenge to FFP was brought before the European Commission by the Belgian football player agent Daniel Striani. He argued that

---

[149] Caldow 2002.

[150] UEFA publication: The European Club Footballing Landscape—Club Licensing Benchmarking Report Financial Year 2008, p. 21.

[151] For definitions of break even requirement and temporal scope of a monitoring period see Articles 57–63 of UEFA Club Licensing and Financial Fair Play Regulations 2012.

[152] Articles 64–68 of UEFA Club Licensing and Financial Fair Play Regulations 2012.

[153] Chelsea and Manchester City are the most well-known examples of such clubs.

[154] Portsmouth Football Club was the only FA Premier League club to enter the formal insolvency proceedings in 2010. See Szymanski 2012, p. 2, available at http://college.holycross.edu/RePEc/spe/Szymanski_Insolvency.pdf.

[155] Andreff 2009, p. 695. For more on financing of the football clubs see Sect. 2.3.2.

the break even rule restricts outside investment into clubs and slows down the transfer market and salary levels, thus negatively affecting his revenue and income. He also argued that the break even rule effectively entrenches the hegemony of already dominant clubs, by preventing other clubs from breaking through by operating at a loss (for example, by exploiting the benefactor owner model that would allow them to compete with dominant clubs who utilised the benefits of this model for years).[156] Hence, free of movement of capital, free movement of workers and freedom to provide and receive services were at stake.

It has been generally accepted that a club's ranking is directly correlated with the club's wage spending so that spending more on wages translates to on-pitch success.[157] At the time of writing, the Commission has not yet responded to Striani's complaint. In general, however, it has been supportive of FFP. Answering to a Parliamentary Question in August 2010 (E-4628/10) Commissioner for Internal Market and Services, Michel Barnier, declared that

> [t]he Commission would also like to draw the Honourable Member's attention to self-regulatory measures taken by the football sector to reduce the overall level of debt of clubs. On 27 May 2010, UEFA's Executive Committee approved the Financial Fair Play Regulations with the aim of ensuring the long-term financial stability of European football clubs. The Commission considers that the rationale of UEFA's plan seems to be in accordance with one of the objectives of the EU's action in the field of sport, namely with the promotion of fairness in sporting competitions (Article 165 TFEU). The Commission also notes that any measure taken in this framework has to respect the EU's Internal Market and competition rules.[158]

Furthermore, on 21 March 2012 the Commission issued a joint statement with UEFA, drawing a parallel between the broad objectives of FFP and EU State Aid rules under Article 107 TFEU, both of which are directed at encouraging undertakings (i.e. the clubs) to operate within their own means without the need for additional financial injections.[159] EU State Aid rules are designed to prevent unauthorised public assistance in cases of undertakings in financial difficulties, as all market operators should compete on a level playing field without receiving any special advantage. According to the joint statement, there is a significant risk that football clubs will increasingly apply for financial help to the public authorities in order to be able to continue playing professional football.[160] This might be more related to fear that the application for assistance from the public purse could not be

[156] See Nixon 2013, available at http://e-comlaw.com/sportslawblog/.

[157] See, for example, Highlights of Deloitte Annual Review of Football Finance (2012), p. 10. Available at http://www.deloitte.com/assets/DcomUnitedKingdom/Local%20Assets/Documents/Industries/Sports%20Business%20Group/uk-sbg-annual-football-finance-review-2012-highlights.pdf. See also Kuper and Szymanski 2012, p. 14.

[158] Cited in Szymanski 2013 (guest post by Professor Stephen Weatherill), available at http://www.soccernomics-agency.com/?p=469.

[159] Joint Statement by Vice-President Joaquín Almunia and President Michel Platini, 21 March 2012, available at http://ec.europa.eu/competition/sectors/sports/joint_statement_en.pdf.

[160] Ibid. para 12.

refused to clubs, than to the fact of application itself. As Weatherill points out, 'in a "normal" industry [the over-indebtedness] would be disciplined by bankruptcy. In football we cannot simply send famous clubs into oblivion.'[161]

There is a general consensus among both economists and lawyers that FFP will further reduce rapidly fading competitive balance in European football. Weatherill says that 'FFP does not contribute to competitive balance' and 'it may even turn out to be a mechanism that stabilises competitive imbalance.'[162] Simmons agrees and contends that 'overzealous application of the [FFP] rules generates a significant risk that the dominance of the strong clubs will be enhanced, while the financial instability of lower division teams in national associations is not addressed.'[163] Having researched the direct correlation between wages and the sporting success Flanagan noted that 'it is ostensibly in the interest of healthy competition to obviate imbalance. FFP will not do this; clubs remain at liberty to spend the money they generate and there is a significant variation thereby.'[164] This could be one of the reasons for strong support given to FFP by the ECA.[165] Had the ECA been dissatisfied with the new regulations and had FFP had positive effect on competitive balance

> Europe's leading clubs could chose to simply relieve themselves of UEFA's regulations altogether by forming a breakaway European competition, perhaps in the form of a European 'Super League', the prospect of which has been mooted by leading authorities within the game (for example, in 2009, Arsenal manager Wenger suggested that a European Super League may be formed 'in 10 years' with the addition that such a change would be more likely 'if the rules become too restrictive for these [leading European] clubs').[166]

Commenting on FC Barcelona's EUR 69 million loss on its 2009/10 balance sheet, Simmons said that 'a threat by UEFA to exclude Barcelona from the Champions League cannot be credible. These clubs could join with others to threaten formation of a rival league similar in format to the Champions League.'[167] This could have been the case had UEFA introduced in its initial proposal to apply the rule only to the clubs with turnover of more than EUR 50 million. ECA rejected this proposal and thought that all clubs should be treated in the same way. However, treating the different situations (for example, clubs in

---

161 See his guest post in Szymanski 2013.

162 Ibid.

163 Simmons 2012, available at http://www.voxeu.org/article/own-goal-uefas-financial-fair-play-initiative-misguided.

164 Flanagan 2013, p. 162. See also the comment of Bosman's lawyer Jean-Louis Dupont in 'Football's Anticompetitive Streak' Wall Street Journal, 25 March 2013.

165 European Club Association 'ECA Calls on Member Clubs to Adhere to Financial Fair Play Rules' 11 September 2012. Available at http://www.ecaeurope.com/news/eca-calls-on-member-clubs-to-adhere-to-financial-fair-play-rules/.

166 Flanagan 2013, p. 157.

167 Simmons 2012.

the FA Premier League and clubs in the Estonian Premium Liiga) in the same way may amount to discrimination as much as treating the same situations in a different way. It also goes against competitive balance. Once again, wealthy clubs that run the ECA improved their position in relation to the rest of the European clubs who, if they had any vote in European football governance, would certainly not reject UEFA's initial proposal.

As the CLFFP Regulation demonstrates, the prospect of formation of breakaway league by European elite clubs is deeply ingrained in the mind of the governing body. UEFA will therefore continue to take outmost care of the wealthy clubs' interests when adopting important rules and regulations to govern European football.

3.5 Risks in the Commercial and Legal Environment

There are several reasons which can explain why the breakaway league in football has not materialised by now. First and foremost, there are certain commercial risks involved. Operating within the wider regulatory and organisational monopoly of UEFA is safer than going it alone. Were the clubs able to accurately anticipate a positive response from the demand market in its broadest sense, and a favourable response in the legal environment it would make commercial sense to part ways with UEFA. However, economic evidence tells us that, in general, quantitative increase in output (more games) will not necessarily create more profit.[168] Data from 2006 revealed the process of slowing down in TV rights fees paid to professional football,[169] but the more recent figures illustrate that broadcasting market has not reached its ceiling.[170] Large adjustments in the production of the sporting contests most often occur where the nature of the existing arrangements was 'clearly not meeting objectives' of the clubs, or where it failed to meet the demand of the fans.[171] Europe in general does not have problems with fan interest nor does the current structure of the production process clearly go against clubs' objectives. The Chief Executive of Liverpool FC was of the opinion that an alternative league did not materialise thus far because the Champions League was so successful and the clubs were broadly happy with it.[172] Nevertheless, he did not exclude the possibility that a trend of increase in foreign ownership may provoke a change of heart. Indeed, there is no doubt that if an investment company from, say, China, the UAE, or Russia offered the clubs a 10-figure sum that they cannot refuse, and a

[168] See Andreff 2009, p. 693.

[169] Andreff and Bourg 2006, p. 37.

[170] See Sect. 1.2.

[171] Borland 2009, p. 24.

[172] An interview with Rick Parry, Chief Executive of Liverpool Football Club 1998–2007 and a former head of the Premier League, 2 June 2011.

deal that UEFA could not match with any concessions, the structure of football in Europe would change. Basic economic theory suggests that sunk costs should not be allowed to affect one's investment decisions. In addition, the elite clubs themselves would probably have disagreements concerning their joint strategies and the compromises made would entail missing out on many Pareto improvements. This would be counterproductive to the economic efficiency objectives of a breakaway league.

Secondly, as will be discussed in Sect. 7.9, clubs in breakaway leagues themselves may breach EU laws (in fact, they might already be doing so by abusing collective dominant position), so there are legal issues which might interfere with the optimal running of the league. Depending on the degree of separation from the rest of the football community (i.e. how closed or open it would be to other entrants, what access criteria would it adopt, its relationship with national associations, etc.), it is possible that the new league would be treated as a purely commercial entity rather than as an entity that possesses specificities which can earn it a soft application of the law and exempt it from, for example, application of Article 101 TFEU to collective sales of broadcasting rights. The breakaway leagues have to remain integrated into the system of promotion and relegation, must make solidarity contributions to the rest of the football, and must remain under regulatory purview of UEFA and national governing bodies to comply with the EU law.[173] In addition, the legal environment for the sporting industry is still in the process of development, which makes it relatively unpredictable in certain situations (in this case because the prospect of pan-European breakaway is a new issue that has never been raised before). Both new and established rules are being challenged in court and although the tests employed are familiar, the outcome might be surprising. One of the examples is the recent *Murphy* case.[174] The *Murphy* case was thought of as having the potential to bring big changes in the way that governing bodies and leagues sell their rights, which could also have repercussions for the alternative league's prospects. Another potential constraint on such prospects might be presented by the Article 14 of the Audiovisual Media Services Directive[175] that provides a possibility for Member States to draw up a list of events which they consider to be of major importance for society to ensure that broadcasters under their jurisdiction do not broadcast on an exclusive basis in such a way as to deprive a substantial proportion of the public in that Member State of the possibility of following such events via live coverage or deferred coverage on free television. Judgments of the Court in a series of cases known as *FIFA and*

---

[173] See Sect. 7.6.

[174] For detailed analysis of this case see Sect. 4.10.

[175] Directive 2010/13/EU of the European Parliament and of the Council of 10 March 2010 on the coordination of certain provisions laid down by law, regulation or administrative action in Member States concerning the provision of audiovisual media services (Audiovisual Media Services Directive), OJ L 95, 15/4/2010, pp. 1–24.

UEFA v Commission[176] confirmed that sporting events such as the FIFA World Cup and the UEFA EURO are single events and may be enlisted by the EU Member States to be shown on free-to-air TV in their totality (as opposed to enlisting only individual matches of major interest to society). This ruling may apply to club competitions at least in the countries where club football is important to big number of people, such as the 'big five' which are also the most lucrative football markets for sale of football media rights. Because it may reduce the value of broadcasting rights for the rights holders and exclusive broadcasters, Article 14 of the Audiovisual Media Services Directive is at least potentially affecting the development of a pan-European breakaway league.[177]

Perhaps the most telling of the risks involved in the formation of a breakaway structure is the statement by Tom Dunmore who thought that 'breaking away, whilst possible, would be a huge gamble of unprecedented proportions in world sports: never would so much money and prestige have been staked on a venture of unknown dimensions'.[178]

3.6 Is the UEFA Champions League an Open Competition?

The issues discussed in this chapter lead to the conclusion that the elite clubs in Europe should be generally content with their status and influence in European football structures. They play top football, have unmatched financial resources, employ the top players, and may exert decisive influence over the matters pertaining to European (and sometimes global) football. Institutionally, they have gained a supreme status among clubs in Europe and run the show in the ECA. UEFA rules and regulations facilitate the consolidation of their supremacy, ease their access to prestigious pan-European competitions, and add to their budget at the expense of slogans such as competitive balance and the system of promotion and relegation. Solidarity contribution, which does not enhance the competitive balance, is a small price to pay to remain in the structure that enables such a state of affairs and in which there is not much external commercial risk to be concerned about. It is a system that has been tried over long period of time and that has worked well thus far.

Regarding participation in the UEFA Champions League, a number of clubs per UEFA member association is determined in accordance with Article 2 of the

[176] Case T-385/07 *Fédération Internationale de Football Association (FIFA) v. Commission*, judgment of 17 February 2011, Case T-55/08 *Union des associations européennes de football (UEFA) v. Commission*, judgment of 17 February 2011; and Case T-68/08 *Fédération Internationale de Football Association (FIFA) v. Commission*, judgment of 17 February 2011.

[177] See Hoehn and Kastrianki 2012, p. 12.

[178] 'The G-14, Michel Platini, and the Bluff of the European Superleague' Tom Dunmore, Pitch Invasion, 7 November 2007.

Regulations of UEFA Champions League 2012/13.[179] Each association may enter a certain number of clubs for the Champions League, in accordance with its position in the coefficient rankings. The numbers of representative clubs that an association may enter ranges from one (winner in the top domestic league) to four (winner, runner-up, third- and fourth-placed clubs in the top domestic league). Accordingly, the top domestic leagues in England, Spain and Germany have four places reserved for their clubs, while Italian and French associations may enter three of their top domestic clubs. Associations occupying spots 16–53 on the UEFA coefficient rankings may enter only one team (Estonia, Croatia, Northern Ireland, Poland and Slovakia are some of these associations).[180] The percentage of titles won by three most successful clubs in the period between seasons 2000/2001 and 2011/2012 is 92 % in England, 100 % in Spain, 83 % in Germany, 92 % in Italy, and 75 % France (similar numbers are also found in other countries). In the same period an average of 50 % of titles were won by one and the same club.[181] The margin remaining for all other clubs is slim, and those clubs that only occasionally qualify for the Champions League are usually the same clubs. Clubs that participate on a regular basis gain a major competitive advantage over other clubs in their domestic league due to the financial rewards brought about by participation in, and progress through the different stages of, the UEFA Champions League. The clubs from the big five that progress to the final stages of the UEFA Champions League have most to gain (benefits such as TV exposure, popularity, value of current and future sponsorship agreements, prize money, etc., increase the longer that a club remains in the championship race). It was commented that

> [t]he UEFA CL makes some concessions to being a Europe-wide club competition that is open to clubs from smaller countries but in reality the [Champions League] only comes alive in the later stages when it is the top clubs from the top leagues who have the largest share of places and greatest chances of qualifying for the final stages. In other words we do have a de facto European Superleague system but one that largely excludes large clubs from small countries. The four or five top leagues act as successful platforms benefiting from economies of scale, network effects and cross-platform effects which leagues from smaller countries cannot match. The platform effects have been magnified by Pay TV which taps into the willingness to pay of viewers for a well-defined fixture list of races, matches and games with an uncertain outcome.[182]

Similarly, the study on transfer of players (2013) funded by the European Commission finds that Europe is slowly embracing a *de facto* system of closed leagues at elite level.[183] It is clear that for most of the football clubs in Europe even a mere participation in the top domestic and European leagues would not be

---

[179] The Regulation is available at http://www.uefa.com/MultimediaFiles/Download/Regulations/competitions/Regulations/01/79/68/69/1796869_DOWNLOAD.pdf.

[180] Ibid. Annex IA.

[181] Study on the Economic and Legal Aspects of Transfers of Players (2013), p. 7. Available at http://ec.europa.eu/sport/library/documents/f-studies/cons-study-transfers-final-rpt.pdf.

[182] Hoehn and Kastrianki 2012, p. 30.

[183] See Sect. 4.4.3.1 for details of the study.

a realistic aspiration but a fantasy: they have not much say in governance, and solidarity payments are clearly insufficient to remedy their situation to the extent that can give them any conceivable chance to benefit from the defining features of the open league model. The study on transfer of players (2013) recognises the latter point and proposes that solidarity schemes managed by UEFA and FIFA should better address competitive imbalance. The study concludes that the solidarity system 'is skewed towards supporting the most successful clubs, which happen to be the wealthiest in their respective leagues' and thus 'contributes to consolidating existing supremacies and fails to address the competitive imbalance. It is reflected in the results of UEFA competitions year after year'.[184]

With competitive balance and the system of promotion and relegation becoming more catchphrases than concepts in action, it appears that the elite clubs have nothing to complain about and that they are already a part of a semi-closed system.

Therefore, the elite breakaway will materialise only if the alternative presents clear advantages with low financial risk involved, or if the current structures fail to produce comparable benefits as thus far (for example, due to overhaul of UEFA rules to enhance competitive balance and make promotion and relegation workable in practice; changes in legal environment and adverse consequences on the exploitation market, etc.) to the extent that even a medium to high risk alternative becomes economically more rational choice. Calculation of risks is a matter of detailed and long-term planning that requires concerted efforts of all the parties involved, in particular by the entity that will perform the league functions. Also, any possible elite breakaway could not happen abruptly due to the running commitments by the clubs—broadcasting and sponsorship deals, obligations to national associations and a Memorandum of Understanding with UEFA are some of such commitments.

3.7 Conclusion

Pyramid structure as a classical European sports model has found its support in many of the EU policy documents to the delight of the governing bodies, including UEFA. However, the Commission makes clear that despite the fact that governing bodies have the right to organise their sport in a way they see fit, this is conditional on respect for EU law.[185] The EU policy also includes the requirements of openness, transparency and democratic representation of all affected stakeholders in the decision-making by the governing bodies. Therefore, in a single federation system the standard of governance ought to correspond to these requirements.

Until very recently UEFA had virtually exclusive power to decide on issues affecting all aspects of European football. A power shift in the commercially sensitive football governance structure emerged from the strategy of breakaway and

[184] Study on the Economic and Legal Aspects of Transfers of Players (2013), p. 7.

[185] See para 4.1 of the Commission Staff Working Document.

litigation threats by the elite clubs. It brought about the establishment of the bodies like the ECA and the PFSC. This chapter argued that the form of decentralisation and co-regulation that has emerged is not a positive development for football as a whole. Due to the structure of the Executive Boards and their representation on the Social Dialogue Committee, the PFSC and the CCC, the only stakeholders that are properly represented in the governance of football are the elite clubs and their players. Even without a formal voice, they were able to steer the decisions of the governing body in the desired direction whenever their commercial interests were at stake, using the threats of litigation and breakaway. The effect of this new model of governance so far has been wealth redistribution that favours the wealthiest to the disadvantage of those worse-off. This further widens the gap that exists in the competitive strength of the football clubs. For more than one reason, the process of social dialogue in professional football has a long way to go. Before it can be used in its normative function, the social partners need to change from within to give a formal voice that represents the rich clubs and rich players, as well as the worse-off clubs and players, equally. The current broad membership is just a smokescreen giving external legitimacy to otherwise undemocratic bodies. The changes that have so far taken place are neither the right basis nor a step in the right direction to alter the pattern in, and establish a truly representative model of governance in European football.

References

Andreff W (2009) Team sports and finance. In: Andreff W, Szymanski S (eds) Handbook on the economics of sport. Edward Elgar, Cheltenham, UK, pp 689–699

Andreff W, Bourg J-F (2006) Broadcasting rights and competition in European football. In: Jeanrenaud C, Késenne S (eds) The economic of sport and the media. Edward Elgar, Cheltenham, UK, pp 37–64

Borland J (2009) The production of professional team sports. In: Andreff W, Szymanski S (eds) Handbook on the economics of sport. Edward Elgar, Cheltenham, UK, pp 22–26

Caldow BA (2002) The European dimension: is the licensing of football clubs that wish to participate in European competitions a way ahead? Sports Law Admin Pract 9(4)

Carvalho O (2020) European social dialogue. EPFL Sports Law Bull 7:48–51

Flanagan CA (2013) A tricky European fixture: an assessment of UEFA's financial fair play regulations and their compatibility with EU law. Int Sports Law J 1–2:148–167

Freeman RE (1984) Strategic management: a stakeholder approach. Pitman Publishing, London

Halgreen L (2004) European sports law—a comparative analyses of the European and American models of sport. Forlaget Thomson, Copenhagen

Hoehn T, Kastrianki Z (2012) Broadcasting and sport: value drivers of TV right deals in European football. CompetitionRx, online paper. http://www.competitionrx.com/documents/SportsRights/Value-drivers-of-TV-Rights-deals-in-Sport-May2012.pdf

Kuper S, Szymanski S (2012) Soccernomics. HarperSport, London

Martins RB (2009) Agenda for a social dialogue in the European professional football sector. In: Gardiner S, Parrish R, Siekmann RCR (eds) EU, sport, law and policy: regulation, re-regulation and representation. T.M.C Asser Press, The Hague, pp 345–400

Nixon A (2013) UEFA's financial fair play regulations and compliance with EU law. World Sports Law Report, 22 May 2013. http://e-comlaw.com/sportslawblog/

Newbould GD, Luffman GA (1979) Successful business policies. Gower Press, Aldershot, UK
Parrish R (2011) Social dialogue in European professional football. Eur Law J 17:213–229
Parrish R, Miettinen S (2008) Sporting exception in European Union law. T.M.C Asser Press, The Hague
Siekmann R (2006) Study into the possible participation of EPFL and G14 in a social dialogue in the European professional football sector. Int Sports Law J 3–4:69–85
Siekmann R (2008) Some thoughts about the European Club Association's possible participation in a social dialogue in the European professional football sector. Int Sports Law J 1–2:95–96
Simmons R (2012) Financial foul play? An analysis of UEFA's attempts to restore financial discipline in European football. http://www.voxeu.org/article/own-goal-uefas-financial-fair-play-initiative-misguided
Supporters Direct (2008) The social value of football research project for supporters direct. http://www.supporters-direct.org/wp-content/uploads/2012/08/2.-SD-Social-Value-Working-Paper-Ownership-Social-Value1.pdf
Szymanski S (2012) Insolvency in English professional football: irrational exuberance or negative shocks? International Association of Sports Economists, Working Paper Series, Paper No. 12-02. http://college.holycross.edu/RePEc/spe/Szymanski_Insolvency.pdf
Szymanski S (2013) Financial fair play and the law Part III: guest post by Professor Stephen Weatherill. Soccernomics blog. http://www.soccernomics-agency.com/?p=469
Thompson JL (2001) Understanding corporate strategy. Thomson Learning, London
Thorp S, Shah S (2008) Breakaway leagues: justifying restrictions under EU law. World sport law report, March 2008. http://www.onsidelaw.co.uk/binary_data/147_world_sport_law_report.pdf
Weatherill S (2009) The influence of EU Law on sports governance. In: Gardiner S, Parrish R, Siekmann RCR (eds) EU, sport, law and policy: regulation, re-regulation and representation, T.M.C Asser Press: The Hague, pp 79–100

Chapter 4
EU Internal Market Law and Sport

Contents

4.1 Introduction to the General Principles and Analytical Framework 101
4.2 Case 36/74 *Walrave* and *Koch* [1974] 102
4.3 Case 13/76 *Donà* [1976] 103
4.4 Case C-415/93 *Bosman* [1995] 104
4.4.1 Factual Background 104
4.4.2 The Judgment of the Court 105
4.4.3 Comment 108
4.5 Joined Cases C-51/96 and C-191/97 *Deliège* [2000] 118
4.6 Case C-176/96 *Lehtonen* [2000] 120
4.7 Case C-438/00 *Kolpak* [2003], Case C-265/03 *Simutenkov* [2005], and Case C-152/08 *Kahveci* [2008] 121
4.8 Case C-325/08 *Bernard* [2010] 123
4.8.1 Facts of the Case 123
4.8.2 Analytical Overview of the Judgment 124
4.9 Cases T-385/07, T-55/08 and T-68/08 *FIFA and UEFA v Commission* [2011] 134
4.10 Joined Cases C-403/08 and C-429/08 *Murphy* [2011] 136
4.10.1 Facts of the Case 136
4.10.2 Analytical Overview of the Judgment 137
References 147

This chapter and Chap. 5 share a common purpose: to set out and discern the principles underlying the application of the EU economic law to legal disputes in the sports sector. Relevant economic provisions of the Treaty are centred on the concept of an internal or single market, the accomplishment of which represents a principal economic rationale for the EU. Article 26(2) of the Treaty defines the internal market as comprising 'an area without internal frontiers in which the free movement of goods, persons, services and capital is ensured in accordance with the provisions of the Treaties'. An important tool through which the Union acts in

K. Pijetlovic, *EU Sports Law and Breakaway Leagues in Football*,
ASSER International Sports Law Series, DOI 10.1007/978-94-6265-048-0_4

achieving the goals of the internal market is the development of competition policy that adheres to the principles of an open market economy with free competition, and ensuring freedom of movement of all factors of production. Together with the customs and monetary union and the common commercial policy, these areas form the core of the economic constitutional law of the European Union.[1]

During the integration process and introduction of non-market elements by various Treaty amendments, Europe moved from a purely economic constitution designed for a market-oriented system to the constitutional model which resembles characteristics of a modern welfare state. Hence, the realisation of the internal market project necessarily implicates the questions on interrelationship and balance between economic and social dimensions of the Union's policy.

In very broad terms, the TFEU provides some answers on this interrelationship. The horizontal social clause in Article 9 TFEU states that 'in defining and implementing its policies and activities, the Union shall take into account requirements linked to the promotion of a high level of employment, the guarantee of adequate social protection, the fight against social exclusion, and a high level of education, training and protection of human health'. This article provides a mechanism which obliges the Union (and its Member States) to mainstream social protection and include social objectives across all other policy areas.[2] Article 165 TFEU does not contain such a horizontal clause and it does not have to be taken into account in the administrative and legislative actions of the Union that are not specifically connected to the exercise of contributory competence related to sport. However, all the social policy provisions of the Treaty, including Article 165 TFEU, give the horizontal social clause a specific expression and must be fully respected when it is applied. The reference in Article 165 TFEU to 'the specific nature of sport, its structures based on voluntary activity and its social and educational function' gave an additional boost to the relevance of those factors when examining the legality of restrictions to freedom of movement.[3] But in terms of innovation, this reference 'merely reinforces judicial possibilities which were already open prior to the passage of the Lisbon Treaty'.[4]

In more concrete terms, the social dimension of the internal market was acknowledged much earlier by both the Court and the EU legislation. For instance, even back in the days of the European Economic Community, a worker was recognised as more than just a factor of production and issues regarding workers were therefore placed and treated in their broader social context.[5] Justifications for the

---

1 Baquero 2002, p. 85.

2 Articles 11 and 12 TFEU, the environmental protection must be integrated and consumer protection must be taken into account in the definition and implementation of the Union's policies. Articles 8 and 10 are aimed at eliminating all inequalities between men and women, and all forms of discrimination.

3 See Case C-325/08 *Bernard*, discussed in Sect. 4.8.

4 The Lisbon Treaty and EU Sports Policy Study (2010), p. 10.

5 See Preamble of Regulation 1612/68 on freedom of movement for workers within Community *OJ L 257* 19.10.1968; and the Opinion of AG Trabucchi in Case 7/75 *Mr and Mrs F v Belgian State* [1975] ECR 679.

breach of free movement provisions include an open list of public interest objectives, to the exclusion of economic objectives. Conversely, with regard to competition law provisions, many authors consider that the available exceptions should not be polluted by non-competition arguments that cannot be translated into economic efficiencies/benefits.[6] The tensions created by similar considerations form the underlying layer for many EU sports law analyses. Sports cases provide a good example of the interplay between the Union's economic and socio-cultural and educational policy goals, as well as between certain aspects of the free movement and competition law.

4.1 Introduction to the General Principles and Analytical Framework

The relevant TFEU provisions on free movement are those applicable to: workers in Articles 45–48; establishment in Articles 49–54; services in Articles 56–62 and goods in Articles 28–37. The aim of these Treaty provisions is to eliminate all physical, technical, fiscal and other obstacles to trade between Member States in order to merge their markets into a single market reproducing as close as possible the conditions of a domestic market.[7] Moreover, the provisions conferring substantive rights onto their respective subjects of protection are directly effective and as such can be relied on before the national courts.[8] In the case of conflict between any directly effective provision of EU law and any Member State national law, the conflicting national law will be 'disapplied' to the case at hand in accordance with the principle of supremacy.[9]

Market access, and non-discrimination on the basis of nationality (equal treatment) are at the core of the free movement provisions, and any departure from these principles has to be justified. Offending Member States may rely on an exhaustive list of derogations in the Treaty, or a non-exhaustive judicially-recognised set of derogations, to objectively justify their restrictive or discriminatory measures. The latter set of derogations is generally reserved only for indirectly discriminatory measures (the measures which are non-discriminatory in law but are discriminatory in fact) and non-discriminatory measures (measures which are genuinely non-discriminative but impede market access). Finally, where it is accepted that the measure pursues a legitimate aim in the public interest and therefore justifies the restriction on the economic freedoms, a Member State will have to show that

---

[6] See, for example, Semmelmann 2008, p. 15.

[7] See Case 270/80 *Polydor Limited and RSO Records Inc. v. Harlequen Records Shops Limited and Simons Records Limited*, [1982] ECR 329, para 18; and Case 15/81 *Gaston Schul Douane Expediteur BV v. Inspecteur der Invoerrechten en Accijnzen, Roosendaal* [1982] ECR 1409.

[8] See Barnard 2010, pp. 233–235.

[9] See Case 106/77 *Amministrazione delle Finanze dello Stato v. Simmenthal SpA* [1978] ECR 629; and Cases C-10-22/97 *Ministero delle Finanze v. IN.CO. GE'90 Srl* [1998] ECR I-6307.

the measure is proportionate (i.e. suitable and necessary for the achievement of the objective).

The debate surrounding the nature of the relationship between EU law and sport began in 1974 with the *Walrave* judgment. Ever since, the Court has followed the standard 'restriction-justification-proportionality' analytical framework in the application of internal market rules in legal disputes involving the sports sector. The only structural irregularity in the Court's analysis is the opening of the avenue of justification on the basis of non-Treaty derogations for directly discriminatory measures. This irregularity became the rule rather than the exception in sport-related cases. It is submitted that this exception should have general application in internal market law. An open list of justifications should be available to all measures whether directly discriminatory, indirectly discriminatory or merely restrictive. The proportionality test is a sufficient means of control and directly discriminatory rules will seldom satisfy its requirements. And should they satisfy it, what is the harm in having the legitimate aim protected in the least restrictive way?

Despite the seemingly standard approach, accompanied by one structural irregularity, matters are in fact more complicated by the notion of 'sporting exception', to which we will revert in Chap. 6 after having set out the application of the internal market and competition law in sports cases.

4.2 Case 36/74 *Walrave* and *Koch* [1974]

Two Dutch professional pacemakers, Walrave and Koch, competed in motor-paced bicycle races. In this sport, each participant on a pedal-powered bicycle (the so-called 'stayer') follows his own motor-powered pacemaker ('pacer'). Due to the vacuum that the pacers create, the stayers can achieve speeds of up to 100 km/h. A stayer and a pacer form a team. Walrave and Koch were among the best pacers in the world. When the Dutch representatives did not perform well in international competitions, Walrave and Koch decided to offer their services to stayers of other nationalities, in particular Belgians and Germans. But the rules of the Union Cycliste International changed and provided that as of the year 1973, the pacer and stayer in international competitions had to be of the same nationality. Walrave and Koch saw this rule as discriminatory on the basis of nationality and as a severe restriction on their professional opportunities. Therefore, they claimed a breach of the general non-discrimination provision under Article 18 TFEU, of free movement of employed persons under Article 45 TFEU, and of freedom to provide services under Article 56 TFEU.

The Court had never before dealt with a sports case and it first had to be considered whether the Treaty extended to the area of sport. In para 4 of the judgment the Court famously held that 'the practice of sport is subject to Community law only in so far as it constitutes economic activity [...]'.[10] As to the prohibition on nationality

[10] Case 36/74 *Walrave and Koch v. Union Cycliste Internationale and others* [1974] ECR 1405.

discrimination in Articles 18, 45 and 56 the Court said in para 8 that it 'does not affect the composition of sport teams, in particular national teams, the formation of which is a question of purely sporting interest and as such has nothing to do with economic activity', adding in para 9 that 'this restriction on the scope of the provisions in question must however remain limited to its proper objective'. This holding became known as the sporting exception in EU law. Accordingly, the Treaty would also not apply to economic sporting activities so long as the motive for the rules was non-economic, in other words, 'purely sporting'.

One of the important questions for general EU law that was raised in the *Walrave* case related to the horizontal direct effect of the Treaty Articles 18, 45 and 56. The respondent in the case, Union Cycliste International, was not a governmental body governed by public law but a private organisation. The Court held that the prohibition on discrimination in those articles 'does not only apply to the action of public authorities but extends likewise to rules of any other nature aimed at regulating in a collective manner gainful employment and the provision of services'.[11] A different approach by the Court would risk creating inequality in the application of the law to legal relationships in the private and public sectors and would jeopardise the accomplishment of the internal market. Later in the non-sporting cases of *Defrenne*[12] and *Angonese*[13] it was clarified that the respondent body need not regulate gainful employment in a collective manner to be a subject of the discrimination prohibition, and that the rule on horizontal direct effect in *Walrave* extends to contracts between individuals.[14]

4.3 Case 13/76 *Donà* [1976]

Under the rules of the Italian Football Federation (FIGC), players are required to have a federation membership card. Only the FIGC could issue such cards and, in principle, only players of Italian nationality residing in Italy could be issued a card. As an exception from this rule, foreign nationals who have never been members of a foreign federation, who were residents in Italy and who asked to be enrolled as youths, amateurs or for recreational purposes could also obtain the membership card. Thus, the precondition to take part in matches as professional or semi-professional players (i.e. affiliation to the federation) was in practice limited almost exclusively to Italian nationals. A challenge to these rules was brought by Mr. Donà, an agent in Italy who was recruiting players from abroad at the request of the president of an Italian football club. In essence, the Court was asked to decide on whether the nationality requirement for playing professional football

[11] Ibid. para 17.

[12] Case 43/75 *Gabrielle Defrenne v Société anonyme belge de navigation aérienne Sabena* [1976] ECR 455.

[13] Case C-281/98 *Roman Angonese v Cassa di Risparmio di Bolzano SpA* [2000] ECR I-4139.

[14] However, see Barnard 2010, p. 234, for the argument that the direct effect in this and other sports cases is an extended form of vertical direct effect.

matches in Italy was compatible with Articles 18, 45 and 56 of the Treaty (originally in the case Articles 7, 48 and 59).

In *Donà*,[15] the Court reformulated and confirmed the sporting exception from *Walrave*. In paras 14 and 15 it held that those provisions of the Treaty do not prevent

> 14. [...] the adoption of rules or of a practice excluding foreign players from participation in certain matches for the reasons which are not of an economic nature, which relate to the particular nature and context of such matches and are thus of sporting interest only, such as, for example, the matches between national teams from different countries.
> 15. This restriction on the scope of the provisions in question must however remain limited to its proper objective.

The rule in *Donà* modified and restricted the rule in *Walrave* to the extent that the exception for composition of national teams was reformulated to the exclusion of the players from participation in certain matches for the reasons of 'sporting interest only'.

Almost two decades after *Donà*, Advocate General Lenz said in the *Bosman* case that

> [...] the wording of the *Donà* judgment represents a limitation of the proposition adopted in *Walrave*. That is evident merely from the fact that the *Donà* case concerned the composition of teams. If the question of the composition of teams was indeed 'of purely sporting interest', as the Court appeared to assume in *Walrave*, the Court could have contented itself in *Donà* with a simple reference to that judgment. It rightly did not do so, since it was presumably not unaware that the question of the composition of teams may very well be dominated by non-sporting motives.[...] Neither the basis of the 'exception' nor its extent can be deduced with certainty from the judgments.[16]

In an answer to the referring national court, in para 19, the Court specifically mentioned professional and semi-professional players as subjects of protection. The reason for this was to distinguish the rules covering their activity from the rules applicable to amateur, non-economic activities which presumably do not fall under the protection afforded by the Treaty freedom of movement provisions.

4.4 Case C-415/93 *Bosman* [1995]

4.4.1 Factual Background

In *Bosman*,[17] the Court was asked to consider a directly discriminatory '3+2' rule and non-discriminatory international transfer rules which restricted the professional activities of football players. As regards the latter, the international and national football associations had developed a detailed set of rules governing the transfer of players from one club to another. At the material time, football players' contracts ran until 30 June and were normally entered into for the period of one to a maximum of

---

15 Case 13/76 *Gaetano Donà v. Mario Mantero* [1976] ECR 1333.

16 Paragraphs 138–139 of his Opinion in Case C-415/93 *Bosman*.

17 Case C-415/93 *Union Royale Belge Sociétés de Football Association and others v. Bosman and others* [1995] ECR I-4921.

5 years. If they wished to retain the player, clubs had to offer a new contract before the expiry of the contract, by 26 April of that year at the latest. In the event the player was either not offered another contract or he did not accept the terms, they were placed on a 'compulsory' transfer list between 1 and 31 May, subject to payment of a compensation fee for 'training' calculated by multiplying the player's gross annual income by a factor varying from 2 to 14 depending on the player's age. If no transfer took place in this period, a period of 'free' transfer commenced on 1 June in which the transfer fees were negotiated and had to be agreed upon by the acquiring club and the vendor. In any event, a club interested in hiring a player had to immediately notify the old club, which in turn was to notify the national association, which issued an international clearance certificate necessary for the international transfer to take place. However, should the player's transfer fail in the 'free' transfer period as well, his old club was obliged to offer him a contract for one season on the same terms as prior to April 26, and if the player refused he faced a suspension.

Jean Marc Bosman was a football player in the Belgian club, SA Royal Club Liègeois (RC Liège). At the expiry of his contract in 1990 he refused an offer to extend the contract at less favourable terms. After no club showed interest in him on a compulsory transfer and the free transfer period started, he found a French club, US Dunkerque, that wanted to hire him and agreed with RC Liège on the transfer fee. However, concerned with the financial standing of the acquiring club, RC Liège failed to apply for the necessary international clearance certificate from the Belgian football association and the contracts between Bosman and US Dunkerque and between RC Liège and US Dunkerque were not concluded. In accordance with the rules of the Belgian football association, Bosman was then suspended by RC Liège for the new season, which effectively prevented him from working anywhere. Via a court order, Bosman secured the possibility to enter into a contract with any club without the payment of transfer fee. However, he found it difficult to find steady employment and suspected that he was being boycotted by most European clubs. These transfer rules were challenged in the Belgian national court.

The other rule challenged was the so-called '3+2' rule according to which each national association was permitted to limit to three the number of foreign players whom a club may field in any first division match in their national championships and matches organised by *Union des Associations Européennes de Football* (UEFA), plus two players who have played in the country of the relevant national association for an uninterrupted period of 5 years, including 3 years as a junior ('assimilated players'). The effect of '3+2' rule was to impose quotas on clubs as regards nationality and residence of their players.

4.4.2 The Judgment of the Court

4.4.2.1 Transfer Rules

Interpreting Article 45 TFEU with regard to its application to transfer rules, the Court cited *Donà* and emphasised 'the difficulty of severing the economic aspects from the sporting aspects of football', thus in a clear language extending the 'sporting exception' originating in *Walrave* to further exclude from the scope of the Treaty non-discriminatory sporting practices and rules which, although economic in nature, can be justified on non-economic grounds related to the particular nature and context of certain matches, and which are limited to their proper objectives.[18] This was, in fact, implied in paras 14 and 15 of *Donà*, however, in the context of nationality restrictions and directly discriminatory rules. Having established that Article 45 applied to transfer rules at issue because those rules regulated the terms on which professional sportsmen can engage in gainful employment, and regardless of the fact that those rules regulated business relationships between clubs, and not between a club and a player, the Court found the existence of an obstacle to freedom of movement for workers.

It then brought the case under the standard objective justification analytical framework established in *Kraus* and *Gebhard*[19] under which those rules that (1) pursued a legitimate aim compatible with the Treaty and were justified by pressing reasons of public interest, and that (2) were compatible with the principle of proportionality will not breach the provisions on freedom of movement for persons. Against this setting, 'in view of the considerable social importance of sporting activities and in particular football in the [Union]', the Court accepted as legitimate the objectives of 'maintaining a balance between clubs by preserving a certain degree of equality and uncertainty as to results', and of 'encouraging the recruitment and training of young players' in para 106 of the judgment. Finally, transfer rules were found unsuitable for the attainment of the said objectives and failed the proportionality test:

> 107. [...] the application of the transfer rules is not an adequate means of maintaining financial and competitive balance in the world of football. Those rules neither preclude the richest clubs from securing the services of the best players nor prevent the availability of financial resources from being a decisive factor in competitive sport, thus considerably altering the balance between clubs.
> 108. As regards the second aim, it must be accepted that the prospect of receiving transfer, development or training fees is indeed likely to encourage football clubs to seek new talent and train young players.
> 109. However, because it is impossible to predict the sporting future of young players with any certainty and because only a limited number of such players go on to play professionally, those fees are by nature contingent and uncertain and are in any event unrelated to the actual cost borne by clubs of training both future professional players and those who will never play professionally. The prospect of receiving such fees cannot, therefore, be either a decisive factor in encouraging recruitment and training of young players or an adequate means of financing such activities, particularly in the case of smaller clubs.

This quote gained increased importance in the comparative perspective in the *Bernard* case discussed below.

After the Court's holding on the transfer system, the international transfer rules had to be remodelled. The new rules provided that the players whose contract with

[18] Ibid. para 76.

[19] Case C-19/92 *Kraus* [1993] ECR I-1663 para 32; and Case C-55/94 *Gebhard* [1995] ECR I-4165 para 37.

their club had expired were 'free agents' and could be transferred without any fees. The transfer fees were still applicable for in-contract players. The decision does not concern the following: internal transfer rules between the clubs in the same national association regarding their national players as it concerns a wholly internal situation (although national transfers must also abide by the same rules as a matter of football regulations); transfer of non-EU nationals from one EU Member State from another; transfers from the EU to third countries[20] and the composition of national teams. The legal principles devised in the judgment are applicable to all sports, not only to football.

4.4.2.2 Nationality Clauses

Interpreting Article 45 of the Treaty with regard to nationality clauses, the Court took an 'obstacle approach' and referred to Article 4 of Regulation 1612/68[21] to find that quotas such as those described are as much a restriction in the sporting community as they would be in any other sector. Next, it assessed the application of non-Treaty objective justifications with regard to the directly discriminatory '3+2' rule, after it found that the rule cannot benefit from the exception established in *Walrave* and *Donà* because it affected not just the participation in certain matches but applied to all official matches and thus to 'the essence of the activity of professional players'. It brushed aside attempts to justify the '3+2' rule under the ordinary justification framework. First, it did not accept the argument that quota clauses served to maintain the traditional link between each club and their country, a factor submitted as enabling the public to identify with their favourite teams and to ensure that clubs effectively represented their countries when taking part in international competitions. The Court considered that a club's link with a Member State is no different than its link with locality, town or region in it that there is no limit on fielding the players on the basis of those links when playing national championships. Clubs participating in international competitions are not chosen on the basis of nationality of their players but on the basis of results achieved in their national leagues. Second, the Court dismissed the argument that the quotas were necessary to create a sufficient pool of top national players to be fielded in national representative team, by referring to the rule on compulsory release of the players for representative matches which does not require players to be registered with a club of the country they represent. Third, quotas were not

[20] However, Fédération Internationale de Football Association (FIFA) later adapted its worldwide international transfer rules to *Bosman* ruling as well.

[21] Regulation (EEC) No. 1612/68 of the Council of 15 October 1968 on freedom of movement for workers within the Community (OJ, English special edition, 1968 (II), p. 475). Article 4(1) of this regulation reads: Provisions laid down by law, regulation or administrative action of the Member States which restrict by number or percentage the employment of foreign nationals in any undertaking, branch of activity or region, or at a national level, are not to apply to nationals of the other Member States'.

suitable to maintain competitive balance between clubs, because the richest clubs will be able to secure the services of the top national players just as they would be able to engage the best foreign players. Finally, the fact that the quota rule was drawn up in collaboration with the Commission did not shield it from judicial scrutiny or provide any guarantees as to its compatibility with the Treaty as the Commission does not have the power to authorise rules and practices that are contrary to the Treaty.[22]

4.4.2.3 Competition Law

Finally, it is interesting to note that the questions forwarded to the Court for preliminary ruling also concerned the interpretation of competition law provisions under Articles 101 and 102. Having found both types of rule contrary to Article 45, the Court considered it unnecessary to rule on the interpretation of competition articles of the Treaty.[23]

4.4.3 Comment

Much has been said and written about every aspect of *Bosman* by academic lawyers and economists, including its effects on the football industry and its application to various issues in sport today.[24] Therefore, rather than going into details of everything that has already been said, the comment here is intended to contribute a new perspective on certain aspects of the judgment to the extent possible in regard to such a 'congested' research topic. *Bosman* has been credited as a case that instigated the birth of EU sports law[25] and increased player mobility.[26] It is commonly blamed for deepening the competitive imbalance between the rich and other clubs in European football, and is criticised for refocusing the clubs' business strategies on buying players from the international market for football players rather than working to develop homegrown talent and investing in youth training programmes, thus inflating the value of the players on the international transfer market and contributing to the financial instability of the clubs.

---

22 After this judgment, Arsenal and Chelsea were the first clubs to field an all-foreign start-up line in their official matches. On a different note, even though the Court in *Bosman* was explicit about prohibition of nationality quotas, in basketball they are maintained until today and nobody has challenged them in a private action.

23 But see the Opinion of AG Lenz in Case C-415/93 *Bosman* that did address the competition law issues.

24 See, for example, Blanpain 2003; Miettinen and Parrish 2008; Blanpain and Inston 1996; and Késenne 2009.

25 See Parrish 2003, p. 17.

26 Gardiner and Welch 2000, pp. 107–126.

The judgment in *Bosman* loosened the grip of monopsony held by the clubs and the federations on the player labour market. In 2005, UEFA identified the following problems that, in its opinion, threaten to damage the long-term interest of European football: lack of investment in player training, reduction in competitive balance, hoarding of players, weakening of national teams and erosion of local identity.[27] Although UEFA never directly referred to these problems as being the results of the Court's judgment in *Bosman*, this was clearly implied for it would be impossible for some of these problems to arise without the prior liberalisation of the player market.

4.4.3.1 The Current Transfer System in Football

The overhaul of the transfer system had far less effect on the player labour market in comparison to abolition of quotas. The clubs easily adapted to modified transfer rules as the system of rolling contracts became a part of their new strategy. Such a system ensured that clubs maintained a transfer value of employed players who were effectively prevented from acquiring a free agent status. This contractual strategy is aided by Articles 13–18 of the *Fédération Internationale de Football Association* (FIFA) Regulations on the Status and Transfer of Players outlining the principles for maintenance of contractual stability between players and clubs (which apply particularly strictly during the course of a season). Accordingly, a player wishing to terminate his employment relationship with his club unilaterally and without just cause may be subject to a buy-out clause set out in his contract requiring him to compensate damages suffered by the club. The amount of compensation is usually set so high, making it extremely unattractive, if not impossible, for a player to leave. In addition, under Article 17(4) of the said FIFA Regulations, sporting sanctions of up to 6 months of restriction on playing in official matches may be imposed on a player, while a ban on registration of new players for two entire and consecutive seasons is imposed upon the club signing him up. Regardless of these regulations and contractual restrictions, that were always present in football in one or another form, professional players have been one of the principal beneficiaries of *Bosman* as their wages have significantly increased due to the liberalisation of the labour market by the abolition of the quota system.

In general, transfer of a player may be made against the following payments, as applicable: fixed transfer fee between the clubs, fee compensation for breach of contract due to the former club, conditional transfer fees, training compensation and solidarity contribution.[28] Players can also be temporarily transferred (on loan) to another club and such transfer is a subject to the same rules that apply to 'ordinary' transfers.[29] In January, the study on transfer of players commissioned by the European Commission revealed that in the period between 1995

[27] UEFA—Investing in Local Training of Players: Key Messages. Available at http://www.uefa.com/multimediafiles/download/uefa/uefamedia/273604_download.pdf.

[28] FIFA Regulations on the Status and Transfer of Players (2012), Annexe 3, Article 4(2).

[29] Ibid. Article 10(1) of the Regulations.

(when the *Bosman* judgment was published) and 2011 the clubs' transfer expenditure in the EU (including both international and domestic transfers) increased by 744 % (from ca. EUR 400 million to ca. EUR 3 billion) while the number of transfers increased by 320 % (from 5,735 to 18,307).[30] These increases may be largely ascribed to two factors: one is the abolition of quotas by the decision in *Bosman*, and another is the technological and structural changes that took place in the media sector. The part of the judgment that relates to transfers did not have such profound impact on the number of transfers or their value. It simply enables those players that find themselves unemployed to be free from any additional restrictions on their prospects to become employed again. An aspect of the study on transfers that is relevant for the overall theme of this volume relates to the competitive imbalance between clubs in European football and the inability of the existing solidarity payments to positively affect such imbalance. The line of logic that emerges from the study is as follows:

1. The study reports that 60 % of the value of transfer market is generated by the clubs in the 'big five' leagues that include the German Bundesliga, the English Premier League, the Italian Serie A, the Spanish La Liga and the French Ligue 1[31] (the value of transfer of superstar players reached a record EUR 94 million in Cristiano Ronaldo's transfer from Manchester United to Real Madrid[32]); the evolution that has taken place in the transfer market affects the openness of the competitions and questions the system of promotion and relegation and the 'imperative of uncertainty' in sport results[33]; and the percentage of titles ranging from 75 % in France to 100 % in Germany were won by the three most successful teams in the domestic league.[34] Therefore, the study says, there is a 'strong link' between transfer expenditures and competitive strength/sporting results at both national and European level—and current transfer rules do not effectively address the competitive imbalance.[35]
2. Training compensations and solidarity mechanisms that are directly linked to transfers account for only 1.84 % of the fixed transfer fees in Europe. This is insufficient to affect competitive balance in a positive way. At the same time, solidarity schemes operated by UEFA tend to support the most successful and wealthiest clubs in their domestic leagues. Solidarity payments to clubs that do not participate in the UEFA Champions League represent less than 6 % of the total received by 32 clubs that do participate in that competition. Contrary to its goal of enhancing competitive balance, this system is 'consolidating existing supremacies'.[36]

[30] Study on the Economic and Legal Aspects of Transfers of Players, p. 159. Available at http://ec.europa.eu/sport/library/documents/f-studies/cons-study-transfers-final-rpt.pdf.

[31] Ibid. p. 242.

[32] Ibid. p. 196.

[33] Ibid. p. 6.

[34] Ibid. p. 7.

[35] Ibid. p. 6.

[36] Ibid. p. 7.

3. The UEFA Champions League increasingly demonstrates the characteristics of a closed league in which the same clubs compete for the title and they are the main beneficiaries of the current transfer system which reinforces their dominance at domestic and European level. Therefore, Europe is slowly embracing the system of de facto closed leagues at the elite level.[37]

This conclusion is not surprising, but it is significant that an independent study spelled it out and supported it with robust data. It is, however, submitted that the conclusions drawn from the facts that exist on the transfer market are symptomatic conclusions. The real causes of competitive imbalance are to be found elsewhere. First and foremost, they may be traced back to the structure of the bodies that participate in the governance of European football and the European social dialogue (the European Club Association in particular), as well as in the possibility of formation of a breakaway structure by big clubs that have used that prospect as a threat in the game of power struggles with UEFA. Transfer rules are far from being the only set of rules that produce data indicating the consolidating supremacy of the elite clubs. As discussed in Chap. 3, creating the pool to compensate clubs for player release for international representative matches of their national teams benefited mostly rich clubs (18 clubs of G14 alone supplied 22 % of the participating players in the World Cup 2006) and added to their budget.[38]

4.4.3.2 Legality of the Current UEFA Home-Grown Players Rule

In order to counter some of the negative effects of quota abolition by the Court's judgment in *Bosman*, UEFA proposed the introduction of the 'home grown players rule'.[39] The rule requires clubs participating in the competitions organised by UEFA (the Champions League, UEFA Europa League, and UEFA Super Cup) to have a minimum number of home-grown players, i.e. players who, regardless of their nationality, have been trained by their club or by another club in the same national association for at least 3 years between the ages of 15 and 21. This number was set at 4 players in a maximum squad of 25 in the first season of application (2006–2007), and it increased to 6 in 2007–2008. It finally rose to 8 out of the maximum squad of 25 players in the 2008–2009 season.[40]

While the attempts of FIFA to re-introduce the directly discriminatory '6+5' rule[41] did not meet much sympathy in European institutions and was eventually

---

[37] pp. 245–247.

[38] For details see Sect. 3.3.6.1.

[39] At the Ordinary Congress in Estonia in April 2005.

[40] The home-grown players rule can be found in Article 18 of the Regulations of the UEFA Champions League 2010/2011, Article 18 of the Regulations of the UEFA Europa League 2010/2011, and Article 15 of the Regulations of the UEFA Super Cup 2010.

[41] According to the 6+5 rule, at the start of each match football clubs must field in at least six players eligible to play for the national team of the country of the club.

dropped in 2010,[42] some uncertainty still surrounds the legality of the home-grown players rule. Generally, the rule found the support in the Commission[43] and the European Parliament.[44] The latter reaffirmed 'its commitment to the home-grown player rule' considering it as a possible model for other professional leagues in Europe and supporting 'efforts of sports governing bodies that stimulate the training of local young players *within the limits of EU law* thus strengthening the competitive balance within competitions and the healthy development of the European sports model'.[45] The reason for strong support might have been that it was the part of the judgment in *Bosman* that abolished the player quota (rather than the one that abolished the player transfer system and introduced free agency) that has contributed to competitive imbalance and refocused clubs' strategy away from the home talent.[46] But as the Court's decision in *Bosman* coincided with the boom in the commercialisation of the sports industry, it is difficult to apportion the negative effects on competitive balance in football between player market liberalisation and a changing commercial environment. Influences were presumably shared and the problems were brought about by a blend of both. In any case, taking a proportionate action to reverse some of the identified evils in order to attain legitimate objectives is likely to be permitted under EU law. The Commission considered that these requirements were met by the home-grown players rule.[47]

To continue with a novel perspective on the issue of quotas, it should not be overlooked that, although commonly referred to as directly discriminatory, there were in fact two distinct parts of the '3+2' rule in *Bosman*: one that was indeed directly discriminatory as it limited the number of foreign players in clubs, and the other one that limited the number of 'assimilated players' and as such was only indirectly discriminatory. Nevertheless, the Court did not distinguish between 3 and 2 in '3+2' rule at any stage of analysis and instead it assessed the rule in its entirety. The exact wording of the rule is contained in the Regulations of the European Champion Club's Cup for the 1992–1993 season, Title VIII on 'Eligibility of Players', Article 12 of which reads:

> [...] 3. The sixteen (or fewer) players chosen by a club to take part in any match in the competitions as indicated on the referee's report form under article 10 para 3, of these Regulations, shall not include more than three players who are not eligible to play for the national team of the national association to which that club belongs.

---

[42] At the 60th FIFA Congress meeting in Johannesburg in June Barnard 2010 it was decided to withdraw the 6+5 proposal.

[43] See Commission Press Release IP/08/807 'UEFA Rule on 'Home-Grown Players': Compatibility with the Principle of Free Movement of Persons' 28 May 2008.

[44] See, for instance, European Parliament Resolution on the White Paper on Sport, 2007/2261(INI) and European Parliament Resolution of 2 February 2011 on the European Dimension in Sport, 2011/2087(INI).

[45] Ibid. 2011/2087(INI), para 72.

[46] Ibid. p. 638.

[47] Commission Press Release IP/08/807 'UEFA Rule on 'Home-Grown Players': Compatibility with the Principle of Free Movement of Persons' 28 May 2008.

> 4. In addition, two names of assimilated (*) players may also appear on the referee's official report form if they have played for an uninterrupted period of five years in the country of the National Association concerned, three years of which must have been spent in playing youth football. Players who fulfil these conditions on the 1st July 1992 will be considered retrospectively assimilated.
> [...]
> (*) In clause 2 of the agreement between EC Commission and UEFA concerning the reduction in the number of "non-selectable" players, the term "matches in the youth sector" is understood to mean all competitive activity by players younger than 19 years of age on the deadline of 1st August. The matches must be played under the auspices of the National Association of affiliated organisations.

Hence, in isolation from the first part, the second part of the '3+2' rule reads as follows:

> The sixteen (or fewer) players chosen by a club to take part in any match in the competitions as indicated on the referee's report form under article 10 para 3, of these Regulations, shall not include more than two names of assimilated (*) players.

In the eyes of EU law, the second part of the '3+2' rule largely resembles the home-grown players rule. It provides for the maximum of two assimilated players of any nationality to be included in the list of 16 players who, when read in isolation from the first part of the '3+2' rule, may be of any nationality. There are some quantitative differences between the indirect discrimination under the home-grown rule and the isolated 'assimilated players rule' contained in Article 12(4) of the Regulations of the European Champion Clubs' Cup for the 1992–1993 season. Whereas the latter limits the number of 'assimilated players' to *maximum* of two in the squad of sixteen, the former has eight places *reserved* for home-grown players in the squad of twenty-five. The home-grown rule also differs in terms of relevant definitions. The assimilated player is someone who has 'played for an uninterrupted period of 5 years in the country of the National Association concerned, 3 years of which must have been spent in playing youth football' defined to include 'all competitive activity by players younger than 19 years of age'. The home-grown player is a 'locally-trained player' which includes 'club-trained' and 'association-trained' players. 'Club-trained' is any player who, between the ages of 15 and 21 has been registered with his current club for a period, continuous or not, of three entire seasons. The only differing criteria to qualify as 'association-trained' is that a player has been registered with a club or clubs affiliated to the same national association as his current club. There is a limit of four 'association-trained players' per eight places reserved for 'locally-trained players'. The main distinction, however, is that under the home-grown rule, the match list of 18 players to be submitted before each match *must have a minimum* of one locally-trained player who does not have to be fielded during the official matches, whereas the rest of the squad may be all-foreign. Under the assimilated player rule, a *maximum* of two assimilated players *may be* included on the match list of 16, or the club can choose to have all-foreign list. The clubs that do not have eight home-grown players in their current squad are still able to comply with the UEFA rule by reducing the size of their squad accordingly. In reality a club could contain no home-grown players, but it would only be able to register 17 players in the squad.[48] This would make the home-grown rule equal to the assimilated players rule.

In accordance with the principles of subsidiarity and proportionality set out in Article 5 of the Treaty on the European Union (TEU), the Court does not have the competence to nullify Member States' laws, private agreements between parties, or rules of sporting organisations that are severable and can function independently from the part of the law, agreement, or rule that was held in breach of any provision of EU law, including the Treaty. In the context of competition, the Court held that

> [t]he automatic nullity [...] only applies to those parts of the agreement affected by the prohibition, or to the agreement as a whole if it appears that those parts are not severable from the agreement itself. Consequently any other contractual provisions which are not affected by the prohibition, and which therefore do not involve the application of the Treaty, fall outside [Union] law.[49]

Principles of subsidiarity and proportionality dictate that the equivalent rule should apply in the free movement area. In fact, Article 7(4) of Regulation 1612/68 on the free movement of workers makes a reference to nullifying 'clauses in collective or individual agreements', implying their severability from the rest of the agreement.[50] By the same token, paragraphs in articles should be severable from the articles wherever possible, and only the paragraph(s) of an article of sporting rules and regulations that are held in breach of EU law should be amended, replaced or deleted.

The '3+2' rule is severable, as it is possible for Article 12(4) of the Regulations of the European Champion Clubs' Cup to exist and operate without the third paragraph of that article, in other words, the assimilated player rule is logically and operationally distinct from the nationality clause. Thus, treating the '3+2' rule in its entirety and declaring it in breach of Article 45 TFEU in its entirety, could be read as the Court's signal that indirect discrimination imposing player quotas on all club's matches will be treated in the same manner as nationality clauses imposing player quotas on all club's matches. Looking at UEFA's current home-grown rule through this prism, it appears *prima facie* that the ruling in *Bosman* unequivocally dismissed any possible justifications for such an indirectly discriminatory

[48] Study on the Assessment of the UEFA's 'Home Grown Players Rule', negotiated procedure EAC 07/2012, 30 April 2013, p. 58.

[49] Case 56/65 *Société La Technique Minière v. Maschinenbau Ulm GmbH* [1966] ECR 235. Similarly, in *CEPSA*, the Court held that 'the automatic nullity provided for in Article [101(2)] EC affects a contract in its entirety only if the clauses which are incompatible with Article [101(1)] are not severable from the contract itself. Otherwise, the consequences of the nullity, in respect of all the other parts of the contract, are not a matter for [Union] law'. See Case 279/06 *CEPSA Estaciones de Servicio SA v. LV Tobar e Hijos SL*, judgement of 11 September, 2008, para 80.

[50] The full text of this provision is: 'Any clause of a collective or individual agreement or of any other collective regulation concerning eligibility for employment, employment, remuneration and other conditions of work or dismissal shall be null and void in so far as it lays down or authorises discriminatory conditions in respect of workers who are nationals of the other Member States'.

quota-setting rule: the '3+2' rule as a whole was not suitable to maintain competitive balance, maintain the traditional link between each club and its country or create a sufficient pool of national players to provide the national team with top players. Additionally, the fact that the rule was drawn up in collaboration with the Commission did not shield the rule from the law nor did it provide any guarantees in that regard. Aware of the principles of subsidiarity and proportionality, and the severability of Article 12(4) in the Regulations of the European Champion Clubs' Cup for 1992–1993 season, the Court would have clearly taken out of its reasoning the indirectly discriminatory 'assimilated players' rule, had it intended to produce no effects upon it. The home-grown rule being analogous to the 'assimilated players rule' in its legal denomination as indirectly discriminatory (and being more restrictive in quantitative terms as explained below) would clearly breach Article 45 TFEU if one is to formalistically apply this line of reasoning. However, things are more complicated than this and there are two important qualifications to this conclusion.

First, the reference to nationality alone in the Court's answer in para 137 of the judgment is somewhat puzzling:

> ...Article [45] of the Treaty precludes the application of rules laid down by sporting associations under which, in matches in competitions which they organize, football clubs may field only a limited number of professional players who are nationals of other Member States.

One explanation for this reference might be, as already mentioned, that in the eyes of the Court there is no difference between the direct and indirect nationality discrimination when it comes to player quotas being imposed on all of the club's matches, and this attitude is merely reflected in the answer to the national court. However, in the next paragraph the point will be made that the Court has only treated *this particular* indirectly discriminatory rule as if it were directly discriminatory, and that such treatment will not always apply in relation to rules which can be formally classified as indirectly discriminatory quota-setting rules. Another possible explanation, a more radical one and going against all *Bosman* interpretations for the past 18 years, would be that the Court never intended for its decision to affect 'the assimilated players' rule. Taking into consideration that in applying Article 101 TFEU in the area of competition law, the Court held that the questions of severability of any clause in the agreement must be decided by national, not Union law,[51] perhaps the wording of the answer in para 137 was an indication to the referring national court that it is only the nationality rule that is prohibited in the '3+2' rule? This line of argument would render the current UEFA home-grown rule valid under the EU law, and all the past and ongoing discussions on the subject of its legality would become meaningless. But this is probably not the case.

Second, the inclusion of the sports article in the Treaty might prove significant enough of a factor to warrant a different approach to the home-grown, in contrast to 'assimilated', player rule, especially when it is considered in conjunction with

---

[51] See, for example, Case 319/82 *Société de Vente de Ciments et Bétons de l'Est v. Kerpen & Kerpen GmbH & Co KG* [1983] ECR 4173, para 11.

the fact that the Court's recognition of the sporting arguments in the post-Lisbon judgment of *Bernard* has somewhat changed due to the specificity of sport and its socio-educational function, the relevance of which has been 'corroborated by their being mentioned in the second subparagraph of Article 165(1) TFEU'.[52] Namely, in *Bernard* the Court reversed the point made in para 109 of *Bosman* regarding the unsuitability of transfer and training fees for the attainment of the objective of encouraging recruitment and training of young players. This will be explained in detail below when addressing the *Bernard* ruling, where I will argue that this reversal is attributable to the additional weight that Article 165(1) TFEU gave to the sporting arguments within the analytical framework of the Treaty's economic provisions. Analogical reasoning implies that this should be good news for UEFA's home-grown rule.

4.4.3.3 Study on the Home-Grown Players Rule

As a part of the strategy of moving towards evidence-based sports policies set out in the White Paper on Sport, para 3.1, the European Commission has recently funded a study[53] to assess the impact of the home-grown players rule on competitive balance and the training and development of young players, the two objective justifications put forth by UEFA in defence of the restrictive effects of that rule on the free movement of employed persons (Article 45 TFEU). If the home-grown players rule could be shown to contribute to the achievement of these objectives, and that other less-restrictive measures are not available, this would lead to the conclusion that it is compatible with Article 45 TFEU. The statistics produced by the study indicated that

> [t]he number of home grown players actively taking part in both Champions League and Europa League matches has increased dramatically since 2007 from 30 % to over 50 % in 2012. While it was a concern that home grown players were simply 'making up the numbers' and not actually participating in starting XIs this has been found not to be the case. The data suggests that the Rule is not restricting the free movement of players across borders; in fact there has been an increase in the number of foreign players that qualify as home grown.[54]

As it was not possible from that data alone to infer causation in relation to the impact of the home-grown players rule, a regression analysis was performed (separately for the Champions League and the Europa League). From such analysis it emerged that, by the time the home-grown players rule had been fully implemented, there was a reduction in the performance of the teams in the Champions League group stages possibly due to the fact that the teams' purchases of players from the international market were also somewhat reduced. Similar evidence was

[52] Case C-325/08 *Bernard*, para 40.

[53] Study on the Assessment of the UEFA's 'Home Grown Players Rule', negotiated procedure EAC 07/2012, 30 April 2013.

[54] Ibid. p. 58.

found, to a more modest extent, in the Europa League group stages. There was no perceptible effect on the success of teams in reaching the finals' stages of the Champions League or becoming Champion. The contrary evidence of effects on finals' stages was found in the Europa League regarding the quarter-finals and semi-finals, possibly due to the fact that the teams in that competition have less access to the international market than the typical Champions League team.[55] While it did appear from these facts that 'some limitation of the players' labour market through encouraging the recruitment and retention of players from a home association can constrain the success of higher ranked teams', and while there has been a small improvement in competitive balance in certain areas as a direct result of the home-grown players rule, the study team considered it insufficient to make an accurate scientific assessment of trajectory in the long run and avoided speculating on whether the effect of the rule on competitive balance will increase or decrease in the future.[56] Therefore, '[f]or the purposes of the legal analysis, future trajectory should be viewed as neutral until further data is available to measure the effect over the longer term'.[57] This recommendation suggests that the study was undertaken too soon after the introduction of the rule to make any conclusive statements in regard to the legality of the rule under Article 45 TFEU. Nevertheless, the findings might provide useful data for other purposes.

Quantitative data regarding the effect of the home-grown players rule on the training and development of young players in the clubs in the EU was inconclusive. Qualitative interviews with UEFA, the Federation Internationale Des Associations De Footballeurs Professionnels (FIFPro), the European Clubs Association (ECA), the Association of European Professional Football Leagues (EPFL), and a number of domestic federations and leagues revealed that the rule had 'between "no impact" and "little impact" upon their strategies for training and development of players'.[58] Some clubs, particularly those with smaller turnovers and/or based in smaller member states, suggested 'that this was because the minimum number of home grown players was too small' to have any impact.[59] Translated to the legal language of Article 45 TFEU analysis, this means that, in the opinion of these clubs, the home-grown players rule is unsuitable (i.e. incapable of achieving the goal) because it is not restrictive enough. Only four clubs said that the home-grown players rule had a significant positive impact on their strategy and investments in the training and development of young players.[60] Thus, very little evidence was found 'that the [home grown players rule] has had any significant impact on the quality of, or investment in, the training and development of young EU players'.[61]

---

55 Ibid. pp. 60–61.

56 Ibid. pp. 61–62.

57 Ibid. p. 62.

58 Ibid. p. 68.

59 Ibid.

60 Ibid. p. 70.

61 Ibid. p. 71.

As the study team implied, these data should be taken as providing an interim result. Similar information should be gathered again (in ca. 5 years) in order to assess the real effect of the rule and reach more conclusive results, while at the same avoiding the *post hoc ergo propter hoc* logical fallacy to the extent possible. The legal analysis of the rule on the basis of data available revealed that 'the neutrality or very limited positive effect' of the home-grown players rule on the twin objectives it was set to attain 'must be balanced against the impact the rule has on restricting a player's freedom of movement' as the restriction is currently not manifestly restrictive. Therefore, the rule seems proportionate as its 'limited restrictive effects do not appear to be disproportionate to the modest benefits generated thus far'.[62] This outcome was conditioned by two considerations:

> [f]irst, should the benefits of the Rule diminish over time, the cost/benefit balance would shift, thus rendering current proportionality arguments less persuasive. In order to establish this, an additional future study into the Rule would be required. Second, alternative measures could potentially achieve a more uniform and substantial impact in terms of competitive balance and youth development, and be less restrictive on the fundamental freedoms of EU workers. If this were the case, the proportionality of the measure could not be made out.[63]

So the proportionality of the home-grown players rule could not be conclusively established. It was proposed that UEFA should demonstrate that less restrictive alternative measures are not capable of securing the said objectives by discussing the alternative measures with key stakeholders—a further study (in 3 years) should assess the outcome of these discussions and report the results to the Commission.[64]

4.5 Joined Cases C-51/96 and C-191/97 *Deliège* [2000]

The governing body for judo in Belgium refused to give authorization to a Belgian judoka, Christelle Deliège, to participate in a series of international competitions (some of which were taking place in other EU Member States) because she failed to achieve the necessary qualification criteria. Although judo governing bodies classified its members as amateurs, she believed she was carrying out an economic activity and relied on the economic rights guaranteed by Articles 56, 101 and 102 of the Treaty. She brought two separate proceedings before the Tribunal de Première de Namur. On a preliminary reference procedure, the Court was asked to rule on whether it was contrary to those articles to 'require professional or semi-professional athletes, or persons aspiring to professional or semi-professional activity, to be authorised by their federation in order to be able to compete in international competition which does not involve national teams competing against each other'.[65]

---

[62] Ibid. p. 110.

[63] Ibid.

[64] Ibid. p. 112.

[65] Joined Cases C-51/96 and C-191/97 *Christelle Deliège v. Ligue francophone de judo et disciplines associées ASBL, Ligue belge de judo ASBL, Union européenne de judo and François Pacquée* [2000] ECR I-2549, para 22.

The Court first reiterated its previous decisions.[66] It confirmed that sport is subject to EU law 'only in so far as it constitutes an economic activity' (*Walrave* para 4 and *Bosman* para 73), and that sporting activities are of considerable social importance (*Bosman* para 106). It then added:

> That case law is also supported by the Declaration on Sport (Declaration 29) annexed to the final act of the Conference which adopted the text of the Amsterdam Treaty, which emphasises the social significance of sport and calls on the bodies of the European Union to give special consideration to the particular characteristics of amateur sport. In particular, that declaration is consistent with the abovementioned case law in so far as it relates to situations in which sport constitutes an economic activity.[67]

The Court also confirmed the scope of the sporting exception as set out in *Donà* (paras 14 and 15) and *Bosman* (paras 76 and 127), but found that the selection rules at issue cannot benefit from it. Henceforth, it confined itself to assessing the nature of the activity in question in the light of Article 56 on freedom to provide services. It said that 'the mere fact that a sports association or federation unilaterally classifies its members as amateurs does not in itself mean that those member do not engage in economic activities'.[68] The Court referred to the rule from *Levin* (para 17) and *Steymann* (para 13) which requires that 'the work performed must be genuine and effective and not such as to be regarded as purely marginal and ancillary',[69] and the rule from *Bond* which essentially states that services do not have to be paid by those for whom they are performed.[70] A high-ranking athlete's participation in international competitions, such as the Olympic Games, involves a number of separate but closely related services which may fall under Article 56.[71] First, organising a sporting contest offers an opportunity for athletes to compete while giving exposure to their personal sponsors as a result of their sporting activity. Second, it allows organisers to exploit the broadcasting rights and sell tickets to events, which is in turn a great commercial interest to sponsors and advertisers. Finally, Deliège received grants to train and compete on the basis of her sporting achievements. Amateur athletes therefore do not automatically fall outside the Treaty scope, but their activity has to be examined in the light of criteria as specified by the Court. If, after such examination, it transpires that the activity in question constitutes an economic activity (provision of services), it is necessary to consider whether the rules governing the exercise of that activity (the rules on selection of athletes) constitute a restriction within the meaning of Article 56 of the Treaty.[72]

The Court considered that selection rules which limited the number of participants in the high-level international competitions, and which did not involve

---

[66] It cited paras 4, 17 and 18 from *Walrave*, paras 14 and 15 from *Donà* and paras 73, 76, 82, 83 and 127 from *Bosman*.

[67] Joined cases C-51/96 and C-191/97 *Deliège*, para 42.

[68] Ibid. para 46.

[69] Ibid. para 54.

[70] Ibid. para 56.

[71] Ibid.

[72] Ibid. para 60.

national teams competing against each other, could not in themselves constitute an obstacle on the freedom to provide services under Article 56 because 'such a limitation is *inherent* in the conduct of an international high-level sports event, which necessarily involves certain selection rules or criteria being adopted'.[73]

Inherent rules therefore constitute yet another category of the sporting exception.[74] The sports organisations also must be able to demonstrate that selection rules are based on objective criteria unconnected with the personal circumstances of the athletes.[75]

Finally, it is noteworthy that in *Deliège*, much like in *Bosman*, the Court did not touch upon the questions related to competition law provisions. Unlike in *Bosman*, where the Court already found both rules contrary to Article 45 TFEU and considered it unnecessary to rule on the interpretation of competition provisions in Articles 101 and 102, in *Deliège* it considered the competition questions inadmissible due to the insufficient factual information provided by the referring national court.

4.6 Case C-176/96 *Lehtonen* [2000]

Finnish basketball player Jyri Lehtonen was transferred from his Finnish team to the Belgian basketball team Castors Braine. However, the necessary license, which should have been approved by International Basketball Federation (FIBA) to allow Lehtonen to play for Castors Braine, was refused because the transfer had not taken place within the specified time period, the so-called 'transfer window'. This in turn meant that he could not compete in Belgian competitions for that season. But Castors Braine already fielded him in one game and listed Lehtonen on a team sheet in another official game, both of which it won. The results were overturned and registered as a 20:0 defeat because the club fielded the unregistered player. In order to avoid further sanctions, Castors Braine did not select or play Lehtonen in the remaining play-off matches. Jyri Lehtonen and Castors Braine brought the case to the *Tribunal de Première Instance* in Brussels which forwarded to the Court the question on the legality of the transfer windows under Articles 18, 45, 101 and 102 of the Treaty.

The Court confirmed its previous case law in a virtually identical manner as in *Deliège*, including a reference to the Amsterdam Declaration, and found that the rules on transfer windows created an obstacle to freedoms guaranteed under Article 45 even though they related to fielding players and not to employing them.[76] Citing para 120 of *Bosman*, the Court explained that being fielded is the

---

73 Ibid. para 64, (emphasis added).

74 See Parrish and Miettinen 2008, p. 90. For discussion on sporting exceptions see Chap. 6, and specifically on inherent rules see Sect. 6.3.3.

75 Joined cases C-51/96 and C-191/97 *Deliège*, para 65.

76 Case C-176/96 *Jyri Lehtonen and Castors Canada Dry Namur-Braine ASBL v. Fédération royale belge des sociétés de basket-ball ASBL (FRBSB)* [2000] ECR I-2681.

'essential purpose of a professional player's activity' and the rules prohibiting fielding therefore restrict the chances of being employed. However, such rules were found to be justified on non-economic grounds, by the need for proper organisation of the game because mid-season transfers could substantially alter the sporting strength and thus the competition between teams in the course of a championship.

Nevertheless, the transfer windows in this particular case were found to be disproportionate and in breach of Article 45 of the Treaty because they were opened substantially longer for the players from outside the EU. Differential treatment between international and EU players proved that the transfers could have taken place even after the deadline for EU players and not stood in the way of effective organisation of the game. In para 59 of the judgment, the Court suggested that there might be an objective justification for this discrimination, but it did not elaborate on or give any examples of such a justification, and the respondent did not raise any arguments in this regard to support its case. The questions on the interpretation of EU competition law provisions were, like in *Deliège*, considered inadmissible due to the insufficient factual information provided by the referring national court.

4.7 Case C-438/00 *Kolpak* [2003], Case C-265/03 *Simutenkov* [2005], and Case C-152/08 *Kahveci* [2008]

The *Kolpak* case[77] concerned a Slovakian handball player who was under contract with a German handball club. The rules of the German Handball Federation stated that the licenses of all non-EU players should be marked with the letter 'A'. Clubs were allowed to use only two players with 'A' licenses in their competition matches. The *Simutenkov* case[78] involved a Russian football player who was employed by a Spanish football club Deportivo Tenerife. There was a limit of three 'non-Community' players allowed on the clubs playing in the Spanish First Division. In *Kahveci*[79] the factual background was virtually the same as in *Simutekov,* involving a Turkish player in a Spanish football club. At the time Kolpak brought his claim, Slovakia was not an EU Member State but it had entered into an Association Agreement with the EU.[80] Russia had a Partnership

[77] Case C-438/00 *Deutscher Handballbund v. Kolpak* [2003] ECR I-4135.

[78] Case C-265/03 *Igor Simutenkov v. Ministerio de Educación y Cultura, Real Federación Española de Fútbol* [2005] ECR I-2579.

[79] Case C-152/08 *Real Sociedad de Fútbol SAD and Nihat Kahveci v Consejo Superior de Deportes and Real Federación Española de Fútbol* [2008] ECR *I-6291.*

[80] Europe Agreement establishing an association between the European Communities and their Member States, of the one part, and the Slovak Republic, of the other part, signed in Luxembourg on 4 October 1993 and approved on behalf of the Communities by Decision 94/909/EC, ECSC, Euratom of the Council and the Commission of 19 December 1994 (OJ 1993 L 359, p. 1) ('the Association Agreement with Slovakia').

and Cooperation Agreement[81] and Turkey had an Association Agreement (the so-called 'Ankara Agreement' with an annexed Additional Protocol).[82] The sportsmen challenged the restrictive rules of the sporting federations on the basis of their countries' agreements with the EU, relying in particular on non-discrimination provisions in those agreements.[83]

The Court held that the provisions in the agreements on which the sportsmen were relying had direct effect. They laid down, in clear, precise and unconditional terms, a prohibition precluding any Member State from discriminating on grounds of nationality against non-Union workers vis-à-vis their own nationals as far as their conditions of employment, remuneration and dismissal were concerned. The quotas on numbers of the non-Union players related to 'working conditions' within the meaning of those provisions, which were considered analogous to Article 45 of the Treaty. Furthermore, the provisions apply to rules drawn up by a sports federation which determines the conditions under which professional sportsmen engage in gainful employment.

The judgments, however, did not create rights concerning the cross-border movement of workers from the countries with which the EU has entered into similar agreements.[84] The benefits were confined to equal treatment with regard to conditions of work, remuneration, or dismissal in a Member State in which they are already lawfully employed, i.e. have already entered the labour market. In contrast to Article 45 of the Treaty, those provisions therefore do not extend to national rules, or rules of private bodies, including sporting organisations,

[81] Agreement on partnership and cooperation establishing a partnership between the European Communities and their Member States, of the one part, and the Russian Federation, of the other part, signed in Corfu on 24 June 1994 and approved on behalf of the Communities by Decision 97/800/EC ECSC, Euratom: Council and Commission Decision of 30 October 1997 (OJ 1994 L 327, p. 1) ('the Communities-Russia Partnership Agreement').

[82] The Additional Protocol, signed on 23 November 1970 in Brussels and concluded, approved and confirmed on behalf of the Community by Council Regulation (EEC) No 2760/72 of 19 December 1972 (OJ 1973 C 133, p. 17) ('the Additional Protocol'), annexed to the Agreement establishing an Association between the European Economic Community and Turkey, signed at Ankara on 12 September 1963 by the Republic of Turkey, of the one part, and by the Member States of the EEC and the Community, on the other part, and concluded, approved and confirmed on behalf of the Community by Council Decision 64/732/EEC of 23 December 1963 (OJ 1973 C 113, p. 1) ('the EEC-Turkey Association Agreement').

[83] Article 23(1) of the Partnership and Cooperation Agreement provides: 'Subject to the laws, conditions and procedures applicable in each Member State, the Community and its Member States shall ensure that the treatment accorded to Russian nationals, legally employed in the territory of a Member State shall be free from any discrimination based on nationality, as regards working conditions, remuneration or dismissal, as compared to its own nationals.' Article 38 of the Europe Agreement between the Community and Slovakia reads: 'Subject to the conditions and modalities applicable in each Member State: treatment accorded to workers of Slovak Republic nationality legally employed in the territory of a Member State shall be free from any discrimination based on nationality, as regards working conditions, remuneration or dismissal, as compared to its own nationals'.

[84] For example, Georgia, Serbia, Moldova, Ukraine, Algeria, Morocco, Armenia and many others.

concerning access to the labour market. This means that those employed and subjected to discriminatory conditions of work in a Member State could have a valid basis to challenge a rule imposing nationality restrictions, while those that have difficulty accessing the labour market of a Member State due to the very same rule, do not have a claim against the body that laid it down.

4.8 Case C-325/08 *Bernard* [2010]

In December 2009, the Lisbon Treaty amendments gave 'complementary' competence to the Union in the area of sport and introduced the concept of 'specificity of sport' in Article 165(1) TFEU. The ruling of the Grand Chamber of the Court in *Bernard*[85] is the first to make reference to this 'sports article' (even though the facts of the case pre-date the entry into force of the Lisbon Treaty). It is therefore necessary to dissect the case and examine each part of the judgment in detail with the purpose of identifying the extent and the nature of changes in legal approach to the sports sector in the EU, if any. *Bernard* embraces the sentiment of European sports policy and insists on certain parameters for the application of law in the sports sector within the established objective justification framework. It legitimises restrictions on player mobility by means of proportionate training compensation schemes which rely on 'real training costs'. Although this case does not conflict with *Bosman*, in the sense that it does not depart in any way from the well-established analytical framework applied in the free movement case law, it nevertheless does conflict with that judgment in terms of the Court's appraisal of the suitability of training compensation within the confines of the free movement framework and, ultimately, in the effects produced. It is exactly this fact that gives some weight to the otherwise largely symbolic and unnecessary reference to Article 165(1) TFEU in *Bernard* and leads to the assumption that a new 'sport article' might have led to minor but permanent alteration on the score board in favour of sporting autonomy. Nevertheless, until we have another case to confirm or deny this assumption, it would be premature to draw any firm conclusions about the impact of *Bernard* in this respect.

4.8.1 *Facts of the Case*

In 1997, the French football club Olympique Lyonnais (Lyon) and the 17-year old Olivier Bernard entered into a training contract for three seasons with effect from 1 July that year. The legal dispute between the parties arose three seasons

[85] Case C-325/08 *Olympique Lyonnais SASP v. Olivier Bernard and Newcastle United FC* judgment of grand Chamber of the Court delivered on 16 March 2010. The following case comment was first published in Pijetlovic 2010 Another Classic of EU Sports Jurisprudence: Legal Implications of *Olympique Lyonnais SASP v. Olivier Bernard and Newcastle UFC* (C-325/08) *European Law Review* (35), pp. 858–869.

later when Bernard refused to accept a 1-year professional contract offered to him by Lyon, which was to take effect as of 1 July 2000. Instead, in August 2000, he signed a professional contract with Newcastle United FC and moved to England.

At the material time, the employment of football players in France was regulated by the *Charte du Football Professionne* (the Charter), which had the status of a collective agreement. Trainee players between the ages of 16 and 22 and employed by a professional club under a fixed-term training contract belonged to a category known as *joueurs espoir*. Article 23 of the Charter provided that the club is entitled to require a trainee to sign a contract as a professional player on the expiry of the training contract. Should the player refuse, he was prohibited from signing with another French club for a period of 3 years without the written agreement of the club in which he was a *joueur espoir*. If the club did not offer him a professional contract, he was free to sign with a club of his choice without any compensation being due to the club that trained him. Although this rule implied that compensation is due if the player refuses to sign a professional contract with that club, the Charter contained no scheme for compensation. The club could nevertheless rely on Article L. 122-3-8 of the French *Code du travail* (Employment Code) to bring an action for 'damages corresponding to the loss suffered' against the *joueur espoir* for breach of contractual obligations flowing from Article 23 of the Charter.

When Bernard left for Newcastle United FC, Lyon considered that the compensation principle should extend outside of France and sued him and his new club. It sought an award of EUR 53,357 in damages, the amount corresponding to the remuneration Bernard would have received over the period of 1 year under the professional contract with Lyon which he had refused to sign. The judgment of the *Conseil de prud'hommes*, ordering Bernard and Newcastle United FC jointly to pay Lyon damages of EUR 22,867, was quashed by the *Cour d'appel* which considered that the obligation on *joueurs espoir* under Article 23 of the Charter contravened freedom of movement under Article 39 EC (now Article 45 TFEU). Lyon then appealed to the *Cour de cassation* which, in July 2008, referred two related questions to the Court of Justice for a preliminary ruling, essentially asking (i) whether Article 39 EC (now Article 45 TFEU) precludes the provision of a national law requiring *joueurs espoir* to pay damages in the described context, and (ii) if so, does the need to encourage the recruitment and training of young professional players constitute a legitimate objective capable of justifying such a restriction.

4.8.2 Analytical Overview of the Judgment

Bernard faithfully follows the standard analytical structure applied in order to consider measures restricting free movement. However, three themes are of key importance for understanding the impact of the judgment: (i) the standard of application of the proportionality principle in the sports sector outlined in para 40 of *Bernard*, which surely provides classic lines to be cited in sports cases still to come before the Court; (ii) the suitability of training compensation schemes as a means to attain the aim of encouraging training and recruitment of young players and (iii) criteria for accepted methods of calculating training compensation. Following a brief overview of the restriction and justification elements of the free movement framework as applied in *Bernard*, these themes will then be discussed in turn, considering the Opinion of the Advocate General in *Bernard* and the Court's judgment in *Bosman* where relevant.

4.8.2.1 The Existence of a Restriction on Freedom of Movement for Workers

The Court first dealt with the question of the restrictive nature of the compensation scheme. This part of the judgment does little but confirm settled case law. Citing *Bosman* (and the reference to *Walrave and Koch* in that judgment), the Court reminded us that Article 45 TFEU applies not only to actions of public authorities but also to rules of any other nature aimed at regulating gainful employment in a collective manner, thus bringing the Charter under the scope of the Treaty.[86] Furthermore, the Court used the obstacle approach to find that the Charter, constituting neither a prohibition on signing a contract with a club in another Member State nor discrimination on the basis of nationality, nevertheless discourages the player from exercising his right of free movement and makes the exercise of that right less attractive. Thus, it constitutes a restriction contrary to Article 45 TFEU. The Court makes no distinction between sport and any other sector at this stage of its analysis. The contested rules or practices are either restrictive or not, notwithstanding the specific characteristics of the sector.[87]

4.8.2.2 Justification of the Restriction: Legitimate Objective

Paragraph 38 of the Court's judgment follows a familiar roadmap for analysing the existence of justifications for measures restricting the free movement provisions of the Treaty. Accordingly, a restriction may be accepted only if it pursues 'a legitimate aim compatible with the Treaty and is justified by overriding reasons in the public interest', and the application of that restrictive measure is (a) capable of ensuring achievement of that aim and (b) does not go beyond what is necessary for that purpose. The Court goes on to confirm para 106 of *Bosman*:

> [...]in view of the considerable social importance of sporting activities and in particular football in the European Union, the objective of encouraging the recruitment and training of young players must be accepted as legitimate.[88]

---

[86] C-325/08 *Bernard*, para 30.

[87] Paragraph 30 of the AG Sharpston's opinion in C-325/08 *Bernard* says that 'the specific characteristics of sport in general, and football in particular, do not seem to me to be of paramount importance when considering whether there is a prohibited restriction on freedom of movement. [...]'.

[88] Case C-325/08 *Bernard*, para 39.

Therefore, the said objective was easily recognised as legitimate by reference to previous case law. It is apparent from the language of the Court that the social importance of sport plays a crucial role in legitimating this objective and that it would probably not be accepted as such in (m)any other employment sectors.

4.8.2.3 Standard of Application of the Proportionality Principle

This aspect of the judgment deserves more attention. The Court states that

> In considering whether a system which restricts the freedom of movement of such players is suitable to ensure that the said objective is attained and does not go beyond what is necessary to attain it, account must be taken, as the Advocate General states in points 30 and 47 of her Opinion, of the specific characteristics of sport in general, and football in particular, and of their social and educational function. The relevance of those factors is also corroborated by their being mentioned in the second subparagraph of Article 165(1) TFEU.[89]

For the first time, the Court mentions the social and educational function of sport at this stage of analysis and refers expressly to sport as a sector which requires specific characteristics to be taken into account in the examination of possible justifications. This does not represent a novelty in terms of the relevant factors taken into account by the Court at different stages of objective justification analysis. The novelty is in the express language of the Court, coupled with the reference to Article 165(1) TFEU.

Although not relevant in *Bernard* itself (since, here, a non-discriminatory restriction was at issue), it is interesting to remember that under the traditional approach, the analytical framework first required labelling the measure as directly discriminatory, indirectly discriminatory or non-discriminatory but restrictive on the exercise of the freedoms conferred. By allowing the directly discriminatory '3+2' rule in *Bosman*, discriminatory transfer windows in *Lehtonen,*[90] and quotas on foreign players in *Kolpak*[91] and *Simutenkov*[92] to be considered under the objective justification framework as opposed to the express derogation framework, and therefore treating these measures as if they were indirectly discriminatory or non-discriminatory restrictions, it could be thought that the Court has effectively introduced the concept of the 'specificity of sport' to the traditional classification process.[93] Sport is not the only sector in which the Court has taken such a detour for directly discriminatory measures.[94] But

---

[89] Ibid. para 40.

[90] Case 176/96 *Lehtonen* [2000] ECR I-2681.

[91] Case C-438/00 *Kolpak* [2003] ECR I-4135.

[92] Case C-265/03 *Simutenkov* [2005] ECR I-2579.

[93] The traditional measure-classification stage in the analysis is nonetheless still evident in the Court's analytical structure in several cases. See Barnard 2010, pp. 246–257.

[94] See, for e.g., Case C-67/97 *Bluhme* [1998] ECR I-6717 (biodiversity), Case C-2/90 *Commission v. Belgium (Walloon Waste)* [1992] ECR I-4431 (environmental protection), Case C-19/92 *Kraus* [1993] ECR I-1663 (protection of public against misleading use of academic titles).

sport is the only sector where it has taken this approach consistently, thus making it a rule in the application of EU free movement law to sports, which could be attributed to the specificity of sport. In *Bernard*, the Court's novel reference to Article 165(1) TFEU might signal that the provision has not just confirmed but has in fact given some additional weight to the specificity and socio-educational function of sport, which could prove just enough to influence the outcome in certain cases. This is, however, evident only when considered in the context of the suitability assessment and the Court's departure on that matter from the judgment in *Bosman*. The discussion in the following section illustrates this point.

4.8.2.4 Suitability of Training Compensation Systems

Turning to the issue of the suitability of training compensation schemes in light of the specificities of sport and its social and educational function, it is important for purposes of discussion to set out the Court's reasoning at paras 41–45 of the judgment in full:

> The prospect of receiving training fees is likely to encourage football clubs to seek new talent and train young players (see *Bosman*, para 108). The returns on the investments in training made by the clubs providing it are uncertain by their very nature since the clubs bear the expenditure incurred in respect of all the young players they recruit and train, sometimes over several years, whereas only some of those players undertake a professional career at the end of their training, whether with the club which provided the training or another club (see, to that effect, *Bosman*, para 109). [...] Under those circumstances, the clubs which provided the training could be discouraged from investing in the training of young players if they could not obtain reimbursement of the amounts spent for that purpose where, at the end of his training, a player enters into a professional contract with another club. [...] It follows that a scheme providing for the payment of compensation for training where a young player, at the end of his training, signs a professional contract with a club other than the one which trained him can, in principle, be justified by the objective of encouraging the recruitment and training of young players. However, such a scheme must be actually capable of attaining that objective and be proportionate to it, taking due account of the costs borne by the clubs in training both future professional players and those who will never play professionally (see, to that effect, *Bosman*, para 109).

This reasoning can be compared with para 109 of *Bosman*, in which the Court held that '[...] because it is impossible to predict the sporting future of young players with any certainty and because only a limited number of such players go on to play professionally, those fees are by nature contingent and uncertain and are in any event unrelated to the actual cost borne by clubs of training both future professional players and those who will never play professionally. The prospect of receiving such fees cannot, therefore, be either a decisive factor in encouraging recruitment and training of young players or an adequate means of financing such activities, particularly in the case of smaller clubs'.[95] Thus, in *Bosman*, training compensation schemes were viewed as unsuitable for the achievement of the objective of *encouraging* the recruitment and training of young players, in *Bernard* they were deemed suitable. Furthermore, in para 46 of her Opinion in

[95] C-415/93 *Bosman*, para 109.

Bernard, AG Sharpston said: '[...] Rules such as the one in question here are therefore perhaps not decisive in encouraging clubs to recruit and train young players. None the less, such rules ensure that clubs are not discouraged from recruitment and training by the prospect of seeing their investment in training applied to the benefit of some other club, with no compensation for themselves'.

Interpreting the word 'encourage'[96] as meaning to 'not discourage' seems to be a linguistic modification, enabling the Advocate General to depart from the decision in *Bosman* as regards the suitability of training compensation schemes.[97] But why would AG Sharpston undertake such a linguistic manoeuvre and why would the Court follow her Opinion on that point? One possible reason is discussed above and relates to the change of direction with regard to the weight given to the socio-educational functions of sport. The other explanation would be that the Court simply did not expressly acknowledge the departure from *Bosman* in this respect, when it in fact changed its opinion as regards the importance of the contingent and uncertain nature of compensation fees in assessing the suitability of the measure. AG Lenz in *Bosman* did not find that the nature of compensation fees prevented him from reaching the conclusion that they are appropriate means for attaining the aim of encouraging training and recruitment of young players, but the Court, back then, did not follow him on this point.

4.8.2.5 Proportionality: Calculation of Training Compensation

Finally, addressing the system of compensation in *Bernard* in paras 46–48 of the judgment, the Court said that payment of damages to the club which provided training calculated on the basis of total loss for breach of contractual obligations by the player (the amount of which was unrelated to the 'real training costs'), went beyond what was necessary to encourage recruitment and training of young players and to fund those activities. The Court offered only very general guidelines on the accepted methods of calculating compensation. Accordingly, such methods should be related to compensation for the real training costs incurred by the club (the criteria for calculation of which should ideally be determined in advance). What constitutes 'real training cost' is the issue left open. Moreover, para 45 tells us that the costs to take into account in designing a scheme are not just those associated with training future professional players but, also, costs associated with training those players who will never turn professional.

---

[96] As required by the objective accepted as legitimate in para 39 of C-325/08 *Bernard* and para 108 of C-415/93 *Bosman*.

[97] The objective required that the restrictive rule *encourages* clubs to train and recruit young players, and not that it did not discourage clubs from doing so. The aim of 'not discouraging' presents a lower bar in terms of finding the restrictive rule suitable for the attainment of the objective than the aim of 'encouraging'. Therefore, the restrictive rule (training compensation) used to attain the objective as re-worded and modified in *Bernard* will more likely be found suitable in the former (i.e. not discouraging) but not in the latter.

Weatherill suggests that interpreting the criteria noted in paras 46–47 of the judgment in *Bernard* to mean that only a scheme tied directly to the actual costs of training one player is permitted 'might be too narrow an interpretation', and that the criterion in para 45 'might conceivably be interpreted to mean that the compensation payable by those who succeed as professionals might be inflated beyond the costs incurred in their particular case to allow also some coverage of training costs incurred but wasted on those players who fall by the wayside'.[98] Lindholm also argues that the Court favoured a total-training-cost-model and 'appeared' to have rejected the Advocate General's suggestions of an individual-training-cost-model.[99] Although this is a possible interpretation of the judgment, there is an alternative explanation which, although not as straightforward, appears more convincing. There are several considerations which lead to the conclusion that the criterion in para 45 is an *additional* criterion that applies *only* in schemes in which the new employer, as opposed to a player, is liable to pay the compensation, and that the Court has in fact followed the suggestions of AG Sharpston on the point of setting different criteria for 'employer pays' and 'player pays' schemes.

First, para 45 appears in the part of the judgment in which the Court addresses compensation schemes in general and not 'player pays' schemes in particular, whereas paras 46–47 address the scheme in the main proceedings, i.e. a 'player pays' scheme. It would be unreasonable to expect the *Cour de cassation* to recognise this criterion as applicable to the case before it. The Court has left out the criterion of 'and those who never play professionally' in its answer to the preliminary reference because it did not want the *Cour de cassation* to reach the decision using that criterion to determine the dispute. If it were applicable, the Court could easily have added this criterion at the end of para 49.[100] Additionally, in para 45, as well as in the preceding reasoning, the Court cites *Bosman*, in which the 'employer pays' scheme was at issue. It would have made all the difference were the attainment of the ends in that case dependant on 'player pays' means. If it were, the Court in *Bosman* would not have implied that training compensation had to be related to the 'actual cost borne by the clubs of training both future professional players and those that will never play professionally'.

This leads to my second point. Namely, the Court could not have intended to subject a young trainee to the burden of a total-training-cost-model, because that could have the disproportionate effect of actually preventing him from moving to a club in another Member State. This is especially true with respect to sports other than football in which the costs of training might be as high but the players' services are much less valued. Such an approach would fail to satisfy proportionality *stricto* sensu. To illustrate this in more concrete terms, we can look at the FIFA training compensation system, according to which an employer is liable to pay up to EUR 90,000 per year of training if it offers the first professional contract to a

---

[98] Weatherill 2010, p. 5.

[99] Lindholm 2010, p. 1192.

[100] See Sect. 4.8.2.6 below for the text of para 49.

young player. The costs are supposed to reflect approximate total training costs. According to a FIFPro comment on FIFA's compensation rules, history has shown that 'such fees operate as a significant and sometimes definite restraint that can not only undermine player earnings but also put players out of the game'.[101] If there is any truth to this claim regarding the FIFA 'employer pays' scheme, for football trainees to be held liable for similar total-training-cost-covering-sums, and for trainees in other sports to be held liable for equivalently restrictive amounts in their respective sports (which could be legally attached to any sport if para 45 is interpreted as applying to 'player pays' schemes), would mean preventing most players from moving anywhere after completing their training. Has the social and educational function along with the specificity of sport really been raised to *such* high level of importance to be capable of justifying these consequences for freedoms guaranteed by Article 45 TFEU? Although it could become more important in the future, depending on how the sport governing bodies react to *Bernard*, this discussion is currently of more theoretical than practical value when placed in the context of the present-day state of affairs, to which we now turn.

In the 10 years since the litigation started, FIFA has introduced a system operated on the 'employer pays' basis, France has changed its rules for internal transfers in football to reflect that system, Bernard finished his footballing career, and Lyon's lawyers probably forgot they ever started the litigation as the club's budget would not be affected at any detectable level by whatever Bernard would have been held liable to owe. In addition, sports today do not apply 'player pays' schemes. For example, basketball, handball, football and rugby run 'employer pays' schemes. Cricket, fencing, hockey, cycling, polo, volleyball, ice-hockey, skiing, swimming and baseball have no training compensation at all. One explanation which renders the judgment valuable in the present day is that the criterion in para 45 applies to any type of scheme including 'player pays' schemes, which is something that I have argued against above. The only other possible explanation is that the para 45 criterion is strictly intended to apply to systems in which employer bears the burden of training compensation.

This explanation of the judgment is in line with AG Sharpston's suggestions. She rejected two models of compensation: one based on the player's prospective earnings, because it is susceptible to manipulation; and the other based on the club's prospective loss of profits, because it is too uncertain.[102] Two other models discussed in the Opinion were the total-training-cost-model and the individual-training-cost-model: '[…] If it is necessary to train *n* players in order to produce one who will be successful professionally, then the cost to the training club (and the saving to the new club) is the cost of training those *n* players. It seems appropriate and proportionate for compensation between clubs to be based on that cost. For the individual player, however, only the individual cost seems relevant', regardless of the overall training costs.[103] So, the Advocate General suggested the

[101] FIFPro report on the Joint FIFA/UEFA Negotiation Document (International Transfer of Players).

[102] See paras 50–51 of her Opinion in Case C-325/08 *Bernard*.

[103] Ibid. para 57.

total-training-cost-model as appropriate for 'employer pays' schemes and the individual-training-cost-model in any instance of 'player pays' schemes.

Weatherill considers that the Court chose not to explore the nuances suggested by AG Sharpston because 'calculation is in any event complicated by the practical reality that players are trained in groups, not individually: the cost of training twenty players is lower than the cost of training one multiplied by twenty thanks to realisation of economies of scale'.[104] But it may well be that the Court has left the nuisance of the nuances to the clubs and/or their governing bodies. After all, football clubs nowadays, especially those playing in the higher divisions of a national league, are professional undertakings with huge turnovers that must have proper accounting systems to manage their revenues and expenditures and, therefore, they should be able to assess quite precisely the expenses involved in the training of young players.[105] It does not seem to be too different or too much harder to calculate the costs of training one player than it is to calculate the costs of training one player plus the fluctuating number of other players but not of entire trainee squad.[106] It is true that the calculations may prove to be more difficult for smaller clubs. However, even small clubs have to manage their accounts during the financial year. If they do not have an in-house accountant, they can hire one specifically to devise a cost template and demonstrate how to calculate costs of training, which fixed and variable costs to include/exclude, which deductions to make, and so on. It is a one-time hire and a one-time expense (which can then possibly be labelled as a cost of training and shifted to another party).

Regardless of the method used for calculating costs, sums of compensation must be set between suitability and necessity, i.e. they must be high enough to be capable of attaining the objective but they must be the lowest possible that can achieve that objective. It can be rightfully claimed that 'player pays' schemes based on the individual-training-cost-model are not suitable to achieve the objective of encouraging clubs to train and recruit young players, simply because of the very low amounts of compensation involved. This is also recognised by AG Sharpston: '[…] investment in training would be discouraged if only the cost of training the individual player were taken into account when determining the appropriate compensation'.[107] Therefore, in team sports, 'employer pays' schemes based on total training cost seem to be the only model that can satisfy all of the legal criteria, and are therefore the right way to go. The reason that the Court ruled that individuals should compensate only for the costs of their own training (under the interpretation of judgment presented in this article) in a team sport such as football is to enable the *Cour de cassation* to settle the issue between the parties to the main proceedings. This ruling can also be important for the future, however, in

---

[104] Weatherill 2010, p. 5.

[105] Van den Bogaert 2005, pp. 256–257.

[106] It takes an average of 10 players to produce one professional. See European Commission, Education of Young Sportspersons, Final Report by PMP in partnership with the Institute of Sport and Leisure Policy Loughborough University (August 2004), p. 49, and Blanpain 2003, p. 52.

[107] See para 52 of her Opinion in Case C-325/08 *Bernard*.

the event of the establishment of mixed systems where the duty to compensate is divided between the player and the employer, or the player and the common compensation pool (which would make the system pass the suitability test).

Regarding the applicability of the judgment to schemes existing today, the criteria for team sports and 'employer pays' schemes are set out in para 45 of the judgment. In addition to this, 'real training costs' (in paras 46 and 50) should be taken as meaning (i) costs for training one individual player in 'player pays' schemes (to settle the case at hand and any eventual future systems where individual would be liable to pay) and (ii) costs for training one individual player plus the number of players that do not make it professionally taking into consideration the appropriate 'player factor' (the ratio of players who need to be trained to produce one professional player) in 'employer pays' schemes. Paragraphs 46 and 50 refer only to the link between the compensation payable and the actual costs incurred—the Court does not insist on precise congruence.[108] It is enough that the relevant calculations are based on the broad criteria set by the Court.

4.8.2.6 The Answer to the Questions Referred

> [...] the answer to the questions referred is that Article 45 TFEU does *not* preclude a scheme which, in order to attain the objective of encouraging the recruitment and training of young players, guarantees compensation to the club which provided the training if, at the end of his training period, a young player signs a professional contract with a club in another Member State, provided that the scheme is suitable to ensure the attainment of that objective and does not go beyond what is necessary to attain it.[109]

Here, the Court omitted to complete the sentence with the para 45 criterion 'taking due account of the costs borne by the clubs in training both future professional players and those who will never play professionally'. The final word flowing from the reasoning in paras 46–48 was that the 'player pays' scheme in *Bernard* failed to satisfy the necessity principle because damages were calculated, 'in a way *which is unrelated to the actual costs of the training*'.[110] So the ruling of the Court was in favour of Bernard and Newcastle United FC. But the reason for that is not because the Court considered training compensation schemes in sports illegal, but because this particular compensation scheme was considered illegal.

4.8.2.7 The Current FIFA Training Compensation System

Article 20 and Annex 4 of the FIFA Regulations for the Status and Transfer of Players set out the rules for training compensation. Accordingly, training compensation shall be paid to a player's training club(s): (1) when a player signs his first

---

[108] See Weatherill 2010, p. 4.

[109] Case C-325/08 *Bernard*, para 49.

[110] Ibid. para 50 (emphasis added).

contract as a professional and (2) on each transfer of a professional until the end of the season of his 23rd birthday.[111] The obligation to compensate applies whether the player is transferred during or at the end of his contract.[112] A special provision that applies for transfers from one association to another within the EU/EEA stipulates that if the former club does not offer the player a contract, no training compensation is payable unless the former club can justify that it is entitled to such compensation. Such an offer must be at least of an equivalent value to the current contract.[113]

In order to calculate the compensation due for training and education costs, national football associations divide their clubs into a maximum of four categories in accordance with the clubs' financial investment in training players. The training costs are set for each category and are said to correspond to the amount needed to train one player for 1 year multiplied by an average 'player factor', which is the ratio of players who need to be trained to produce one professional player. The flat amounts of training costs are established on a confederation basis for each category of club.[114] UEFA has established the following sums for Europe: category I clubs EUR 90,000, category II clubs EUR 60,000, category III clubs EUR 30,000 and category IV clubs EUR 10,000.[115] So, when a player that has been trained for 5 years by club X, a category III club refuses to sign their first professional contract with club X and instead signs with club Y, a category II club, club Y will owe 45,000 EUR times the number of years that the player spent with club X (when a player moves from a lower to a higher category, the average amount between the two categories applies). The total amount owed for 5 years of training a player in this case would come to EUR 225,000. If a player were to move after 5 years of training from a club belonging to the first category to another club also categorised as belonging to the first category, EUR 450,000 would be the applicable amount. In Europe, only six national associations have clubs classified as belonging to category I. About half of the national associations have only category III and IV clubs.

The FIFA Dispute Resolution Chamber reviews disputes concerning the amount of training compensation payable and has discretion to adjust this amount if it is clearly disproportionate in the case under review.[116] A question which has received increased attention after *Bernard* is whether the FIFA training compensation system is compatible with the requirements of EU law. *Prima facie*, it appears that Article 20 and Annex 4 of the FIFA Regulations satisfy the general criteria of the judgment in *Bernard*. The European Commission has already given an informal green light to these rules. However, until someone actually pursues a challenge, we will not be able to say with certainty which provisions are perhaps precluded by the EU law and need amendment.

---

[111] Ibid. Article 20.

[112] Ibid.

[113] Annex 4, FIFA Regulations for the Status and Transfer of Players.

[114] Ibid.

[115] FIFA circular letter nr. 1223.

[116] Annex 4, FIFA Regulations for the Status and Transfer of Players.

The feature of the system that appears most controversial is the fact that payable flat sums are set on the level of confederation.[117] The actual costs of training are not the same or even similar in all European countries due to differences in economic conditions. Therefore, it seems more desirable that the flat rate sums for different categories of clubs should be set by national associations to reflect more accurately the real costs of training incurred, as required by *Bernard*.[118] On the other hand, the existence of a FIFA Dispute Settlement Chamber that has the power to adjust the sums in individual cases is a positive feature of the system which can be used as an argument against claims that sums are clearly disproportionate. It follows implicitly from the judgment in *Bernard* that the *precise* sum of the real training costs is not a must.

4.8.2.8 Final Remarks

Let us remind ourselves that the judgment in *Bosman* led to the abolition of transfer fees for out-of-contract professional players who then became free agents whereas, under *Bernard*, out-of-contract trainee players were not considered to be free agents and compensation fees were given a green light. This differential treatment of young trainees who embark upon a professional career and professional players can, *inter alia*, be considered to be an exception to the prohibition on age discrimination in EU law.[119] It can also be a preliminary indication of the validity of FIFA rules that have for years maintained, contrary to *Bosman*, transfer fees for out-of-contract trainees. In this sense, *Bernard* represents a restriction on, or clarification of, the scope of *Bosman*. Given what could prove to be a minor but permanent increase in the significance of the specific characteristics and socio-educational function of sport, now captured by Article 165(1) TFEU, the judgment in *Bernard* may yet become the 'classic' touchstone in EU sports law.

4.9 Cases T-385/07, T-55/08 and T-68/08 *FIFA and UEFA v Commission* [2011]

On 17 February 2011, the General Court delivered three separate but closely related judgments in the cases *FIFA and UEFA v Commission*.[120] Article 14(1) of the Council Directive 2010/13/EU on Audiovisual Media Services (AVMS

[117] In other words, UEFA as a confederative body sets sums for all European national football associations, and other regional governing bodies set the sums in their respective regions.

[118] See on this point also Van den Bogaert 2005, pp. 256–257, and Drolet 2009, pp. 167–190.

[119] See Article 10 TFEU and Council Directive 2000/78 establishing a general framework for equal treatment in employment and occupation OJ L 303/16, 2 December 2000.

[120] Case T-385/07 *Fédération Internationale de Football Association (FIFA) v. Commission*, judgment of 17 February 2011, Case T-55/08 *Union des associations européennes de football (UEFA) v. Commission*, judgment of 17 February 2011; and Case T-68/08 *Fédération Internationale de Football Association (FIFA) v. Commission*, judgment of 17 February 2011. See also the General Court's Press Release No. 9/11 'Judgments in Cases T-385/07, T-55/08 and T-68/08 FIFA and UEFA v Commission' Luxembourg, 17 February 2011.

Directive) provides a possibility for Member States to draw up a list of events which they consider to be of major importance for society to ensure that broadcasters under its jurisdiction do not broadcast on an exclusive basis in such a way as to deprive a substantial proportion of the public in that Member State of the possibility of following such events via live coverage or deferred coverage on free television.[121] According to Article 14(2), Member States exercising this possibility are to send the list of 'designated events' to the Commission for confirmation that they are compatible with EU law.

The Commission approved the lists sent to it via this procedure by the Belgian federal authorities, and the UK. The list included, among other events, all matches of the FIFA World Cup and the UEFA EURO football championship. The applicants, FIFA and UEFA, argued that all such matches cannot be regarded as events of major importance for the public of those States.

The General Court referred to Article 10 of the European Convention of Human Rights on the freedom of expression, including the right to receive information, as a fundamental right capable of justifying the restrictions on the economic freedoms guaranteed by the Treaty. As the measures contemplated in Article 14 of the AVMS Directive are intended to protect the right to information and to ensure wide public access to television broadcasts of national or non-national events of major importance for society, they were held justified by overriding reasons in public interest. The General Court further clarified that the World Cup and EURO are to be regarded as single events rather than as a series of individual events divided into 'prime' and 'non-prime' matches (the semi-finals, the final and the matches involving the relevant national team of the country in question are considered as 'prime') or into 'gala' and 'non-gala' (opening match and final match are 'gala') matches. It cannot be specified in advance, at the time when the national lists are drawn up or broadcasting rights acquired, which matches will be decisive for the subsequent stages of those competitions or which ones may affect the fate of a given national team. For that reason, the Court held that a Member State's decision to consider that all of the matches of those competitions are of major importance for society may be justified. The restrictions on freedom to provide services under Article 56 TFEU and freedom of establishment under Article 49 TFEU were therefore found to be compatible with EU law.

An obvious question after these judgments is their effect on the commercial value of the property rights for the listed events held by FIFA and UEFA. The General Court admits that the legislation in question and the contested Commission decisions are liable to negatively affect the property rights, but that such fact does not destroy their commercial value as FIFA and UEFA are not obliged to sell them on whatever conditions they can obtain. Earlier in the judgment it was held that 'the principle of protection of the fundamental right to property under [Union] law is not absolute but must be viewed in relation to its social function'. As in this balance of social interests and property rights

[121] Directive 2010/13/EU of the European Parliament and of the Council of 10 March 2010 on the coordination of certain provisions laid down by law, regulation or administrative action in Member States concerning the provision of audiovisual media services (Audiovisual Media Services Directive), OJ L 95, 15/4/2010, pp. 1–24.

the former prevailed, it is interesting for a moment to think of this reference to social function as a reference to specificity of sport. Indeed, the AVMS Directive (much like its predecessor, Council Directive 89/552/EEC) was adopted primarily with sport in mind and the designated events are usually exclusively sports events. In this sense, the judgments quite paradoxically represent a victory for specificity of sport, but a loss for FIFA and UEFA, the main proponents of the concept. Deciding a case in favour of the socio-cultural function of sport will not necessarily produce benefits for sporting organisations. Specificity of sport is therefore a double-edged sword.

4.10 Joined Cases C-403/08 and C-429/08 *Murphy* [2011]

4.10.1 Facts of the Case

The English Football Association Premier League (FAPL) grants its licensees the right to live broadcasting and exploitation of Premier League matches within the specific country-wide territory on an exclusive 3-year basis. In order to safeguard their exclusivity and the value of the rights for FAPL, the broadcasters are at the same time required by their license agreements to prevent their broadcasts from being viewed outside the specified broadcasting area. In practice, this is done by requiring broadcasters to encrypt the programme-carrying satellite signal and restrict the circulation of authorised decoder cards only to persons residing within their exclusive territory.

In one of the *Murphy* joined cases,[122] FAPL and other applicants brought proceedings against suppliers whose business included importing and marketing in the United Kingdom foreign decoder cards and equipment used to access foreign satellite transmissions of live Premier Leagues football matches in pubs and bars.[123] They also brought an action against four pub operators who used foreign decoder cards to screen live Premier League matches.[124] In another joined case, unhappy with the price that exclusive broadcaster in UK charged pubs for its Sky Sports services,[125] one of those pub operators, Karen Murphy, obtained a cheaper decoder from Greece and begun showing Premier League matches in her Portsmouth pub. In criminal proceedings launched against her in the UK, she was fined on the ground that the Greek decoder card was an illicit access device. Ms Murphy appealed to the High Court, which then referred the case to the Court under Article 267 TFEU.[126]

[122] Joined Cases C-403/08 and C-429/08 *FAPL and others v. QC Leisure and others;* and *Karen Murphy v Media Protection Services Ltd.*, judgment of 4 October 2011. Section 4.10 on the Murphy case has been analysed in detail by Pijetlovic and Nyman-Metcalf 2013.

[123] Case C-403/08 *Football Association Premier League v QC Leisure YouTube.* that was joined with Case C-429/08 *Karen Murphy v Media Protection Services Ltd.*

[124] Ibid.

[125] The price was ca. £1000 per month.

[126] Case C-429/08 *Karen Murphy v Media Protection Services Ltd.* that was joined with Case C-403/08 *Football Association Premier League v QC Leisure YouTube*.

The FAPL and others complained that the practice of importing and marketing foreign decoders, as well as their use, constituted an infringement of their rights under the provisions of national law[127] designed to implement Conditional Access Directive (CAD) 98/84[128] and of the copyright in various artistic and musical works, films and sound recordings embodied in the Premier League match coverage. The main issue in these cases was whether Articles 56 TFEU and 101 TFEU preclude national legislation and licence agreements that prohibit the use of foreign decoding devices.

4.10.2 Analytical Overview of the Judgment

4.10.2.1 Preliminary Issues Under the Conditional Access Directive: Notions of 'Illicit Device' 'Abuse of Rights' Under the EU Law

The main objective of the CAD is the approximation of Member State laws concerning measures against illicit devices giving unauthorised access to broadcasting services.[129] Under Article 4 CAD, Member States are obliged to take measures to prohibit on their territory

> (a) the manufacture, import, distribution, sale, rental or possession for commercial purposes of illicit devices; (b) the installation, maintenance or replacement for commercial purposes of an illicit device [...]

On the other hand, Article 3 CAD specifies that Member States are not allowed *for these reasons* to restrict the provision of protected services (broadcasting) which originate in another Member State or the free movement of conditional access devices (decoders). Should they do so, they have to provide an objective justification (i.e. *a different reason* from those listed under Article 4 CAD) for their restrictive measures, and satisfy the requirements of proportionality to escape falling foul of TFEU free movement provisions. When such restrictions on economic freedoms originate from agreements or practices of private undertakings they have to comply with the competition provisions of the TFEU. The distinction between a decoding device having the status of a 'conditional access device' and one falling under the definition of 'illicit device' therefore plays a crucial role in the initial assessment of the legality of Member States' measures that restrict commercial activities in decoding equipment. The sole difference between the two is that the latter is used *without the authorisation of the service provider.*[130]

---

[127] See sections 297(1) and 298 of the UK Copyright, Designs and Patents Act of 1988, as amended.

[128] Council Directive 98/84/EC on the legal protection of services based on, or consisting of, conditional access. OJ L 320/54, 28.11.1998.

[129] Article 1 of CAD.

[130] Article 2(c) and (e) of CAD.

The Grand Chamber of the Court first answered questions concerning the meaning of these crucial concepts under the factual circumstances *in casu*. It found that a foreign decoding device does not constitute an 'illicit device' within the meaning of Article 2(e) CAD.[131] This is because 'illicit device' within the meaning of the CAD covers access to broadcasting 'free of charge' (see para 6 the preamble), and placing it on market 'without the authorisation of the service provider'. In *Murphy*, decoding devices were purchased in Greece and remuneration had been duly paid to the Greek service provider who authorised their marketing within its exclusive broadcasting territory. Importantly, this conclusion was not affected by the fact that the foreign decoders were procured by provision of a false name and address, and that they were used in breach of a contractual limitation permitting use only for private purposes.[132] In essence, the Court here, in the framework of CAD, added another specific use of EU-conferred rights to the list of those it accepted as not constituting 'abuse of rights'.

The prohibition of abuse of rights has been recognised as a general principle of EU law, although the Court's approach in most areas has been to treat it solely as an interpretative principle (which is not directly effective without national anti-abuse measures), rather than as a self-standing general principle.[133] In *Emsland-Stärke*, the Commission contended that the prohibition of abuse of rights is a general principle that exists in the legal systems of all Member States and that it has already been applied in the case law of the Court without being expressly recognised as a general principle.[134] However, the Court did not recognise it expressly as such in *Emsland-Stärke*. Only later, in *Kofoed*, did the Court hold that the anti-abuse provision in Directive 90/434 *reflects the general [EU] law principle that abuse of rights is prohibited*.[135] After a series of incoherent cases, the current position is that an act of an individual who is exercising fundamental freedoms under the Treaty can only constitute abuse if the two cumulative conditions laid down by the Court in *Emsland-Stärke* are met:

> A finding of an abuse requires, first, a combination of objective circumstances in which, despite formal observance of the conditions laid down by the [EU] rules, the purpose of those rules has not been achieved. It requires, second, a subjective element consisting in the intention to obtain an advantage from the [EU] rules by creating artificially the conditions laid down for obtaining it.[136]

The entire CAD could possibly be seen as an anti-abuse measure, for it listed the specific situations when Member States can and must restrict abuses of freedom of

[131] Joined Cases C-403/08 and C-429/08 *Murphy*, paras 62–67.

[132] Ibid. paras 68–74.

[133] Generally, there are three types of abuses of rights under EU law: circumvention (or U-turn transactions), fraud and misuse. For explanation of the concepts see, for example, Kjellgren 2000, pp. 179–194.

[134] Case C-110/99, *Emsland-Stärke GmbH v Hauptzollamt Hamburg-Jonas*, (2000) ECR I-1569.

[135] Case C-321/05, *Hans Markus Kofoed v Skatteministeriet* (2007), ECR I-05795, para 38.

[136] Case C-110/99, *Emsland-Stärke*, paras 52–53.

movement: namely, in the case of 'illicit devices'. In such cases, traders cannot rely on economic freedoms to claim their rights under the TFEU because, according to a 'ghost provision' of the CAD, that would amount to abuse of rights. Therefore, the Court did not have to fall back on the general case law and *Emsland-Stärke* criteria discussed above, but instead focused on the meaning of 'illicit device'. That, in itself, was an exercise in finding out whether there was an abuse of rights in the area as specifically covered by the CAD. Deciding that the decoders were not illicit devices meant that traders were not abusing their rights, and vice versa.

Against this background, the Court in *Murphy* could have gone either way in determining whether the provision of a false name and address to procure decoders and their supply to another EU Member State constituted abuse of rights. It could have easily interpreted the concept of 'illicit device' under Article 2(e) CAD as meaning that the authorisation given by the Greek broadcaster was not genuine and valid because the broadcaster was unaware that the devices would be used outside its authorised territory and in breach of a contractual limitation permitting the use of decoders only for private purposes. Authorization implies conscious agreement, and not an agreement given on the basis of a fraudulent misrepresentation by another party. This is a fundamental rule of any law of obligations and the Greek broadcaster could have brought an action for breach of contract before a national court. It is true that placing devices on the market was authorised, but 'authorization' is an expandable concept and can be interpreted as entailing conditions under which the devices are placed on the market. The broadcaster was relying on the terms of the contract for the conditions of use and had given an authorization only for a particular purpose.

Thus, the outcome of the case could have been different, and in reaching such a different outcome the Court would not even have had to apply counter-textual interpretation. Instead, the decoders procured by the provision of a false name and address were considered 'conditional access devices' within the meaning of Article 2(c) CAD. As seen above, Article 3 CAD neither imposes a mandatory requirement on such devices, nor prohibits EU Member States from restricting their use. Having found that the CAD does not harmonise national legislation prohibiting their use,[137] the Court did not further elaborate on the legality of the devices and instead turned its attention to the compatibility of UK measures under the TFEU provisions on the internal market.

4.10.2.2 Existence of the Restriction Under Article 56 TFEU

Examining the case under Article 56 TFEU, the Court did not take much time to find that the national legislation conferring legal protection on contested contractual clauses in broadcasting agreements restricts the freedom to provide services by preventing the access to service by recipients outside the Member State of

[137] This finding indirectly subsequently freed Ms Murphy from criminal liability in the national proceedings. See *Murphy v. Media Protection Services Ltd* [2012] EWHC 466 (Admin).

broadcast.[138] It then considered the applicability of two objective justifications put forth: protection of intellectual property rights and encouraging the public to attend football matches at stadia in person.

4.10.2.3 Objective Justification: Intellectual Property Protection

The protection of intellectual property rights was accepted as a part of the public policy derogation already in previous case law.[139] Sporting events were held in *Murphy* as forming the subject of that protection. Importantly, however, the starting point in reaching this conclusion was the Court's refusal to classify Premier League matches as 'works' within the meaning of the Copyright Directive as they were not original product of the author's own intellectual creation. It was also made clear that the EU has no other basis in intellectual property legislation to protect sporting events.[140] But the Court then held sporting events to be of such unique and original character as to make them capable of being transformed into a subject-matter of protection by intellectual property law.[141] Thereafter the Court made a reference to Article 165(1) for the second time ever.[142] Accordingly, it was held permissible for the Member States to employ various means to protect sporting events, including by virtue of protection of intellectual property rights, even if they restrict free movement, as long as the restrictions are proportionate.

Thus the judgment made it clear that EU law has no basis to protect any form of intellectual property of sporting events, but since sporting events are so specific in their nature, Member States' legislation may provide such protection. Article 165(1) TFEU played a role in opening this avenue of protection by domestic legal systems. It must be acknowledged that it has not been a decisive role as the Court already held the sporting events to be of a unique and original character capable of forming a subject of protection *before* making a reference to Article 165(1) TFEU. However, constructing the subsequent reasoning around the Treaty-based obligation to take into account specificity of sport and its social and educational functions certainly strengthened the soundness of the argument and furnished it with a firm constitutional support. Even before the coming into force of the Lisbon Treaty amendments the Court would probably have reached the same conclusion based on the 'specific nature of sports' alone, a concept entirely based on the state of affairs in the sporting industry and their recognition in the Court's jurisprudence. Objectives specific to the sporting industry accepted as legitimate before the inclusion of Article 165(1) TFEU were, for example, ensuring regularity of competitions,[143] maintaining the balance

[138] Ibid. paras 85–89.

[139] Paragraph 94 of Joined Cases C–403/08 and C–429/08 *Murphy*.

[140] Ibid. paras 96–99.

[141] Ibid. para 100.

[142] Ibid. para 101. The first time the Court mentioned Article 165(1) was in C-325/08 *Bernard*.

[143] Case C-176/96 *Lehtonen and Castors Braine* [2000] ECR I-2681.

between clubs by preserving a certain degree of equality and uncertainty as to results, encouraging the recruitment and training of young players[144] and combating doping in order for competitive sport to be conducted fairly including the need to safeguard equal chances for athletes, athletes' health, the integrity and objectivity of competitive sport and ethical values in sport.[145] After *Murphy*, the protection of intellectual property rights of sporting events can be added to the list of aims accepted as legitimate in the interpretation and enforcement of the EU law in the area of sport. The difference between pre- and post-Article 165(1) TFEU methodology in generating this list is the introduction of the constitutional nature of the obligation to take into consideration the specificity of the sport, as opposed to a loose obligation not delineated in clear and express terms in either the Treaty or the Court's jurisprudence that does not have a strict precedential value. This part of the judgement has not yet affected the interpretation of intellectual property legislation at EU level. However, by including sporting events in the derogation based on intellectual property protection, it has slightly broadened the scope of that derogation under the EU free movement law.

The *Murphy* case also illustrates that the restrictions do not necessarily have to originate from sporting bodies to benefit from the legitimate aim recognised on the basis of specificity of sport. An objective worthy of protection is to be taken as such regardless of who adopts the restrictive measures as long as the infringing party can be considered an addressee under the internal market provisions. This particular justification, placed within the broader derogation of intellectual property rights protection, is rooted in the specific nature of sporting events in general (as opposed to being confined to particular sporting events) and the interpretation of EU law in accordance with Article 165(1) TFEU, so as to allow for proportionate national law to be consistent with the EU free movement provisions.

The proportionality of a measure taken at the national level to protect intellectual property in sporting events was emphasised by the Court in para 105 of the *Murphy* case. On the facts of the case, the restrictions in broadcasting agreements were held to be disproportionate. The specific subject-matter of the intellectual property did not guarantee the rights holders concerned the opportunity to demand the highest possible remuneration. Protection of intellectual property rights which included payment of a premium by broadcasters to obtain absolute territorial protection partitioned national markets and maintained artificial price differences, and went beyond what is necessary for 'appropriate remuneration' to the right holders.[146] Hence, a premium paid in exchange for territorial exclusivity in itself would form a part of 'appropriate remuneration' and would be proportionate, but only if that exclusivity is not accompanied by export prohibitions on decoding devices granting absolute territorial protection. In other words, the system of sole licensed broadcaster per territory which encrypts programme-carrying signal is

---

144 Case C-415/93 *Bosman* and Case C-325/08 *Bernard*.

145 Case 519/04 *Meca-Medina*.

146 Paragraphs 105–117.

allowed, but restricting trade in decoder devices on the top of such territorial exclusivity is not. The possibility of provision of cross-border services to TV viewers in other Member States should not be affected by exclusivity clauses in broadcasting agreements. The Court followed the opinion of the Advocate General in the case who considered that offsetting the price differences between Member States by trade is a part of the idea behind the internal market and marketing the broadcasting rights by the Premier League on this basis amounts to 'profiting from the elimination of the internal market'.[147]

There is no clearly recognisable pattern regarding the intensity of the proportionality test carried out by the Court in different cases. Generally, the intensity will vary depending on the restriction in question. From the *Meca-Medina* case[148] it does not follow that the Court has given any special consideration to sport in this regard. Kaburakis et al. correctly note that the proportionality test applied in *Murphy* was stricter than the one carried out in *Bernard*,[149] in which the Court for the first time ever referred to Article 165(1) TFEU and it did so in the context of the required standard of application of the proportionality test.[150] This reference was omitted at the proportionality stage of analysis in *Murphy* because there were no specificities and social and educational functions of sport involved and the issues considered were strictly commercial.

4.10.2.4 Objective Justification: Encouraging the Public to Attend Matches

UEFA's Regulations governing the implementation of Article 48 of the UEFA Statutes allow, but do not require, national associations to set a two-and-a-half-hour period on Saturdays or Sundays during which no live football matches can be transmitted. The purpose of this so-called 'closed period' or 'blocked hours' rule is to ensure that people are not deterred from going to the stadiums to watch local matches, or participate in amateur or youth matches on the account of live transmission.[151] The Football Association in England designated this closed period for Saturday afternoons. As required by the UEFA rules, this is the time corresponding to the domestic fixture schedule when the majority of the games in the top national leagues are played. The local broadcasters are required to respect this rule by the terms of their license agreements. Also, national associations are required to observe blocked hours in their agreements with broadcasters when selling in the territory matches from other national associations that have designated their own closed periods.

[147] Paragraph 192 of her Opinion in Joined Cases C-403/08 and C-429/08 *Murphy*.

[148] Case C-519/04 *David Meca-Medina and Igor Majcen v. Commission* [2006] ECR I-6991.

[149] Kaburakis et al. 2012, p. 313.

[150] See para 40 of Case C-325/08 *Bernard*. For discussion see Pijetlovic 2010, pp. 862–867.

[151] Opinion of AG in Joined Cases C-403/08 and C-429/08 *Murphy*, para 206.

FAPL claimed that the importation of decoder cards would make it impossible to enforce closed periods. But the Court rightfully dismissed this argument in para 123 saying that:

> [...] even if the objective of encouraging such attendance of stadiums by the public were capable of justifying a restriction on the fundamental freedoms suffice it to state that compliance with the aforementioned rule can be ensured, in any event, by incorporating a contractual limitation in the licence agreements between the right holders and the broadcasters, under which the latter would be required not to broadcast those Premier League matches during closed periods. It is indisputable that such a measure proves to have a lesser adverse effect on the fundamental freedoms than application of the restriction at issue in the main proceedings.

It is indeed far less restrictive, and yet as effective, to contractually oblige foreign broadcasters to respect the sellers' local rules on closed periods.

Regarding the precedential value of the justification put forth, the Court left us without a clear indication on whether the goal of encouraging the public to attend football stadiums and participate in matches was capable of justifying restrictions. Its wording 'even if the objective of encouraging such attendance of stadiums by the public were capable of justifying a restriction' would suggest that it is not. But the Court then goes on to dismiss the proportionality of the measure (which is not necessary for objectives not considered worthy of protection). The reason for this ambiguity in analysis might be that the Court did not necessarily have to be more specific as the restrictions themselves were easily proven disproportionate; the outcome of the analysis would have been the same in either case. Unlike the Court, the Advocate General seems to have accepted the attendance at stadiums and participation in matches as capable of constituting a legitimate goal under EU internal market law.[152] It is important to note here that in assessing the value of the objective the Advocate General relied on Article 165 TFEU but the Court did not. Siding with the Court on this issue, it is submitted that encouraging attendance at stadiums and participation in sporting activities should not be held in such high regard as worthy of protection at the expense of free movement and partitioning of internal market. Merely creating opportunities for the general public to engage in sports participation and attendance at stadiums is sufficient. Once the opportunities exist, even the public health argument would not justify a different conclusion. People usually like to de-stress during weekends and the choice of how should be entirely up to them, as long as choices exist. Some prefer staying at home and being far from football crowds and socialising; who is to say that this might not be a more suitable personal health choice for both mental and physical workers. Besides, attendance at stadiums, participation in matches and watching a live transmission are three qualitatively different activities that are poor substitutes for one another.[153]

Furthermore, under the contemporary model of financing employed by the clubs in the Premier League, revenues from gate receipts are by far superseded by revenues derived from the sales of media rights and are no longer crucial to the

[152] This follows from paras 206–210 of her Opinion.

[153] Ibid. (suggested in para 209).

financial survival of the clubs.[154] But in lower football leagues, or in other sports, gate receipts still represent a major part of the clubs' budgets and the Court might have been more receptive towards the justification put forth if the arguments were repackaged and objective renamed as, for example, a solidarity mechanism, enhancing competitive balance between leagues, or improving training conditions for young talent (given that clubs in lower leagues are a breeding ground for young talent). So, protecting gate receipts of the lower division clubs by closed periods for reasons such as solidarity and competitive balance by means of blocked hours is an objective likely to be accepted by the Court, but restricting free movement and partitioning the internal market with the objective to encourage public attendance at stadiums and participation in sport—which the public can anyway do at will—should not be given the status of justification in EU law.

In either case, accepting the objective as legitimate does not mean that the contested rule is in accordance with the Treaty provisions. The rule still has to be suitable and proportionate. To demonstrate suitability in this particular case would be a challenging task, to say the least, especially in the light of the intensity of the application of the proportionality test as suggested by the Advocate General. She assumed that the blocked hours rule might have been designed at least in part to safeguard the economic interests of Premier League clubs by partitioning the internal market and considered that 'a particularly strict test is therefore to be applied to the demonstration of the need for closed periods'.[155] Then she seems to have suggested that using closed periods to attain *any* objective can hardly ever be suitable because economic evidence and practice from other countries is heavily weighted towards the conclusion that the attendance at stadiums and sport participation is not affected by live transmission.[156] Thus, even the public health, solidarity, competitive balance and any other initially accepted legitimate objective, would all be predestined to fail. As a matter of sound legal advice, the Advocate General ultimately left the burden for FAPL to prove that different conditions prevailed in English football which necessarily required protection by means of closed periods and which would in turn justify a different conclusion on the point of suitability of the restricting rule. The strictness of the application of proportionality makes any such burden particularly onerous as the FAPL evidence would have to show that live transmissions have '*substantial detrimental effects* on attendance at matches and/or participation in football matches in order for enforcement of the closed periods to be able to prevail over the adverse effects on the internal market'.[157]

[154] See Deloitte Annual Report of Football Finance (2011).

[155] Paragraph 208 of her Opinion.

[156] Ibid. para 209 reads: '[...] in an investigation of the closed periods under competition law the Commission found that only 10 of 22 associations had actually adopted a closed period. No closed periods were adopted in France, Germany, Italy and Spain, or in Northern Ireland, that is to say, within the sphere of influence of English football. Furthermore, in Germany today all Bundesliga matches are evidently transmitted live without attendance at matches in the top two leagues suffering as a result'.

[157] Paragraph 210 of her Opinion in Joined Cases C-403/08 and C-429/08 *Murphy*.

4.10.2.5 Competition Law Aspects

Unsurprisingly, the Court confirmed the result obtained under the free movement provisions: clauses in the exclusive license agreements which include an obligation on broadcasters not to supply decoding devices outside their exclusive territories restrict competition *by object* and are prohibited by terms of Article 101(1) TFEU.[158] Even though the restraint to trade under both national legislation and the broadcasting license agreements was identical and posed identical legal questions, the national legislation was examined under free movement law, and clauses in agreements under EU competition law, the latter set of provisions being addressed to private undertakings and the former to the Member States. This was merely a technicality enabled by the specific circumstances of the case. Had there not been any national legislation on the subject, and the restrictions originated from a sporting body, a single source, it would have been possible to bring those restrictions in private agreements under the scope of internal market rules. The result would be the same as for national legislation. In that case, the Court would refer to its findings under free movement to say that there is no need to answer the competition law questions, as it did in *Bosman*. But had the Court found no restriction under the internal market law, it would have to examine the case under competition law.

The competition law aspects of *Murphy* are discussed in Sect. 5.5.4.4. As parts of the case provide contribution to the convergence between the two sets of TFEU economic provisions, Sect. 6.4 will look at the relevant paragraphs in the light of the convergence theory.

4.10.2.6 Protecting Copyrights and Associated Works Under the Copyright Directive

Having found that the EU internal market and competition law principles require that a European citizen should be able to purchase a cheaper decoder card from another Member State to gain access to foreign satellite transmissions, the Court answered a set of questions regarding the use of the broadcast once they are received. Although the live transmission was not subject to copyright, the associated works such as the opening video sequence, the Premier League anthem, pre-recorded films showing highlights of recent Premier League matches and various graphics were.[159] The reproduction within the memory of a satellite decoder and on a television screen to enable the broadcasts to be transmitted and received constituted ‘reproduction’ within the meaning of Article 2(e) of the Copyright Directive, but since the reproduction fulfilled the exemption conditions under Article 5(1) of that directive, (*inter alia,* it was temporary and transient and had no independent economic significance) it did not require the authorisation of the copyright holder.[160] However, with regard to the works that are ‘communicated to

[158] Joined Cases C-403/08 and C-429/08 *Murphy*, paras 134–146.

[159] Ibid. para 149.

[160] Ibid. para 182.

the public' within the meaning of Article 3(1) of the Copyright Directive, the transmission of broadcast works to a new public (i.e. a public which was *not taken into account by the authors of the protected works when they authorised their use by the communication to the original public*) constituted a new communication to the public.[161] The Court here assumes that when authors 'authorise a broadcast of their works, they consider, in principle, only the owners of television sets who, either personally or within their own private or family circles, receive the signal and follow the broadcasts'.[162] This might indeed hold true in all other broadcasts but certain sports broadcasts in which the right owners are well-aware of the fact that their copyrighted material is going to be used widely in the public establishments, pubs in particular. The transmission of the copyrighted works in pub settings was considered to have satisfied the formula of a new 'communication to the public' and thus required authorisation.[163] So the Court distinguished between the authorisation requirement for use in private homes and the use containing element of 'communication to public' which includes transmission of broadcast works in places where people gather such as cafés, restaurants, pubs, clubs, offices, airplanes, etc. However, the key to the proper reading of the judgment should not be the objective test related to the place where the works are shown, but the subjective test related to the public 'considered by the authors when they authorised the broadcasts of their works'. The Court could not have been unaware of the fact that authors of the works *in casu*, the FAPL, already take into account and know that exclusive broadcasters will be serving both private homes and pubs. It is therefore submitted that pub-clients of the broadcasters should not need any additional authorisation from the authors of works, whether they are domestic or foreign clients. Such authorisation is clearly given to exclusive broadcasters for both types of clients when the rights are sold, and the public in the public house should therefore constitute 'original public' when it comes to broadcasting of Premier League. Recital 17 of the Satellite Broadcasting Directive stands in support of this interpretation. It provides that 'in arriving at the amount of the payment to be made for the rights acquired, the parties should take account of *all aspects* of the broadcast, such as the actual audience, the potential audience and the language version'.[164] Such aspects also include the copyrights associated with the broadcast.

4.10.2.7 Final Remark

Ever since the Advocate General delivered her opinion, it was thought that liberalising the service market for satellite transmission of sports, and as a necessary corollary, creating an internal market for trade in decoder cards, could result in

161 Ibid. para 197.

162 Ibid. para 198.

163 Ibid. paras 199 and 207.

164 Council Directive 93/83/EEC of 27 September 1993 on the coordination of certain rules concerning copyright and rights related to copyright applicable to satellite broadcasting and cable retransmission *OJ L 248 ,06/10/1993* pp. 0015–0021.

reorganisation of the entire broadcasting sector in Europe,[165] as without the protection by national segmentation, the rights holders would probably have to find a new way to sell their rights to make up for the loss of profits resulting from parallel trade in decoder cards. It was further thought that the judgement may 'have serious implications for European football [...] which might lose a significant share of their profits from the sale of broadcasting rights'.[166] Looking at the staggering figures in post-*Murphy* sale of broadcasting rights by the FAPL (for seasons 2013–2016),[167] these concerns now appear unjustified. Restricting the commentary included in broadcasting signal to different language versions might have created 'a sufficiently effective practical delimitation of the markets in order to continue to serve the different national markets at different prices'.[168]

References

Barnard C (2010) The substantive law of the EU, 3rd edn. Oxford University Press, Oxford

Baquero Cruz J (2002) Between competition and free movement: the economic constitutional law of the European Community. Hart Publishing, Oxford

Blanpain R (2003) The legal status of sportsmen and sportswomen under international, European and Belgian national and regional law. Kluwer Law International, The Hague

Blanpain R, Inston R (1996) The Bosman case: the end of the transfer system? Sweet & Maxwell, London

Doukas D (2012) The sky is not the (only) limit—sports broadcasting without frontiers and the Court of Justice: comment on Murphy. Eur Law Rev 37:605–626

Drolet J-C (2009) Extra time: are the new FIFA transfer rules doomed? In: Gardiner S, Parrish R, Siekmann R (eds) EU, sport, law and policy. TMC Asser Press, The Hague, pp 167–190

Gardiner S, Welch R (2000) Show me the money: regulation of the migration of professional sportsmen in post-*Bosman* Europe. In: Caiger A, Gardiner S (eds) Professional sport in the EU: regulation and re-regulation. T.M.C. Asser Press, The Hague, pp 107–126

Kaburakis A, Lindholm J, Rodenberg R (2012) British pubs, decoder cards and the future of intellectual property licensing after Murphy. Columbia J Eur Law 18:307–322

Késenne S (2009) The Bosman case and European football. In: Andreff W, Szymanski S (eds) Handbook on the economics of sport. Edward Elgar, Cheltenham, pp 636–642

Kjellgren A (2000) On the border of abuse—the jurisprudence of the European Court of Justice on circumvention, fraud and other misuses of community law. Eur Bus Law Rev 11:179–194

Lindholm J (2010) Case C-325/08, *Olympique Lyonnais SASP* v. *Olivier Bernard and Newcastle United UFC*, judgment of the Court of Justice (Grand Chamber) of 16 March 2010, not yet reported. Common Market Law Rev 47:1187–1197

Miettinen S, Parrish R (2008) Nationality discrimination in community law: an assessment of UEFA regulations governing player eligibility for European club competitions (the Home-Grown Player Rule). Entertain Sports Law J 5(2). http://www2.warwick.ac.uk/fac/soc/law/elj/eslj/issues/volume5/number2/miettinen_parrish

Parrish R (2003) Sports law and policy in the European Union. Manchester University Press, Manchester

---

[165] Ward and Amor 2012, pp. 86–90.

[166] Doukas 2012, p. 626.

[167] See Sect. 1.2.1.

[168] Opinion of AG in Joined Cases C-403/08 and C-429/08 *Murphy*, para 202.

Parrish R, Miettinen S (2008) Sporting exception in European Union law. T.M.C. Asser Press, The Hague

Pijetlovic K (2010) Another classic of EU sports jurisprudence: legal implications of *Olympique Lyonnais SASP v. Olivier Bernard and Newcastle UFC* (C-325/08). Eur Law Rev 35:858–869

Pijetlovic K, Nyman-Metcalf K (2013) Liberalising the market for satellite transmission: interplay between intellectual property rights, specificity of sport and TFEU economic provisions in Murphy (joined cases C-403/08 and C-429/08). Int Sports Law J 13:82–96

Semmelmann C (2008) The future role of the non-competition goals in the interpretation of Article 81 EC. Glob Antitrust Rev 1:15–47

Van den Bogaert S (2005) Practical regulation of the mobility of sportsmen in the EU post bosman. Kluwer Law International, The Netherlands

Ward C, Amor D (2012) Significant change to the European media rights landscape. Comput Telecommun Law Rev 18:86–90

Weatherill S (2010) The *Olivier Bernard* case: how, if at all, to fix compensation for training young players? Int Sports Law J 1–2:3–6

Chapter 5
EU Competition Law and Sport

Contents

5.1 Article 101 TFEU 150
  5.1.1 Prohibition Provision: Article 101(1) TFEU 150
  5.1.2 Exemption Provision: Article 101(3) TFEU 154
  5.1.3 Nullity Provision: Article 101(2) 157
  5.1.4 Commercialisation Agreements 157
5.2 Article 102 TFEU 158
  5.2.1 Definition of Relevant Market 158
  5.2.2 Establishing Dominance 159
  5.2.3 Abuse of Dominant Position 160
  5.2.4 Objective Justification and the Efficiency Defence 161
5.3 Oligopolistic Market Structures and the Concept of Collective Dominance 162
  5.3.1 The Oligopoly Problem 162
  5.3.2 Collective Dominance 163
5.4 Simultaneous Application of Articles 101 and 102 TFEU 167
5.5 Articles 101 and 102 TFEU in the Sporting Context 168
  5.5.1 Basic Elements 168
  5.5.2 Relevant Market 170
  5.5.3 Collective Dominance 172
  5.5.4 Analytical Framework for Commercial Rules in Sport 173
  5.5.5 Analytical Framework for Regulatory Rules: C-519/04 *Meca-Medina* [2006] 179
5.6 Blocking Competing Organisations 187
  5.6.1 C-49/07 *MOTOE* [2008] 187
  5.6.2 Commission Investigation in *FIA/Formula One* Case 196
  5.6.3 Case C-250/92 *DLG* [1994] 199
5.7 Superdominance and Special Responsibility 202
  5.7.1 The Concept of Superdominance 203
  5.7.2 Special Responsibility of Dominant Undertakings: The Sliding Scale Approach 206
  5.7.3 The Content of Special Responsibility of Superdominant Sports Undertakings 208
5.8 Conclusion 211
References 212

K. Pijetlovic, *EU Sports Law and Breakaway Leagues in Football*,
ASSER International Sports Law Series, DOI 10.1007/978-94-6265-048-0_5

European Union competition provisions that apply to undertakings are set out in the Title VII, Chap. 1, Sect. 1.1, Articles 101–106 of the Treaty. Article 101 is the main instrument to control cartels between undertakings, Article 102 prohibits the abuse of a dominant position by one or more dominant undertakings, while the application of these two provisions (as well as other Treaty articles) to state measures in respect of public undertakings, undertakings granted special or exclusive rights and undertakings entrusted with services of general economic interest are regulated by Article 106 of the Treaty.

What follows in the sections below is a description of these articles, custom-tailored to suit the purpose of this volume. They will set up the framework for analysis of breakaway structures under Chap. 7, and focus on the application of competition law in the sporting context.

5.1 Article 101 TFEU

For the purposes of application of competition law provisions contained in Articles 101 and 102 of the Treaty, any entity engaged in an economic activity,[1] irrespective of its legal form and the way in which it is financed is categorised as an undertaking.[2] Together with Regulation 1/2003, Article 101 provides a principal tool to control anti-competitive behaviour by cartels in the Union. The legal rules in this article are divided into three functionally distinct paragraphs: the prohibition provision under para 1, the nullity provision under para 2, and the exemption provision under para 3 of the article.

5.1.1 Prohibition Provision: Article 101(1) TFEU

Article 101(1) prohibits agreements between undertakings, decisions by associations of undertakings, or concerted practices, which are considered capable of affecting trade between Member States and that have as their object (i.e., subjectively intend)

[1] Any activity consisting in offering goods or services on a given market is an 'economic activity'. See Case C-35/96 *Commission* v *Italy* [1998] ECR I-3851, para 36, and Joined Cases C-180/98 to C-184/98 *Pavlov and Others* [2000] ECR I-6451, para 75. In addition, in Case C-222/04 *Cassa di Risparmio di Firenze and Others* [2006] ECR I-289, paras 122 and 123, the Court stated that the fact that the offer of goods or services is made without profit motive does not prevent the entity which carries out those operations on the market from being considered an undertaking, since that offer exists in competition with that of other operators which do seek to make a profit.

[2] Case C-41/90 *Höfner and Elser* [1991] ECR I-1979, para 21, and Joined Cases C-264/01, C-306/01, C-354/01 and C-355/01 *AOK Bundesverband and Others* [2004] ECR I-2493, para 46. See also Guidelines on the Application of Article 81(3) OJ C 101 27.4.2004, para 22.

or effect (i.e., objectively cause)[3] the prevention, restriction, or distortion of competition within the common market. The term 'agreement' has a broad definition, and is inclusive of agreements between independent undertakings that might distort competition within the internal market, regardless of whether or not they constitute contracts under national laws, whether or not they are intended to be legally binding, whether they are in oral or in written form, and whether or not they provide sanctions for the breach.[4] Falling short of the 'agreement', mental consensus regarding conduct on the market that substitutes cooperation for the risks of competition is considered concerted practice,[5] while all conduct which is meant to coordinate the activities of the members of any association, in particular a trade association, will amount to a decision by an association of undertakings.[6] The object of the agreement is discerned by examining 'the aims pursued by the agreement [...] in the light of the economic context in which the agreement is to be applied', rather than looking at common intention of the parties.[7] Once the anti-competitive object of the agreement is established, there is no need to demonstrate its adverse effects on competition. The scope of this article is very broad since no actual and direct effect on trade is required and *prima facie* any agreement made may be caught by this provision. However, there are a number of exceptions within the framework of this provision, primarily for the agreements that restrict the competition by effect.

First, certain agreements are deemed harmless and never fall under Article 101(1) because they do not have an appreciable impact on trade between Member States.[8] This is known as the *de minimis* doctrine which automatically places agreements of minor importance outside of the scope of Article 101(1).[9]

---

[3] For the concept of 'effects on trade' see C-56/65 *Societe Technique Miniere v. Maschinenbau Ulm (STM)* [1966] ECR 235, para 7; and Case 56/64 *Consten and Grundig* [1966] ECR 299, para 27. See also Commission Notice—Guidelines on the effects on trade concept contained in Articles 81 and 82 of the Treaty, OJ C 101, 27.04.2004, pp. 81–96.

[4] See, in particular, Cases 56 and 58 *Etablissements Consten SA and Grunding-Verkaufs-GmbH v. Commission* [1966] ECR 299, Case *41/69 ACF Chemiefarma NV. v. Commission (the Quinine Cartel)* [1970] ECR 661, Case C-227/87 *Sandoz Prodotti Farmaceutici Spa. v. Commission* [1990] ECR I-45, and Case IV/30.804—Nuovo Cegam [1984] OJ L 99/29, [1984] 2 CMLR 484.

[5] Case 48/69 *ICI v. Commission* [1972] ECR 619, para 64.

[6] See, for example, Case 8/72 *Vereeniging van Cementhandelaren v. Commission* [1972] ERC 977.

[7] Cases 29 and 30/83 *Compagnie Royale Asturienne des Mines SA and Rheinzink GmbH v. Commission* [1984] ECR 1679, para 26; Case C-551/03 P *General Motors BV v. Commission* [2006] ECR I-3173, para 77; and Joined Cases C-501/06 P, C-513/06 P, C-515/06 P and C-519/06 P *GlaxoSmithKline Services and Others v. Commission and Others* [2009] ECR I-9291, para 58.

[8] Case 23/67 *Brasserie de Haecht SA v. Wilkin* [1967] ECR 407. For discussion on appreciable impact of agreements see Case 5/69 *Völk v Vervaecke* [1969] ECR 295.

[9] Under this principle, agreements are permissible between parties that do not collectively exceed 10 % of the relevant market, or 15 % in the case where the undertakings are not competitors, though certain agreements such as price fixing, output or sales limitations or market allocations are impermissible in all instances. See the Commission Notice on agreements of minor importance which do not appreciably restrict competition under Article 81(1) of the Treaty establishing the European Community (de minimis), OJ C 368/07, 22.12 2001.

Second, ancillary restraints, i.e., the restrictions on competition that are directly related and objectively necessary for the implementation of the main, non-restrictive transaction and are proportionate to it, fall outside of the ambit of the prohibition provision.[10] In *STM* the Court held that the term conferring exclusivity on a distributor may not infringe Article 101(1) if it seems 'really necessary for the penetration of a new area by an undertaking'.[11] In *Metro* the restrictions in a selective distribution scheme were held to fall outside of Article 101(1) where they satisfy objective qualitative criteria and are applied in non-discriminatory manner.[12] The closest analogy to breakaway structures is supplied by the *DLG* case decided in 1994 in the context of agriculture.[13] Therein, a cooperative purchasing association was permitted to place a restriction on their members' participation in alternative agricultural cooperatives, on the basis that the restriction in fact benefited competition and was necessary to protect legitimate goals necessary for the functioning of the cooperative. In the Court's own words:

> [a] provision in the statutes of a cooperative purchasing association, forbidding its members to participate in other forms of organized cooperation which are in direct competition with it, is not caught by the prohibition in Article [101(1)] of the Treaty, so long as the abovementioned provision is restricted to what is necessary to ensure that the cooperative functions properly and maintains its contractual power in relation to producers.[14]

The same test was carried out under Article 102 for the same restrictive provision in the statutes of the cooperative and the same result was reached.[15] Moreover, proportionate restrictions in franchising agreements designed to protect intellectual property rights of the franchisor, and to maintain the common identity of the franchise system,[16] as well as proportionate non-competition obligations on the vendor where they are necessary to effect the transfer of undertaking,[17] will not breach the prohibition provision. Whish referred to the type of ancillary restrains seen in these cases as 'commercial ancillarity' restraints because the restrictions on competition were ancillary to a legitimate *commercial* purpose.[18]

Third, in *Wouters* the Court introduced an exception, characterised by Monti as a 'European-style rule of reason'[19] and by Whish, perhaps more accurately, as a

---

[10] See Guidelines on the Application of Article 81(3) OJ C 101 27.4.2004, paras 28–31; and Case T-112/99 *Métropole télévision (M6) and others* [2001] ECR II-2459.

[11] Case 56/65 *Société La Technique Minière v. Maschinenbau Ulm GmbH* [1966] ECR 234.

[12] Case 26/76 *Metro (I)* [1977] ECR 1875.

[13] Case C-250/92 *Gøttrup-Klim e.a. Grovvareforeninger v Dansk Landbrugs Grovvareselskab AmbA* [1994] ECR I-5641.

[14] Ibid. para 45.

[15] Ibid. para 52.

[16] Case 161/84 *Pronuptia de Paris GmbH v Pronuptia de Paris Irmgard Schillgallis* [1986] ECR 353.

[17] Case 42/84 *Remia BV and Others v. Commission* [1985] ECR 2545.

[18] Whish 2009, p. 126.

[19] Monti 2002, pp. 1087–1088.

'regulatory ancillarity'.[20] The judgment does not really introduce the rule of reason in Article 101(1) because balancing of the pro- and anti-competitive effects of restrictions involves economic arguments on both sides, whereas *Wouters*[21] introduces the balancing of the Union's competition law objectives against the non-economic public interests that may or may not be a part of the Union's objectives in other areas. The *Wouters* test was confirmed in the sporting case of *Meca-Medina*.[22] Accordingly, certain types of agreements or decisions that restrict the commercial behaviour of undertakings do not violate the prohibition in Article 101(1) TFEU, if, because of their *context and objectives*, the restrictions in those agreements or decisions are *inherent* to, and *proportionate* for, the realisation of non-competition objectives.[23] From the scarce case law on regulatory ancillarity, it appears that the exception is applicable only in cases of regulatory restrictions imposed by collective private bodies in public interests, whether at national, European or global level. So far, the Court has applied it only to rules having a public law character deemed necessary for the proper organisation and (ethical) conduct of a certain profession. The private bodies that laid those restrictive rules down, the Bar of the Netherlands and the International Olympic Committee, derived their powers from national law and public international law, respectively. It is submitted that these facts do not imply that the framework developed under that case law cannot be used to accommodate other kinds of non-competition objectives, in particular those under policy-linking clauses of the Treaty, the importance of which has been enhanced by the Lisbon amendments.[24] To allow a reliance on the public interest defence for agreements concluded by private parties that do not derive their powers from public laws, especially private collective bodies such as the *Fédération Internationale de Football Association* (FIFA) and *Union des Associations Européennes de Football* (UEFA), in an area where no responsible public authority vested with powers to enforce the laws protecting those public interests exists,[25] is a necessary constitutional fine-tuning of the Union's competition law in view of the increase in private governance and self-regulation of certain sectors and the corresponding decrease in the private/public divide in EU law. It is noteworthy, however, that in the *ENIC* case concerning the UEFA rule prohibiting multiple ownership of clubs the Commission applied the

---

[20] Whish 2009, p. 126.

[21] Case C-309/99 *J.C.J Wouters, J.W. Savelbergh, Price Waterhouse Belastingadviseurs BV v. Algemene Raad van de Nederlandse Orde van Advocaten* [2002] ECR I-1577.

[22] Case C-519/04 *David Meca-Medina and Igor Majcen v. Commission* [2006] ECR I-6991.

[23] Paragraph 97 of Case C-309/99 *Wouters*, and para 42 of Case C-519/04 *Meca-Medina.*

[24] The EU for the first time has a duty to mainstream the policy objectives under Article 7 of the TFEU after Lisbon amendments: '[t]he Union shall ensure consistency between its policies and activities, taking all of its objectives into account and in accordance with the principle of conferral of powers.'

[25] However, the General Court held that where there is public authority with powers, for example, in relation to product safety, it is not for private undertakings to take the initiative to eliminate the products which are not safe. See case T-30/89 *Hilti*, para 118.

Wouters test and thus recognised that necessity. It will be demonstrated in Chap. 6, in the context of the sporting exception, that the foregoing considerations present one of the reasons why the principle of convergence ought to be formally introduced between competition and internal market provisions to the extent possible.[26] The Court has anyhow made some competition decisions on the basis of single market considerations, which then, due to misunderstandings and a lack of any reference to convergence, attracted a lot of criticism.[27]

Finally, the approach presented is in line with the Court's jurisprudence in the *Albany*, *Brentjens* and *Drijvende Bokken* cases, where it was held that agreements concluded in the context of collective bargaining between an employee and an employer association that improve working and employment conditions fall outside the scope of Article 101(1).[28] In addition, agreements between two or more persons forming a single economic entity, full-function joint ventures, individual employment agreements, and agreements between an agent and principal, will normally also fall outside the scope of prohibition provision.[29]

5.1.2 Exemption Provision: Article 101(3) TFEU

Agreements, decisions or practices that are incompatible with Article 101(1) but that satisfy the conditions under Article 101(3) of the Treaty, are valid and enforceable, with no prior decision to that effect being required.[30] The rationale behind the provision is connected to the fact that certain agreements may have both, pro-competitive and anti-competitive features. This recognition of the dual nature of economic effects usually involves complex economic analysis weighting the beneficial and harmful effects to determine whether the agreement qualifies for the exemption. Accordingly, those agreements, decisions or practices that fulfil the four conditions outlined in this provision will benefit from an exemption. Two positive conditions state that an agreement must improve the production or distribution of goods or promote technical or economic progress, and at the same time allow consumers a fair share of the resulting benefits. Two negative conditions

[26] See also Sect. 5.4.

[27] See, for example, discussion on Case 56/64 *Consten and Grundig* in Jones and Sufrin 2011, pp. 204–209.

[28] Case C-67/96 *Albany International BV v. Stichting Bedrijfspensioenfonds Textielindustrie* [1999] ECR I-5751, Cases C-115, 116 and 117/97 *Brentjens' Handelsonderneming BV v Stichting Bedrijfspensioenfonds voor de Handel in Bouwmaterialen* [1999] ECR I-6025 and Case C-219/97 *Drijvende Bokken* [1999] ECR I-6121.

[29] See Whish 2009, p. 146.

[30] See Article 1(2) of the Council Regulation (EC) No 1/2003 of 16 December 2002 on the implementation of the rules on competition laid down in Articles 81 and 82 of the Treaty OJ L 1, 04.01.2003, pp. 1–25.

state that an agreement cannot contain any restrictions that are not essential to the attainment of the objectives under agreement (i.e., disproportionate restrictions) and cannot lead to elimination of competition in substantial part of the product in question. Balancing of anti-competitive and pro-competitive effects is conducted exclusively within the framework laid down by Article 101(3),[31] and there is no scope in this provision for non-competition arguments that cannot be translated into economic efficiencies.[32] The Treaty, however, pursues a number of policy objectives and some of them must be taken into consideration in the pursuit of other policies. Under Article 101(3), public policy objectives may be taken into account only if they can be subsumed under one of its four conditions,[33] so as a supplement to economic benefits that the agreement generates. Jones and Sufrin argue that 'a pursuit of a sole consumer welfare objective may produce a result inconsistent with other Treaty policies [...] and actions should take account of certain policy-linking clauses, such as environmental protection, employment, culture, health, consumer protection, industrial policy and/or elimination of regional disparities.'[34] However, instead of going so far as to contaminate the exemption provision with the non-competition arguments, which could potentially create more problems than solutions, it is submitted, first, that in the light of the Court's case law and the Commission practice so far, Article 101(1) offers a more suitable analytical platform for policy integration. In fact, the framework established by *Wouters* is ideal to accommodate any other policy objectives in accordance with Article 7 TFEU and at the same time to stay faithful to the already established and persistently defended paradigms that balancing of anti-competitive and pro-competitive effects is conducted exclusively within the framework of

[31] See Commission Guidelines on application of Article 81(3), para 11, and Commission Guidelines on application of Article 101 on horizontal agreements para 20. See also Case T-65/98 *Van den Bergh Foods* [2003] ECR II-4653, para 107; and Case T-112/99 *Métropole télévision (M6) and others* [2001] ECR II-2459, para 74, where the General Court held that it is only in the framework of Article 101(3) that the pro- and anti-competitive aspects of a restriction may be weighed.

[32] See also Semmelmann 2008, p. 15. The Commission has accepted arguments on the basis of environmental protection in Case IV/F 1/36/718—CECED [2000] OJ L 187/47. In Case 26/76 *Metro (I)* [1977] ECR 1875, the Court has accepted that 'the establishment of supply forecasts for a reasonable period constitutes a stabilising factor with regard to the provision of employment which, since it improves general conditions of production, [...] comes within the framework of the objectives to which reference may be had pursuant to Article [101(3)]', para 43. The stabilising effect of an agreement on employment may translate into cost savings and other efficiency gains.

[33] Commission Guidelines on the application of Article 81(3), para 42. So far, the other policy objectives have been considered under the first condition. See also Commission White Paper on Modernisation of the rules implementing Articles 81 and 82 of the EC Treaty, Commission Programme No 99/027 1999/OJ C 132/1, which states that Article 101(3) is meant to 'provide a legal framework for the economic assessment of restrictive practices and not to allow the application of the competition rules to be set aside because of political considerations', para 56.

[34] Jones and Sufrin 2011, p. 245.

Article 101(3), and that only economic efficiencies are to be taken into account in that provision, including public policy objectives that can be subsumed under one of its four conditions. Namely, an agreement or decision that restricts competition but genuinely pursues a public policy objective under some of the policy-linking clauses[35] or outside of it,[36] that is not already protected by public regulation,[37] and that fulfils the *Wouters* criteria could thus escape the application of the prohibition provision. Should the outcome of the *Wouters* test be different, the agreement or decision will have to satisfy the four conditions of Article 101(3). If the public policy objective that it pursues can be translated into economic benefits, it should be taken into account also in the framework of the exemption provision although it is likely to fail the indispensability requirement in the cases where it already failed to satisfy the proportionality under *Wouters*. This is the true face of the European-style rule of reason and to interpret the exemption provision as suitable for purely non-competition arguments would have the effect of completely blurring the distinction between the different paragraphs of Article 101. As a second point, it is submitted that the consumer welfare standard includes the protection of goals in the public interest, and that consumers are not just concerned with having cheap, high-quality products and services. The European Union, correspondingly, has 'not only an economic but also a social purpose'[38] and this purpose ought to be reflected in the interpretation of the law, especially in regard to the issues involving policy linking clauses.

Although the Commission and the Court take the view that hard core cartels restricting competition by object are generally incapable of meeting the four conditions of Article 101(3),[39] this possibility nevertheless remains available.[40] Alternatively, restrictions on competition can also be considered compatible with Article 101 if they satisfy the criteria for application of one of the block exemption regulations that grants exemptions to certain categories of agreements.

---

[35] Such as, for example, clauses related to environmental protection in Article 11 TFEU, consumer protection in Article 12 TFEU, achieving high level of employment in Article 147(2) TFEU, respect for cultural diversities in Article 167(4) TFEU, health protection in Article 168(1) TFEU, competitiveness of the Union's industry in Article 173(3) TFEU, and regional development under Article 175 TFEU.

[36] See, for e.g., Case C-309/99 *J.C.J Wouters, J.W. Savelbergh, Price Waterhouse Belastingadviseurs BV v. Algemene Raad van de Nederlandse Orde van Advocaten* [2002] ECR I-1577; Case C-519/04 *David Meca-Medina and Igor Majcen v. Commission* [2006] ECR I-6991; Case C-250/92 *Gøttrup-Klim e.a. Grovvareforeninger v Dansk Landbrugs Grovvareselskab AmbA* [1994] ECR I-5641.

[37] See Case T-30/89 *Hilti v Commission* [1991] ECR II-1439.

[38] Case C-438/05 *Viking Line* [2007] ECR I-10779, para 79; Case C-341/05 *Laval* [2007] ECR I-11767, para 105.

[39] Cases C-403/04 P and 405/04 P *Sumitomo Metal Industries Ltd. v. Commission*, judgment of 25 January 2007, para 43.

[40] See Commission Decision in COMP/29.373—Visa International—Multilateral Interchange Fee [2000] OJ L 318/17, [2003] 4 CMLR 283.

5.1.3 Nullity Provision: Article 101(2)

Article 101(2) of the Treaty simply provides that agreements, which were caught by Article 101(1) and have not qualified for exemption under Article 101(3), are automatically void and unenforceable without the need for a prior decision to that effect.[41] This automatic nullity applies only to individual clauses in the agreement affected by the prohibition.[42]

5.1.4 Commercialisation Agreements

Agreements restricting competition can be vertical and horizontal. Commercialisation agreements[43] are a common type of horizontal restraints. They involve co-operation between competitors in the selling, distribution, or promotion of their interchangeable products and cover a wide spectrum of agreement. 'At one end of the spectrum are joint selling agreements that may lead to a joint determination of all commercial aspects related to the sale of the product, including price.'[44] As a rule of thumb, these agreements will almost always breach Article 101(1). At the other end of the spectrum, there are agreements that only address one specific commercialisation function, such as distribution, after-sales service, or advertising.[45] Some of the main competition concerns of commercialisation agreements include price fixing, output limitation and market partitioning, all of which ultimately lead to a reduction in consumer welfare. According to the Guidelines on horizontal cooperation agreements, price fixing cannot be justified, unless it is indispensable for the integration of other marketing functions, and this integration will generate substantial efficiencies.[46] The question of indispensability is therefore especially important for those agreements involving hard-core cartels such as price fixing or market allocation, which can only, under exceptional circumstances, be considered indispensable to achieve efficiency gains.[47]

---

[41] See Article 1(1) of the Council Regulation (EC) No 1/2003 of 16 December 2002 OJ L 1, 04.01.2003, pp. 1–25.

[42] See Case 56/65 *Société La Technique Minière v. Maschinenbau Ulm GmbH* [1966] ECR 234; and Case 279/06 *CEPSA Estaciones de Servicio SA v. LV Tobar e Hijos SL*, judgement of 11 September, 2008, para 80.

[43] See Communication from the Commission—Guidelines on the applicability of Article 101 of the Treaty on the Functioning of the European Union to horizontal co-operation agreements OJ C 11, 14.1.2011, pp. 1–72, paras 225–256.

[44] Ibid. para 225.

[45] Ibid. para 225.

[46] Ibid. para 246.

[47] Ibid. para 249.

5.2 Article 102 TFEU

Article 102 prohibits abuse of market power by undertakings in a dominant position in one or more relevant markets. Dominance can be held by one undertaking (single dominance) or more than one undertaking (collective dominance). The thrust of this policy is not to prohibit the acquisition and existence of power per se, but is directed at controlling the unilateral behaviour of a dominant firm(s) with market power. In essence, three related enquiries must be conducted when determining the existence of an abuse of the dominant position.[48]

5.2.1 Definition of Relevant Market

First, the relevant market should be defined from its product, geographic and, if applicable, temporal market.[49] In defining the product market, cross-elasticity of demand is analysed to determine the extent to which the goods or services offered are interchangeable (substitutable) with other products or services from the point of view of the consumer.[50] The degree of interchangeability or substitutability is based upon a hypothetical SSNIP[51] test which asks whether the undertaking's customers would switch to readily available substitutes or suppliers in response to a small but significant non-transitory increase in price (5–10 %) in the products or services and areas being considered. If the degree of substitution resulted in loss of sales and made the price increase unprofitable, additional substitutes and areas are included in the relevant market until the set of products and geographic areas is such that increases in relative prices would become profitable.[52] In defining the product market from the supply side, cross-elasticity is measured according to the possibility for suppliers to switch production to the relevant product (in response to its relative price increase) and market it in the short term without incurring significant additional costs. The broader the definition of the relevant product market, the less likely that the element of dominance will be found. The undertakings under investigation will therefore always endeavour to include as many other

---

[48] The Court has laid down the definition of the concept of dominant position in Case 27/76 *United Brands v. Commission* [1978] ERC 207, para 65.

[49] See Commission Notice on the definition of relevant market for the purposes of Community competition law, OJ C 372, 9.12.1997, pp. 5–13.

[50] In order to answer this question, cross-elasticity of demand and supply are analysed. See Case 27/76 *United Brands* which provides a good example of the application of product and geographic market test by the Court.

[51] Small but significant non-transitory increase in price.

[52] Commission Notice on the relevant market, para 17. The same rule was provided in, the now obsolete, Form A/B for applications for negative clearance of agreements or practices which may fall under Article 85(1) or 86 [now Articles 101(1) and 102 TFEU], Section 6.

suppliers and products into the definition as possible. In determining the geographic market, only the Member States in which the conditions of trade are sufficiently homogenous for the market to be considered in its entirety are taken into account,[53] and conversely, those Member States markets where the dissimilar conditions of competition exist are excluded from the definition.

The definition of relevant market is also important in the cases under Article 101(1) when considering whether an agreement has a restrictive or distortive effect on competition.

5.2.2 Establishing Dominance

Second, the definition of the relevant market will be used to determine whether an undertaking was dominant within that market. The concept of a dominant position is defined as a position of economic strength enjoyed by an undertaking which enables it to prevent effective competition being maintained on the relevant market by giving it the power to behave to an appreciable extent independently of its competitors, customers and ultimately of its consumers.[54] Market power is assessed on the basis of market share held by the undertaking,[55] the existence of potential competitors, barriers to entry, level of vertical integration, specificity of the product in question, and other indicators of dominance.[56] The existence of a dominant position derives from a combination of several of these factors which, taken separately, are not necessarily decisive.[57] Undertakings in a dominant position have a special responsibility not to allow their conduct to impair genuine and undistorted competition.[58]

---

[53] For details on approach and overview of the relevant case law see Commission Notice on the definition of the relevant market.

[54] See, in particular, the judgments in Case 27/76 *United Brands v Commission* [1978] ECR 207, paras 65–66; and Case T-30/89 *Hilti v Commission* [1991] ECR II-1439, para 90.

[55] In Case 27/76 *United Brands* a market share of 45 % in combination with other factors established dominance, in Case 322/81 *Michelin* it was 57–65 %, in Case 62/86 *AKZO* the Court said that where market share is 50 % there is a presumption of dominance; the lowest share at which an undertaking was found to be dominant was 39.7 % in Case T-219/99 *Virgin/British Airways* [2004] ECR II-5917.

[56] Market share is therefore only an indicator of market power. See for e.g. Case 62/86 *AKZO v. Commission* [1991] ECR I-3359, Case T-30/89 *Hilti AG v. Commission* [1991] ECR II-1439, Case 85/76 *Hoffmann-La Roche v. Commission* [1979] ECR 461. See also paras 53–55 of Commission Notice on the definition of the relevant market for the purposes of Community competition law OJ C 372, 9.12.1997, pp. 5–13. See Jones and Sufrin 2011, pp. 324–355.

[57] See, for example, Case 27/76 *United Brands v Commission* [1978] ECR 207, paras 65 and 66; Case T-30/89 *Hilti v Commission* [1991] ECR II-1439, para 90; and Case C-250/92 *Gøttrup-Klim e.a. Grovvareforeninger v Dansk Landbrugs Grovvareselskab AmbA* [1994] ECR I-5641, para 47.

[58] Case 322/81 *Michelin* [1983] ECR 3461, paras 10 and 57. See also Sect. 5.7.2.

5.2.3 Abuse of Dominant Position

The third and final enquiry relates to the element of abuse of the dominant position within the specified market. Instances of abuse are outlined in Article 102 TFEU in a non-exhaustive list. They can be in the form of overpricing, predatory pricing, refusal to supply, imposition of unfair trading conditions, discrimination between trading partners, tying, exclusive dealing (single branding) contracts, or any other form of abuse. Unlike purely unilateral abuses, such as predatory pricing, contractual abuses involve implied or express participation of another undertaking such as in, for example, exclusive supply agreements. Much like under Article 101(1), the element of effect on trade between Member States is required for abusive behaviour to be held incompatible with Article 102.[59]

Refusal to supply is a broad concept and covers many practices including vertical and horizontal foreclosures, and refusal to deal with existing and new customers.[60] More specifically, it covers practices such as, for example, refusal to supply in the aftermarket (even where the offending undertaking is not dominant in the primary product market but only in the market for its own spare parts),[61] refusal to supply with the purpose of excluding a competitor from an ancillary market,[62] refusal to supply to prevent parallel trade,[63] or refusal to grant access to so-called essential facilities.[64]

The concept of essential facilities was defined as 'a facility or infrastructure without access to which competitors cannot provide services to their customers'.[65] It can be anything from physical infrastructure such as ports, gas pipelines, or telecommunication wires, to property rights related to premium TV content or intellectual property.[66] An undertaking which refuses its competitors access to essential facilities or grants access to competitors on discriminatory terms in relation to its own

---

[59] The same test for effects on trade is applicable as in Article 101(1). See Commission Notice—Guidelines on the effect on trade concept contained in Articles 81 and 82 of the Treaty OJ C 101, 27.4.2004, pp. 81–96.

[60] For more on the concept of refusal to supply see Communication from the Commission—Guidance on the Commission's enforcement priorities in applying Article 82 of the EC Treaty to abusive exclusionary conduct by dominant undertakings, OJ C 45, 24.2.2009, paras 75–90.

[61] Case 22/78 *Hugin Kassaregister v. Commission* [1979] ECR 1869.

[62] Cases 6 and 7/73 *Istituto Chemioterapico Italiano Spa and Commercial Solvents Corp. v. Commission* [1974] ECR 223.

[63] Cases C-468-478/06 *Sot. Lelos kai Sia and others EE v. GlaxoSmithKline AEVE Farmakeftikon Proionton* [2008] ECR I-7139.

[64] See, for example, Cases C-241-242/91 P *RTE & ITP v. Commission* [1995] ECR I-743. See Joined Cases T-374-5, 384 and 388/94 *European Night Services v. Commission* [1998] ECR II-3141 for application of essential facilities doctrine in the context of Article 101 TFEU. See also Anderman 2009, pp. 87–98.

[65] See, for instance, Commission Decision in Case IV/34.174—Sealink/B&I Holyhead: Interim Measures [1992] OJ 378/4, 5 CMLR 255, para 41, and Commission Decision in Case IV/31.990—Port of Rødby [1994] OJ L 55/52, [1994] 5 CMLR 457, para 12.

[66] See Whish 2009, pp. 697–699 for facilities to which the essential facilities doctrine has been applied.

services, thereby placing it at a competitive disadvantage, infringes Article 102 TFEU.[67] Mandatory dealing, however, interferes into contractual freedom of private parties and acts as a disincentive for innovation for undertakings that have incurred big expenses over a long period of time to develop their services. This is why the application of the essential facilities doctrine should be narrowly construed and the obligation to contract based on Article 102 TFEU imposed only in very exceptional circumstances.[68] In order to find this type of abuse of dominant position, the Court specified the following four criteria: the refusal must be likely to eliminate all competition in the downstream market, the access to essential facilities must be indispensable (as opposed to merely desirable and convenient) for carrying on the business, and there must be no potential substitute for the essential facility in question.[69] In addition, an undertaking owning or controlling an essential facility will not commit an abuse if it has an objective justification for the denial of access[70] such as, for example, issues with the creditworthiness of an undertaking seeking access, capacity constraints, or the fact that other competing undertakings already having access to the facilities maintain effective competition in the downstream market.

5.2.4 Objective Justification and the Efficiency Defence

Unlike Article 101 TFEU, Article 102 TFEU does not have an exemption provision. Nevertheless, in the practice of the Court and the Commission, the use of the concept of objective justification coupled with the requirement of proportionality provides the necessary flexibility to the otherwise overly formalistic approach in the application of Article 102 TFEU.[71] It would appear from the decisional practice of the Commission, as well as from the Commission Guidance,[72] that objective justifications may include non-economic objectives and amount to an equivalent of public policy justification under Article 101(1) TFEU. Furthermore, in its 2005 Discussion Paper the Commission outlined the conditions under which a dominant company may also rely on the efficiency defence in cases of abusive exclusionary conduct. These conditions, which reproduce four cumulative criteria of Article 101(3) TFEU, were later confirmed in the Commission Guidance,

---

67 Ibid.

68 Case C-7/97 *Oscar Bronner GmbH & Co. KG v. Mediaprint Zeitungs* [1998] ECR I-7791, para 26. In liberalised sectors where the facilities were built with public money it is easier to find an abuse.

69 Ibid. para 41.

70 Ibid. See also Commission Decision in Case IV/34.174—Sealink/B&I Holyhead: Interim Measures [1992] OJ 378/4, 5 CMLR 255, para 41.

71 Case 27/76 *United Brands*, Case T-65/89 *BPB*, Case T-30/89 *Hilti*, Case 311/84 *Centre Belge d'Etudes du Marché-Télémarketing (CBEM) v. CLT SA* [1985] ECR 3261.

72 Communication from the Commission—Guidance on the Commission's enforcement priorities in applying Article 82 of the EC Treaty to abusive exclusionary conduct by dominant undertakings, OJ C 45, 24.2.2009, pp. 7–20.

reflecting the overall reform of the approach to Article 102 TFEU and shifting the focus from the form-based towards a more effect-based analysis.[73] The mirroring of the cartel exemption provision makes the efficiency defence the functional and analytical equivalent of Article 101(3) TFEU in the framework of Article 102 TFEU. Conversely, the objective justification defence under Article 102 TFEU is more related to the specific framework developed by the Court in *Wouters* and confirmed in the sporting case of *Meca-Medina*, because a dominant undertaking that engages in an abusive but objectively justified and proportionate conduct will be, as a matter of technicality, considered as not having committed an abuse in the first place.[74] *A fortiori*, it is submitted that the defence of objective justification has been replaced by the *Wouters* test when applying Article 102 TFEU to the regulatory (organisational) acts of collective bodies that pursue a public policy interest, as after *Meca-Medina* in the light of *DLG*, it is clear that the *Wouters* test is applicable in the abuse of dominant position cases as well.

5.3 Oligopolistic Market Structures and the Concept of Collective Dominance

5.3.1 The Oligopoly Problem

Undertakings operating in oligopolistic markets are sometimes able to coordinate their behaviour and raise prices substantially above the competitive level or restrict their output without entering into any explicit agreement or concerted practice. Structural conditions prevailing in tight oligopolies predispose the market to a type of conduct that resembles that of a concerted practice. Under Article 101 TFEU a mere commercial parallelism is not caught by its prohibition provision and must be distinguished from concerted practices which are so caught.[75] Nevertheless, the

[73] Ibid. para 30.

[74] On the last point see the Opinion of Advocate General in Case C-53/03 *Synetairismos Farmakopoion Aitolias and Akarnanias (Syfait) and Others v. GlaxoSmithKline plc and GlaxoSmithKline AEVE, formerly Glaxowellcome AEVE*, delivered on 28 October 2004, para 72.

[75] The Court said that '71.[...] it must be noted that parallel conduct cannot be regarded as furnishing proof of concertation unless concertation constitutes the only plausible explanation for such conduct. It is necessary to bear in mind that, although Article 85 of the Treaty prohibits any form of collusion which distorts competition, it does not deprive economic operators of the right to adapt themselves intelligently to the existing and anticipated conduct of their competitors. 72. Accordingly, it is necessary in this case to ascertain whether the parallel conduct alleged by the Commission cannot, taking account of the nature of the products, the size and the number of the undertakings and the volume of the market in question, be explained otherwise than by concertation.' Joined Cases C-89, 104, 114, 116, 117, 125 to 129/85 *Ahlström Osakeyhtiö and others v Commission of the European Communities* (*Wood Pulp II*) [1993] ECR I-1307. See also Commission Decision in Case IV/30.350—Zink Producer Group [1984] OJ L 220/27, [1985] 2 CMLR 108, para 75 that reads: '[...] parallel pricing behaviour in an oligopoly producing homogenous goods will not in itself be sufficient evidence of a concerted practice'.

effects that tacit coordination can produce on the market (coordinated effects) are the same as would be produced by undertakings that entered into illegal cartels.[76] However, not all oligopolies are uncompetitive. There are many highly competitive markets with only few major sellers, and conversely, there exist polypolies with a failure of competitive market mechanisms. Although a four-firm concentration ratio is a quantitative description often utilised to describe oligopoly, the truth is that they exist, as Whish puts it, 'somewhere on the continuum that begins at monopoly and ends at perfect competition.'[77]

Oligopolies present a regulatory problem for competition law. Both the Court and the Commission have struggled to find a balanced approach to collective dominance in their application of substantive rules on concentrations with the 'Union dimension' and Article 102. On the one hand, it makes no sense to prohibit intelligent adaptations by undertakings regarding transparency on the market and to require them to conduct their business irrationally by not taking account of their rivals' behaviour. On the other hand, what is commercially rational for participants in an oligopoly is not always good for consumers and competition. Hence, even the non-collusive commercial parallelism can be quite detrimental to consumer welfare.

5.3.2 Collective Dominance

Collective dominance (also referred to as 'coordinated effects', 'tacit collusion', 'tacit coordination' and 'joint dominance') implies the absence of effective competition within an oligopoly and between an oligopoly and other firms on the relevant market.[78] With the case law raising more questions than it answers, a lot of uncertainties surround this blurry concept in EU law and the subject is still overly open to conjecture.

Article 102 refers to 'abuse by *one or more* undertakings of a dominant position within the common market' [emphasis added]. This wording implies the possibility for the *independent* undertakings to be found collectively dominant, a proposition which was not accepted in early decisions. The Court was invited by the Commission to adopt the theory of collective dominance in 1988 in the *Alsatel* case on the basis of structural links between undertakings.[79] However, the Court did not comment on this point and its judgements prior to *Alsatel* appeared to have rejected such a theory. For example, in *Hoffmann-La Roche* the Court suggested that it was not appropriate to control tacit collusion by the Article 102 mechanism,

---

[76] Non-coordinated effects (non-collusive oligopoly) occur when one of the undertakings in an oligopoly, without being individually dominant, can derive benefits from their market power without the coordinated response from the other undertakings in an oligopoly.

[77] Whish 2009, p. 545.

[78] O'Donoghue and Padilla 2006, p. 137.

[79] Case 247/86 *Société alsacienne et lorrainne de telecommunications et d'électronique v. SA Novasam* [1988] ERC 5987, paras 21–22.

presumably because oligopolistic conduct amounting to agreements or concerted practices would be caught by Article 101,[80] while in *Continental Can*[81] it stated that Article 102 covers a situation where dominance is held by undertakings that belong to the same economic unit or corporate group. This narrow view on collective dominance was subsequently expanded and the issue raised in *Alsatel* was finally addressed by the General Court in the *Italian Flat Glass* judgment:

> There is nothing in principle to prevent two or more *independent economic entities* from being, on a specific market, untied by such *economic links* that, by virtue of that fact, together they hold a dominant position vis-à-vis the other operators on the same market.[82]

Italian Flat Glass represents the acceptance of the concept of collective dominance. This decision has also created the possibility for the conduct by the oligopolists that is not caught by Article 101 to fall under Article 102, an approach previously rejected by the Court in *Hoffmann-La Roche*.[83] Although many questions in relation to collective dominance still remain without answers, the subsequent case law has clarified that: the concept of 'economic links' mentioned in *Italian Flat Glass* can be structural (such as for example cross-shareholding or common directorship),[84] contractual,[85] or provided by the structure of the market which allows for the parallel behaviour between undertakings operating on an oligopolistic market.[86] Further, 'the undertakings in the group must be linked in such a way that

---

[80] Case 85/76 [1979] ECR 461, para 39 stated that: 'A dominant position must also be distinguished from parallel courses of conduct which are peculiar to oligopolies in that in an oligopoly the courses of conduct interact, whilst in the case of undertaking occupying a dominant position the conduct of an undertaking which derives profits from that position is to a great extent determined unilaterally.'

[81] Case 6/72 *Europemballange Corporation and Continental Can Company Inc. v. Commission* [1973] ECR 215.

[82] Cases T-68/89 etc. *Società Italiano Vetro SpA v. Commission* [1992] ECR II-1403, para 358, (emphasis added).

[83] Case 85/76 [1979] ECR 461, para 39 stated that: 'A dominant position must also be distinguished from parallel courses of conduct which are peculiar to oligopolies in that in an oligopoly the courses of conduct interact, whilst in the case of undertaking occupying a dominant position the conduct of an undertaking which derives profits from that position is to a great extent determined unilaterally.'

[84] Opinion of AG Fennelly in Joined Case C-395/96 P and C-396/96 P *Compagnie Maritime Belge Transports and Others* v. *Commission* [2000] ECR I-1365.

[85] Case T-191/98 *Atlantic Container Line AB v Commission of the European Communities* [2003] ECR II-3275. Commission Decisions in Commission Decision in Case IV/31.990—Port of Rødby [1994] OJ L 55/52, [1994] 5 CMLR 457; Case IV/30.373—P&I Clubs [1999] OJ L 125/12; or Opinion of Advocate General Lenz in Case C-415/93 *Bosman* and in Case C-66/86 *Ahmed Saeed Flugreisen v Zentrale zur Bekampfung Unlauteren Wettbewerbs* [1989] ECR 803.

[86] See, for instance, Case T-102/96 *Gencor Ltd. v. Commission* [1999] ECR II-0753. In this case the Commission relied on other elements to prove collective dominance including a high degree of market concentration, the similarity of cost structures of the undertakings holding the collective dominant position, market transparency, product homogeneity, moderate growth in demand, price inelastic demand, high entry barriers, and a lack of negotiating power on the part of purchasers.

they adopt the same conduct on the market'[87] (i.e., engage in tacit collusion) and 'links must be sufficiently strong for there to be a collective dominant position in a substantial part of the common market'.[88]

In para 79 of the Notice on Access Agreements in the Telecommunication Sector the Commission took the approach that:

> [...] for two or more companies to be jointly dominant it is necessary, though not sufficient, for there to be no effective competition between the companies on the relevant market. This lack of competition may in practice be due to the fact that the companies have links such as agreements for cooperation or interconnection agreements. The Commission does not, however, consider that either economic theory or [Union] law implies that such links are legally necessary for a joint dominant position to exist. It is a sufficient economic link if there is the kind of interdependence which often comes about in oligopolistic situations. There does not seem to be any reason in law or in economic theory to require any other economic link between jointly dominant companies [...].[89]

In *Compagnie Maritime Belge* the Court confirmed the Commission's approach, introduced the notion of collective entity into the definition of collective dominance, and reaffirmed the analytical framework under Article 102. It said that

> [...] a dominant position may be held by two or more economic entities legally independent of each other, provided that from an economic point of view they present themselves or act together on a particular market as a *collective entity*. [...F]or the purposes of analysis under Article [102] of the Treaty, it is necessary to consider whether the undertakings concerned together constitute a *collective entity* vis-à-vis their competitors, their trading partners and consumers on a particular market. It is only where that question is answered in the affirmative that it is appropriate to consider whether that collective entity actually holds a *dominant position* and whether its conduct constitutes *abuse*.[90]

Whether or not independent undertakings will constitute a collective entity is determined on the basis of 'economic links or factors which give rise to a connection between the undertakings concerned', and which 'enable them to act together independently of their competitors, their customers and consumers'.[91] The Court took the opportunity to spell out that agreements or other links in law are not a pre-requisite to a finding of a collective dominant position; other connecting factors may be a basis for such finding, and economic assessment and the structure of the relevant market can play the decisive role.[92] 'The analysis whether there exists links sufficient to establish firms as a collective entity is therefore inextricably bound to the question whether the firms individually occupy a dominant

---

[87] Case C-393/92 *Almelo v. NV Energiebedriff IJsselmij* [1994] ECR I-1477, para 42.

[88] Ibid. para 43.

[89] Notice on the application of competition rules to access agreements in the telecommunications sector OJ [1998] C 265/2, 5 CMLR 521.

[90] C-396/96 P *Compagnie Maritime Belge* [2000] ECR I-1365, paras 38 and 39, (emphasis added).

[91] Ibid. paras 41 and 42, respectively.

[92] Ibid. para 45.

position.'[93] *Compagnie Maritime Belge* confirmed that the rule from *Gencor* decided under the Merger Regulation[94] that economic interdependence alone as imposed by the market structure will suffice to find the undertakings concerned in a collectively dominant position (or as Whish puts it, the 'essence of collective dominance is parallel behaviour within an oligopoly'[95]) is applicable in Article 102 cases as well.

In para 62 of the *Airtours* judgment, also belonging to the sphere of concentrations, on the basis of the facts in which no structural or contractual links existed, three cumulative conditions were deemed necessary for a finding of collective dominance:

> - first, each member of the dominant oligopoly must have the ability to know how the other members are behaving in order to monitor whether or not they are adopting the common policy. [...]; - second, the situation of tacit coordination must be sustainable over time, that is to say, there must be an incentive not to depart from the common policy on the market. [...]; - third, to prove the existence of a collective dominant position to the requisite legal standard, the Commission must also establish that the foreseeable reaction of current and future competitors, as well as of consumers, would not jeopardise the results expected from the common policy.[96]

In *Piau* the General Court cited the *Airtours* criteria in the context of Article 102 assessments of joint dominance.[97] Later in the year, the Commission outlined the same criteria in the Discussion Paper on the application of Article 102 to exclusionary abuses,[98] but it is instructive that it has not done so in the subsequent Guidelines adopted after public consultation on the Discussion Paper and focusing only on single dominant undertakings. Some argue that a reference to *Airtours* in *Piau* is misplaced because *Piau* dealt with the links in law (contractual links *in casu*) and not tacit collusion,[99] while others see the *Airtours* criteria as applicable to any case of collective dominance, be it a case of tacit or explicit collusion, because it would make no sense to have two distinct tests for reviewing cases of collective dominance.[100] The 2005 Discussion Paper makes a difference between links in law and tacit collusion and appears to lend support to the former view.[101]

Regarding the final limb of the Article 102 analytical framework, the 2005 Discussion Paper states that 'a finding of abuse of a collective dominant position is

---

[93] Jephcott and Withers 2001, p. 301.

[94] Case T-102/96 *Gencor Ltd. V. Commission* [1999] ECR II-0753.

[95] Whish 2009, p. 564.

[96] T-342/99 *Airtours plc. v. Commission* [2002] ECR II-2585, judgment of 6 June 2002, (emphasis added).

[97] Case T-193/02 *Laurent Piau v. Commission*, judgment of 26 January 2005, para 111.

[98] European Commission DG Competition Discussion Paper on the application of Article 82 to exclusionary abuses, Brussels (December 2005) paras 48–50.

[99] Mezzanotte 2009, pp. 137–142.

[100] O'Donoghue and Padilla 2006, p. 152.

[101] Commission Discussion Paper on the application of Article 82 to exclusionary abuses, paras 45–50.

typically based on showing that the collectively dominant undertakings have tacitly or expressly been following a common policy on the market, at least in regard to the abusive conduct'.[102] The General Court spelled out in *Irish Sugar* that a collectively-held dominant position does not necessarily need to be abused collectively, but that undertakings individually may commit an abuse which needs only be a manifestation of, and undertaken from the position of, such collective dominance.[103] This case established vertical collective dominance and showed that only a flimsy line separates a situation in which firms form a single economic unit from the situation where two independent firms are united by economic links.[104]

5.4 Simultaneous Application of Articles 101 and 102 TFEU

Already in its early judgment of *Continental Can* the Court held that Articles 101 and 102 TFEU seek to attain the same aim of maintaining effective competition within the common market.[105] According to settled case law, the two competition provisions can be applied simultaneously.[106] In many cases, the strategy of the dominant undertaking(s) turns on the reinforcement of their market power by means of contractual clauses, such as tying, exclusivity, and other clauses. The agreements between two or more undertakings containing such clauses might create or reinforce a position of dominance which is, or may become, subject to abuse. Such agreements may be incompatible with both, Articles 101 and 102 TFEU. If the case involves a tacit collusion in an oligopolistic market then only Article 102 applies,[107] and if the collusion is explicit than Article 101 will apply simultaneously. The conduct resulting from the terms of restrictive agreements

[102] Ibid. para 74.

[103] Case T-228/97 *Irish Sugar plc v. Commission* judgment of 7 October 1999.

[104] Mezzanotte 2009, pp. 137–142.

[105] Case 6/72 *Europemballage Corporation and Continental Can Company Inc. v. Commission* [1973] ECR 215, para 11. See also Case T-51/89 *Tetra Pack Rausing SA v. Commission* [1990] ECR II-309.

[106] See Case 85/76 *Hoffmann-La Roche* [1979] ECR 461, para 116; Case 66/86 *Ahmed Saeed Flugreisen and Silver Line Reisebüro GmbH v Zentrale zur Bekämpfung unlauteren Wettbewerbs e.V.* [1989] ECR 803; Joined Cases C-395/96 P and C-396/96 *P Compagnie Maritime Belge Transports SA, Compagnie Maritime Belge SA and Dafra-Lines A/S v Commission* [2000] ECR I-1365, para 33.

[107] This conclusion follows from the case law discussed above. However, see para 4.125 of Faull and Nikpay 2007, p. 343, for an argument that 'it is very unlikely that a case could be taken under Article [102] against oligopolists for engaging in tacit collusion per se. It is submitted that, if the collusion is not such that it is capable of being addressed under Article [101], it would not be appropriate to do so "through the back door:" under Article [102]'.

between the undertakings constituting the single economic entity is considered unilateral and not collusive so Article 102 alone will be applicable, but only if the undertakings concerned are dominant on the relevant market. Consistency requires that Article 101(3) be interpreted as precluding any application of this exemption to restrictive agreements that constitute an abuse of a dominant position. On the other hand, a company holding a dominant position may benefit from an exemption under Article 101(3) of the Treaty when its conditions are fulfilled.[108] In the *Piau* case, decided in the sporting context, the General Court held that if the conduct of a dominant company satisfies all the conditions of Article 101(3) such conduct should not be classified as an abuse under Article 102 of the Treaty.[109] Rousseva has convincingly argued that the element of dominance is the only difference between Articles 101 and 102 when it comes to vertical contractual restraints involving a dominant undertaking.[110] Therefore, as the current division of labour between Articles 101 and 102 is difficult to sustain from a legal and economic point of view, she suggests that discarding Article 102 and relying exclusively on Article 101 would be a pragmatic solution which would bring many advantages including carrying out a de facto modernisation of Article 102 without entering into explicit conflict with existing precedents.[111]

5.5 Articles 101 and 102 TFEU in the Sporting Context

Provided that the sporting activity in question falls within the scope of the Treaty, the rules which govern the conditions for engaging in that activity must satisfy the requirements of Articles 101 and 102.[112]

5.5.1 Basic Elements

It has been recognized that national and international sporting associations, clubs and independent athletes can constitute 'undertakings'[113]; sporting federations

---

[108] See also Commission Notice Guidelines on the application of Article 81(3) of the Treaty, OJ C 101, 27.04.2004, pp. 97–118, para 106.

[109] See Case T-193/02 *Piau*, para 119.

[110] Rousseva 2005, p. 590.

[111] Ibid. p. 637.

[112] Case C-519/04 P *Meca-Medina and Majcen v. Commission* [2006] ECR I-6991, para 28, and C-49/07 *MOTOE*, [2008] ECR I-4863.

[113] For national and international sporting associations as undertakings see; Case T-193/02 *Piau* paras 69–72; Commission Decision in COMP IV/37.806—ENIC/UEFA [2002] unpublished decision of 27 June 2002, para 25; Opinion of Advocate General Lenz in *Bosman* points 255

can, in addition, also constitute an 'association of undertakings'[114] or an 'association of associations of undertakings'[115]; their rules can amount to 'agreements or decisions,'[116] distort the competition within the relevant markets and affect trade between Member States within the meaning of Articles 101 and 102.[117] Article 102 TFEU does not include the concept of 'association of undertakings' but applies to unilateral conduct of dominant 'undertakings'. The General Court has held that even where a sports federation such as FIFA is not itself active on a given market, it may be considered an 'undertaking' under Article 102 TFEU to the extent that it represents the emanation of its members that are active on that market.[118] Furthermore, when they directly engage in economic activity, sporting federations usually acquire a status of an undertaking in a monopolistic position,[119]

Footnote 113 (continued)
et seq; Commission Decision in Case Cases 33.384 and 33.378—Distribution of package tours during the1990 World Cup [1992] OJ L 326/31, paras 47 and 52–53. For individual athletes as undertakings see Joined Cases C-51/96 and C-191/97 *Christelle Deliège v. Ligue francophone de judo* etc. ECR 2000 I-2549, paras 56 and 57. According to AG Lenz in C-415/93 *Bosman* para 263 football players employed by a football club do not constitute undertakings, as they are workers and not providers of services. Commission Staff Working Document, The EU and Sport: Background and Context, Accompanying Document to the White Paper on Sport, COM (2007) 391 final, Annex I, para 2.1.3 clarifies that 'even if athletes are employed by a sport club, they may be considered undertakings insofar as they carry out economic activities independent thereof, e.g., by entering into sponsoring agreements.'

[114] See Case T-193/02 *Laurent Piau v. Commission*, judgment of 26 January 2005 where the General Court held that '69. [...] FIFA's members are national associations, which are groupings of football clubs for which the practice of football is an economic activity. These football clubs are therefore undertakings within the meaning of Article [101 TFEU] and the national associations grouping them together are associations of undertakings within the meaning of that provision. 70. The fact that the national associations are groupings of 'amateur' clubs, alongside 'professional' clubs, is not capable of calling that assessment into question.[...] 72. Since the national associations constitute associations of undertakings and also, by virtue of the economic activities that they pursue, undertakings, FIFA, an association grouping together national associations, also constitutes an association of undertakings within the meaning of Article [101 TFEU].' See also Opinion of AG Lenz in C-415/93 *Bosman* paras 255–257, and the Commission Decision of 23 July 2003 in Case COMP/C.2-37.398 Joint Selling of the Commercial Rights of the UEFA Champions League.

[115] Commission Decision Case COMP/C.2-37.398 UEFA Champions League, para 106.

[116] Case T-193/02 *Piau,* para 75. Rules drawn up unilaterally by sporting associations consisting of undertakings will usually constitute decisions by an association of undertakings (see, e.g., Commission decision in COMP IV/37.806—ENIC/UEFA, para 26, for a rule drawn up by the UEFA Executive Committee, and C-519/04 P *Meca-Medina,* para 45 for a rule drawn up by the International Olympic Committee and implemented by the International Swimming Federation).

[117] For general guidance see 'Guidelines on the effect of trade concept contained in Articles 81 and 82 of the Treaty', OJ 2004 C 101/7.

[118] Case T-193/02 *Piau*, paras 112 and 116.

[119] Commission Staff Working Document, Annex I, para 2.1.4 recognises that: 'sports associations usually have practical monopolies in a given sport and may thus normally be considered dominant in the market of the organisation of sport events under Article [102] EC.'

whereas clubs organised in a league may be held collectively dominant within the meaning of Article 102, as interpreted by the relevant case law.[120]

Rules adopted by international sporting organisations will normally affect trade between Member States due to their scope of application. Rules of national sports associations usually affect only the territory of their respective country but in light of the high level of internationalisation and mobility in professional sport, those rules may also affect trade between Member States. The same can be said for the agreements between clubs affiliated to national and international federations.

5.5.2 Relevant Market

An element that Articles 101 and 102 have in common is, *inter alia*, a need to define the relevant market from both the geographic and the product market points of view.

According to the generally–accepted Stix-Hackl and Egger classification, the relevant product market for professional sport can be of three types.[121] The first is the *exploitation market* in which clubs and federations exploit their performances and commercial rights, for example, through sales of broadcasting rights, ticketing, and merchandising. Upstream of the exploitation market is the *contest market* in which the final product, the sporting contest, is jointly produced by the clubs, players being the most important factor of production.[122] In order to effectively stage a contest, sport governing bodies design the rules that regulate competition between participants and rules limiting access to competitions. Since in European football the leagues are open and they apply the system of promotion and relegation, the market cannot be strictly demarcated according to leagues. The third is the *supply market* which essentially comprises of the buying and selling of players by the clubs. It is upstream of the contest market. Substitutability is generally quite low in the first two types of markets but it is equally low when it comes to the top players in the supply market.

In addition, some economists have made a useful description of the structure of sporting competition which distinguishes between the product market, the labour market, and the capital market.[123] The product market in a sporting competition incorporates structure of competition (playing rules for the contest and the organisation of the competition), league structure (organisation and composition of the league), and revenue (corresponds to the exploitation market according to the

---

120 For discussion on the concept of collective dominance in the sporting context see Case T-193/02 *Piau*, paras 113–115; Opinion of AG Lenz in C-415/93 *Bosman* para 285. See also Sect. 5.3.2.

121 Stix-Hackl and Egger 2002, pp. 81–91.

122 Other factors are, for example, trainers and physiotherapists.

123 See Borland 2009, p. 23.

Stix-Hackl and Egger classification, plus allocation of the league revenue). The structure of a labour market in a sporting competition incorporates: player assignment to teams, player payment and wage determination, and size of the player list. The capital market structure in a sporting competition deals with the types of ownership arrangements. One missing aspect in this classification is governance, i.e., the way that rules and policies are decided, and the degree of vertical integration.[124]

In *Piau*, the rules of the FIFA Players' Agents Regulations relating to agent licensing requirements were challenged on the basis of Articles 101 and 102. The relevant market was held to be 'the market affected by the rules in question' i.e., 'a market for the provision of services where the buyers are players and clubs and the sellers are agents'.[125]

In *ENIC*,[126] the Commission examined the rule that prohibited ownership of multiple football clubs, according to which two or more clubs participating in the same UEFA competition cannot be directly or indirectly controlled by the same entity or managed by the same person. The English National Investment Company (ENIC) owned stakes in six professional clubs. It argued that the relevant market is the market for capital investment in football clubs in Europe that is 'characterised on the demand side by football clubs seeking capital and/or investment and on the supply side by individuals or corporations interested in investing in a European football club. Football clubs are competing in this market for access to capital.'[127] Interestingly, the relevant market defined by the Court of Arbitration for Sport (CAS) in this case[128] was considered to be 'the market for ownership interests in football clubs capable of taking part in UEFA competitions'.[129] What was seen as the demand side of the market by ENIC was identified as the supply side by CAS and vice versa. On the supply side of the relevant market, according to CAS, are the potential sellers of ownership interests in football clubs. In point 135 of its arbitral award, CAS considered this narrow market to be the relevant market since: 'because of the peculiarities of the football sector, investment in football clubs does not appear to be interchangeable with investments in other businesses, or even in other leisure businesses'. In addition to the definition of the relevant market, ENIC also considered the market for players, the sponsorship market, the football merchandising market, the media rights market, and the market for gate revenues as the ancillary markets.[130]

---

124 Ibid. pp. 23–24.

125 Case T-193/02 *Laurent Piau v. Commission* [2005] ECR II-0209, para 112.

126 Commission Decision in Case COMP IV/37.806—ENIC/UEFA.

127 Ibid. para 10.

128 CAS arbitral award of 20 August 1999 in Case CAS 98/200 *AEK Athens and Slavia Prague v. UEFA*.

129 Ibid. para 133. See also Case COMP/37.806—ENIC/UEFA, para 10.

130 Case COMP/37.806 ENIC/UEFA, para 12.

In *Mouscron*,[131] the UEFA 'home and away' rule according to which each club must play its home matches at its own ground was challenged on the basis of Article 102 by the French Communauté Urbaine de Lille after UEFA refused to allow the Belgian club Excelsior Mouscron to play its home match against French club Metz in Lille. The Commission considered that Lille was active in the market for the renting of stadiums, but it left open the question on whether UEFA was dominant in the market for organising European club competitions in football.[132]

In *1998 Football World Cup* the Commission investigated the implementation of discriminatory ticket sales arrangements by the local organising committee of the 1998 Football World Cup in France towards non-French residents. The practical effect of such discrimination was to deny the overwhelming majority of consumers outside France access to a significant proportion of entry tickets for finals matches. The relevant product market was determined on the basis of a detailed analysis under the SSNIP test, and it was held to comprise only the market for the tickets for Football World Cup 1998 due to the very low cross–elasticity of demand.[133] The relevant geographic market was held to comprise 'at least all countries within the EEA'.[134]

5.5.3 Collective Dominance

In its judgment in *Piau*, the General Court addressed the issue of collective dominance in the sporting sector. Citing the previous judgement in *Compagnie Maritime Belge*[135] it said that legally independent economic entities may be found collectively dominant 'provided that from an economic point of view they present themselves or act together on a particular market as a collective entity'.[136] Thereafter the Court restated the three cumulative conditions for a finding of collective dominance as set out in para 62 of the *Airtours* decision.[137] Implementation by the clubs of a decision such as the FIFA Players' Agents Regulations was seen as potentially resulting in clubs being so linked as to their conduct on a particular market that they present themselves on that market as a collective entity vis-à-vis

---

[131] Case COMP/E3/36.85—Lille/UEFA ('the Mouscron case') [1999] unpublished decision of 3 December 1999. Commission Press Release IP/99/965 'Limits to Application of Treaty Competition Rules to Sport: Commission Gives Clear Signal' 9 December 1999. See also XXIXth Report on Competition Policy 1999, pp. 166–167.

[132] Commission Staff Working Document, Annex I, para 2.2.1.2.

[133] Case IV/36.888—1998 Football World Cup [2000] OJ 2000 L 5/55, paras 66–74.

[134] Ibid. para 77.

[135] C-396/96 P *Compagnie Maritime Belge*, para 36.

[136] Case T-193/02 *Laurent Piau v. Commission* [2005] ECR II-0209, para 110.

[137] Ibid. para 111.

their competitors, their trading partners, and consumers.[138] FIFA, national football associations, and the clubs forming them were held collectively dominant on the market for the provision players' agents' services:

> Because the regulations are binding for national associations that are members of FIFA and the clubs forming them, these bodies appear to be linked in the long term as to their conduct by rules that they accept and that other actors (players and players' agents) cannot break on pain of sanctions that may lead to their exclusion from the market, in particular in the case of players' agents. [...] such a situation therefore characterises a collective dominant position for clubs on the market for the provision of players' agents' services, since, through the rules to which they adhere, the clubs lay down the conditions under which the services in question are provided.[139]

FIFA is included even though it is not active on the market for players' agents' services; it is enough that it constitutes the emanation of the national associations and the clubs, the actual economic operators on the relevant market. FIFA therefore operates on the market through its members. The element of abuse of the collective dominant position was not subsequently found in this case.

This is not the first time that the issue of collective dominance was considered in the sporting sector. In the *Bosman* case, Advocate General Lenz considered that football clubs in a professional league could be 'united by such economic links' as to be regarded as collectively dominant.[140] However, the Court decided this case under the internal market rules and therefore omitted to provide guidance on the competition questions.[141]

5.5.4 Analytical Framework for Commercial Rules in Sport

It is clear from the General Court judgment in *Piau* that the rules enacted by sporting organisations to regulate economic activity not connected to the specific nature of sport, are to be assessed under the ordinary competition law framework applicable to any other commercial rule. Therein it was held that FIFA regulations governing

> the activity of players' agents, an economic activity involving the provision of services which does not fall within the scope of the specific nature of sport as defined by the case

---

[138] Ibid. para 113.

[139] Ibid. para 114.

[140] Opinion of AG Lenz in C-415/93 *Bosman,* para 285.

[141] Case law and practice have assimilated the treatment of collective dominance under the Council Regulation 139/2004 (Merger Regulation) and the Article 102 TFEU, and the Court has used the cases decided in one area to solve the legal problems related to collective dominance in another area. Having said this, it is important to nevertheless keep in mind the differences in objectives between the two areas. EU merger control is concerned with preserving a market structures and a 'creation or strengthening of the dominant position' whereas Article 102 TFEU does not condemn the dominance as such.

> law of the Court of Justice, constitutes a decision by an association of undertakings within the meaning of Article [101(1)] EC, which must comply with the [Union] rules on competition where it has effects in the [Union].[142]

The activity of players' agents was treated as being ancillary to sport, which was not sufficient to merit a different treatment than any other profession. The same treatment applies to Article 102 cases in as far as the sporting rules that govern the economic activity which have nothing to do with the special nature of sport have been unilaterally adopted by a dominant or collectively dominant undertaking.

5.5.4.1 Commercialisation Agreements and Sports Broadcasting Market

The Nice Declaration acknowledges that the sale of television broadcasting rights is one of the largest sources of income today for certain sports. Football is most definitely one of those sports, in contrast to say, Formula 1 races, which generate the main part their of revenues from sponsorship agreements. The position of the European Council in the Nice Declaration was that 'moves to encourage the mutualisation of part of the revenue from such sales, at the appropriate levels, are beneficial to the principle of solidarity between all levels and areas of sport.'[143]

The market for sports broadcasting used to be, and to a good extent still is, organised in a monopoly/monopsony structure, i.e. it is characterised by the presence of a dominant seller and a dominant buyer. The buying side was decartelised, but the selling side stayed highly centralised, which had implications for the ability of sporting federations to affect the competition between broadcasters in the downstream market. What makes the definition of the relevant market particularly difficult in the media sector is that the product and services are not clearly separable, and due to technological or economic convergence they are often marketed in a bundle.[144]

Sport events and films are the most popular pay-TV products.[145] In *TPS*, the Commission suggested that a separate market might exist for rights to broadcast sports events.[146] Today, not only is it universally accepted that sports broadcasting rights indeed constitutes a separate market, but that the definition has become

---

[142] Case T-193/02 *Laurent Piau v. Commission* [2005] ECR II-0209, para 5 summarising paras 73–75 of the judgment.

[143] 'Declaration on the Specific Characteristics of Sport and its Social Function in Europe, of which Account Should be Taken in Implementing Common Policies', Presidency Conclusions following the Nice European Council Meeting of 7, 8 and 9 December 2000.

[144] Organisation for Economic Co-operation and Development—Competition Committee, Roundtable on Competition and Sports: Note by the European Union, DAF/COMP/WD(2010)56.

[145] Commission Decision in Case No IV/36.237—TPS [1999] OJ L 90/6, para 34.

[146] Ibid. See also Commission Decision in Case M.779—Bertelsmann/CLT [1996] OJ C 364/3, para 19, where this was acknowledged for the first time.

more sophisticated and narrower.[147] Particular characteristics of sports programmes include their ability to generate high viewing figures and reach an identifiable audience specially targeted by certain advertisers.[148] In the examination of the joint selling of commercial rights in *UEFA Champions League*, the Commission considered the following markets relevant to an assessment of the effects of such arrangements:

> (a) the upstream markets for the sale and acquisition of free-TV, pay-TV and pay-per-view rights; (b) the downstream markets on which TV broadcasters compete for advertising revenue depending on audience rates, and for pay-TV/pay-per-view subscribers; (c) the upstream markets for wireless/3G/UMTS rights, Internet rights and video-on-demand rights, which are emerging new media markets at both the upstream and downstream levels that parallel the development of the markets in the pay-TV sector; (d) the markets for the other commercial rights namely sponsorship, suppliership and licensing.[149]

With regard to the geographic markets, both the downstream and upstream markets are usually of a national character.[150] This is due to the national character of distribution as a result of national regulatory regimes, linguistic differences and cultural factors.[151]

5.5.4.2 Competition Concerns with Regard to Joint Selling and Exclusivity Clauses

In most European sports, the condition for participation in a league is the transfer of the commercial rights to a governing body by the clubs. Governing bodies then create a single point of sale and bundle the rights for offer to broadcasters on an exclusive basis. One broadcaster per country will win the bidding for the rights. Such collective selling amounts to horizontal price fixing, a hard-core cartel specifically referred to in Article 101(1)(a). One of the justifications cited in support of this arrangement is the need to maintain competitive balance between league participants which is achieved by the subsequent distribution of profits acquired by means of joint selling. In addition, exclusivity clauses in the broadcasting contracts with national operators segment the market along national lines. This is,

---

[147] Mangeat 2004 Sports Media Rights and Competition law: What are the Relevant Markets?—Economics of the Sports Media Rights/Appraisal of the Relevant Markets with Regard to Their Acquisition and Sale. *Jusletter*, (6 September).

[148] Commission Decision in COMP/37.398 UEFA Champions League, OJ 2003 L291/25, para 60 (summarising the *TPS* case).

[149] Ibid. para 56.

[150] See, for example, Commission Decision in UEFA Champions League OJ 2003 L291/25, para 90, and Case M.993 Bertelsmnann/Kirch/Premiere, OJ 1999 L 53/1, para 22.

[151] Commission Decision in UEFA Champions League OJ 2003 L291/25, para 88. For more on product and geographic market see also Commission Staff Working Document, Annex I, para 3.1.

however, seen as the norm in the industry reflecting the predominantly national set-up of the sports market that differs culturally and linguistically from one Member State to another. Also, it protects the value of the rights for both buyers and sellers, and encourages investments in innovative programming. Exclusivity is not prohibited per se and will be examined in the light of the duration of commitments in relation to the time needed for the broadcasters to recoup their investments as well as in the light of the foreclosure effect on potential new market entrants. Availability and conditions of licensing will play a role in assessing the nature of exclusivity. Apart from this restriction on competition in the downstream market, two other effects of broadcasting agreements are of particular concern to the competition enforcers: the impact it has on consumers in terms of choice and price, and the restrictions on commercial undertakings (clubs) to exploit their rights on an individual basis.

5.5.4.3 UEFA Champions League, Bundesliga, and the FAPL Cases

The Commission was dealing with the issue of collective sales of Champions League rights on an exclusive basis by UEFA[152]; Bundesliga rights by the German Football League[153]; and Premier League rights by the Football Association Premier League.[154] In all three cases, the joint selling arrangements were considered horizontal restrictions on competition contrary to Article 101(1) because they hindered competition between the clubs in terms of prices and innovation, and create the preconditions for offering to broadcasters the single (bundled) packages on an exclusive basis. On the other side of the coin are the efficiencies identified by the Commission under Article 101(3). They relate to the improvement of the media product and its distribution with the resulting benefits for broadcasters, viewers and the football clubs. Specifically, the creation of a single point of sale for acquisition of a packaged league product provides efficiencies by reducing transaction costs for football clubs and media operators, while the branding of the output creates efficiencies as it establishes a recognisable homogenous product that is more attractive for the viewers, more valuable for broadcasters, and leads to more objectivity in media coverage than would be present with individual selling by clubs. In *UEFA Champions League* the UEFA convincingly argued that

> the creation of a single point of sale is a prerequisite for the existence of the UEFA Champions League product. Since no individual club knows before the start of the season

[152] The Champions League is one of the most watched events on television. Commission Decision Relating to a Proceeding Pursuant to Article 81 of the EC Treaty and Article 53 of the EEA Agreement (Comp/C.2-37.398 Joint Selling of the Commercial Rights of the UEFA Champions League) 2003/778/EC, OJ 2003 L291/25.

[153] Decision 2005/396 OJ 2005 L134/46.

[154] Commission Decision in Case COMP/C-2/38.173—Joint Selling of Media Rights to the FA Premier League [2006] C 2006/868 final.

> how far it will get in the tournament it could not sign a commercial agreement with a broadcaster giving the broadcaster any certainty that the football clubs will make it to the very end of the UEFA Champions League season. This provides an element of uncertainty for broadcasters.[155]

In order to make the identified efficiencies count so as to outweigh the negative effects the joint selling agreements have on competition, the Commission has attached a number of commitments to its exemption decisions. The collectivity and exclusivity were not condemned per se, but the unbundling of rights to make them accessible to the wider range of operators, a shorter duration of exclusive commitments, a transparent and non-discriminatory bidding procedure, selling of some of the rights by the clubs, and reverting unsold rights back to the clubs were all among the conditions for exemption depending on the specific circumstances of each case. UEFA proposed a revised, unbundled selling policy based on segmentation of exploitation of TV rights, radio, internet, Universal Mobile Telecommunications Systems and physical media such as DVD, VHS and CD-ROM. Although the case finally ended in an exemption under Article 101(3), in the Staff Working Document the Commission nevertheless identified the remaining restraints after the commitments entered into have been put into practice. Namely, 'the exclusive sale of live rights by UEFA still prevented individual clubs from competing in the sale of those rights, a single price was fixed, broadcasters only had one point of supply in respect of most live rights and the exploitation of deferred rights was subject to limitations.'[156] The Bundesliga had entered into similar unbundling commitments and has limited the period of the duration of the contracts with operators to 3 years maximum. Similarly, in the Premier League, the commitments were shortened from 5 to 3 years and the league has entered into a series of other undertakings including an increase in the number of matches available for live TV transmission and the sale of rights in packages with no buyer being able to acquire all of them. The end result was that British Sky Broadcasting (BskyB), a broadcaster which used to hold all the exclusive rights, acquired four out of the six packages available.[157]

Therefore, a common set of principles emerged from the three decisions allowing collective selling as long as tendering of the media rights is open and transparent, the duration of exclusive commitments is limited to 3 years, rights are unbundled to be accessible on all media platforms and to a wider range of operators, and the unsold rights are reverted back to the clubs. These were some of the ways in which

---

[155] Commission Decision in Case COMP/37.398—Joint Selling of Commercial Rights (UEFA Champions League) [2003] OJ L 291/25, para 140.

[156] Commission Staff Working Document, Annex I, para 3.1.3.1.3.

[157] For more on this topic see Rubenstein 2005 Unbundling of Sports Media Rights. *Sports Law: Administration and Practice* 12(1), pp. 14–16; Editorial 2005 Sports Broadcasting: What Next?. *Sports Law: Administration and Practice* 12(5), pp. 5–7; Thomas and Thomson 2004 Negotiation, Bundling and Competition Law—Current Issues Facing Those Involved in Sports Broadcasting Rights. *Sports Law: Administration and Practice* 11(5), pp. 1–5.

the exclusivity of the media deals was made less exclusive. However, Hoehn and Kastrianki identified case-specific differences between *FAPL* and *Bundesliga* related to different circumstances that exist in the UK and Germany.[158] In the UK, the pay TV market was more mature than in Germany which justified the FAPL's commitments related to no-single-buyer rule, whereas Bundesliga's commitments related to substantially unbundling its media rights according to different platforms. In the UK, the auctioning of packages was platform-neutral. Today, all of the big domestic European leagues have adopted, or plan to adopt, a system of collective selling.[159]

5.5.4.4 Joined Cases C-403/08 and C-429/08 Murphy

The facts of *Murphy*,[160] along with the parts of the judgement related to the internal market and intellectual property law were set out in Sect. 4.10. With regard to competition law, the Court unsurprisingly reached the analogous conclusions as under Article 56 TFEU. Whereas granting the exclusive right to broadcast protected subject-matter by satellite to a sole licensee was essentially in accordance with the Satellite Broadcasting Directive,[161] accompanying such exclusivity with the prohibition on provision of cross-border services (i.e. supply of decoding devices outside exclusive territory) constituted restriction of competition *by object* under Article 101 TFEU.[162] Absolute territorial exclusivity in the area covered by the licence eliminated all competition between broadcasters.[163] This arrangement could not be exempted by the terms of Article 101(3) because the Court found it disproportionate earlier in the judgment in the context of the objective justification framework under Article 56 TFEU.[164]

The Advocate General suggested the same outcome and considered that a contractual obligation requiring the broadcaster to prevent its satellite decoder cards which enable reception of the licensed programme content from being used outside the licensed territory has the same effect as an agreement to prevent parallel exports.[165] The exemption under Article 101(3) is theoretically possible, but because the Advocate General indicated that it should be subject to similar considerations as in the examination of whether a restriction of freedom to provide

[158] Hoehn and Kastrianki 2012, p. 11.

[159] Ibid. p. 12.

[160] Joined Cases C-403/08 and C-429/08 *FAPL and others v. QC Leisure and others;* and *Karen Murphy v Media Protection Services Ltd.*, judgment of 4 October 2011.

[161] Ibid. para 138. Article 1(2)(b) of the Directive 93/83/EEC of 27 September 1993 on the coordination of certain rules concerning copyright and rights related to copyright applicable to satellite broadcasting and cable retransmission (Satellite Broadcasting Directive) [1993] OJ L 248/15.

[162] Ibid. paras 139–140.

[163] Ibid. para 142.

[164] Ibid. para 145.

[165] Paragraph 248 of her Opinion in Joined Cases C-403/08 and C-429/08 *Murphy*.

services is justified, it is very unlikely on the basis of her Opinion that the license agreements in question would benefit from that exemption.[166] We will come back to this point below in Sects. 6.3 and 6.4 in the context of convergence between internal market and competition law provisions of the Treaty.

5.5.5 *Analytical Framework for Regulatory Rules: C-519/04* Meca-Medina *[2006]*

The first time that the Court directly addressed the application of competition provisions to regulatory rules in sport was in the *Meca-Medina* judgment[167] of 2006. Hence, the case deserves special attention.

5.5.5.1 Factual Background

The case involved two professional swimmers who were found to have breached the sport's anti-doping rules adopted by the International Olympic Committee (IOC). They tested positive for nandrolone and were suspended for a period of 4 years by the Doping Panel of the International Swimming Federation that implemented the rules for their discipline.[168] Contesting the anti-doping rules, the applicants asserted that they were in breach of Articles 101 and 102, and 56 on freedom to provide services.

> [...] First of all, the fixing of the limit at 2 ng/ml is a concerted practice between the IOC and the 27 laboratories accredited by it. That limit is scientifically unfounded and can lead to the exclusion of innocent or merely negligent athletes. In the applicants' case, the excesses could have been the result of the consumption of a meal containing boar meat. Also, the IOC's adoption of a mechanism of strict liability and the establishment of tribunals responsible for the settlement of sports disputes by arbitration (the CAS and the

---

166 Ibid. para 250.

167 Case C-519/04 *David Meca-Medina and Igor Majcen v. Commission* [2006] ECR I-6991. Before this case the Court has had a number of opportunities to clarify the relation between competition law and sports (notably in C-415/93 *Bosman*) but it has avoided this problem by deciding the cases on the basis of internal market rules. In the absence of Union legislative competence, it was only the Commission decisional practice that shed some light on the competition law issues in sports.

168 The appeal against the suspension was first launched before the Court of Arbitration for Sports which confirmed the decision of the doping panel but later, when scientific experiments showed that nandrolone's metabolites can be produced endogenously by the human body at a level which may exceed the accepted limit when certain foods have been consumed, they reduced the sanctions to 2 years. In 2001, however, the applicants launched the complaint with the Commission whose decision they appealed to the General Court, and finally the decision of the General Court was brought before the Court.

ICAS) which are insufficiently independent of the IOC strengthens the anti-competitive nature of that limit. [...].[169]

The athletes raised their claim under both the freedom to provide services and the competition provisions of the Treaty.

5.5.5.2 Judgment of the Court

The Court started off by reiterating and confirming the rules developed in its previous case law. The orthodox rule that originated in *Walrave*[170] provides that 'sport is subject to Community law only in so far as it constitutes an economic activity [...]'.[171] Rules of 'purely sporting' interest with nothing to do with economic activity are excluded from the scope of the Treaty.[172] The Court cited paras 14 and 15 of *Donà* and held that freedom of movement provisions 'do not preclude rules or practices justified on non-economic grounds which relate to the particular nature and context of certain sporting events,' and are limited to their proper objective.[173] Such a restriction on the scope of the freedom of movement provisions 'cannot be relied upon to exclude the *whole* of a sporting activity from the scope of the Treaty'.[174] The Court here states the obvious: that the sporting activity in question (say, the activity of a football player) cannot altogether be excluded from the scope of the Treaty in relation to all other sporting rules. The restriction on the scope of the Treaty by the rule that fulfilled the requirements for exception enabled by *Walrave* and *Donà* cannot be relied on to say that the sporting activity that that rule governed therefore as a whole falls outside of the scope of the Treaty. There is no such thing as a general exception for the sporting activity in question. This interpretation of the judgement comes from the fact that when the Court in para 76 of *Bosman* cited paras 14 and 15 from *Donà* adding to them the sentence 'it cannot therefore be relied upon to exclude the whole of a sporting activity from the scope of the Treaty' it did so in response to the arguments raised by the German Government that sport such as football is not an economic activity, that it is akin to culture and should be treated as such. Also, it addressed UEFA arguments which essentially called for exception due to the particular nature of sport.

---

169 C-519/04 *Meca-Medina*, paras 16–17.

170 Case 36/74 *Walrave and Koch* [1974] ECR 1405, para 4. This paragraph was subsequently confirmed in Case 13/76 *Donà* [1976] ECR 1333, para 12; Case C-415/93 *Bosman* [1995] ECR I-4921, para 73; Joined Cases C-51/96 and C-191/97 *Deliège* [2000] ECR I-2549, para 41; and Case C-176/96 *Lehtonen and Castors Braine* [2000] ECR I-2681, para 32.

171 C-519/04 *Meca-Medina*, para 22.

172 Ibid. para 25 (citing *Walrave* para 8).

173 Ibid. para 26.

174 Ibid. para 26 (Citing *Bosman*, para 76, and *Deliège*, para 43). Emphasis added.

The Court itself said it is addressing the arguments 'on the question of application of Article [45 TFEU] to rules laid down by sporting associations'.[175]

In the following paragraph, the Court used the new language that resulted in giving the paragraph the false reputation of severely limiting the scope of sporting exception that originated in paras 8 and 9 of *Walrave*. Having set out its position from the previous case law, it said that

> it is apparent that the mere fact that a rule is purely sporting in nature does not have the effect of removing from the scope of the Treaty the person engaging in the activity governed by that rule or the body which has laid it down.[176]

All the Court does here is re-state the obvious in the light of the above considerations: if a rule is motivated by purely sporting interests (which is what the Court meant by 'purely sporting in nature') it is not the end of the story—a person engaged in the economic activity governed by that rule and a body that laid it down will fall under the scope of the Treaty, and the rule may be examined for its compatibility with the Treaty provisions. In order to receive what is classified below in Chap. 6 as a category II sporting exception, the rule will have to fulfil the other requirements of paras 14 and 15 of *Donà*/paras 8 and 9 of *Walrave*. A rule referred to in para 17 of *Meca-Medina* is any rule that produces an economic effect. If it were a rule that has no effect of an economic nature the Court would refer to para 4 in *Walrave* and that is where the story would begin and end.

The Court therefore implied that purely sporting motives of the rule are not sufficient to escape scrutiny for the body that laid it down when it produces effects on the economic activity. In either case, the fact that it uses the language of 'it is apparent' would imply that it does not change anything in regard to the previous case law.

Thereafter the Court set aside the reasoning in the decision of the General Court by finding an error in the interpretation of law. It held that:

> even if those rules do not constitute restrictions on freedom of movement because they concern questions of purely sporting interest and, as such, have nothing to do with economic activity, that fact means neither that the sporting activity in question necessarily falls outside the scope of Articles [101 TFEU] and [102 TFEU] nor that the rules do not satisfy the specific requirements of those articles. However, in para 42 of the contested judgment, the [General Court] held that the fact that purely sporting rules may have nothing to do with economic activity, with the result that they do not fall within the scope of Articles [45 TFEU] and [56 TFEU], means, also, that they have nothing to do with the economic relationships of competition, with the result that they also do not fall within the scope of Articles [101 TFEU] and [102 TFEU]. In holding that rules could thus be excluded straightaway from the scope of those articles solely on the ground that they were regarded as purely sporting with regard to the application of Articles [45 TFEU] and [56 TFEU], without any need to determine first whether the rules fulfilled the specific requirements of Articles [101 TFEU] and [102 TFEU], as set out in para 30 of the present judgment, the [General Court] made an error of law.[177]

---

[175] C-415/93 *Bosman*, para 69.

[176] C-519/04 *Meca-Medina* para 27.

[177] Ibid. paras 31–33, (emphasis added).

Therefore, the rules found to be purely sporting for the purpose of freedom of movement provisions are not by the virtue of that fact also excluded from the assessment under competition provisions. They have to satisfy the requirements of both sets of the Treaty rules separately. A generous approach of the General Court to the scope of sporting autonomy was quashed and tighter legal requirements for compatibility of the rules of governing bodies with EU law were set by the Court. Weatherill saw the setting aside of the General Court judgment not as a criticism to the convergence thesis but as the Court first pointing out the inadequacy of the General Court analysis and then putting the interpretation of Article 101 on the right track setting the convergent course for other economic law provisions in the Treaty that affect sport.[178] Section 5.5.5.5 and Chap. 6 below develop a detailed convergence theory.

Finally, the Court turned its attention to the application of Article 101(1). Relying on its previous ruling in *Wouters* the Court emphasised the need for contextual approach:

> Not every agreement between undertakings or every decision of an association of undertakings which restricts the freedom of action of the parties or of one of them necessarily falls within the prohibition laid down in Article [101(1) TFEU]. For the purposes of application of that provision to a particular case, account must first of all be taken of the overall context in which the decision of the association of undertakings was taken or produces its effects and, more specifically, of its objectives. It has then to be considered whether the consequential effects restrictive of competition are inherent in the pursuit of those objectives (*Wouters and Others*, para 97) and are proportionate to them.[179]

The fact that the doping rule was intended to safeguard the objective of fair play and ethics in sports did not remove it from the scope of competition rules; the economic effects that it produced had to be considered in the light of the *Wouters* inherency test and the requirement of proportionality. The rule was found to restrict athletes' freedom of action, but as the general objective was to provide a level playing field and preserve integrity of sporting competition and the sanctions were necessary to ensure compliance with the doping ban, the restrictions were deemed inherent in the rule. The Court also found that athletes had not demonstrated that the rule was disproportionate and upheld the previous finding of the Commission on this point.

So the athletes lost. Of particular importance for understanding of the development of law in this field is to remember that they did not lose because the rules were of 'purely sporting' interest, but because these rules satisfied the test laid down by the Court in para 42.[180]

---

[178] Weatherill 2008b, p. 342.

[179] C-519/04 *Meca-Medina*, para 42.

[180] Weatherill 2007, p. 57.

5.5.5.3 Comments

It follows from the test in para 97 of *Wouters*, as absorbed by para 42 of *Meca-Medina*, that an organisational sporting rule or practice that is found to restrict the freedom of action under Article 101(1) or 102 may not breach those provisions to the extent that the rule in question pursues a legitimate objective, its restrictive effects are inherent in the pursuit of that objective and are proportionate to it.[181] Hence, the objective justification defence developed in the framework of Article 102, coupled with proportionality requirement, has been remodelled for the purposes of its application to organisational rules of collective (sports) bodies that pursue non-competition objectives, to the extent that the criterion of inherency has been added to it. This seems to be a peculiar twist in the overall approach to the application of EU law to sport which is known to be sensitive; it looks as if a regulatory sporting rule is held to a higher standard than a commercial rule or practice adopted in an ordinary sector relying on the ordinary objective justification defence which does not include the inherency requirement. Although on this level of analysis the Court takes into consideration the specificity of sport, the effect of which could be thought to bring back the necessary balance and stay faithful to the overall approach via the adjusted intensity of the application of different parts of the test, in particular the criterion of proportionality, the practice shows that in *Meca-Medina*, just like in *Wouters*, the Court has applied a moderate intensity proportionality test.[182] Usually the intensity will vary depending on the restriction in question. It does not follow from *Meca-Medina* that the Court has given any special consideration to sport in this regard.

Meca-Medina is not the first time that the *Wouters* test was applied in the sporting case, but it is the first time that the judgment hit so close to the core of sporting autonomy and it was passed by the Court itself. Several years earlier, in *ENIC*[183] and in the unpublished *Mouscron* decision,[184] the Commission directly applied para 97 of *Wouters* in its positive assessment of the UEFA rule on multi-club ownership and the 'home and away rule', respectively. Advocate General Lenz

[181] Case C-519/04 *David Meca-Medina and Igor Majcen v. Commission* [2006] ECR I-6991. See also Commission Staff Working Document, Annex I, para 2.1.2.

[182] Lavrijssen 2010, pp. 636–659.

[183] Commission Decision in Case COMP/37.806—ENIC/UEFA. See also Commission Press Release IP/02/942 'Commission Closes Investigation into UEFA Rule on Multiple Ownership of Football Clubs' Brussels 27 June 2002.

[184] Case COMP/E3/36.85—Lille/UEFA ('the Mouscron case') unpublished Commission Decision of 3 December 1999. Commission Press Release IP/99/965 'Limits to Application of Treaty Competition Rules to Sport: Commission Gives Clear Signal' 9 December 1999. See also XXIXth Report on Competition Policy 1999, pp. 166–167.

in *Bosman*,[185] Advocate General Cosmas in *Deliège*,[186] and Advocate General Alber in *Lehtonen*[187] explicitly referred to the *DLG* case, a precursor to *Wouters*.

The rule or practice which is found to satisfy the cumulative criteria of the test is considered compatible with Articles 101 and 102. One the other hand, should the rule or practice fail to meet any of the criteria, and it has a negative effect on trade between Member States, it will breach Article 101(1) and will constitute an abuse contrary to Article 102, which can be made valid only by satisfying the conditions for exemption common to both articles (i.e., Article 101(3) and the efficiency defence conditions). Here, it must be acknowledged that it is highly unlikely that a rule of a sporting organisation pursuing a non-competition goal that cannot be translated into economic efficiencies, or a rule that has failed the *Meca-Medina/Wouters* test on the point of proportionality, would satisfy the requisite economic conditions.[188] That presents yet another *raison d'être* of the *Wouters* test in the sporting context, for without it, the broad scope of Article 101(1) would most likely render virtually any organisational rule of sport that restricts the freedom of action and relies on the non-competition justification incompatible with the entire Article 101. Even without a test case, it can be assumed on the basis of the case law so far, that neither the Court and the Commission are prepared to take the specificity of sport into consideration at this level of analysis when it cannot be translated into economic efficiency arguments, nor does the exemption provision lends itself to non-economic assessments.

5.5.5.4 Reactions

The *Meca-Medina* judgment hit closer to the core of sporting autonomy than any other sporting judgment prior to it. Needless to say, it was not welcomed by the sporting bodies. In particular, the IOC and the two largest football governing bodies (FIFA and UEFA) saw it as an attack on their authority and an unnecessary intrusion into the scope of sporting autonomy they had thus far. *Meca-Medina* has brought to an end the constitutionally based distinction in para 4 of *Walrave and Koch* between economic and 'purely sporting' rules, leaving the sporting exception applicable to only a small number of rules which, in all probability, no athlete or club would even think to challenge.[189] Weatherill thought that a possible

[185] Opinion of AG Lenz in C-415/93 *Bosman*, paras 269–270.

[186] Opinion of AG Cosmas in Joint cases C-51/96 and C-191/97 *Deliège*, para 112.

[187] Opinion of AG Alber in C-176/96 *Lehtonen*, paras 107–108.

[188] The Commission in Commission Staff Working Document, Annex I, para 2.1.6, says that '[s]uch a justification is most likely to apply where a rule is not inherent in the organisation or proper conduct of sport so as to justify the application of *Wouters* but where the beneficial effects of a rule outweigh its restrictive effects.'

[189] Such as the rules of the game.

interpretation of the decision in *Meca-Medina* would hold that the so-called rule of 'purely sporting interest', originating in *Walrave and Koch*, has now been eliminated as a basis for immunising sports rules which have an economic effect from review under EU law.[190] UEFA's Director of Legal Affairs commented on the judgment in *Meca-Medina* saying that it has opened up a possibility for almost any sports sanction for any offence (e.g. doping, match-fixing, gambling, bad conduct, etc.) to be described as representing a condition 'for engaging in' sporting activity and be challenged under EU competition law.[191] Speaking for the Financial Times, the IOC president Jacques Rogge also expressed his concern and thought that proportionality of sentences has always been counted with and there is no reason for the EU to interfere. He described bringing doping rules under EU competition law as 'frightening'[192]

On the other hand, the fact that the rule will be scrutinised under the competition provisions does not mean that it will be found in breach of those provisions. But the concern of the sporting bodies seems to be there regardless of this fact. The case has opened a door for the possibility to challenge most of the sporting rules and there will be a consequential increase in the amount of litigation, regardless of their positive outcome for the governing bodies in sport. While it is not hard to sympathise with some of the concerns raised, the fact is that none of the criticisms of the judgment presented well-reasoned, convincing arguments on the basis of EU law, not just amongst sport bodies and their representatives but also in the relevant academic circles. UEFA's Director of Legal Affairs further recalled that in the General Court's reasoning a sports rule that was 'non-economic' in character and so outside free movement law, meant that it was also outside the scope of competition law. He saw this reasoning as superior because the Treaty applied only to economic activities, and if the rule is non-economic it should be the end of the story, meaning that the Treaty does not apply altogether. Paragraph 31 of the decision of the CJEU in *Meca-Medina* was described as a 'strange twist' to this logic.[193]

While reflecting the opinion of most of the sporting world, this comment is based on a flawed interpretation of the judgment because it alludes to the category I sporting exception while it is clear that the Court was referring to the category II sporting exception.[194] The Court had merely reminded us that the two sets of provisions protect different freedoms of action and include different elements and that those differences deserve recognition. This is considered next as an answer to the criticism of the Court's decision in *Meca-Medina*.

---

[190] Weatherill 2008b, p. 345.

[191] Infantino 2006, pp. 3–4.

[192] See 'Olympic Chief Fears EU Grip on Doping' by Roger Blitz, Financial Times, 17 October 2007.

[193] Infantino 2006, pp. 3–4.

[194] On this point, see Sect. 6.3.

5.5.5.5 Paragraph 31 of Meca-Medina Reversed

The constitutional limitations on the action of the Union institutions operate generally, but their specific expression might be different in different substantive Treaty provisions. With regard to the principle of subsidiarity in Article 5 of the Treaty on the European Union (TEU), purely internal situations are outside of the scope of internal market rules and therefore outside of Union competence,[195] but the competition rules may, at least theoretically, apply even if the situation is purely internal, as long as there is the required effect on competition. Similarly, the notion of appreciability delimits the respective competences between Member States and the Union with regard to competition provisions, but the notion has no counterpart in the internal market area. Hence, the restriction on competition which does not produce an appreciable effect on the trade between Member States is outside of the EU competence in respect to competition provisions, but it may fall to be examined by the EU institutions under the free movement articles. To give a hypothetical example, it is possible that regulatory rules restricting *by effect* the numbers of non-national players in, say, the third national league of a certain sport in a Member State could escape review under Article 101(1) on the basis of their unappreciable effect on trade between Member States. The competition provisions are not as concerned with individual freedoms as much as with general market structures and preservation of viable, undistorted competition. However, because the doctrine of unappreciable effect is virtually unknown in the freedom of movement provisions,[196] the same nationality restrictions might impede market access and fall afoul of Article 45 TFEU and Article 7 of Regulation 492/2011,[197] unless objectively justified and proportionate. *A fortiori*, a completely amateur, recreational sports league ran by volunteers which has nationality quotas could be condemned on the basis of differential treatment in regard to social advantages for workers employed in the Member State in another capacity (e.g., as construction workers), or on the basis of making the move to that Member State less attractive for workers that practice the sport in

[195] See, for example, Case 175/78 *Regina v. Saunders* [1979] ECR 1129 and Cases C-225-227/95 *Kapasakalis, Skiathis and Kougiagakas v. Greece* [1998] ECR I-4329.

[196] In the freedom of movement of goods that is not the subject of this convergence discussion some rules can be seen as performing the same function: in C-267 and 268/91 *Criminal Proceedings against Keck and Mithouard* [1993] ECR I-6097 rule on certain selling arrangements; Cases C-69/88 *Krantz v Ontvanger der Directe Belastingen* [1990] ECR I-583 para 11, and C-93/92 *Motorradcenter v Pelin Baskiciogullari* [1993] ECR I-5009, para 12 state that restrictive effects which it might have on the free movement of goods are too uncertain and indirect for the obligation which it lays down to be regarded as being of a nature to hinder trade between Member States. In Case C-190/98 *Graf v Filzmozer Maschinebau GmbH* [2000] ECR I-493, para 23, the Court stated that if a measure is non-discriminatory and it does not substantially hinder access to market or its effect on free movement is too remote, it falls outside of Article 45 TFEU. This has some functional resemblance to the *de minimis* and appreciability concepts, but it was never formally recognised, it involves the non-discriminatory measures only and it is, in any case, a far higher threshold to cross to have it produce the same effect as *de minimis* and appreciability.

[197] Regulation (EU) No. 492/2011 of the European Parliament and of the Council of 5 April 2011 on the freedom of movement of workers in the Union OJ L 141, 27.5.2011, pp. 1–12.

question. A worker that is a national of another Member State (or their family member) who does not have access to the sport they want to practice due to the imposed quotas is de facto being discriminated against in terms of social advantages and would have a right to bring a claim to the national court against the body which laid the rule down. This situation is of no concern to competition law.

The illustration presented proves that para 31 of *Meca-Medina* also works in reverse with regard to the constitutional limits. Rules of sports bodies would have to satisfy the specific requirements of each of the articles of the Treaty separately in order to be considered outside of the Union competence. So in the *reverse* wording of the Court in para 31 of the judgment:

> even if those rules do not constitute restrictions on competition because they do not produce appreciable (economic) effect on trade between Member States and, as such, are not subject of Union competence under competition provisions, that fact means neither that the (sporting or other) activity in question necessarily falls outside the scope of the free movement provisions nor that the rules do not satisfy the specific requirements of those articles.

Whatever the degree and type of convergence between competition and free movement provisions, the reflection of the general constitutional principles may be different in the course of their enforcement, depending on the factual background of each case. This is due to the fact that there is no, there cannot be a, total convergence in the application of the two sets of rules, for they protect different economic rights. The core constitutional provisions of the Union, such as the principle of subsidiarity in Article 5 TEU, are therefore to be taken functionally from provision to provision. This functional approach is dictated on the constitutional level by the difference in the analytical elements, scope and content of prohibitions, exceptions and protection in articles, but also by the demands of each article on a case-by-case basis.[198] The formalistic application in which the effect of the basic Union principles under one article could determine the outcome under another would deprive those other Treaty articles of their proper function. Put simply, the competence to act is generally not transplantable from competition to internal market articles and vice versa. The article-specific exceptions and limitations, as well as general constitutionally–based limitations cannot produce a generic effect of removing the case from the scope of all of the Treaty articles under which they fall.

5.6 Blocking Competing Organisations

5.6.1 C-49/07 MOTOE *[2008]*

5.6.1.1 Article 106(1)

Addressed to Member States, Article 106(1) applies to state measures of a regulatory nature which are directed at activities of an economic nature. It does

[198] This comes through, for e.g., in paras 29 and 30 of Case C-519/04 *Meca-Medina*.

not have an independent application because it is a reference provision which can be applied only in conjunction with other TFEU articles. The rationale behind Article 106(1) is that in certain circumstances a Member State can be held liable for the breaches of the Treaty by undertakings. It reflects in more specific terms the principle of loyalty enshrined in Article 4(3) TEU according to which Member States shall, *inter alia,* refrain from any measure that can jeopardise the attainment of the Union's objectives. Article 106(1) TFEU reads:

> In the case of public undertakings and undertakings to which Member States grant special or exclusive rights, Member States shall neither enact nor maintain in force any measure contrary to the rules contained in the Treaties, in particular to those rules provided for in Articles 18 and 101–109.

5.6.1.2 Facts

MOTOE[199] is the second sports case decided under the TFEU competition provisions concerned Articles 102 and 106 in the context of the organisation and regulation of motorcycling in Greece. Article 49 of the Greek Road Traffic Code provides that a license to organise motorcycling events would be issued to the organisers by the Minister for Public Order, or the authorities empowered by him, only after the organiser secures the consent from the official representative in Greece of the *Fédération Internationale de Motocyclisme* (the International Motorcycling Federation). Accordingly, the power to grant consent for the organisation of motorcycling events was given to ELPA (*Elliniki Leskhi Aftokinitou kai Periigiseon*—Automobile and Touring Club of Greece), a legal person and a non-profit association who was itself organising the same kinds of events in Greece.

MOTOE (Greek Motorcycling Federation) planned to organise a motorcycling competition in Greece but was refused the consent from ELPA for no apparent reason and therefore failed to obtain authorisation from the competent ministry. After being refused an authorisation, MOTOE claimed pecuniary damages from the government in the Greek national court relying on Articles 102 and 106(1) TFEU. Article 49 of the Greeks Road Traffic Code conferred on ELPA a position of monopoly power over the organisation of motorcycle events in Greece which in itself does not breach Article 102 of the Treaty to the extent that the power is not abused. MOTOE claimed that ELPA had abused its monopolistic position because it refused to grant the consent needed for authorisation of its planned event.

5.6.1.3 Judgment and Comments

The Courts first held that ELPA constitutes an undertaking regardless of the fact that it has been formally classified as non-profit organisation under Greek law, and

[199] Case C-49/07 *Motosykletistiki Omospondia Ellados NPID* (*MOTOE*) v *Elliniko Dimosio* [2008] ECR I-4863.

that it has been vested with public powers in regard to its special right to grant consent. For the remainder of its activities, the organisation and marketing of sporting events, it was an undertaking, and this conclusion cannot be changed because the offer of goods or services is made without a profit motive since that offer is in competition with other undertakings that do seek to make profit.[200] The fact that MOTOE was itself classified as a non-profit organisation could not change this conclusion either, as 'non-profit-making associations which offer goods or services on a given market may find themselves in competition with one another' and their economic survival ultimately depends on imposing their services on the relevant market to the detriment of those offered by the other operators.[201] This is not a novelty in the Court's jurisprudence.[202] Furthermore, the product market was defined as consisting of 'first, the organisation of motorcycling events and, second, in their commercial exploitation by means of sponsorship, advertising and insurance contracts. Those two types of activities are not interchangeable but are rather functionally complementary.'[203] Confirming the well-established case law, the Court then went on to say that a geographic market which is confined to a single Member State does not imply that trade between Member States is not affected; the effect of the conduct in a single Member State may be the partitioning of markets on a national basis and preventing economic interpenetration.[204]

There was no doubt that ELPA was dominant on the relevant market as defined by the Court. Granting special or exclusive rights to an undertaking to control whether and under which conditions other undertakings can gain access and engage in activities on the relevant market entails such conclusion. ELPA's monopoly to grant the necessary consent was statutory and therefore the examination of Article 106 TFEU was needed. The classification of ELPA as an undertaking entrusted with the operation of 'services of general economic interests' for the purposes of application of exception in Article 106(2) TFEU was dismissed on the following ground: the undertaking's economic activities related to the organisation and commercial exploitation of motorcycling events were not conferred by an act of entrustment by the public authority, an element needed for the application of this provision. The power to grant consents to applications for authorisation to organise motorcycling events, although stemming from an act of public authority, namely Article 49 of the Greek Road Traffic Code, could not be classified as an economic activity and consequently Article 106(2) TFEU was held inapplicable also to this part of ELPA's activities.[205]

---

200 Paragraphs 25 and 27 of C-49/07 *MOTOE.*

201 Ibid. para 28.

202 See, for example, Case 96/82 *IAZ International Belgium v. Commission* [1983] ECR 3369.

203 Paragraph 33 of C-49/07 *MOTOE.*

204 Ibid. para 42.

205 Paragraphs 44–47 of C-49/07 *MOTOE.*

The Court then turned its attention to Article 106(1) TFEU in conjunction with Article 102 TFEU. The mere creation or reinforcement of a dominant position through the grant of special or exclusive rights within the meaning of Article 106(1) TFEU was not in itself considered incompatible with Article 102 TFEU. However,

> a Member State will be in breach of the prohibitions laid down by those two provisions if the undertaking in question, merely by exercising the special or exclusive rights conferred upon it, is led to abuse its dominant position or where such rights are liable to create a situation in which that undertaking is led to commit such abuses (*Höfner and Elser*, cited above, para 29; *ERT*, cited above, para 37; Case C-179/90 *Merci convenzionali porto di Genova* [1991] ECR I-5889, paras 16 and 17; and Case C-323/93 *Centre d'insémination de la Crespelle* [1994] ECR I-5077, para 18). In this respect, it is not necessary that any abuse should actually occur (see, to that effect, Case C-55/96 *Job Centre* [1997] ECR I-7119, para 36). In any event, Articles [102 TFEU and 106(1) TFEU] are infringed where a measure imputable to a Member State, and in particular a measure by which a Member State confers special or exclusive rights within the meaning of Article [106(1) TFEU], gives rise to a risk of an abuse of a dominant position (see, to that effect, *ERT*, cited above, para 37; *Merci convenzionali porto di Genova*, cited above, para 17; and Case C-380/05 *Centro Europa 7* [2008] ECR I-0000, para 60).[206]

As emphasized by the Court in numerous judgments, including *MOTOE*, Article 102 is not breached by the mere existence or reinforcement of a dominant position, even if the position is attained through the grant of special or exclusive rights within the meaning of Article 106(1), but by the circumstances in which the undertaking is led to abuse that position is created. The key question is the discretion that a Member State leaves for the regulatory bodies to abuse the conferred powers. Should an undertaking be under an obligation to engage in abusive practices, the Member State is responsible for the abuses that take place, and conversely, if an undertaking has discretion not to abuse its special powers the Member State will not be held responsible for the committed abuses.[207] The judgment in *MOTOE*, paras 49 and 50, clearly indicate that the Court will consider Article 106(1), in conjunction with Article 102, breached where the dominant position creates the mere possibility which can lead the undertaking to commit an abuse. The concept of abuse is interpreted expansively to include creating 'a risk of an abuse of a dominant position'. This is more reminiscent of the approach to oligopolistic markets, and even to substantive assessment of concentrations, than it is to the well-established approach to Article 102 TFEU alone under which abuse has to take place in order to find violation. On the facts of the case, ELPA was itself organizing and commercially exploiting motorcycling events, and in addition was in charge of giving consent to other undertakings to organise and commercially exploit motorcycling events. These different powers placed ELPA in apparent

[206] Ibid. paras 49 and 50.

[207] For analytical comment on *MOTOE* that details this point see Miettinen 2009, pp. 137–149.

advantage over its competitors whereby it could restrict access to the relevant market for the other operators.[208]

Weatherill has posed the question if the *MOTOE* judgment therefore implies that sporting federations must ruthlessly separate their regulatory functions from any whiff of commercial advantage in order to avoid condemnation under Article 102 and that the State too must withdraw special rights granted to such sporting bodies in order to escape condemnation under Article 106? He said that 'it certainly pushes in that direction.'[209] The conflict of interests between regulatory and commercial functions has been held to per se violate a combination of Articles 106(1) and 102 also in *Corbeau,*[210] whereas in cases such as *ERT* and *La Crespelle*[211] the mere risk of abuse was not sufficient to find Member State liability. The final word of the Court was that:

> [...] a rule, which gives a legal person such as ELPA the power to give consent to applications for authorisation to organise motorcycling events *without that power being made subject by that rule to restrictions, obligations and review*, could lead the legal person entrusted with giving that consent to distort competition by favouring events which it organises or those in whose organisation it participates. In the light of the foregoing, the answer to the questions referred must be that a legal person whose activities consist not only in taking part in administrative decisions authorising the organisation of motorcycling events, but also in organising such events itself and in entering, in that connection, into sponsorship, advertising and insurance contracts, falls within the scope of Articles [102 EC and 106 EC]. Those articles preclude a national rule which confers on a legal person, which organises motorcycling events and enters, in that connection, into sponsorship, advertising and insurance contracts, the power to give consent to applications for authorisation to organise such competitions, without that power being made subject to restrictions, obligations and review. [emphasis added].[212]

This wording provides a lifeline for the sporting bodies: although paras 49 and 50 considered the mere existence of a conflict of interest in breach of Article 106(1), in conjunction with 102, this breach could have been avoided if the power granted to ELPA were subject to an appropriate standard of control. On the facts of this case there was no such control placed upon ELPA and the Greece lost the case.

---

208 Paragraph 51 of the C-49/07 *MOTOE.* In Case C-41/90 *Höfner and Elser v. Macrotron* [1991] ERC I-1979 it was held that the state measure within the meaning of Article 106(1) will be unlawful where by exercising exclusive rights conferred on it an undertaking cannot avoid abusing dominant position. In Case C-203/96 *Dusseldorp* [1998] ECR I-4075 the Court held that Article 106(1) in conjunction with Article 102 will be breached where the Member State 'adopts any law, regulation or administrative provision which enables an undertaking on which it has conferred rights to abuse its dominant position.'

209 Weatherill 2008a, p. 6.

210 Case C-320/91 *Corbeau* [1993] ERC I-2533, where the Court appears to have implied that the monopoly not justifiable under Article 106(2) would amount to measure contrary to Article 106(1).

211 Case C-260/89 *ERT* [1991] ECR I-2925, and Case C-323/93 *Centre d'Insémination de la Crespelle v. Coopérative de la Mayenne* [1994] ECR I-5077.

212 C-49/07 *MOTOE,* paras 51 and 52.

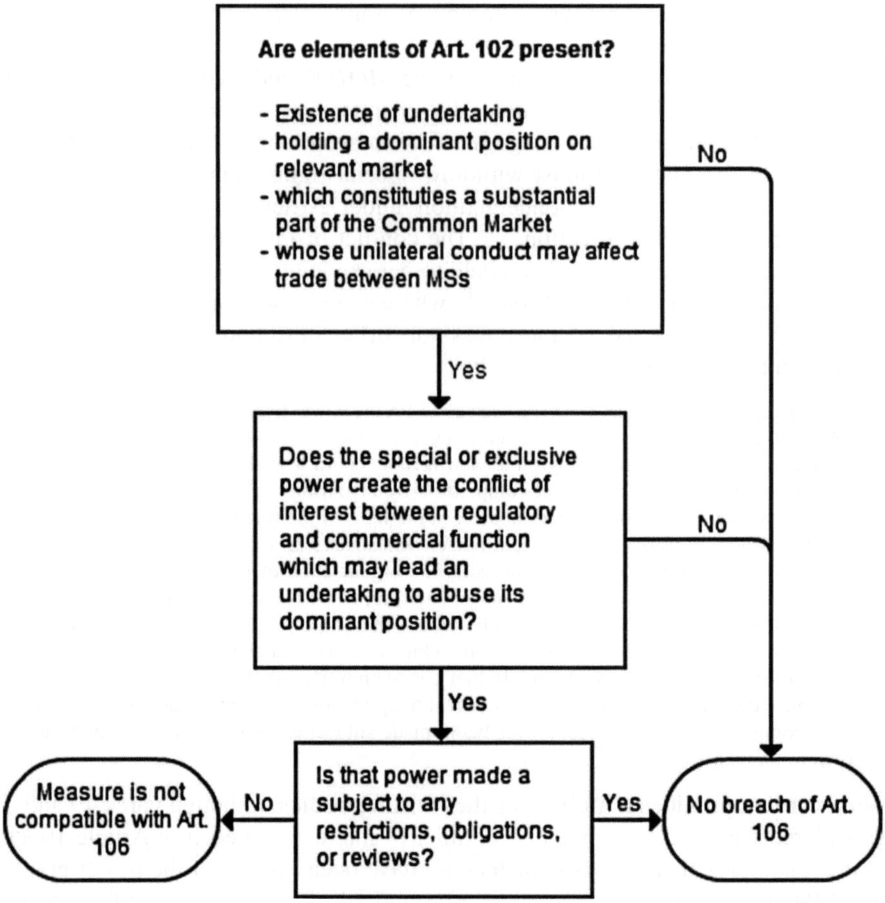

Fig. 5.1 Checklist under C-49/07 *MOTOE* judgment

Nevertheless, as a matter of the rule supplied by the *MOTOE* judgment, justification for the inevitable abuse is possible. Miettinen concludes that, 'as a consequence of *MOTOE*, it could be argued that since all undertakings that are endowed with regulatory powers are placed in a dominant position, regardless of whether they abuse that position they must be subject to "restrictions, obligations and review."'[213] (see Fig. 5.1)

What kind of supervisory control on the exercise of special powers is required has not been explained by the Court. Reflecting part of the Opinion of Advocate General Kokott, Weatherill suggests that the correct interpretation of the judgment is that giving exclusive rights which lead to conflict of interests is not a problem in itself, as long as sporting federations thus endowed have 'transparent, objectively

[213] Miettinen 2009, p. 147.

justified, and non-discriminatory procedures and criteria for selection which are followed faithfully and openly'.[214] Moreover, the applicant promoter should be afforded a right to a hearing and be given reasons for decisions taken, which should be reviewable by an independent body.[215]

5.6.1.4 Applying Article 106(2) to Sport is Undesirable and Superfluous

In addition to the exceptions under internal market provisions, and Articles 101 and 102 TFEU, 106(2) TFEU provides a further exception from the application of the rules contained in the Treaty which applies only to cases involving provision of services of general economic interest. It reads:

> Undertakings entrusted with the operation of services of general economic interest or having the character of a revenue-producing monopoly shall be subject to the rules contained in the Treaties, in particular to the rules on competition, in so far as the application of such rules does not obstruct the performance, in law or in fact, of the particular tasks assigned to them. The development of trade must not be affected to such an extent as would be contrary to the interests of the Union.

Article 106(2) thus excludes from the application of the Treaty certain categories of agreements, decisions and certain types of conduct by undertakings in as far as they do not significantly affect trade contrary to the Union interests. The Article 106(2) exception is of a dual nature in as far as it is capable of being invoked by both, undertakings entrusted with the operation of a public service to justify breaches of, for example, Articles 101 and 102, and by Member States to justify the adoption of certain measures which are deemed necessary to guarantee the functioning of the public services, the operation of which was entrusted to certain undertakings. In order to qualify for the Article 106(2) TFEU exception, four cumulative criteria must be fulfilled. Firstly, there must be an act of entrustment, whereby the State confers responsibility for the execution of a certain task to an undertaking.[216] Secondly, the entrustment must relate to a service of general

[214] Weatherill 2008a, p. 8.

[215] Ibid.

[216] Entrustment requires an official act(s) by the Member State, no particular form being prescribed. It can be for example, a legislative measure or follow from the terms and conditions of a concession agreement (see Case 30/87 *Corinne Bodson v. Pompes Funèbres* [1988] ECR 2497, [1989] 4 CMLR 984). Commission Decision 2005/842/EC on the application of Article 86(2) of the EC Treaty to State aid in the form of public service compensation granted to certain undertakings entrusted with the operation of services of general economic interest, OJ L 312/67, 29/11/2005, Article 4(a), requires the state entrusting an undertaking for the execution of a certain task to specify the nature and duration of the public service obligation; Article 4(b) the undertaking and territory concerned; Article 4(c) the nature of any special or exclusive right assigned to undertaking; Article 4(d) parameters for calculating, controlling and reviewing the compensation, and; 4(d) the arrangements for avoiding and repaying any overcompensation.

economic interest.[217] Thirdly, the exception has to be necessary for the performance of the tasks assigned and proportional to that end. If the market is in a state of healthy competition, providing a product or a service to the consumers is not considered necessary.[218] Finally, the development of trade must not be affected to such an extent as would be contrary to the interests of the Union.[219] If these requirements are satisfied, the Member State measure or conduct of undertaking(s) will be deemed compatible with the Treaty.

The proposals in the Arnaut Report aimed at European institutions included the adoption of the 'Guidelines to the application of competition law to sport' according to which it should be assumed that sport organisations fulfil a task of general economic interest in the sense of Article 106(2).[220] However, any such 'assumptions' would constitute a double breach of the EU law. First, Union law is clear that without the official act of entrustment by the state in the exercise of its functions as a public authority there can be no performance of the task of general economic interest within the meaning of Article 106(2) by any undertaking and therefore no exception granted on that basis.[221] Second, it could also be construed as an intrusion into Member States' authority and a breach of the principle of subsidiarity to imply any such entrustment in relation to the undertakings that have not been so entrusted by the Member States themselves.

It is debatable whether sport would qualify as a 'general service' or a 'service of general economic interest'. Although Member States are in principle free to choose which services they want to guarantee for its citizens, their discretion is subject to principles of necessity and proportionality. The concept of 'services of general economic interests' is a Union concept which sets a maximum standard. Therefore, the Court and the Commission could refuse to accept that the public

[217] Commodities that states are obliged to provide to their citizens due to their essential character. The functioning of the general economic interest can be provided through state aid measures only if a normal market economy cannot provide for it without state intervention. Also, the measure must be so essential to the consumers that it is considered to be a necessity in their everyday life, must benefit the citizens of the state in general and not be aimed at giving an advantage to an industry or generally boost the economy of the state. Whereas the provision only applies to general interests of economic nature, the aim cannot be economic but it must be of social, cultural, or other non-economic nature. For the specific requirements to qualify as service of general economic interest see, for example, Faull and Nikpay 2007, pp. 626–646, or Whish 2009, pp. 234–335.

[218] The industry that does not need state regulation to allow it to function in a manner that will guarantee the consumer constant access to the product at a competitive price is not a good candidate for this exception.

[219] Case law in C-56/65 *STM* [1966] ECR 235 has demonstrated that there is no need to show the measures actually produce effect in distorting the trade between Member States, it is sufficient to show that there is potential threat.

[220] Paragraph 6.27 of the Arnaut Report.

[221] Opinion of Advocate General Jacobs in Case C-203/96 *Chemische Afvalstoffen Dusseldorp and others v. Minister van Volkshuisvesting, Ruimtelijke Ordening en Milieubeheer* [1998] ECR I-4075, para 103.

service guaranteed by a Member State was a 'service of general economic interest' within the meaning of Article 106(2). Any other approach would send an invitation to Member States to use the Article 106(2) as a protectionist mechanism to exclude the entire sectors of economy from the application of the Treaty rules.

In the opinion of the Arnaut Report authors, there is no doubt that sport organisations perform services of general economic interest within certain geographic areas. They cite access to sport, bringing people together, social inclusion, measures to combat doping, social significance, fight against xenophobia etc., in support of that suggestion.[222]

Due to the multiplicity of tasks and the stark difference between stakeholders' interests that one sport federation ought to protect in accordance with the principles of good governance, and whereas the Article 106(2) implies the States pursuing the goals of, *inter alia*, social policy, and whereas the social policy goals might indeed qualify as 'general services', it is difficult to reconcile this social role with the role of the sporting organization in regulating the highly commercial professional sport. Partial entrustment could therefore be thought to be the way to go. But the practical difficulties prevent this approach: there is no clear distinction between sports bodies' regulation of professional and amateur sports. They are interconnected on many levels, and so the rules passed by the bodies often have implications for both. Taking into account the current sporting structures in Europe there is no space for this exception.

The ultimate question is if the sport bodies would even (a) want to be entrusted, or (b) need to be entrusted with the task of providing a service of general economic interest. In relation to the 'need to be entrusted', national sport organisations already have the same objectives enshrined in their functions. Promoting sport at all levels and making it generally and widely accessible within their respective geographic areas is a part of what they already (ought to) do. They have a monopoly over such activities so there is no need to protect them from competition. In addition, they comply with the rules of international governing bodies that already fight against xenophobia and racism, doping, protection of minors, etc. Hence, an act of entrustment would be unnecessary. More importantly, there is no reason to go through Article 106(2) to achieve the effect of excluding the rules of the sport organisations from the scope of application of the Treaty. The EU institutions have already designed a system of enforcement in which the rules for performance of tasks in the general public interest by sporting bodies are sufficiently protected. To push for the status of undertakings entrusted with operation of services of general economic interest would therefore be unnecessary.

In relation to the 'want to be entrusted', it has already been observed by some authors that sporting bodies themselves have not promoted the arguments put forth by the Arnaut Report, and it is indicative that the White Paper on Sports does not mention sport in this context.[223] Every sporting body seeks the maximum level of

---

[222] Paragraphs 6.53 and 6.54 of the Arnaut Report.

[223] Parrish and Miettinen 2008, pp. 133–134.

autonomy and self-governance without interference from any other regulators. With the act of entrustment, a Member State would impose a legal obligation on the sporting organisations to perform the specific service of general interest (which they already perform), and this would in turn require state supervision of the performance and accountability for financial compensation. This is not what the sport organisations want. Also, Member States are not very keen on promoting this exception in sporting context for it brings extra expenses and administrative burden. For instance, in the *MOTOE* judgment the Greek Government did not even try to claim that ELPA has been entrusted with the exercise of their activities through an act of public authority.

5.6.2 Commission Investigation in **FIA/Formula One** *Case*

In sport involving motor races, unlike in football, it is hard to see any socio-educational function. The *FIA/Formula One* case[224] is therefore significant for the management and governance of motor sports, in which there is no element of specificity of sport, but also for sports in general when the issue under investigation is purely commercial.

The access to financial resources at all levels of the sport is a prerequisite for participation, and it has been said that Formula One is first business and then sport.[225] Unlike in football where financing is heavily reliant on broadcasting rights, in motor sport events such as Formula One, organisers, promoters and teams mostly depend on sponsorship for finance. Television coverage is vital to the success of a motor sport event mostly because the level of sponsorship generated depends to a large extent on the television coverage a promoter or organiser can guarantee.

5.6.2.1 Restrictive/Abusive Conduct

A case concerning the conflict of interest between the regulatory and commercial functions of a sport association involved the *Fédération Internationale d'Automobile* (FIA), the international association for motor sport. FIA was the organiser and promoter of motor sport championships, including Formula One. It issued licences to any party wishing to take part in international motor sport events authorised by FIA, including track owners, vehicle manufacturers, organisers of motor sport events and drivers. License holders were allowed to organise or enter

[224] Notice published pursuant to Article 19(3) of Council Regulation No 17 concerning Cases COMP/35.163—Notification of FIA Regulations, COMP/36.638—Notification by FIA/FOA of agreements relating to the FIA Formula One World Championship, COMP/36.776—GTR/FIA and others (2001/C 169/03).

[225] Cygan 2007, p. 76.

only those events authorised by FIA. Entering or organising events not authorised by FIA would mean the loss of their license and the virtual end of any commercial activity in motor sport. This way, FIA was able to control everyone and everything needed stage a rival championship that could compete with FIA's events. The Commission found evidence that the competing GTR Organisation was forced out of the market by these rules, and its GTR series was replaced by the FIA GT Championship. Further, FIA claimed the television rights to all events incorporating the FIA name into their title, which were then transferred to International Sportsworld Communicators (ISC). It also forced the Formula One teams by the terms of tripartite Concorde Agreement to assign to it all broadcasting rights in the Formula One championship, which it then transferred to Formula One Administration Ltd (FOA), a commercial rights holder. The same agreement also prevented Formula One teams from racing in any other series comparable to Formula One for a very long period of time. The promoters' rights were taken directly by FOA which has been given the power by the FIA to determine who can and cannot be a promoter of a grand prix. Interesting to note here is that a vice-president of FIA, Bernie Ecclestone, was controlling both FOA and ISC. An agreement between FOA and the various broadcasters and promoters which are involved in the Formula One championship was reinforcing already substantial difficulties for those who wished to stage a series competing with Formula One. The promoters' contracts prevented circuits used for Formula One races from being used for races which could compete with Formula One, while the agreements with broadcasters placed a massive financial penalty, ranging from between 33 and 50 % of the price paid, if they televised anything deemed by FOA to be a competitive threat to Formula One.[226]

5.6.2.2 Statement of Objections and Settlement

In 1999, the Commission issued a Statement of Objections. It came to the preliminary conclusion that the rules described were contrary to Articles 101(1) and 102 TFEU as they gave FIA the control to block the organisation of races which competed with the events FIA promoted or organised, in particular Formula One from which it derived the biggest commercial benefit. The Commission also objected to certain terms of the contracts between the FOA and broadcasters because they made it possible to block the organisation of motor sport events that would compete with Formula One races. Finally, the Commission objected to FIA rules according to which FIA automatically acquired TV rights to all the motor sport events it authorises even if these were promoted by a different promoter. The core of all of the

[226] Commission Press Release IP/99/434 'Commission opens formal proceedings into Formula One and other international motor racing series' Brussels 30 June, 1999.

objections is the conflict between the FIA's legitimate role as the regulator of international motor sport and its interests in the commercial side of motor sport.[227]

In 2001 the Commission closed the case after reaching a settlement with FIA's president Max Mosley, and CEO of FOA, Bernie Ecclestone. The settlement provided that FIA would

> limit its role to that of a sport regulator without influence over the commercial exploitation of the sport and thus removing any conflict of interest (through the appointment by FIA of a 'commercial rights holder' for 100 years in exchange for a one-off fee); guarantee access to motor sport to any racing organisation and to no longer prevent teams to participate in and circuit owners to organize other races provided the requisite safety standards are met; waive its TV rights or transfer them to the promoters concerned; and remove the anticompetitive clauses from the agreements between FOA and broadcasters.[228]

Later in 2001, after consultation with all the interested parties, the Commission closed its investigation in the *FIA/Formula One* case, satisfied that the agreed amendments will remove the competition concerns.[229] In 2003 it ended the monitoring of compliance with the 2001 settlement.[230]

5.6.2.3 Comparison with MOTOE

Much like *MOTOE*, *FIA/Formula One* was a case of sporting 'conflict of interest' examined under the TFEU competition rules. In both cases the core issue was conflation of regulatory and commercial functions in one body, which ultimately led to blocking of competing organisations and preventing market access. Both cases involved sporting bodies protecting private interests, rather than acting on behalf of public interests in general. Neither of the cases involved specificity of sport in any form. Unlike in *MOTOE*, in *FIA/Formula One* there was no element of State involvement, as the powers which enabled it to control the relevant markets were not endowed by an act of public authority but by its own rules and web of private agreements. Whereas in *MOTOE* the requirement on the Member State was to create a system of safeguards against abuse (by ELPA's refusal to grant the consent necessary for the issuance of license) of the dominant position it enabled, in *FIA/Formula One* the mere fact that the body was issuing licenses was not a problem. Rather, it was the restrictions on competition that those licenses entailed under the

[227] Commission Press Release IP/01/120 'Commission welcomes progress towards resolving the long-running FIA/Formula One case' Brussels, 26 January 2001.

[228] Commission Staff Working Document, Annex I, para 2.2.2.1.

[229] Commission Press Release IP/01/1523 'Commission closes its investigation into Formula One and other four-wheel motor sports', Brussels, 30 October 2001.

[230] Commission Press Release IP/03/1491 'Commission ends monitoring of FIA/Formula One compliance with 2001 settlement', Brussels, 31 October 2003.

disputed rules.[231] The safeguard against unjustified refusal of licenses in the *FIA/ Formula One* case was the obligation to insert a new clause ensuring that legal challenge against FIA decisions would be available not only within their structure but also before national courts.

5.6.3 Case C-250/92 DLG *[1994]*

5.6.3.1 Facts

A Danish cooperative association, DLG, which distributed farm supplies, provided its members with farm supplies at the lowest prices and negotiated the best prices for its members' produce. DLG's members were divided into four categories from A to D. B members were local associations or other cooperatives whose objective was trading in and/or producing goods appearing in the range of products offered by DLG. They were entitled to some extent to take part in DLG's management. The plaintiffs, 37 local associations specialising in distribution of farm supplies that were B members of DLG, were also members of the National Union of cooperative associations (LAG) formed in 1975 by the B members of DLG. During the 1980s, some B members, dissatisfied with the prices charged by DLG on the sale of fertilizers and plant protection products, took the initiative and began to import those products themselves. As a result, they started to cooperate amongst themselves within LAG.

DLG reacted by amending its statutes as regards B members because of increasing competition from LAG. According to the amended statutes, B members were prohibited from membership in any other cooperative organisations or participation in any other forms of organised membership in competition with this association on the wholesale market, with regard to the purchase and sale of fertilizers and plant protection products. The B members were still free to make wholesale purchases of farm supplies through suppliers other than DLG, as long as those substitute purchases were not made through any organised membership of or participation in other associations. Members who were participating in any such association, society or cooperative were required to cease that membership or resign from DLG. Some of the B members refused to comply with the

[231] This is evident from the Statement of Objections and from the Sect. 5.6 of the Notice (Notice published pursuant to Article 19(3) of Council Regulation No 17 concerning Cases COMP/35.163—Notification of FIA Regulations, COMP/36.638—Notification by FIA/FOA of agreements relating to the FIA Formula One World Championship, COMP/36.776—GTR/FIA and others (2001/C 169/03)), which says that '[t]he notified agreements as amended will remove those barriers which had prevented in the past the use of FIA licensed products and circuits or the participation of FIA licensees in different disciplines or in competing events in the same discipline. The proposed changes to the notified agreements will, for example, result in the availability of racetracks in Europe for rival series to use, even if these circuits already host FIA Formula One championship events.'

amendments to the statutes, with the result that 37 local associations which were B members were excluded from DLG.

5.6.3.2 Judgment

The compatibility of the statutes of a cooperative purchasing association, a voluntary association of persons established in order to pursue common *commercial* objectives, with EU competition law cannot be assessed in the abstract but will depend on the particular clauses in the statutes and the economic conditions prevailing on the markets concerned.[232] In a market where product prices vary according to the volume of orders, the activities of cooperative purchasing associations may, relative to the size of their membership, constitute a significant counterweight to the contractual power of large producers and bring about more effective competition in some markets.[233] A dual membership in competing cooperatives would jeopardize both the proper functioning of the cooperative and its contractual power in relation to producers making each association less capable to pursue its objectives. In this sense, prohibition of dual membership does not necessarily constitute a restriction of competition and may even have beneficial effects on competition.[234] On the other hand, the amendments also have adverse effects on competition because they restrict the opportunity for members to join other types of competing cooperatives and thus discourage them from obtaining supplies elsewhere.[235]

The Court held that the statutes of a cooperative purchasing association, forbidding its members to participate in other forms of organised cooperation which are in direct competition with it, are not caught by the prohibition in Article 101(1) TFEU and do not amount to abuse of a dominant position under Article 102 TFEU, so long as they are restricted to what is necessary to ensure the achievement of the legitimate commercial objectives (in casu, the proper functioning of the cooperative and ensuring its contractual power in relation to producers).[236]

On the facts of the case it did not appear that amendments went beyond what was necessary to ensure that the said objectives are met. First, the restrictions covered only the farm supplies in respect of which there existed a direct relationship between sales volume and price.[237] Second, non-members of DLG, including the plaintiffs, were free to make any purchases from it on the same commercial terms and at the same prices as members, except that 'non-members' were not entitled to

[232] Case C-250/92 *Gøttrup-Klim e.a. Grovvareforeninger v Dansk Landbrugs Grovvareselskab AmbA* [1994] ECR I-5641, para 31.

[233] Ibid. para 32.

[234] Ibid. paras 33–34.

[235] Ibid. para 35.

[236] Ibid. paras 35, 45 and 52.

[237] Ibid. para 37.

annual discount on the amount of the transactions carried out.[238] Finally, DLG's statutes authorize its members to buy fertilizers and plant protection products without using DLG as an intermediary, provided that such transactions are carried out otherwise than through an organised consortium.[239]

5.6.3.3 Comment and Comparison with *Wouters* and *Meca-Medina*: The Shared Test

In *DLG*, much like in the subsequent *Wouters* and *Meca-Medina* judgments, the Court made it clear that a restriction on commercial freedom is not the same as a restriction on commercial freedom that restricts competition. The aims of EU competition law and policy are centred on the preservation of free competition and do not contain guarantees on unfettered commercial conduct of the all the parties. In fact, the success of many pro-competitive agreements depends on the ability to restrict conduct of some of the parties.

The judgment in *DLG* is often referred to as a precursor to *Wouters*, but some important differences should be recognised. First, DLG was probably not a dominant undertaking having only 36 % of the market share and it was established as voluntary association of persons to pursue common commercial objectives. In contrast, the Bar of the Netherlands in *Wouters* and the IOC in *Meca-Medina* were both regulatory monopolies with delegated public functions. Second, DLG acted in the interest of its members, whereas the two regulatory monopolies laid down rules that were in public interests. Third, the objectives of the rules in *DLG* statutes were strictly commercial while the rules in *Wouters* and *Meca-Medina* had a deontological purpose. Fourth, the plaintiffs in DLG were its members but also competitors, while the parties whose conduct was restricted as a result of the rules of Bar of the Netherlands and IOC were not either actual or potential competitors of those bodies. Finally, it is clear that the *Wouters* and *Meca-Medina* cases involved weighing of the public interest (i.e., non-competition) objectives against the TFEU competition objectives, but it is equally clear that the *DLG* case involved weighing pro and anti-competitive effects of the statutes within the framework of Article 101(1). The last-mentioned matter applies regardless of the formal rejection by the Court and the Commission of the rule of reason analysis in this provision. Thus, whereas it is easy to explain why the Court would design the test in regard to the cases involving public policy non-economic interests that are ill-suited for the exclusively economic analysis in Article 101(3), it is hard to see why it would do so for the *DLG*-type of cases that could in any case benefit from the Article 101(3) as they are well-suited for the economic analysis and exception criteria contained therein.

---

[238] Ibid. para 38.

[239] Ibid. para 39.

The significance that the outlined differences hold is prone to conjecture, but before getting caught in any such discussion it must be recognised that the test supplied by these cases is essentially the same. The difference is that the Court had not been careful in *DLG* to neatly separate the different parts of the test it later spelled out in *Wouters*. Nevertheless, it implicitly recognised the objectives that DLG was carrying out as legitimate and it considered as necessary (i.e., inherent) the restrictions on the conduct of its B members. The recognition that something is 'limited to what is necessary' for the attainment of its objectives is an automatic acceptance of those objectives as legitimate by the Court, and automatic recognition that they are 'necessary' or 'inherent'. In the judgment the Court did deal with the question of inherency in paras 32–34 without specifically mentioning it.

Furthermore, paras 35, 45 and 52 of *DLG* illustrate that the test applicable to Article 101(1) TFEU along with its outcome, also applies to Article 102 TFEU. The same is, of course, valid for the *Wouters* and *Meca-Medina* test. It would make no sense to hold the proportionate rules adopted in the public interest that outweigh the restrictions on free competition under Article 101(1) in breach of Article 102. The two provisions protect the same undistorted competitive process and consumer welfare and once the case falls under both provisions the application of the same test ought to produce a uniform result. In *Meca-Medina*, the Court itself did not mention Article 102 TFEU, one of the articles relied on by the plaintiffs, once it decided the case under Article 101 TFEU. The Commission Staff Working Document confirms that the *Meca-Medina* (and therefore *Wouters*) test is applicable to both competition provisions equally.[240]

5.7 Superdominance and Special Responsibility

Even by the most permissive definition, sports governing bodies tend to constitute dominant undertakings when they engage in economic activity; the decisive question then is whether their acts amount to abuse.[241] This fact can be seen as pointing towards the more specific concept of superdominance. In accordance with the established case law of the Court, 'the actual scope of the special responsibility imposed on a dominant undertaking must be considered in the light of the specific circumstances of each case.'[242]

---

240 See Annex I to the Commission Staff Working Document, para 2.1.2.

241 Parrish and Miettinen 2008, p. 126. Case T-193/02 *Piau* has shown that the engagement in economic activity can be indirect, when federations operate on the relevant market through their members.

242 See, for example, Case C-333/94 P *Tetra Pak International SA v. Commission* [1996] ECR I-5951, para 24.

5.7.1 The Concept of Superdominance

In *Michelin*[243] the Court has formulated the concept of special responsibility of dominant undertakings which has been confirmed in the subsequent case law in the same terms:

> whilst the finding that a dominant position exists does not in itself imply any reproach to the undertaking concerned, it has a special responsibility, irrespective of the causes of that position, not to allow its conduct to impair genuine undistorted competition on the common market (*Michelin*, para 57, and *Irish Sugar*, para 112).[244]

The special responsibility of dominant undertakings is particularly onerous in cases of superdominance where the degree of market power reaches a status of quasi-monopoly.[245] This status might have repercussions for the finding of abuse, which in few cases seemed to be correlated with the degree of market power enjoyed by the undertaking(s).[246] In *GVL*, the Court acknowledged the wide scope of a monopolist's special responsibility in relation to discriminatory conduct on grounds of nationality or residence.[247]

O'Donoghue and Padilla saw several practical, legal, and economic problems with the concept of superdominance. First, Article 102 itself does not make any reference to the degree of dominance and a corresponding level of responsibility. Second, economics does not have a basis for specifying a point at which an undertaking could be said to acquire a position of superdominance. Third, by applying the concept, significant uncertainty would be added to the law and the notion of

[243] Case 322/81 *Michelin* [1983] ECR 3461, paras 10 and 57.

[244] Case T-219/99 *British Airways plc v. Commission* judgment of 17 December 2003, para 242.

[245] The concept of superdominance was first time referred to in the Opinion of Advocate General Fennelly delivered on 29 October 1998 in Joined Cases C-395/96 P and C-396/96 P *Compagnie Maritime Belge Transport SA, Compagnie Maritime Belge and Dafra-Lines A/S v. Commission*, para 137: 'To my mind, Article [106] cannot be interpreted as permitting monopolists or quasi-monopolists to exploit the very significant market power which their superdominance confers so as to preclude the emergence either of a new or additional competitor. Where an undertaking, or group of undertakings whose conduct must be assessed collectively, enjoys a position of such overwhelming dominance verging on monopoly, comparable to that which existed in the present case at the moment when G and C entered the relevant market, it would not be consonant with the particularly onerous special obligation affecting such a dominant undertaking not to impair further the structure of the feeble existing competition for them to react, even to aggressive price competition from a new entrant, with a policy of targeted, selective price cuts designed to eliminate that competitor. [...]' In Case C-333/94 P *Tetra Pak International SA v. Commission* [1996] ECR I-5951, paras 28–31, the Court referred to the quasi-monopolistic position enjoyed by the undertakings.

[246] See Case T-228/97 *Irish Sugar plc v. Commission*, judgment of 7 October 1999, para 185. See also Commission Decision in Case IV/36.888—1998 Football World Cup [2000] OJ L 5/55, para 86, where the Commission considered that the scope of the parties' responsibility must be considered in relation to the degree of dominance held by the parties.

[247] Case 7/82 *GVL* [1983] ECR 483, para 56.

abuse would require re-defining. Finally, the concept might lead to unnecessary intervention in as far as it is related to the high market share, which does not imply the ability to persist or the protection of market power by high entry barriers.[248]

It is submitted that that none of these points is very convincing. First, it is well-known that the Court uses teleological interpretation. Given the countless number of occasions in which the Court construed the provision as necessary to give it full effect in the light of its objectives and context, it would not be too much to conclude that imputing into an article what it does not expressly provide for, constitutes a rule rather than exception in the interpretation of the Treaty. Here, the Court would not even have to go against the express wording of the article, a path not unfamiliar to its judgments. The fact that Article 102 does not distinguish between varying degrees of dominance is therefore completely irrelevant. In addition, the mere fact that an undertaking occupies the superdominant position does not mean that it breaches Article 102 as some other authors have implied.[249] It merely means that the effects of that undertaking's behaviour on the market are more profound, which merits more rigorous standard of application of the competition rules including amplified concept of special responsibility.[250] Second, superdominance was referred to by the Court as a quasi-monopoly—a term familiar to economists for a long time.[251] Relying on both Whish[252] and Advocate General Fennelly's Opinion in *Compagnie Maritime Belge*, Crocioni and Veljanovski, both economists, defined superdominance, using this very term, as '(a position approaching monopoly) which requires a market share of 80 % or more.'[253] More importantly, there is no need to specify the precise point when dominance turns into superdominance in any quantitative terms. In this respect O'Donoughe and Padilla correctly note that market power exists along a continuum and that

[248] O'Donoghue and Padilla 2006, pp. 167–168.

[249] Appeldoorn 2005, pp. 653–658.

[250] See C-52/09 *Konkurrensverket v TeliaSonera Sverige AB* [2011] ECR I-000 paras 78–82.

[251] See, for example, Taussig 1915, p. 119, where he said that 'if not complete monopoly, a quasi-monopoly, enduring for a considerable time, is likely to appear wherever industry is conducted on a very large scale'.

[252] Whish 2001, pp. 635–637.

[253] Crocioni and Veljanovski 2003, p. 39. In the practice of the Court and the Commission so far, the market share of the superdominant undertakings has been 90 % or more. See for e.g., Commission Decision in Case COMP/C-3/37.792 Microsoft [2005] 4 CMLR 965, IP/03/1025, and Cases T-24/93, T-25/93, T-26/93 and T-28/93 *Compagnie Maritime Belge v Commission* [1996] ECR II-1201. In Commission Decision in Case COMP D3/38.044—NDC Health/IMS Health: Interim measures [2002] OJ L 59/18, the undertaking was held to be in 'quasi-monopoly situation 'according to the Commission, however, the market shares have been deleted as a business secret. This case has withdrawn by the Commission—see Commission Press Release IP/03/1159 'Commission intervention no longer necessary to enable NDC Health to compete with IMS Health' 13 August 2003. Paragraph 92 of the Commission's 2005 Discussion Paper which provided that 'a dominant company is in general considered to have a market position approaching that of a monopoly if its market share exceeds 75 %' has not been subsequently adopted in the subsequent Guidelines. This is an indication that 75 % might be too low a market share for finding of superdominance.

'concerns regarding dominance are at their most acute where a firm's strength approaches a position of near-monopoly'.[254] From the economic point of view there indeed exists a palpable difference in effects between a situation of dominance where an undertaking with, say 45 % of the market share is found dominant, and a dominance that results from an undertaking holding, for example, 90 % of the market share. In the former case, the next largest competitor might be an undertaking holding 20 % that could in the future acquire the ability to exercise competitive pressure on the dominant undertaking individually or via a concentration with a firm that holds, say 12 % of the relevant market, possibly rendering the dominant undertaking no longer dominant. But in the latter case of an undertaking with 90 % of the market share, especially if accompanied by high barriers to entry, there exists no realistic possibility for viable competition to emerge. This sizeable difference in the economic power and effects on the market between the dominant and superdominant undertakings should be matched by corresponding legal regulation, and always according to the individual merits of each case. Third, any call for re-definition of the concept of abuse in order to specify when exactly the conduct of a superdominant undertaking falls foul of Article 102, is a call for the re-introduction of the form-based approach to this provision, or an equivalent of strict liability. The case-by-case approach and treating each case on its own merits is in accordance with the modernisation and effect-based approach. In case of any uncertainty that might result from this approach, the undertakings thought to be in a superdominant position always have the option to seek informal guidance from the Commission on the compatibility of their conduct with the competition law.[255] In response to the final point, suffice it to say that even though the Court takes very high market shares in themselves as evidence of the existence of dominant position, it has nevertheless repeatedly emphasised that 'exceptional circumstances' might merit a different conclusion. For example, in *Compagnie Maritime Belge* the General Court said that *'in the absence of exceptional circumstances,* extremely large market shares are in themselves evidence of the existence of a dominant position.'[256] In its Guidance on the exclusionary conduct, the Commission indicated that in assessing the dominance it takes into account the competitive structure of the market, and in particular the constraints from competitors, constraints imposed by the countervailing buyer power and the credible threat of future expansion by actual competitors or entry by potential competitors.[257] The fact of the matter is that the Court and the Commission *do* take into consideration other factors than market shares in their appraisal of superdominance, as do the

[254] O'Donoghue and Padilla 2006, p. 166.

[255] Paragraph 38 of the preamble of the Regulation 1/2003.

[256] Cases T-24/93, T-25/93, T-26/93 and T-28/93 *Compagnie Maritime Belge v Commission* [1996] ECR II-1201, para 76. See also Case 85/76 *Hoffmann-La Roche* [1979] ECR 461, para 41 [emphasis added].

[257] Communication from the Commission—Guidance on the Commission's enforcement priorities in applying Article 82 of the EC Treaty to abusive exclusionary conduct by dominant undertakings, OJ C 45, 24.2.2009, pp. 7–20, para 12.

relevant authorities of EU Member States. In *Napp* case the UK Competition Appeals Tribunal cited and applied AG Fennelly's Opinion in *Compagnie Maritime Belge* and a number of the Court's judgments. It accepted that the special responsibility of a dominant undertaking is particularly onerous where the quasi-monopolists enjoy 'dominance approaching monopoly', 'superdominance' or 'overwhelming dominance verging on monopoly'.[258] Having moved on to the next stage of analysis the Court will take into consideration the specific circumstances of each case to analyse the existence of the abuse[259] and its effect on the market, which is surely more profound in cases of undertakings with very large market shares. The case-sensitive approach should in principle act as a safety net and provide guarantee against unreasonable outcomes. Indeed, the emergence of the concept of superdominance does little more but emphasise the need to judge each case on the basis of its own facts.[260]

The concept of superdominance, although never referred to by this name by the Court and the Commission,[261] has found its doctrinal space within Article 102 TFEU. For the purposes of that provision, it introduced a new layer in the distinction between undertakings on the basis of degree of their market power: non-dominant, dominant, superdominant (quasi-monopolistic) and monopolistic. Some national authorities have transplanted this concept following developments in the EU competition law and this is indicative of the wider acceptance and that the concept is there to stay.

5.7.2 Special Responsibility of Dominant Undertakings: The Sliding Scale Approach

In order to establish a market-distorting foreclosure effect, the DG Competition Discussion Paper suggested the sliding scale approach. Accordingly, the degree of

[258] In *Napp* case the UK Competition Appeal Tribunal said: 'In our view, Napp's high *and persistent* market shares put Napp into the category of "dominance approaching monopoly"—i.e. superdominance—and the issue of abuse in this case has to be addressed in that specific context' [emphasis added]. Paragraph 219 of the judgement in Case No 1001/1/1/01 *Napp Pharmaceutical Holdings Ltd v. Director General of Fair Trading* [2002] CAT 1, [2002] CompAR 13.

[259] In general, finding the exsistence of abuse is not affected by the market share of undertakings as indicated in C-52/09 *Konkurrensverket v TeliaSonera Sverige AB* [2011] ECR I-000 paras 78–82. In para 81 the Court said that 'the degree of market strength is, as a general rule, significant in relation to the extent of the effects of the conduct of the undertaking concerned rather than in relation to the question of whether the abuse as such exists.'

[260] This was implied by the Court in para 24 of Case C-333/94 P *Tetra Pack II* ECR I-5951 when it said that each case is to be decided on its own merits. See also Cases T-24/93, T-25/93, T-26/93 and T-28/93 *Compagnie Maritime Belge v Commission* [1996] ECR II-1201, para 114.

[261] Instead, it has been called an: 'overwhelmingly dominant position', 'quasi-monopoly situation', 'virtual monopoly', 'a position of dominance approaching monopoly' and 'a position of dominance exhibiting extraordinary features'.

dominance will be a relevant factor to such an assessment and 'the higher the capability of conduct to foreclose and the wider its application and the stronger the dominant position, the higher the likelihood that an anticompetitive foreclosure effect results'.[262] In *General Electric* the Court held that 'the greater the dominance of an undertaking, the greater is its special responsibility to refrain from any conduct liable to weaken further, a fortiori to eliminate, competition which still exists on the market'.[263] Citing *GVL* and *Tetra Pack II*, in *1998 Football World Cup* the Commission said that the actual scope of 'special responsibility must be considered in the light of the specific circumstances of the case, reflecting a weakened competitive situation.'[264] It then went on to assert that the scope of special responsibility should therefore be assessed 'in relation to the degree of dominance held by the parties and to any special characteristics of the market which might affect the competitive situation.'[265] The Commission emphasised the interrelation between the scope of the special responsibility and the degree of dominance in its Guidelines on exclusionary abuses according to which the scope of special responsibility must be considered in the light of the specific circumstances of each case.[266] It is well-established that a special responsibility may deprive a dominant undertaking of the right to adopt a course of conduct that would be unobjectionable if adopted by a non-dominant undertaking.[267] According to this, and in combination with the sliding scale approach, a special responsibility imposed upon a superdominant undertaking may deprive it of the right to adopt a course of conduct that would be unobjectionable if adopted by a dominant undertaking.

This can be contrasted with the approach of the courts in the US who repeatedly held that a monopolist has no special duties under section 2 of the Sherman Act with respect to other market participants, nor should it have to co-operate with its rivals, exercise any special restraint or be held to a standard of behaviour which differs from that of other competitors, as Judge Posner made clear in *Olympia Equipment*.[268] In *Trinko*, the Supreme Court concluded that insufficient assistance in the provision of service to rivals was not a recognized antitrust claim under the Court's refusal to deal precedents as there is no duty to aid competitors.[269] The

262 Paragraph 56 of the Discussion Paper.

263 Case T-210/01 *General Electric v. Commission* judgment of 14 December 2005, para 550.

264 Case IV/36.888, 1998 Football World Cup, OJ 2000 L 5/55, para 85.

265 Ibid. para 86.

266 Paragraph 9 of Commission Guidelines on exclusionary abuses.

267 Case T-111/96 *ITT Promedia v Commission* [1998] ECR II-2937, para 139.

268 *Olympia Equipment Leasing v Western Union Telegraph* 797 F 2d 370 (7th Cir 1986), at 375. For more details see Mcmahon 2009.

269 *Verizon Communications Inc v Law Offices of Curtis V. Trinko* 540 US 398 (2004), 124 S.Ct 872, at 411. Discussed in Mcmahon 2007, pp. 123–172.

source of this attitude can be traced back to the Chicago school of thought and the theory on self-correcting market mechanisms.

5.7.3 The Content of Special Responsibility of Superdominant Sports Undertakings

It is not clear whether the content of special responsibility of dominant undertakings refers to any other obligations but the preservation of undistorted competition. Case law thus far seems to indicate only the concern with this specific obligation. But to interpret the concept this way would imply a redundant approach to the responsibilities upon the dominant undertakings that are nevertheless binding upon them by the terms of Articles 101 and 102 TFEU. The emphasis on special responsibility, therefore, seems completely unnecessary, and as noted by Whish, it is 'a statement of the obvious'.[270] In order to make this concept count, its content has to be expanded beyond the requirements imposed by the mere wording of those articles.

For this purpose it first of all needs to be acknowledged that while the undertakings in the highly fragmented markets already participate in effective competition which delivers all the benefits of competition to the final consumers and customers alike, and in which participating undertakings are relatively easily substitutable from the point of view of demand and supply, the dominant or collectively dominant undertakings operating in the highly concentrated oligopolistic markets possess a degree of independence from the competition and other external pressures.[271] They are not easily substitutable, and in the case of regulatory monopolies, not at all substitutable. It means that their conduct is capable of having a detrimental impact on all interested parties and that they are responsible not just for the undistorted competitive process in downstream and upstream markets, but for the interests of all other stakeholders as well. In relation to stakeholders that have economic interests, the responsibilities of the superdominant undertakings are prescribed and protected by the Treaty. The manifestation of responsibilities that are not legally binding is sometimes effected by the firms through their voluntary investment into various social causes as a part of positive social responsibility.

Corporate social responsibility (CSR) is a concept whereby undertakings consider interests of the society by taking responsibility for the effect of their

---

[270] Whish 2009, p. 184.

[271] This is actually already included in their definition as dominant undertakings. See, for instance, Case 27/76 *United Brands* [1978] ECR 207, para 65.

decisions and conduct on a *voluntary* basis.[272] The new instruments on corporate governance in Europe all include policy proposals relating to CSR. For instance, the new corporate governance principles published by the European Corporate Governance Service (ECGS) brought together best practice standards for large companies and took the view that CSR and corporate governance are interconnected and that social and environmental reporting, as well as the transparency with regard to the management of stakeholder relationships, are all aspects of good corporate governance. ECGS recognizes that a 'one size fits all' approach is inappropriate but that institutional investors support common international standards. The enquiry here is not related directly to CSR as such but rather to the question of whether such ethical business codes can be translated into positive legal obligations when relied on as legitimate aims to seek an exemption from the application of the law by the superdominant private regulatory bodies that, due to their mandate, restrict competition in the public interests.

Only some of the most profound impacts of the activities of corporations are regulated by law and social responsibilities are imposed on them as a matter of statutory obligation. Such is the obligation on environmental reporting under the Environmental Impact Assessment Directive of 1985, as amended.[273] However, these legal obligations are enforced in relation to non-dominant firms on the market as well, and in this regard they cannot be counted on as that extra responsibility borne as a matter of law only by the dominant undertakings. The enquiry should focus on those responsibilities which can be made legally-binding upon superdominant undertakings through the expanded concept of special responsibility. One conceivable option in law is to include into the concept of special responsibility the content of legitimate aims relied on to secure the exemption from the enforcement of the otherwise applicable provisions of competition law.

---

[272] Communication from the Commission to the European Parliament, the Council and the European Economic and Social Committee—Implementing the partnership for growth and jobs: making Europe a pole of excellence on corporate social responsibility, Brussels 22.3.2006, COM(2006) 136 final, defined CSR as '[...] a concept whereby companies integrate social and environmental concerns in their business operations and in their interaction with their stakeholders on a voluntary basis. It is about enterprises deciding to go beyond minimum legal requirements and obligations stemming from collective agreements in order to address societal needs. Through CSR, enterprises of all sizes, in cooperation with their stakeholders, can help to reconcile economic, social and environmental ambitions. As such, CSR has become an increasingly important concept both globally and within the EU, and is part of the debate about globalisation, competitiveness and sustainability. In Europe, the promotion of CSR reflects the need to defend common values and increase the sense of solidarity and cohesion.' Directorate General in charge of Employment, Social Affairs and Inclusion at the European Commission defines the concept in the following terms: 'corporate social responsibility is companies acting voluntarily and beyond the law to achieve social and environmental objectives during the course of their daily business activities.'

[273] Council Directive 85/337/EEC of 27 June 1985 on the assessment of the effects of certain public and private projects on the environment, OJ L 175, as amended.

To illustrate this point with the sporting example, the Nice Declaration states that

> sports federations have a central role in ensuring the essential solidarity between the various levels of sporting practice, from recreational to top-level sport, which co-exist there; they provide the possibility of access to sports for the public at large, human and financial support for amateur sports, promotion of equal access to every level of sporting activity for men and women alike, youth training, health protection and measures to combat doping, acts of violence and racist or xenophobic occurrences. These social functions entail special responsibilities for federations and provide the basis for the recognition of their competence in organising competitions.[274]

It also declared that the Union must 'in its action under the various Treaty provisions, take account of the social, educational and cultural functions inherent in sport and making it special, in order that the code of ethics and the solidarity essential to the preservation of its social role may be respected and nurtured.' The working group on the follow-up to the Nice Declaration recognised the central role of the federations in organising sport in Europe, while at the same time pointing out that the federations also have duties with regard to transparency, solidarity, democracy and development of a sport with a social and educational vocation.[275]

Due to the fact that sports governing bodies rely heavily on public interest justifications that are part of their mandate, such as those related to their social functions, the content of their legitimate aims should be made legally binding on sport bodies every time they rely on them to provide an exemption from EU laws. For instance, the legitimate aim of ensuring competitive balance in European football is something that UEFA can successfully invoke before the EU Courts. The part of the principle of proportionality that should ensure the suitability of the means used to attain ends is most often based on purely hypothetical assessments producing faulty conclusions, as it is seldom evidence-based. False positive results in the test of suitability will secure the exemption, if the rule is otherwise proportionate. But in practice there is no competitive balance in European football, and some of the rules that can be justified by reference to that legitimate aim, in practice produce the opposite result. To make the content of a legitimate aim invoked legally binding when relied on to ensure an exemption, would ensure that competitive balance (i.e., the reason for exception) is actually attained in practice by the restrictive rule (or at least that restrictive effect is in balance with its alleged benefits). This is the only way to effectively protect competition—otherwise, any rule that can be merely hypothetically defended by reference to public interest and proportionality will be found to be compatible with competition articles. The Commission

---

274 'Declaration on the Specific Characteristics of Sport and its Social Function in Europe, of which Account Should be Taken in Implementing Common Policies', Presidency Conclusions following the Nice European Council Meeting of 7, 8 and 9 December 2000.

275 Xth European Sports Forum, Conclusions of the working group on the follow up to the Nice Declaration, Brussels 17–18 October 2001.

decisions in cases of breaches of Article 101 TFEU or abuse of a superdominant position or monopoly by a sport governing body that relies on the legitimate aim could be taken by decisions similar to those under Article 9 of the Regulation 1/2003 which provides for commitment decisions.[276] In cases of undertakings in superdominant or collective superdominant position that rely on a public interest justification to secure an exemption under competition law for otherwise restrictive rules or practices, the decision to exempt that rule or practice could be made conditional upon fulfilment of the content of objective justification. Hence, it could be a conditional decision accompanied by temporal limitation—the time frame of the effect of such decision could be the time in which the superdominant undertaking will be asked to supply the evidence on the real practical effects of the justification.

5.8 Conclusion

The concept of special responsibility of dominant undertakings was developed and recognised under Article 102 TFEU. Nevertheless, if the theory on expansion of the concept of special responsibility for superdominant sport governing bodies is to be accepted, the upshot in the light of the *Meca-Medina/Wouters* test and the convergence theory set out in Chap. 6 is the expanded *legal scope* of special responsibility, i.e., this concept would incidentally apply also under Article 101 TFEU and the free movement provisions analysis. This would, however, add nothing to the obligation upon undertakings resulting from the expanded *content* of the concept under Article 102 TFEU. Simply put, if the entity that is in superdominant position is allowed to justify its rules or conduct that have restrictive effect on the market, then the claimed benefits to the public interest should be proven genuine and not merely hypothetical. So the standard of proof should increase from logical construction of argument to practical effects demonstrable by sufficiently convincing evidence.

[276] Under Article 9 of the Regulation 1/2003, in the cases in which it intends to order the termination of infringement, the Commission may instead adopt decisions accepting commitments by undertakings. These commitments are binding on the addressee, subject to the time limits, and may be invoked by the third parties before national courts. Article 9(2) provides that: 'Commission may, upon request or on its own initiative, reopen the proceedings: (a) where there has been a material change in any of the facts on which the decision was based; (b) where the undertakings concerned act contrary to their commitments; or (c) where the decision was based on incomplete, incorrect or misleading information provided by the parties.' The corresponding penalty provision is introduced by Article 22(2)(c) for failure to comply with the commitments. According to Article 27(4) of the Regulation 1/2003, the Commission publishes its commitment decisions and all interested parties can submit observations within the period no shorter than 1 month. Safeguards ensuring compliance with commitment decisions are fines provided in Article 23(2)(c) and periodic penalty payments in Article 24 of the Regulation 1/2003.

References

Anderman S (2009) The epithet that dares not speak its name: the essential facilities concept in Article 82 EC and IPRs after the Microsoft case. In: Ezrachi A (ed) Article 82 EC: reflections on its recent evolution. Hart Publishing, Oxford, pp 87–98

Appeldoorn J (2005) He who spareth his rod, hateth his son? Microsoft, super dominance and Article 82. Eur Compet Law Rev 26:653–658

Borland J (2009) The production of professional team sports. In: Andreff W, Szymanski S (eds) Handbook on the economics of sport. Edward Elgar, Cheltenham, pp 22–26

Crocioni P, Veljanovski C (2003) Price squeezes, foreclosure, and competition law. J Netw Ind 4:28–60

Cygan A (2007) Competition and free movement issues in the regulation of formula one motor racing. In: Bogusz B, Cygan A, Szyszczak E (eds) The regulation of sport in the European Union. Edward Elgar, Cheltenham, pp 74–94

Editorial (2005) Sports broadcasting: what next? Sports Law: Adm Pract 12(5):5–7

Faull J, Nikpay A (2007) The EC law of competition, 2nd edn. Oxford UP, Oxford

Hoehn T, Kastrianki Z (2012) Broadcasting and sport: value drivers of TV right deals in European Football. CompetitionRx, online paper. http://www.competitionrx.com/documents/SportsRights/Value-drivers-of-TV-Rights-deals-in-Sport-May2012.pdf

Infantino G (2006) Meca-Medina: a step backwards for the European sports model and the specificity of sport? Sports Law: Adm Pract 13:3–4

Jephcott M, Withers C (2001) Where to go now for EC oligopoly control? Eur Compet Law Rev 22:295–303

Jones A, Sufrin B (2011) EU Competition Law, 4th edn. Oxford UP, Oxford

Lavrijssen S (2010) What role for national competition authorities in protecting non-competition interests after Lisbon? Eur Law Rev 35:636–659

Mangeat G (2004) Sports media rights and competition law: what are the relevant markets? Economics of the sports media rights/appraisal of the relevant markets with regard to their acquisition and sale. Jusletter, 6 September 2004

Mcmahon K (2007) Interoperability: "Indispensability" and "Special Responsibility" in high technology markets. Tulane J Tech Intellect Prop 9:123–172

Mcmahon K (2009) A reformed approach to Article 82 and the special responsibility not to distort competition. In: Ezrachi A et al (eds) Article 82 EC: reflections on its recent evolution. Hart Publishing, Oxford

Mezzanotte FE (2009) Tacit collussion as economic links in Article 82 EC revisited. Eur Compet Law Rev 30:137–142

Miettinen S (2009) Policing the boundaries between regulation and commercial exploitation: lessons from the *MOTOE* case. In: Gardiner S, Parrish R, Siekmann RCR (eds) EU, sport, law and policy. T.M.C. Asser Press, The Hague

Monti G (2002) Article 81 and public policy. Common Market Law Rev 39:1057–1099

O'Donoghue R, Padilla AJ (2006) Law and economics of Article 82 EC. Hart Publishing, Oxford

Parrish R, Miettinen S (2008) Sporting exception in European Union Law. T.M.C Asser Press, The Hague

Rousseva E (2005) Modernising by eradicating: how the commission's new approach to Article 81 EC dispenses with the need to apply Article 82 EC to vertical restraints. Common Market Law Rev 42:587–638

Rubenstein A (2005) Unbundling of sports media rights. Sports Law: Adm Pract 12:14–16

Semmelmann C (2008) The future role of the non-competition goals in the interpretation of article 81 EC. Global Antitrust Review 1:15–47

Stix-Hackl C, Egger A (2002) Sports and competition law: a never-ending story? Eur Compet Law Rev 23:81–91

Taussig (1915) Principles of economics, Vol 2. Macmillan, New York

Thomas T, Thomson R (2004) Negotiation, bundling and competition law—current issues facing those involved in sports broadcasting rights. Sports Law: Adm Pract 11(5):1–5

Weatherill S (2007) Overlapping legal orders: what is the 'Purely Sporting' rule. In: Bogusz B, Cygan A, Szyszczak E (eds) The regulation of sport in the European Union. Edward Elgar, Cheltenham, pp 48–73

Weatherill S (2008a) Article 82 EC and sporting 'Conflict of Interest': the judgment in *MOTOE*. Int. Sports Law J 3–4: special addendum

Weatherill S (2008b) Anti-doping revisited—the demise of the rule of 'purely sporting interest? In: Weatherill S (ed) European Union sports law: collected papers. T.M.C. Asser Press, The Hague

Whish R (2001) Competition Law, Butterworths, London

Whish R (2009) Competition Law, 6th edn, Oxford UP, Oxford

Chapter 6
A Quest for Convergence in the Application of EU Internal Market and Competition Law to Sport

Contents

6.1 Introduction 215
6.2 Addressees 216
6.3 Prohibition Level Convergence—Categories I, II and III of Sporting Exception 217
6.3.1 Sporting Rules That Do not Produce Any Economic Effect 218
6.3.2 'Purely Sporting' Rules 218
6.3.3 Inherent Rules 224
6.4 Justification Level Convergence—Category IV Sporting Exception 228
6.5 Burden of Proof 233
References 235

6.1 Introduction

The degree and type of convergence between competition and internal market rules is an obscure, yet important matter. A fundamental tension underlying both fields of law in their application to regulatory rules in sport concerns striking the proper balance between the pro-market regime and the public interests exceptions as reflected in the concept of sporting exception and Article 165(1) TFEU. The issues regarding relationship between the two types of rules, as regards their addressees, prohibitions and exceptions, are the most pronounced in sports cases.[1]

Questions that would need judicial and/or legislative clarification regarding convergence and divergence between internal market and competition rules are many, but for the purposes of this volume, the discussion will focus on the relationship in the area of sport between the elements of the analytical framework under Articles

[1] For detailed treatment of other areas, such as social security, see Sauter and Schepel 2007, available at http://papers.ssrn.com/sol3/papers.cfm?abstract_id=1010075.

K. Pijetlovic, *EU Sports Law and Breakaway Leagues in Football*,
ASSER International Sports Law Series, DOI 10.1007/978-94-6265-048-0_6

45, 49 and 56 TFEU, with the elements in the *Meca-Medina/Wouters* analytical framework, and with emphasis on the proper place for the sporting exceptions in the convergence thesis. It is submitted that, for the sake of legal certainty and clarity, simplification of the legal tests, and development of a logical analytical framework, the Court and the Commission should seek to promote convergence wherever possible. It should be taken that if 'in law, the only things which are comparable are those which fulfil the same function',[2] it follows *a fortiori* that the only things transposable are those which fulfil the same function.

The ideas outlined in this chapter are split into discrete categories for the purposes of clarity. But it is to be kept in mind that there is a good degree of overlap between the different categories of the sporting exception, which will be indicated throughout the text.

6.2 Addressees

The initial dichotomy in the application of the two sets of norms is among their respective circle of addressees. Typically, Articles 101 and 102 TFEU apply to private undertakings, whereas free movement provisions apply to state and quasi-state defendants. Baquero Cruz considered that the heart of the relationship between the provisions on competition and free movement lies in the eventual application of the free movement rules in the private sphere and of the competition rules to state action.[3] The Court has applied competition rules to a government (employment) agency engaged in the business of employment procurement because such activity 'has not always been, and is not necessarily, carried out by public entities',[4] while refusing to apply those rules to private undertakings exercising powers that typically belong to public authorities.[5] Moreover, the Court has given a full effect to free movement provisions in cases against private entities,[6]

[2] Zweigert and Kotz 1987, p. 31.

[3] Baquero Cruz 2002, p. 85.

[4] Case C-41/90 *Höfner and Elsner v Macroton* [1991] ECR I-1979, para 22.

[5] Case C-343/95 *Diego Calì & Figli v SEPG* [1996] ECR I-1547.

[6] Free movement of goods is a notable exception and become applicable only when a private action is attributable to state. See, for example, Case C-470/03 *A.G.M.—COS.MET Srl v Suomen Valtio, Tarmo Lahtinen* [2007] ECR I-2749 and Case C-265/95 *Commission v France (Spanish Strawberries)* [1997] ECR I-6959. For horizontal application of free movement of workers in non-sporting context see, for example, Case C-281/98 *Angonese* [2000] ECR I-4139; for freedom to provide (and receive) services see C-341/05 *Laval un Partneri Ltd v Svenska Byggnadsarberareförbundet* [2007] ECR I-11767; and for freedom of establishment see Case C-438/05 *Viking Line* [2007] ECR I-10779.

and at the same time preserved an appropriate sphere for public authority exceptions under Articles 45(4) and 51 TFEU.[7]

In regard to sporting organisations, however, the public/private distinction is not very pronounced, if at all. As we have seen in cases like *Walrave*, *Bosman*, *Deliège*, *Lehtonen*, *Piau* and *Meca-Medina*, sports federations may be subject to both set of norms without anyone seriously questioning their applicability on the basis on improperness of addressee. It is debatable whether the effect that free movement provisions have when applied to the rules of sport governing bodies constitutes 'an extended form of vertical direct effect'[8] due to the scope of regulatory latitude possessed by these bodies and effect of their decisions, or a restrictive form of horizontal direct effect which encompasses only those private bodies that collectively regulate the entire profession. It is, however, clear that the aspect of convergence pertaining to addressees of competition and internal market provisions is facilitated by the direct effect of both set of norms in regard to their application in the sport sector, the Court's teleological interpretation of Treaty rules and its functional approach to classification of entities.

6.3 Prohibition Level Convergence—Categories I, II and III of Sporting Exception

The nature and scope of the sporting exception in EU law has been thoroughly researched by Parrish and Miettinen.[9] The sporting exception in EU law describes 'both the removal of rules from the scope of the Treaty and the sensitive application of [EU] law to the sports sector'.[10] In this sense, the sporting exception is a misnomer in the latter case, as it does not imply an exception as such. Four categories of rules that will qualify for the sporting exception in its broad meaning can be identified in the examination of the Court's jurisprudence.[11] The first two categories of sporting exceptions have a limited use in practice, but are valid nevertheless. What follows is an explanation of each category in the light of convergence between free movement of persons and competition law in their application to sport.

---

[7] This sphere was defined in Case 149/79 *Commission v Belgium* [1982] ECR 1845 that concerned public service exception under Article 45(4) TFEU, and Case 2/74 *Reyners v Belgian State* [1974] ECR 631 that involved official authority exception under Article 52 TFEU. The scope of these exceptions is narrowly construed.

[8] As argued by Barnard 2010, p. 234.

[9] Parrish and Miettinen 2008.

[10] Ibid. p. 73.

[11] For more detailed treatment of the subject, see Parrish and Miettinen 2008, Chap. 4, in particular pp. 100–101.

6.3.1 Sporting Rules That Do not Produce Any Economic Effect

The Category I exception applies when sport constitutes a non-economic activity within the meaning of *Walrave*, para 4. Both the sporting rule and its effects must be non-economic to merit this exception. The exception applies to a very small group of rules, such as rules of the game (e.g. offside in football, the dimensions of a tennis court) which are unlikely to be challenged before the courts.[12] This is the only category of sporting rules that will not be examined for its compatibility with the Treaty. Although it was developed in the free movement area, this exception can also apply in challenges under competition law to render the rules *ab initio* outside the scope of the Treaty as it sets a *generally applicable* constitutional limitation on the conferred powers of EU institutions.

Many authors confuse this exception with the notion of 'purely sporting' rules, implying that 'purely sporting' rules produce no economic effect.[13] However, as will be illustrated in the section below, the 'purely sporting' rule exception involves sporting rules that *do produce* an economic effect, but because they meet specific requirements, they are nevertheless considered 'purely sporting'. Without economic effects, the sporting rule would fall under para 4 of *Walrave*, as opposed to paras 8 and 9 of *Walrave* and 14 and 15 of *Donà*, and would not require fulfilment of any additional requirements. The lack of economic effect is the sole fact that is sufficient in itself to take the rule outside of the scope of the Treaty and outside of Union competence.

6.3.2 'Purely Sporting' Rules

The Category II exception encompasses sporting rules that (1) produce an economic effect, but (2) that can be justified due to their non-economic ('purely

[12] This is not to say that a few scenarios could not be envisaged where the rules of the game are challenged, especially if the long-standing rules of the game were to be changed so as to produce specific disadvantages for an identifiable group of undertaking (clubs or individual participants), in which case they might be held to have an effect on economic activity and would not benefit from this particular exception.

[13] For example, it has been argued that '[r]ules governing the composition of national sports teams or the conduct of anti-doping controls may plausibly define the nature of sporting competition, in the sense that the very existence of sporting endeavour is undermined without such rules. They are sporting rules. But they are not *purely* sporting rules. They visibly have economic repercussions (for players most of all)'. He also states that '[a]ll that can be intended by the 'purely sporting rule' is a reference to the small category of rules which govern sport but which are devoid of economic effect—such as the offside rule and fixing the height of goalposts. In the unlikely event that such rules were to provoke litigation, they would be found to lie outside the scope of the [TFEU]'. See Weatherill 2009, pp. 78–100.

sporting') motives, (3) that relate to the particular nature and context of certain sporting events and (4) that are limited to their proper objectives. This exception originated in paras 8 and 9 of *Walrave* and it was reformulated in paras 14 and 15 of *Donà* and repeated in subsequent case law. In *Walrave*, the Court held that the prohibition on nationality discrimination in Articles 18, 45 and 56

> 8. [...] does not affect the composition of sport teams, in particular national teams, *the formation of which* is a question of purely sporting interest and as such has nothing to do with economic activity. 9. This restriction on the scope of the provisions in question must however remain limited to its proper objective.

In paras 14 and 15 of *Donà* it confirmed, but somewhat reformulated, the exception and held that those provisions of the Treaty do not prevent

> 14. [...] the adoption of rules or of a practice excluding foreign players from participation in certain matches for the reasons which are not of an economic nature, which relate to the particular nature and context of such matches and are thus of sporting interest only, such as, for example, the matches between national teams from different countries. 15. This restriction on the scope of the provisions in question must however remain limited to its proper objective.

From these paragraphs, it is apparent that it is the *motives* for the rules, and not the rules themselves, that do not produce an economic effect and have nothing to do with economic activity. The *effect* of the rules is undeniably economic. Furthermore, 'purely sporting' interest and 'purely sporting' rules are two different things. 'Purely sporting' rules necessarily have 'purely sporting' interests which is one of the requirements for this exception, but the 'purely sporting' interests of the rule do not imply that the rule will necessarily be considered 'purely sporting'. It still has to fulfil the other two requirements for the exception, i.e. be related to the particular nature and context of certain sporting events, and be limited to its proper objectives (the proportionality requirement).

It was argued that the 'purely sporting' rules exception 'does not apply to sports teams, or to general rules on team composition, but only to nationality rules in national team sports'.[14] However, although it originated in that specific factual context, since *Walrave*, the Court has always repeated the rule, mentioning the national team sports and nationality rules only as an example, or completely leaving that example out. It is hard to see the logic in doing so, unless there is a purpose behind it. In para 25 of *Meca-Medina* the Court cited para 8 of *Walrave*: '[...] the prohibitions enacted by those provisions of the Treaty do not affect rules concerning questions which are of purely sporting interest and, as such, have nothing to do with economic activity'. It does not say that the exception applies only in relation to prohibitions on nationality discrimination, but to 'prohibitions enacted by Articles 45 and 56'. Such prohibitions include both direct and indirect nationality discrimination as well as non-discriminatory obstacles. Clearly, the Court left open the possibility for the other kind of discriminatory and non-discriminatory rules to qualify as 'purely sporting' rules. Unlike in *Walrave* and *Donà*, the factual context in *Meca-Medina* did not involve nationality discrimination and thus the

[14] Parrish and Miettinen 2008, p. 100.

Court left out the reference to 'foreign players' or 'nationality discrimination' from its formula on what constitutes a 'purely sporting' rule. Repeating para 76 of *Bosman* word for word, it then said in para 26 of *Meca-Medina* that

> With regard to the difficulty of severing the economic aspects from the sporting aspects of a sport, the Court has held (in *Donà*, paras 14 and 15) that the provisions of [Union] law concerning freedom of movement for persons and freedom to provide services do not preclude rules or practices justified on non-economic grounds which relate to the particular nature and context of certain sporting events. It has stressed, however, that such a restriction on the scope of the provisions in question must remain limited to its proper objective. It cannot, therefore, be relied upon to exclude the whole of a sporting activity from the scope of the Treaty [...].

The Court first recognises that almost every aspect of sport has something to do with economic activity,[15] but that proportionate rules grounded on purely sporting motives 'which relate to the particular nature and context of certain sporting events' are outside the scope of the Treaty even when they are both sporting and economic. It does not mention national team sports even as an example.

Paragraphs 76 and 127 of *Bosman* make a reference to paras 14 and 15 of *Donà*. Paragraph 127 of *Bosman* restates para 76 of *Bosman* in full, but adds as a specific example of non-economic interests the exclusion of foreign players from certain matches, such as 'matches between national teams from different countries'. Unlike para 76 of *Bosman*, which cited *Donà* in the context of non-discriminatory transfer rules, in which participation in matches was not an issue, the para 127 reference to *Donà* was made in the context of the directly discriminatory 3+2 rule which related to participation in matches. It could be read from this that the Court indeed takes national team matches only as an example, when related to the issue considered, and when not related, the example is left out as irrelevant. The *Donà* rule as clarified and broadened by para 76 of *Bosman* stands regardless of whether the issue involves nationality discrimination in national team sports. The rest of the case law supports this interpretation. In *Lehtonen*, where the participation of a player in team matches was an issue, the Court mentioned an example of excluding players from certain matches, and matches between national teams from different countries. The same goes for *Deliège*, where the selection rules preventing athletes from participation in certain competitions were disputed. *Bernard* did not even mention the notion of 'purely sporting' rules from *Walrave* and *Donà* because the rules were not related to the context and nature of certain matches, nor were they preventing participation of a player in any matches. Advocate General Cosmas in *Deliège*, after citing relevant paragraphs from *Walrave*, *Dona* and *Bosman*, said that the following conclusions can be drawn from that line of cases:

> First, certain rules or practices relating to sport do not fall within the scope of Article [56] of the Treaty. Secondly, in order for that exception to apply, the rules or practices in question

[15] It has been argued in the light of *Meca-Medina*, that, to continue assessing the sporting rules on the basis of their fiscal nature is 'intrinsically flawed since modern sport dictates that financial considerations now impact on almost every aspect of sport'. See Callery 2011, p. 48.

> must be justified by specific, non-economic reasons which relate purely to sport; the organisation of matches between national teams is a prime example of such a reason. […].[16]

Advocate General Alber in *Lehtonen* also referred to the organisation of matches between national teams as a 'prime example' of purely sporting motives.[17] All of this implies that there may be something more to the exception than just directly discriminatory rules in matches between national teams from different countries. If the Court intended the exception to produce only such a limited effect, why would it bother mentioning it only in the role of a prototype, and why would that role be left out in cases in which there is no question of the particular nature and context of certain matches, such as transfer rules in *Bosman*, training compensation fees in *Bernard*, or doping sanctions in *Meca-Medina*?

Further, it may be thought that this interpretation would result in an overbroad exclusion of all sporting rules with economic effects from the scope of the Treaty. But it appears that the requirement that the rules be motivated by 'purely sporting' considerations, be related to the nature and context of certain sporting events, and be proportionate, is a very high threshold, which has in practice so far been met only by directly discriminatory rules in national team sports. This single instance of the application of the exception does not mean that it may not be met by other types of rules not involving national teams or issues of direct discrimination.[18]

Stripped of the requirement for nationality discrimination in national team sport, the exception may well be applicable in competition law instances, although, admittedly, the Court has thus far cited it in relation to free movement of persons only. This neither implies that other Treaty articles are excluded, nor would there be a logical explanation for reserving this type of exception only for free movement cases. In *Meca-Medina*, the reference in para 26 to free movement provisions was specifically directed to overruling the decision by the General Court, while in all other cases the Court dealt only with free movement and ignored the preliminary reference questions about the applicability of competition law. There was no chance to clarify its take on this issue.

In para 31 of *Meca-Medina*,[19] the Court seems to have rejected any parallels between free movement and competition law in the application of this exception.

---

[16] Paragraph 69.

[17] Paragraph 69 of his Opinion.

[18] For example, compulsory uncompensated player release for representative matches of national teams might be a candidate rule for this exception. It produces economic effects, is related to the particular nature and context of certain matches, and there is no doubt that it has been motivated by purely sporting considerations. Its proportionality in the light of its objectives, especially considering solidarity and the need for competitive balance between the teams, as well as solidarity with poorer national associations, might not be at issue either. See Sect. 3.3.6.1.

[19] This paragraph reads: 'even if those rules do not constitute restrictions on freedom of movement because they concern questions of purely sporting interest and, as such, have nothing to do with economic activity, that fact means neither that the sporting activity in question necessarily falls outside the scope of Articles [101 TFEU] and [102 TFEU] nor that the rules do not satisfy the specific requirements of those articles'. See Sect. 5.5.5.5 above for detailed analysis of this paragraph.

But this rejection is only on one level of the analysis of the exception.[20] Weatherill points out that paras 31–33 in *Meca-Medina* should not be read as a general rejection of the convergence thesis because the Court is not 'doing anything more remarkable than drawing attention to the thinness of the [General Court] analysis' that did not even touch on possible differences between the norms.[21] He also says that para 31 of *Meca-Medina* is probably best taken on its own limited terms.[22] This is an excellent point for departure of the illustration that follows.

In the arguments presented above,[23] there is indeed no convergence in regard to EU constitutional competence due to some very individual features of each set of norms, such as internal situations, or the requirement of appreciability. There is also no convergence as regards other required elements for the presumption of restriction, such as the concept of undertaking, agreement or decision, restrictive effects, etc. I will refer to all these features and conditions as 'required economic effects' for moving on to the exception analysis.

The application of the 'purely sporting' rule exception is triggered by the presumption of the restriction of the specific provision. It also implies that the required economic effect was found to exist. The specific scope of the different articles (constitutional competence and certain individual elements giving rise to the required economic effect) and the presumption of restriction are the areas in the analytical process in which convergence does not exist. However, the conditions for exception (e.g. purely sporting motive, participation in certain matches and proportionality) are exactly the same, and concerning them, there exists full convergence. Once the rule satisfies the required economic effect test for application of both sets of provisions, it reaches the common ground for assessment of the applicability of conditions for exemption. In that case there is no need to carry out the exemption test separately. One more element has to be added to complete and clarify these conclusions: presumptions under Article 101(1).

The language in para 31 of *Meca-Medina*, which implies that the rule that already satisfied the requirements for exception under the free movement provisions cannot be taken to automatically satisfy those requirements under competition provisions, can be explained by the difference in presumptions. Namely, in regard to cases that involve the specificity of sport, the internal market does not have the equivalent of the hard-core restrictions in Article 101(1). In sports cases, both directly discriminatory and merely restrictive rules are treated within the same analytical framework. However, under Article 101(1), if a rule constitutes a '*per se*' or hard-core restriction by object, it is not open to the parties to argue that it in fact does not amount to a restriction and the presumption of a breach of that provision is conclusive, as opposed

[20] Level of 'required economic effect'. See Fig. 6.1.

[21] Weatherill 2008, p. 342.

[22] Ibid. p. 341. See also paras 104–105 of Advocate General Alber's Opinion in *Lehtonen* who, in the context of Article 101(1), argued that it must be possible 'to find that trade is affected in a case in which the exercise of fundamental freedoms is obstructed. […] Since the development of economic activities by the clubs, that is, by undertakings, is obstructed by these transfer rules, there is probably also a restriction of competition within the meaning of Article [101(1)] of the EC Treaty'.

[23] See Sect. 5.5.5.5

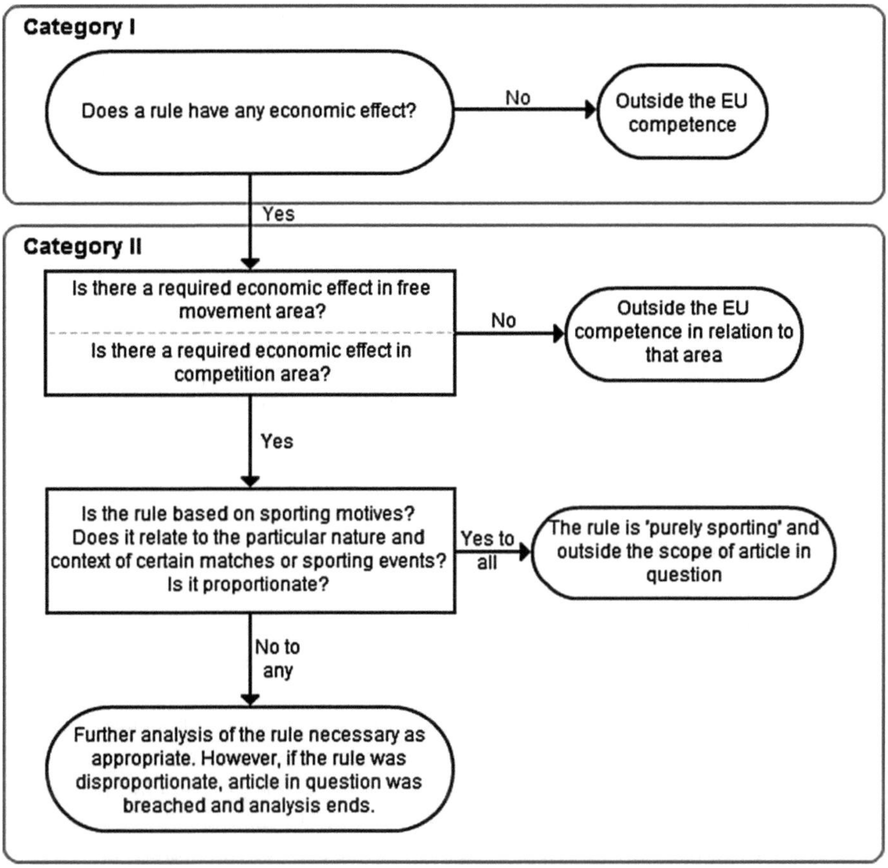

Fig. 6.1 Flowchart for analysis of category I sporting exception and 'purely sporting' rules

to rebuttable. In that case, a rule that has satisfied all the requirements for the category II exception under the free movement provisions cannot benefit from the attempt at that exception under Article 101(1) to which it would otherwise be entitled but for the hard-core restrictions and conclusive presumptions of the breach. A party may rely on Article 101(3) but not on any of the judicially-developed exceptions available on the level of the restriction. Conversely, if there is no conclusive presumption under the competition provisions, and the rule has already been regarded under internal market articles as 'purely sporting' and having nothing to do with economic activity, that result is transplantable to competition law, with no further analysis being required. The para 31 in *Meca-Medina* should be read in this light. Once there is a rebuttable (non-conclusive) presumption on the level of 'required economic effect' established under both sets of provisions, the rest of the conditions for exception are the same.[24]

[24] On convergence of burden of proof see Sect. 6.5

Most recently, this approach to convergence is confirmed in general terms by the Advocate General in *Murphy*, who used her conclusion in regards to freedom of movement law to support her conclusion in competition law. She said that '[…] conflicting assessments of the fundamental freedoms and competition law are to be avoided in principle'.[25]

Finally, it must be added that if rules were not confined to their proper objectives (and thus failed the proportionality criterion for the category II exception) it is very unlikely that they will be exempted in further analyses, which also involve the proportionality requirement under both sets of provisions. When it is determined that the case falls under both areas of law, yet the category II exception did not apply under either set of the articles for a failure to meet the criterion other than proportionality (which is the most likely outcome in sports cases), the results of the analyses that follow should, in principle, be transposable. This is what the discussion turns to next.

6.3.3 Inherent Rules

The Category III sporting exception includes rules that, based on their legitimate objectives,[26] do not constitute restrictions because they derive from the need, and their restrictive effects are, inherent in the organisation of sport, and are proportionate.[27] In the Commission practice and the case law of the Court, including the opinions of the Advocate Generals, 'inherent' is a synonym for 'indispensable', 'necessary' or 'essential'. Inherency can also be seen as one part of a *full* proportionality test, which includes an assessment of suitability (a measure is suitable, if it is capable of achieving the goal both legally and factually), inherency or necessity (a measure is inherent/necessary if, without taking these measures, the legitimate objective cannot be achieved), and proportionality (a measure is proportionate if does not go beyond what is necessary, and there are no less restrictive rules that are capable of achieving the same objective).

The application of the 'inherent sporting rules' concept is not identical under free movement and competition law.[28] In free movement law, only non-discriminatory rules that are not related to market access can satisfy the inherent rule test. The same test under competition law articles is not sensitive to the difference between the discriminatory and non-discriminatory rules, and between market access and exercise of economic activity rules. Its scope is therefore broader and more flexible.

[25] Opinion of AG Kokott in Cases C-403/08 and C-429/08 *Murphy v. Premier League* [2011], para 249.

[26] This criterion is specifically mentioned only in relation to competition provisions (in *Meca-Medina* case) but, as submitted below, it applies in free movement as well.

[27] Ibid.

[28] For more on this discussion see paper by Miettinen S and Parrish R, 'Inherent Rules in EC Sports Law', presented at the Conference on Law and Popular Culture, Onati, Spain (June 2008).

In the context of free movement, in *Deliège*, the Court first dismissed the applicability of the categories I and II sporting exception and then went on to say that

> in contrast to the rules applicable to the Bosman case, the selection rules at issue in the main proceedings do not determine the conditions governing *access* to the labour market by professional sportsmen and do not contain nationality clauses limiting the number of nationals of other Member States who may participate in a competition.[29]

The Court thus considered the selection rules as non-discriminatory rules affecting the exercise of economic activity, rather than as discriminatory market access rules.[30] Only then it proceeded to specify that although the selection rules at issue

> …inevitably have the effect of limiting the number of participants in a tournament, such a limitation is inherent in the conduct of an international high-level sports event, which necessarily involves certain selection rules or criteria being adopted. Such rules may not therefore in themselves be regarded as constituting a restriction on the freedom to provide services prohibited by Article [56] of the Treaty.[31]

Although the Court did not specifically mention that the inherent rules should be proportionate, it is hard to accept that disproportionate rules could satisfy the requirements of the free movement norms, even if they raise issues affecting the exercise of economic activity as opposed to market access. The following paragraph requires the inherent rule to be proportionate:

> …the adoption, for the purposes of an international sports tournament, of one system for selecting participants rather than another must be based on a large number of considerations unconnected with the personal situation of any athlete, such as the nature, the organisation and the financing of the sport concerned.[32]

Accordingly, the discriminatory rule would be considered disproportionate and the inherency test failed. The Commission in its Communication did not differentiate between competition and internal market law when it explained that in order to assess the compatibility of sporting rules with any EU law, it considers the legitimacy of the objectives pursued by the rules, whether any restrictive effects of those rules are inherent in *the pursuit of the objectives*, and whether they are *proportionate* to them.[33] So these are the common requirements under the inher-

---

[29] Joined Cases C-51/96 and C-191/97, para 61.

[30] Under the '*Säger* formula' this would have been enough to find a breach. Paragraph 12 of Case C-76/90 *Säger* [1991] ECR I-4221 provides that Article 56 required: 'not only the elimination of all discrimination against a person providing services on the ground of his nationality but also the abolition of any restriction, even if it applies without distinction to national providers of services and to those of other Member States, when it is liable to prohibit or otherwise impede the activities of provider of services established in another Member State where he lawfully provides similar services'. See on this point Miettinen S and Parrish R, 'Inherent Rules in EC Sports Law', presented at the Conference on Law and Popular Culture, Onati, Spain (June 2008).

[31] Joined Cases C-51/96 and C-191/97 *Deliège*, para 64.

[32] Ibid. para 65 (emphasis added).

[33] Communication from the Commission to the European Parliament, the Council, the European Economic and Social Committee, and the Committee of the Regions 'Developing the European Dimension in Sport' COM(2011) 12 final, 18. 1. 2011, para 4.2.

ency test for both sets of provisions, whether or not explicitly stated. In *Deliège*, the adoption of one system over another is left to sporting bodies and organisers,[34] as long as the selection is made on the basis of objective factors unconnected with the athletes' personal situation. The proportionality of such a system is not questioned by the Court. But this does not imply that the system need not fulfil the requirement of proportionality. It is deemed proportionate by default. Thus, the system adopted in *Deliège* was deemed proportionate because it was neither based on the athlete's personal situation (it was not discriminatory) nor did it create obstacles to market access. The athletes not selected on the basis of their nationality have no chance to ever be selected (unless they change their citizenship or move back to their Member State), but when criteria unrelated to their personal situation is used, all athletes have an equal opportunity to be selected. Only non-discriminatory rules that do not relate to market access can satisfy the inherency test under free movement provisions. Hence, the reason that the Court did not specifically mention the proportionality requirement is because it is built into the concept of inherency under free movement. Parrish and Miettinen argued that

> [a]lthough inherent rules do not constitute restrictions within the meaning of free movement law, the process of analysis involves an examination of proportionality of the rule and the relationship between fundamental rights and the rule purported to be inherent. As a consequence, the distinction between objective justification and the process of determining whether a rule is inherent is limited to the Court's treatment of proportionality of inherent rules: the Court appears less inclined to examine the proportionality of inherent rules and more inclined to require that applicants demonstrate its disproportionality, whereas in the context of objective justification the party purporting to objectively justify the rule is required to demonstrate that no less restrictive means will achieve the same, justified ends.[35]

A discriminatory rule would not be inherent, but would be subject to the objective justification framework as was the case in *Lehtonen*, and is unlikely to satisfy the proportionality test unless objective reasons concerning only sport as such can justify differential treatment.[36] Another possibility for a discriminatory sporting rule to satisfy free movement provisions is to fall under the Category II sporting exception. Rules preventing market access, even if non-discriminatory rules such as the transfer rules in *Bosman*, or training compensation fees in *Bernard*, 'affect the players' opportunities for finding employment and the terms under which such employment is offered'[37] and therefore 'directly affect players' access to the employment market in other Member States'.[38] As such they cannot be considered inherent and must be put through the objective justification framework.

In the field of competition law, the Court set out the inherent rule test in para 42 of *Meca-Medina* which included three analytical points: the existence of a

[34] Joined Cases C-51/96 and C-191/97 *Deliège*, paras 67 and 68.

[35] Parrish and Miettinen 2008, p. 101.

[36] See C-176/96 *Lehtonen*, paras 47–51.

[37] C-415/93 *Bosman*, para 75.

[38] Ibid. para 103.

legitimate aim, inherency and proportionality. The apparent difference with the inherency test in *Deliège* is that the requirement for proportionality of the rules, and the existence of a legitimate aim, are both specifically set out. *Prima facie*, it could be thought that the effect of this difference is that a rule that does not qualify as inherent for the purposes of competition might so qualify for the purposes of free movement law. However, given that proportionality is also a built-in requirement in an inherent rule under free movement law, and given that every inherent rule does in fact pursue a legitimate aim, it is submitted that the result of the tests under both set of provisions should be identical. There is one qualification to this: if the rule satisfies the competition law inherency test, the result can be transplanted to the free movement inherency test only if the rule is non-discriminatory and related to exercise of economic activity rather than to market access—otherwise, the result will be transplanted under the internal market objective justification framework. Substantial equivalence between these tests should in principle produce the same results.

The rules that have been, or are likely to be, considered inherent under competition law provisions are: non-discriminatory transfer windows, non-discriminatory criteria for selection of athletes for competitions, proportionate sanctions for breach of anti-doping rules, proportionate home-and-away rules and proportionate rules preventing multiple ownership of clubs.[39] In the Commission Staff Working Document, Annex I, the 'rules of the game' (category I)[40] and 'purely sporting' rules (category II) are also contained in the notion of inherent rules under competition provisions, which apply to a much broader category of organisational sporting rules.[41] All those rules have 'purely sporting' interests (or motives) in common. The Commission considered that the 'purely sporting' rule from *Walrave* would likely meet the inherency test under *Meca-Medina*.[42] The inherent rule notion *under competition law*, therefore, inevitably encompasses both the non-economic rules of the game and the 'purely sporting' rules. It will be argued in Sect. 6.4 below that it is also apt to encompass the rules objectively justified under free movement articles.

In this sense, at the risk of going too far, the argument could be stretched to claim that the scope of a 'purely sporting' rule was *de facto* broadened by the notion of inherent rules *but only in relation to competition law*: it necessarily fits into the inherent rule test, and in addition, there are many other rules that are not 'purely sporting' that satisfy the same inherency test. The benefit that both categories of sporting exception afford to a sporting rule is essentially the same (it affirms their compliance with the law) and on the same level of analysis in both sets of provisions (that of restriction), however with a different *de jure*

[39] Commission Staff Working Document, The EU and Sport: Background and Context, Accompanying Document to the White Paper on Sport, COM (2007) 391 final, Annex I, para 2.4.

[40] Ibid. para 2.1.5.

[41] Ibid. paras 2.2.1.4 and 2.4.

[42] Ibid. para 2.2.1.4.

result: 'purely sporting' rules do not fall under the scope of the article in question whereas inherent rules do not constitute restrictions even though they restrict freedom of action. For the parties involved in a dispute, this technical difference means nothing. Even though a 'purely sporting' rule is technically outside the scope of the article in question, substantively, it will have to go through a similar analytical process as the inherent rule under competition law to enable that conclusion. At the end of the day, the inherent rule and 'purely sporting' rule tests are nothing more than an application of specific forms of the rule of reason or ancillary restraints doctrine (see Fig. 6.2 in Sect. 6.4).

The test for 'purely sporting' rules as outlined above in Sect. 6.3.2 is capable of incidentally satisfying the inherent rules test in the free movement area. Unlike in competition law, it will not always happen. 'Purely sporting' rules that are discriminatory or that relate to market access will not be capable of satisfying the inherency test in free movement law, unless in the future the Court indicates that the inherency test has replaced the purely sporting rule test in the free movement area. In *Meca-Medina*, the Court reiterated paras 14 and 15 of *Donà* with the purpose of showing that there is no full convergence between competition law and free movement of persons. Nevertheless, it indicated that the 'purely sporting' rule is still alive and well in free movement law, regardless of the fact that its practical use might be limited to those rare rules fulfilling the conditions of the Category II exception.

Discriminatory rules and rules restricting market access that have satisfied the competition law inherency test will be subject to the objective justification framework under free movement (or, in very rare instances, the 'purely sporting' rules test). The submission in the section that follows is that there is a full convergence between the free movement objective justification framework and the competition law *Meca-Medina/Wouters* inherency test. This in turns means that the rules found compatible with Article 101(1) under the inherency test will, in any case, be compatible with free movement provisions (and vice versa, barring the existence of hard-core restrictions).

6.4 Justification Level Convergence—Category IV Sporting Exception

The Category IV exception is not an exception, strictly speaking. It applies to rules that, unlike the other three categories, constitute restrictions. It involves a sensitive application of the law to sport,[43] or rather, the recognition of the specificity of the sports industry. In para 40 of the *Bernard* case, the Court set out the standard of application of the proportionality principle in the objective justification framework, according to which, account must be taken of the specific characteristics of sport and of its social and educational function. The same standard, it is submitted, applies in the interpretation and application of EU competition law to sport.

[43] Parrish and Miettinen 2008, p. 73.

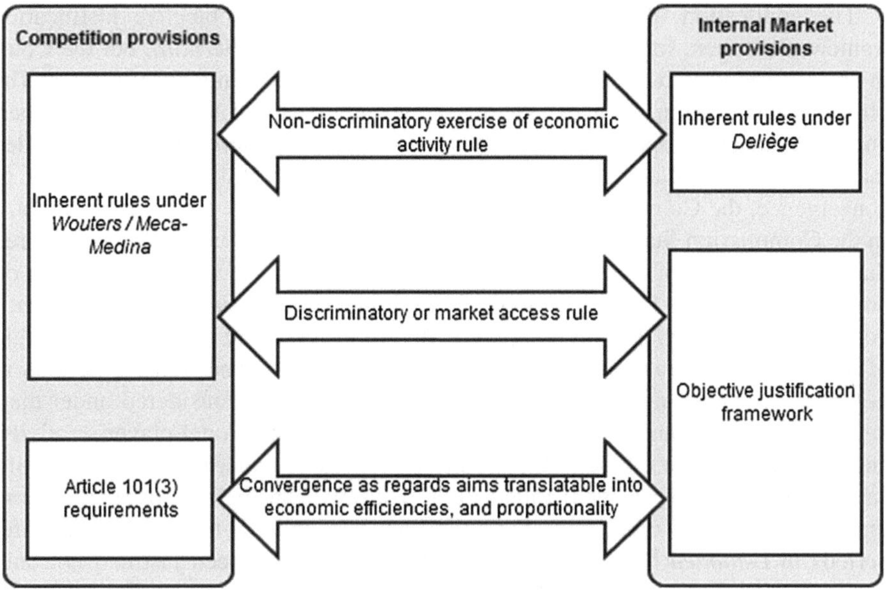

Fig. 6.2 Convergence between inherent rules and objective justification framework

Here it must be emphasised that the category IV exception does not exist separately in application of competition law to sport, but it is contained in the *Meca-Medina/Wouters* test. It is in this way that the convergence occurs between the internal market objective justification framework and competition law. Otherwise, once the sporting rules are found restrictive under Article 101(1), there is no indication in law that they will benefit from any special treatment under Article 101(3), or the efficiency defence under Article 102 in cases where they are found to constitute an abuse of a dominant position. These competition law justifications stand alone and have no counterpart in free movement law that could be taken into account for the purposes of convergence theory, *unless* the legitimate aim in public interest can be translated into economic benefits in which case there would exist at least a possibility for this type of convergence. The sporting rules that failed the requirement of inherency but are proportionate, and can translate their legitimate public interest goals into economic benefits, are apt for the convergent outcome between the Article 101(3) exemption and Article 102 economic efficiency defences on the one hand, and the objective justification test in free movement provisions on the other. The two requirements specific to Article 101(3) regarding affording a fair share of the resulting benefits to consumers and the non-elimination of competition in respect of a substantial part of the product in question are more likely to be satisfied than not, once the requirements of economic efficiency and proportionality are met under that provision.[44]

[44] See Guidelines on the Application of Article 81(3) *OJ C 101* 27.4.2004.

The application of the free movement *Gebhard*-type objective justification framework is seen, for example, in *Lehtonen*, *Bosman* and *Bernard*, but the Court in sport cases uses it for both directly and indirectly discriminatory rules.[45] The objective justification involves essentially the same analytical points as the inherency test under competition provisions. Although the Court has so far avoided making any direct statements about convergence in general, including this type of convergence, the Commission and the Advocates General have been less cautious. In the Commission Staff Working Document, Annex I, the Commission considered that 'the regulation of transfer periods are likely to constitute sporting rules that do not infringe Articles [101(1) and 102 TFEU] under *Meca-Medina* (provided they do not go beyond what is necessary, e.g. do not differentiate as regards the origin of a player or set transfer periods that are too short).'[46] The transfer periods in *Lehtonen*, assessed under internal market provisions, were considered under market access rules relating to the 'essential purpose of professional player's activity' and as such were not inherent; they fell to be examined under the objective justification framework. They were found to be disproportionate. The instruction from the Annex I of the Commission Staff Working Document is that, had the transfer periods in *Lehtonen* been proportionate, they would have been justified not only under free movement law, but also under Article 101(1) and the judicially developed objective justification under Article 102. Objectively justified sporting rules under internal market law satisfy the inherency test under competition law and vice versa.

In the preliminary opinion on the notified *Union des Associations Européennes de Football* (UEFA) rule prohibiting ownership of more than one team participating in the same UEFA club competition, the Commission has drawn the analogy from the area of freedom of movement and automatically applied the objective justification from the *Bosman* case to Article 101(1):

> Taking into account what the Court of Justice has recognised in the Bosman Case as legitimate objectives in the view of the considerable social importance of football in the [Union], the Commission considers that the restrictions imposed by the rule may escape to the prohibition laid down in Article [101(1)] of the Treaty. In order to establish whether this preliminary conclusion can be upheld or not, the Commission has to know if such restrictions are limited to what is necessary to preserve the integrity of the UEFA club competitions and to ensure the uncertainty as to results. In other words, the Commission must confirm whether there are or not less restrictive means to achieve the same objective.[47]

---

[45] Case C-55/94 *Gebhard* [1995] ECR I-4165 para 37 and Case C-19/92 *Kraus* [1993] ECR I-1663 para 32 are normally reserved for non-discriminatory measures only. Discriminatory measures normally can only benefit from the exhaustive list of Treaty-based exceptions such as public policy, public health and public security, but not from an open list of justifications available to non-discriminatory measures. Sport is an exception to this rule.

[46] Paragraph 2.2.1.6.

[47] Communication made pursuant to Article 19(3) of Council Regulation No 17 concerning request for negative clearance or for exemption pursuant to Article 81(3) of the EC Treaty Case No 37.632—UEFA rule on integrity of the UEFA club competitions: independence of clubs 1999/C 363/02.

This represents the transposition of the objective justification framework to Article 101(1) reminiscent of the *Meca-Medina/Wouters* inherency test.

Conversely, in the *EPO* case decided under Article 101, the General Court dismissed the applicant's arguments that the professional codes of conduct pursue an aim in the general interest according to *Van Binsbergen*, *Thieffry* and *Gebhard*,[48] cases decided under the freedoms provisions, and that it was therefore necessary to accept, by application of the rule of reason, that they are indispensable and cannot therefore fall within the scope of Article 101(1) TFEU. The ban on comparative advertising, according to the applicant, was necessary in the context of a regulated activity which is a matter of public policy and does not adversely affect competition.

The General Court replied that:

> ...the case-law which the applicant cites in support of its argument is irrelevant. The judgments in question relate to the principles of freedom of establishment and freedom to provide services. It follows that rules of professional conduct in force in one Member State which pursue an aim in the general interest apply to professionals who come to practise on the territory of that State without infringing those principles. However, no conclusion can be drawn from that case law as concerns the applicability of Article [101 TFEU] in the present case.[49]

Mortelmans considered that it does not constitute a refusal of the convergence approach by the General Court because the goal of the general interest was invoked as an exception after finding a restriction, while under Article 101 it was invoked as an argument, packed up as a rule of reason, in support of non-applicability of the rule, i.e. at the gate of Article 101, in its prohibition paragraph.[50] However, it would seem to be the case that convergence can be properly invoked only in the context of the first paragraph of Article 101(1), because justifications in free movement law are non-economic. Under Article 101(3), the rule faces four cumulative criteria that are specific to economic arguments and in general do not provide space for public policy grounds as exceptions. Any convergence between the two areas of EU law has to involve the possibility of 'diagonal convergence' and this is especially necessary in the area of sport where grounds of justification are non-economic. It makes more sense and is more in line with the Court's overall approach to draw the analogies with regard to their substantive, functional role in the process of analysis. Treating issues formalistically is not known to be the Court's style.

Whish suggested that the Court in *Wouters* was perhaps deliberately trying to reach the convergent outcome to that which would have been attained under Article 56, had it been the Dutch Government and not the Bar that adopted the

48 Case 33/74 *Van Binsbergen v. Bestuur van de Bedrijfsvereniging voor de Metaalnijverheid* [1974] ECR 1299; Case 71/76 *Thieffry* [1977] ECR 765; and Case C-55/94 *Gebhard* [1995] ECR I-4165.

49 T-144/99 *Institute of Professional Representatives before the European Patent Office v. Commission* [2001] ECR II-1087 para 66. This paragraph makes the decision of the General Court in *Meca-Medina* taken a few years later even more surprising.

50 Mortelmans 2001, p. 629.

restrictive rule in question in *Wouters*.[51] It is to be remembered that the early case law of *Van Binsbergen* allows Member States to take measures restricting the freedom to provide services to the extent they are necessary to safeguard professional rules of conduct.[52]

Regarding Article 101(3), Advocate General Lenz in *Bosman* mentioned that

> ...it would admittedly appear theoretically conceivable that the Commission might grant those rules, which are in breach of Article [45], an exemption from the prohibition in Article [101(1)]. Since such an exemption would, however, make no difference to the breach of Article [45], it would make sense for the Commission to take that factor into account in the exemption procedure. A uniform result ought to be aimed at in any case. That would mean that an exemption under Article [101(3)] would also have to be ruled out.[53]

Most recently, in the *Murphy* case, the Advocate General pointed out that

> ...conflicting assessments of the fundamental freedoms and competition law are to be avoided in principle. [...]an anti-competitive agreement within the meaning of Article 101(1) TFEU can be justified pursuant to Article 101(3) TFEU. However, a person who relies on that provision must demonstrate, by means of convincing arguments and evidence, that the conditions for obtaining an exemption are satisfied. In this connection, it would appear that similar considerations should apply as in the examination of whether a restriction of freedom to provide services is justified.[54]

The Advocate General was apparently of the opinion that convergence ought to exist on the level of justification, but also in general, including on the level of prohibition.[55]

However, the utility of establishing the principle of convergence between the free movement ordinary objective justification framework and Article 101(3) TFEU would be relatively limited, and in sporting disputes virtually unusable. If a measure survives the objective justification test and *Meca-Medina/Wouters* test then, of course, there is no reason to look into it further under Article 101(3) TFEU. If a measure fails their shared test, it means that it failed to establish its legality under EU free movement law and as such it does not qualify for the exception. Even if such measure produced economic efficiencies, which outweigh the negative effects of restraints under Article 101(3) TFEU, that fact still does not legalise the measure under the freedom of movement provisions. The measure will be illegal and will have to be abandoned or modified to comply with the

51 Whish 2009, pp. 127–128.

52 Case 33/74 *Van Binsbergen* [1974] ECR 1299.

53 Opinion of AG Lenz in C-415/93 *Bosman*, para 278.

54 Opinion of AG Kokott in Cases C-403/08 and C-429/08 *Murphy v. Premier League* [2011], paras 249–250.

55 In C-222/07 *Presidente del Consiglio dei Ministri v Regione Sardegna* [2009] ECR I-1404 she similarly considered that when the same questions arise under the law of State aid as with regard to the fundamental freedoms, the reply to the latter should not differ from the reply to the former and the same criteria must be applied in both cases to avoid conflicting assessments. See paras 134 and 135 of her Opinion in that case.

requirements of free movement rules. In other words, once the internal market rules apply alongside the competition law, Article 101(3) TFEU becomes obsolete in practical terms and any convergence in regard to the aims translatable into economic efficiencies and proportionality becomes relevant only in theory.[56]

This was confirmed by the Court in *Murphy* when it only referred to its findings on (dis)proportionality of the measure under internal market law to hold that the exemption in Article 101(3) TFEU does not apply in the case. Had the avenue of the *Meca-Medina/Wouters* test been available to the rule under competition law provisions, all of the objective justification findings would have been fully transplantable and the Court would have referred not just to the part of the judgement dealing with the proportionality of the measure, but also to the rest of the considerations under the objective justification framework.[57]

6.5 Burden of Proof

The outstanding question concerns the party that should bear the burden of proof under Article 101(1) in the framework of the *Meca-Medina/Wouters* test. Normally under Article 101 TFEU, in the first paragraph the burden is on the party alleging infringement, and in the third paragraph the burden is borne by the defendant.[58] However, in *Michelin II* the General Court was unequivocal that the burden of proof for elements of the objective justification defence in Article 102 TFEU was on the dominant undertaking.[59] The Discussion Paper addressed this issue and said that

> [e]xclusionary conduct may escape the prohibition of Article [102] in case the dominant undertaking can provide an objective justification for its behaviour or it can demonstrate that its conduct produces efficiencies which outweigh the negative effect on competition. The burden of proof for such an objective justification or efficiency defence will be on the dominant company. It should be for the company invoking the benefit of a defence against a finding of an infringement to demonstrate to the required legal standard of proof that the conditions for applying such defence are satisfied.

---

[56] See also Sect. 7.8

[57] Paragraph 145. The Court's selected reference to paras 105–124 also confirms the point made above in Sect. 4.10.2.4, that encouraging public to attend and participate in matches is probably not accepted as objective worthy of protection under EU law, and that the Court was only dealing with the point of proportionality.

[58] Article 2 of the Council Regulation 1/2003 of 16 December 2002 states that: 'In any national or [Union] proceedings for the application of Articles [101] and [102] of the Treaty, the burden of proving an infringement of Article [101(1)] or of Article [102] of the Treaty shall rest on the party or the authority alleging the infringement. The undertaking or association of undertakings claiming the benefit of Article [101(3)] of the Treaty shall bear the burden of proving that the conditions of that paragraph are fulfilled'.

[59] See Case T-203/01 *Manufacture française des pneumatiques Michelin v Commission (Michelin II)* [2003] ECR II-4071, paras 107–109.

The burden of proof therefore shifts to the dominant undertaking when relying on the efficiency defence in Article 102 TFEU, equivalent to Article 101(3) TFEU, or the objective justification defence in Article 102 TFEU, equivalent to the *DLG* and *Meca-Medina/Wouters* style of exceptions under Article 101(1) TFEU. For the sake of convergence between the two competition law provisions, which is absolutely necessary to preserve the uniform application of the *Meca-Medina/Wouters* test applicable equally to both competition provisions, the structure of Article 101 TFEU should not be allowed to impede the functional equivalence between the elements and analysis common to them. Such equivalence would bring a number of conceptual problems should the burden of proof under the *Meca-Medina/Wouters* test remain with the party alleging the infringement. *Prima facie*, this interpretation seems to go against Article 2 of Regulation 1/2003,[60] but on a more careful examination, Recital 5 of that regulation explains that in the effective enforcement of EU competition law, which respects the 'fundamental rights of defence', the burden of proof under Articles 101(1) and 102 TFEU should be on the authority alleging infringement, but then it goes on to say without specifying the legal provisions involved that the burden of proof 'should be for the undertaking or association of undertakings invoking the benefit of a defence against a finding of an infringement to demonstrate to the required legal standard that the conditions for applying such defence are satisfied'. In other words, it does not matter under which paragraph of Article 101 TFEU the defence takes place, the burden of proof should be on the party seeking to rely on the justification, as a matter of the fundamental right of defence. This interpretation would, moreover, coincide and align the approach with that under the free movement provisions. For these reasons, in the light of the blurring divide between addressees and the pressing need to specify the parameters of convergence, it is submitted that the Court should re-examine para 55 of *Meca-Medina* in which it implied that the burden is on appellants to establish that rules were disproportionate.[61] Examination of the regulatory and organisational sporting rules does not follow the orthodox analytical approach under Articles 101(1) and 102 TFEU, whereas Article 2 of the Regulation 1/2003 was drafted with that approach in mind. When dealing with private regulatory bodies such as sporting organisations where it is clear that both internal market and competition law apply to the same cases, this should not be allowed to create additional confusion. Burden of proof is suitable for convergence in the application of the two sets of provisions.

---

[60] Council Regulation (EC) No 1/2003 of 16 December 2002 OJ L 1, 04.01.2003, pp. 1–25. Article 2 reads: 'in any national or Community proceedings for the application of Articles 81 and 82 of the Treaty, the burden of proving an infringement of Article 81(1) or of Article 82 of the Treaty shall rest on the party or the authority alleging the infringement. The undertaking or association of undertakings claiming the benefit of Article 81(3) of the Treaty shall bear the burden of proving that the conditions of that paragraph are fulfilled'.

[61] In para 55 of C-519/04 *Meca-Medina*, the Court held: 'Since the appellants have, moreover, not pleaded that the penalties which were applicable and were imposed in the present case are excessive, it has not been established that the anti-doping rules at issue are disproportionate'.

References

Barnard C (2010) The substantive law of the EU, 3rd edn. Oxford University Press, Oxford
Baquero Cruz J (2002) Between competition and free movement: the economic constitutional law of the European community. Hart Publishing, Oxford
Callery C (2011) Should the European Union embrace or exorcise Leegin's rule of reason European competition law. Review 32:42–50
Mortelmans K (2001) Towards convergence in the application of the rules on free movement and on competition? Common Market Law Rev 38:613–649
Parrish R, Miettinen S (2008) Sporting exception in European Union law. T.M.C Asser Press, The Hague
Sauter W, Schepel H (2007) State and market in the competition and free movement case law of the EU courts. TILEC discussion paper 2007-024, Tilburg University. http://ssrn.com/abstract=1010075
Weatherill S (2008) Anti-doping revisited—the demise of the rule of 'purely sporting interest? In: Weatherill S (ed) European Union sports law: collected papers. T.M.C. Asser Press, The Hague
Weatherill S (2009) The influence of EU law on sports governance. In: Gardiner S, Parrish R, Siekmann CR (eds) EU, sport, law and policy: regulation, re-regulation and representation. T.M.C Asser Press, The Hague, pp 79–100
Whish R (2009) Competition law, 6th edn. Oxford University Press, Oxford
Zweigert K, Kötz H (1987) An introduction to comparative law, 2nd edn. Clarendon Press, Oxford

Chapter 7
Treatment of UEFA Restrictions on Breakaway Leagues in Football Under EU Law

Contents

7.1 Introduction 237
7.2 The Conflict 239
7.3 Defining the Relevant Market 240
7.3.1 The Market for Organisational Services for Transnational Club Football in Europe 241
7.3.2 Connected Downstream Market: Exploitation Market 244
7.3.3 Connected Upstream Market: The Market for Clubs' Services 246
7.3.4 Relevant Geographic Market 247
7.4 Classification of the Parties and the Restraints 248
7.4.1 Undertaking or Association of Undertakings/Agreement or Decision? 248
7.4.2 Market Power of UEFA on the Relevant Market 253
7.4.3 Article 49 of the UEFA Statutes: Restrictive Effects 259
7.5 Applicable Justification Framework 267
7.6 The Existence of Elements of Justification 268
7.6.1 The Overall Context: Legitimate Aims in Public Interest 269
7.6.2 Suitability of the Article 49 Rule: Effectiveness Test 272
7.6.3 Inherency Requirement 278
7.6.4 Proportionality 281
7.7 Effect on Intra-Union Trade 301
7.8 The Conditions of Article 101(3) TEFU 302
7.9 Collective Dominance and Collusion by Elite Clubs 303
7.10 Concluding Remarks 308
References 309

7.1 Introduction

The questions of breakaway leagues and the legality of the clauses in Article 49(1) and (3) of the *Union des Associations Européennes de Football* (UEFA) Statutes have never been addressed by the Court of Justice of the European Union ('CJEU' or 'the Court'). But as we saw in Chaps. 4 and 5, a compass to navigate through this

K. Pijetlovic, *EU Sports Law and Breakaway Leagues in Football*,
ASSER International Sports Law Series, DOI 10.1007/978-94-6265-048-0_7

legal issue is supplied to us by the Court's jurisprudence and the Commission's practice in the area of sport and beyond. In *DLG*, the Court held that the statutes of a cooperative purchasing association forbidding its members to participate in other forms of organised cooperation was compatible with Articles 101(1) and 102 TFEU because it was restricted to what was necessary to ensure the achievement of the legitimate (commercial) objectives. In its policy documents, the Commission supported the preservation of pyramid structures and open competitions, however, not at the expense of surrendering the breadth of economic freedoms any more than necessary to attain legitimate aims.[1] According to the Commission Communication on Developing the European Dimension in Sport, Article 165 TFEU supports the preservation of European sporting structures as a part of the concept of specificity of sport.[2] Elsewhere in this volume, it has been submitted that Article 165 TFEU has given additional weight to the sporting arguments.[3] This certainly plays into the hands of UEFA as a party that heavily relies on the concept of specificity of sport in the context of breakaway structures. On the other hand, the Court is known to rule in favour of economic considerations every time that rules pursuing legitimate sporting goals have been found disproportionate. It had little hesitation in holding that rules regarding transfer windows in *Lehtonen* or training compensation in *Bernard* went further than necessary in realisation of their legitimate aims. Similarly, the Court liberalised the market for satellite transmission decoders in *Murphy* and the labour market in *Bosman*. It is for the clubs determined to form an alternative league to exploit the logic of the legal arguments in this line of jurisprudence.

According to the Commission, the methodological approach to assessing whether a rule adopted by a sports association relating to the organisation of sport infringes Articles 101 and/or 102 involves a four-step test:

> Step 1: Is the sports association that adopted the rule to be considered an 'undertaking' or an 'association of undertakings'? […] Step 2: Does the rule in question restrict competition within the meaning of Article [101(1) TFEU] or constitute an abuse of a dominant position under Article [102 TFEU]? This will depend, in application of the principles established in the *Wouters[/Meca-Medina]*judgment, on the following factors: a. the overall context in which the rule was adopted or produces its effects and its objectives; b. whether the restrictions caused by the rule are inherent in the pursuit of the objectives; and c. whether the rule is proportionate in light of the objective pursued. […] Step 3: Is trade between Member States affected? Step 4: Does the rule fulfil the conditions of Article [101(3) TEFU]?[4]

Striking the balance between commercial freedoms for the clubs on the one hand and the specificity of sport on the other is at the heart of the conflict that culminates in the application of the proportionality test. On the basis of established legal parameters, this chapter will evaluate the status under EU law of clauses in the UEFA Statutes

[1] See Sect. 3.2.1 for policy statements on the pyramid structure.

[2] Paragraph 4.2 of the Communication, COM (2011) 12 final, 18. 1. 2011.

[3] See Sect. 4.8.

[4] Commission Staff Working Document, The EU and Sport: Background and Context, Accompanying Document to the White Paper on Sport, COM (2007) 391 final, Annex I, para 2.1.2.

prohibiting the unauthorised establishment of alternative cross-border competition in football. It will also briefly touch upon the question of whether the practices in the current governance model as described in Chap. 3 amount to an abuse of a collective dominant position by elite European football clubs.

7.2 The Conflict

The source of potential conflict between elite clubs in a pan-European breakaway league and UEFA arises from the clauses in Article 49(1) and (3) of the UEFA Statutes (hereinafter 'Article 49 rule') that read:

> UEFA shall have the sole jurisdiction to organize or abolish international competitions in Europe in which Member Associations and/or their clubs participate. [...] International matches, competitions or tournaments which are not organized by the UEFA but are played on UEFA territory shall require the prior approval of FIFA and/or UEFA and/or the relevant Member Associations in accordance with the FIFA Regulations Governing International Matches and any additional implementing rules adopted by the UEFA Executive Committee.[5]

Committing to any form of participation in international club competitions not organised or not approved by the concerned governing bodies will entail disciplinary measures as specified in the codes implementing the *Fédération Internationale de Football Association* (FIFA) Regulations Governing International Matches and disciplinary codes of national associations; Article 19 of the FIFA Regulations Governing International Matches (2012) and Article 12 of the FIFA Disciplinary Code (2011); and Article 53 of the UEFA Statutes (2012) and Article 6 of the UEFA Disciplinary Regulations (2013). The sanctions that may be imposed by UEFA provide that any club in breach of the UEFA Statutes may become subject to a withdrawal of their license, full or partial stadium closure, disqualification from competitions in progress and/or exclusion from future competitions, and fines in an amount of no more than €1 million.[6] The European Club Association (ECA) expressly agreed to this rule via Memorandum of Understanding 2012 that governs the relationship between the clubs and UEFA. According to paras D.1, D.3 and D.4, ECA undertakes 'to recognise UEFA as the governing body of football at European level in accordance with its Statutes [...]; to ensure that none of its member clubs participate in any competition that is not organised or recognised by UEFA/FIFA' and 'to ensure that its member clubs are not members of any other association or grouping involving clubs from more than one country [...]'.

In recent years, the UEFA's general attitude to the idea of cross-border leagues became more moderate. After the meeting of the UEFA Management with UEFA Member Association General Secretaries, which was held on 26–27 October 2005

---

[5] UEFA Statutes, edition 2012.

[6] Similarly, the most severe sanction under Article 12 of the FIFA Disciplinary Code involves expulsion from competitions and a fine of no more than CHF 1 million.

in Nyon, UEFA considers that a cross-border competition is conceivable, but only if the proposal for such a project a priori satisfies 13 conditions which are set out and analysed below in Sect. 7.6.4.3. The conditions are particularly onerous: they do not allow a direct access to the exploitation market, the proposed league has to be confined to a specific geographical area, compulsory solidarity contributions are required, regulatory competence remains mostly with UEFA including club licensing and uniform match calendar, clubs presumably have to remain as participants in their national championships, and the approval of national associations, UEFA and FIFA is required. UEFA perceives these rules as a natural and legitimate part of its mandate and a necessary means of the proper organisation and financing of football. Conversely, clubs may claim that the Article 49 rule presents a restriction upon their commercial freedom in breach of TFEU rules on competition and the free movement of services. The Article 49 rule in the UEFA Statutes is not likely to be challenged in the abstract by the clubs, but only when the conflict materialises, i.e. only if the authorisation by the relevant governing body or bodies has not been obtained and/or the clause is used as a basis to impose sanctions on the clubs and/or players participating in an unsanctioned breakaway league.

The first part of the text that follows in this chapter will consider preliminary issues such as the relevant market, classification of parties and their position on the relevant market, classification of restraints under the EU law and the applicable justification framework. Thereafter, the elements in the justification framework will be analysed.

7.3 Defining the Relevant Market

The relevant product market in question is the market for provision of organisational services for transnational club football in Europe. Entry to this market in isolation would however not be the *per se* goal for the clubs involved in an alternative league and for private promoters. The UEFA rules are designed to control access to this market, but their ultimate aim is to prevent the emergence of a rival league in several connected markets, most importantly, in the downstream market for commercial exploitation and the upstream market for services of clubs. In the *DLG* case, the Court considered the commercial activities within the organisation (distribution of fertilisers and plant protection products, *in casu*), rather than the access to mere organised membership in the rival establishment, as the relevant market.[7] In *MOTOE*, the Court defined the relevant market as consisting in 'first, the organisation of motorcycling events and, second, in their commercial exploitation'.[8]

---

[7] Case C-250/92 *Gøttrup-Klim e.a. Grovvareforeninger v Dansk Landbrugs Grovvareselskab AmbA (DLG)* [1994] ECR I-5641, paras 19 and 48.

[8] Case C-49/07 *Motosykletistiki Omospondia Ellados NPID (MOTOE)* v *Elliniko Dimosio* [2008] ECR I-4863, para 33.

Those two types of activities were seen as functionally complementary.[9] Nevertheless, the definition of the relevant market in our case should rather focus on the market for the organisation of football competitions alone. The reason for this difference in approach is that in *MOTOE* and *DLG*, the rival entity already existed and was active on the market for organisation and exploitation. In *MOTOE*, the prior authorisation was exercised by ELPA in relation to MOTOE, a rival already established on the market and an entity already performing organising functions. In *DLG*, the B members had already organised their participation in a rival entity and competed with DLG when DLG decided to change its rules and prohibit dual membership. So the question was less about restricting the access to market for organisation in general and more about restricting the exercise of specific activities that also entailed an element of discrimination between economic operators that were already active on the organisational market. In our case, there is no actual rival organisation and the question is focused more on access to the organisational market itself that will, in either case, bring about access to the exploitation market. The distinction is similar to the distinction between access (take-up of an activity or entry into market) and exercise (pursuit of an activity or operation in a market) in internal market law.

7.3.1 The Market for Organisational Services for Transnational Club Football in Europe

7.3.1.1 Production Processes of Professional Football Contests

There are two stages in the production process of professional football contests. The first stage takes place at the level of individual clubs: owners invest into developing the playing strength of their respective teams.[10] They buy players and hire coaches, buy, build or rent stadia, and provide everything that is necessary for building as successful a team as possible. Under the European model of sport, and taking into consideration the system of revenue distribution, we can assume that club owners focus on win-maximising strategies and not profit-maximising strategies—this is because the two are interconnected and focusing on the club's on-the-pitch success inevitably implies economic success. However, a single club is not capable of producing a marketable product and needs at least one opponent to achieve that. There is significantly less demand in the exploitation market for individual games, such as exhibitions, than games played as a part of an organised

[9] Ibid.

[10] Dietl et al. 2011, Organisational Differences between U.S. Major Leagues and European Leagues: Implications for Salary Cap. International Association of Sports Economists, Working Paper Series, Paper No 11-05, p. 2. Available at http://college.holycross.edu/RePEc/spe/Dietletal_OrganizationalDifferences.pdf.

competition.[11] In order to markedly raise the economic value of such a game, the game needs to be integrated into an organised championship race. Clubs are therefore the producers of inputs (individual games) which, when integrated, deliver the final meta-product—the championship.[12]

The second stage of the production process occurs at the level of the league.[13] For example UEFA has the organisational and administrative responsibility for the UEFA Champions League and Europa League. It conducts the draw procedure; approves the participants; and appoints referees, match delegates, and referee observers, and covers their expenses. It also acts as a disciplinary body supervising and enforcing all aspects of the competition. UEFA selects and appoints a wide range of third-party service providers to provide services that are required in connection with a match, such as product development, sales, after-sales services and client relations with broadcasters, sponsors, suppliers, licensees and participating clubs, media services (booking of commercial spots and broadcast sponsorship throughout the world), legal services, television production services, auditing and monitoring of UEFA Champions League television programmes throughout the world, research services, operational implementation of the commercial concepts, hospitality services, financial and administrative services, and statistical and information services.[14] All of these services are indispensable for creating the best possible value in any professional team sport and for the professional marketing of a final meta-product before it starts producing revenue. UEFA thus performs organising functions in the production process of professional football competitions at a pan-European level.

The market for organisational services for transnational club football in Europe is integrated into the contest production process, and the clubs participate together with UEFA in this process. It is the access to the organisational market that is the subject of the authorisation under the Article 49 rule. Imposing prior authorisation on clubs entering the second stage of production is at the heart of the legal problem and a key to the correct definition of the relevant market in the context. Without such authorisation, it is not possible to produce a marketable product independently of UEFA. Lack of direct control by clubs over the second stage presents a barrier for clubs to become market operators independent of UEFA in the production process of professional football contests. The entry into that stage directly ties with, and provides access to, the exploitation market.

[11] Noll 2003, fn. 1.

[12] Dietl et al. 2011, p. 3.

[13] Ibid. p. 2.

[14] Commission Decision in Case COMP/37.398—Joint Selling of Commercial Rights (UEFA Champions League) [2003] OJ L 291/25, para 13.

7.3.1.2 Cross-Elasticity of Supply and Demand

The relevant market is the market for organisational services for transnational club football in Europe. In this market, clubs are on the demand side and UEFA is on the supply side. Stage one of the production process is identical for both the production of national and European professional club football contests. In stage two of the national championship production process, national leagues or associations, as the case may be, provide the organisational services and perform functions similar to those of UEFA. Service providers for national club football do not have the mandate, aspiration, or realistic chance to provide their services to organise transnational competitions. They will not supply the transnational market in either the short or long term and are not a potential substitute for UEFA, a transnational regulatory and organisational body. The competitive constraint on the supply side might come from independent private entities such as big media firms, the formation of a rival entity by the clubs or the combination of the two. Nevertheless, these parties cannot be said to present an *immediate* competitive threat as supply substitutes, but they will definitely play a role as potential competitors—it is more appropriate to take potential competition into account in the assessment of UEFA's market power than in the assessment of relevant market.

In a market with no *immediate* alternative suppliers, the use of the SSNIP test might not be an ideal measurement for demand substitution as there is no viable option to easily switch to. But due to the existence of potential competitors it is possible to, at the very least, run the test. There is a general consensus among economists and competition law academics that the use of this test provides many advantages. For example Faull and Nikpay argue that 'it is useful to think of the market definition questions in terms of SSNIP. [...] [It] provides for a framework within which to consider the question of economic substitution'.[15]

The way that UEFA 'charges' for its services is to apportion a part of the revenues from the exploitation market to cover its organisational costs. It takes no profit for performing this function. In the circumstances where there are no immediate alternative suppliers, the SSNIP test for the cross-elasticity of demand comes down to one question: would the clubs break away (and organise in a joint venture or assign organising functions to an independent entity) shortly after the cost of organisational services rose by 5–10 %? The answer would probably be 'no'. The UEFA organisational costs for all the competitions in the past four seasons represented 12 % of the overall profits, so the total price increase would roughly be in the range of 0.6–1.2 % of the overall profits. On the basis of this test alone, the conclusion is that it would not make such a significant impact on the important commercial decisions of the clubs. Also, the rise in the cost of services would probably not affect the returns to the clubs, but some other item on the financial report's expenditure sheet. In the past 3 years, the amounts paid to the clubs as well as solidarity payments have been rising due to the rise in the broadcasting revenues.

---

[15] Faull and Nikpay 2007, p. 44.

From the qualitative perspective, input by clubs produced in stage one of the contest production process is compatible with the organisational functions of any entity that has the necessary level of know-how. Should it become evident to a sufficiently big majority of the top clubs that the commercial and legal risks involved in changing the *status quo* are the more rational economic choice than continuing to cooperate with UEFA in their role as organisers, the clubs will break away and create a rival competition that could have the effect of commercially killing off any remaining pan-European competition. As seen throughout the discussion in Chap. 3, regulatory and governance issues affecting the commercial interests of the clubs outside this market may also have repercussions for any breakaway decision.

7.3.2 Connected Downstream Market: Exploitation Market

On the supply side of the exploitation market is UEFA's licensing of the commercial rights to pan-European football club competitions that are played throughout the year, and sales of the related merchandise. The commercial rights include product licensing, broadcasting and new media, sponsorship, suppliership and other intellectual property rights. One of the products that UEFA markets (in partnership with Television Event and Media Marketing AG) is supreme: the Champions League features the highest quality football on the planet and it is the most popular club competition in the world, even ahead of the American National Football League's Super Bowl.[16] The newly rebranded Europa League is, in sheer number of matches, the biggest football competition, with 205 matches per season, but it is considerably less valuable and in the few years of its existence has not managed to break-even financially.[17] However, the quality of football played between the top teams in the Europa League is generally comparable to the quality achieved by the clubs in the Champions League, so there is at least a potential to build up the marketing image. The system of promotion and relegation keeps the membership in the two pan-European leagues fluid, and it is also instructive for the market definition that the Media Partners proposal included most of the clubs from both of those leagues. Since UEFA holds the exclusive right to organise and commercially exploit the two championships, at this stage of product market analysis it appears that there are no actual competitive constraints on the supply side of the market. Potential competition in the exploitation market may come only from clubs organising a pan-European rival league.

On the demand side are the suppliers, sponsors, producers of different goods, broadcasters with a downstream market for their subscribers and advertisers, and football supporters. The demand side is a market for the acquisition and resale of commercial rights to football competitions, typically organised in a tendering contest. There is a close and interdependent vertical relationship between the parties

[16] 'Champions League Final Tops Super Bowl for TV Market', BBC news, 31 January 2010.

[17] UEFA Financial Report 2010/2011, p. 23.

in the demand market: broadcasting companies are willing to invest generously into obtaining exclusive rights to top sporting events as they are considered the most valuable TV content. Broadcasting these events attracts a big number of advertisers and subscribers. The events are followed live by a cumulative audience of hundreds of millions of fans on different kinds of media devices, which makes the events especially interesting for sponsors and advertisers aiming to reach large targeted audiences. The bigger the anticipated audience and the more popular the sporting event, the more lucrative the sponsorship deals for UEFA and the higher the value of advertising space for broadcasters.[18]

The entire demand side of the exploitation market is driven by the appeal a particular sporting event has on the masses as represented by final consumers in this vertical chain of supply. Hence, it is ultimately the substitutability from the perspective of the final consumers that determines the substitutability of demand in the exploitation market.[19] In this context, it was held that viewing sport is not interchangeable with viewing other forms of entertainment[20] and football broadcasts are not interchangeable with other sports broadcasts.[21] The Commission further subdivided the football broadcasting market into regular events and those played intermittently.[22] This was confirmed in the examination of joint selling arrangements in *UEFA Champions League*, where the Commission held that football events in Europe that are played throughout the year constitute a separate relevant product market.[23] Such events included UEFA Champions League, Europa League and national first division leagues and cups. They regularly attract high audience numbers, a specific audience, and provide a certain brand image for the broadcaster which cannot be achieved by means of any other content.[24] Even though UEFA's EURO is the third and FIFA's World Cup is the most-watched sporting event in the world, they were viewed as too infrequent and too short to be considered as presenting an alternative to support the viewing habits of subscribers or to add a temporal dimension to the product market as defined by the Commission. The application of the standard SSNIP test to football broadcasts of regular events would likely reveal zero cross-price elasticity of demand as a competitive

[18] This was recognised by the Commission in Case COMP IV/37.806—ENIC/UEFA [2002] unpublished decision of 27 June 2002, para 41 that said: 'the preferences of viewers determine the value of a programme to advertisers and pay TV broadcasters'.

[19] Analogous to finding in Commission Decision in Case IV/36.539—British Interactive Broadcasting/Open [1999] OJ L 312/1, p. 1.

[20] Commission Decision in Case No IV/36.237—TPS [1999] OJ L 90/6, p. 6.

[21] Commission Decision in COMP/M.2483—Group Canal+/RTL/GJCD/JV [2001] OJ L 2985, para 19.

[22] Ibid. para 21.

[23] Commission Decision in COMP/37.398—Joint Selling of Commercial Rights (UEFA Champions League) [2003] OJ L 291/25, para 59.

[24] Ibid. para 58.

constraint from other kind of sporting events.[25] In relation to a part of final consumers, this position is reinforced by the fans' loyalty to one club, analogous (and perhaps more strongly) to the concept of consumer loyalty to a particular brand mentioned by the General Court in cases such as *BaByliss*[26] or *Kaysersberg*.[27]

7.3.3 Connected Upstream Market: The Market for Clubs' Services

The upstream market to the organisation of European transnational football club competitions is the market for clubs' services. This market is the mirror image of the relevant organisational market discussed above. Here UEFA is on the demand side and is currently the sole buyer of the services of clubs on a European level.[28] This in turn enables the exclusivity of commercial exploitation of pan-European club competitions. It is a peculiarity of professional sport production that championships must possess a monopoly status to achieve consistent ranking and increase their value for consumers.[29] Being a sole buyer of the clubs' services functions as a means to achieve such consistency and to produce a single champion per market area, per sport discipline.

UEFA regulates the European labour market, club licensing and other factors of production. National associations regulate the production of their competitions within the confines of their respective mandates. Operating in this regulatory environment, clubs invest into team building and participate in competitions organised by UEFA and by national associations. By participating in those competitions, clubs supply input services for the production of championship leagues without which UEFA's organisational functions in transnational club competitions, and national associations' organisational functions in national club competitions, would become obsolete. It should be remembered that clubs cannot individually produce a marketable product and that individual games that are not a part of scheduled contest are not in demand. Hence, clubs need an entity performing the organising functions, be it sporting association such as UEFA, or a private promoter.

It may be difficult to define a market in a situation where both levels of the vertical chain of supply, which are represented by parties having a *quid pro quo* arrangement instead of a classic wholesale price (for example cost covering for UEFA organisational services is not a classic charge for services as it has no profit margins). But we need not look far, as the service is unique and not interchangeable: the

[25] This follows from findings by Dietl et al. 2011, p. 10. In either case, it is not irrelevant that the UEFA EURO and the FIFA World Cup, which similarly attract large viewership, are scheduled to avoid overlap with the Champions League, European League or national leagues.

[26] Case T-114/02 *BaByliss SA v. Commission*, judgment of 3 April 2003.

[27] Case T-290/94 *Kaysersberg SA v. Commission*, judgment of 27 November 1997.

[28] But see the discussion below in the subsection on the UEFA market power.

[29] Dietl et al. 2011, p. 3.

relevant market is the market for top football clubs' 'input services'. Since, for UEFA, and any potential pan-European rival organiser, there are no economically viable substitutes for the quality and value of individual games between clubs in the Champions League and the Europa League, only those clubs' services are to be included in the definition of the connected upstream market. Only the input from those clubs is compatible with UEFA's relevant organisational functions (i.e. another part of the final meta-product), because it is capable of being turned into economically valuable product that can be used for the purposes of maintaining crucial solidarity mechanisms. The market at the European level is therefore further subdivided into services for clubs playing top-quality football as represented in European leagues and the rest of the clubs. National associations however might have a different perspective on the interchangeability of the elite clubs' services as only a few of such teams from their top flight league participate in European competitions. For most of them, all the clubs in their first (and in the big football nations, also second) division are capable of creating commercial value at the national level, the only level they can exploit. The input services from both the top clubs and from all others playing in their competitions are compatible with their organisational functions. Hence, the national associations and UEFA can be said to 'compete' only for the services of those clubs playing in the European leagues. However, as the 13 conditions set by UEFA for the approval of alternative cross-border competitions[30] are directed towards geographically delimited leagues (as opposed to pan-European leagues which would not be approved), all the clubs that are capable of producing the commercial value for the national governing bodies belong to the connected upstream market for clubs' services.

7.3.4 Relevant Geographic Market

The relevant geographic market is the European continent. This is the area in which UEFA organisational services are provided and in which sufficiently homogenous conditions of competition exist. Unlike the broadcasting market which is still, even after *Murphy,* national in character, the organisational service market for transnational club competitions is not characterised by linguistic, cultural and legal-regulatory differences or other factors segmenting markets along national lines. Organisational services are provided at a European level and have no connection to any particular country. The upstream market as defined above mirrors this geographic scope. Clubs provide their services and play the matches all over Europe under the unified set of rules. Commercial rights other than broadcasting (such as sponsorship, product licensing and suppliership) are also Europe-wide rather than national as these undertakings associate themselves with the league and not with particular teams.[31]

[30] See Sect. 7.6.4.3.

[31] Ibid. para 89.

7.4 Classification of the Parties and the Restraints

The difficulties involved in applying the traditional competition law concepts to the area of sport are illustrated by the classification of the parties and the restraints under Articles 101 and 102 TFEU. For the purpose of application of those provisions, individually or simultaneously, the preliminary question must be: is UEFA is an undertaking or association of undertakings on the relevant market, and does the Article 49 rule constitute an agreement between undertakings or a decision by an association of undertakings? Article 101 applies to different forms of collusion between *two or more* undertakings, including collusions made through the medium of association, whereas Article 102 TFEU does not include the concept of an association of undertakings, but if the association represents an emanation of its members that are active on the relevant market, it may be considered an undertaking for the purposes of that article.[32] Also, if the association is active itself on the relevant market it will amount to an undertaking.

7.4.1 *Undertaking or Association of Undertakings/ Agreement or Decision?*

Formally, UEFA is a private body that is engaged in economic activities on the relevant market and in both of the connected markets. But even if it could be argued, in order to take its *purchasing* functions outside the definition of economic activity, that *functionally* UEFA is a public body because it discharges social functions in public interest, it would nevertheless be considered as engaged in economic activity because the services of the clubs that it obtains are subsequently used as an input for an economic activity.[33]

On the basis of the considerations in Sects. 5.1 and 5.5.1, it is clear that UEFA can be classified as an 'association of associations of undertakings', an 'association of undertakings' or an 'undertaking' for the purposes of the application of competition law provisions. The precise classification depends on the definition of the relevant market under examination. The Commission decision in para 25 of *ENIC* states that although UEFA is an association of associations of undertakings, it can qualify as an undertaking for the purposes of organisation of European club competitions.[34] An undertaking alone cannot adopt 'decisions by associations of undertakings' or collide with itself by entering into agreements or concerted practices within the meaning of that article. That action requires involvement of at

[32] T-193/02 *Piau*, paras 112 and 116.

[33] In accordance with Case T-319/99 *Federación Nacional de Empresas de Instrumentación Científica, Médica, Técnica y Dental (FENIN) v. Commission* ECR II-351 paras 36–37 as upheld by the Court in Case C-205/03 [2006] ECR I-6295, paras 25–27.

[34] Commission Decision in Case COMP IV/37.806—ENIC/UEFA, para 25.

least two undertakings. Alternatively, it requires an agreement between an association of undertakings and at least one other undertaking. The General Court has held that the wording of Article 101(1) TFEU encompasses agreements between associations of undertakings and other undertakings, including its member undertakings, as long as the association engaged in conduct is separate from that of undertakings in regard to one and the same infringement.[35]

Citing the General Court on this point, the Commission held in para 26 of *ENIC* that 'the UEFA rule on "Integrity of the UEFA club competitions: independence of clubs" is a decision taken by an association of associations of undertakings within the meaning of Article 101(1) of the Treaty, *as it was drawn up by UEFA Executive Committee*.'[36] Does this imply that *any* rule drawn up by the UEFA Executive Committee is a decision by the association? If it does, then the decision in *ENIC* appears to be in conflict with itself because in para 25 the Commission suggested that UEFA 'can be qualified as an undertaking for certain activities such as the organisation of European club competitions'. If UEFA constitutes an undertaking on that market, and the Article 49 rule was drawn up by the UEFA Executive Committee, how could that rule be a decision by the association? Specifically, what is the status under Article 101 TFEU of a rule drawn up by the UEFA Executive Committee that regulates the activities regarding organisation of club competitions? This question is valid in our case even though the Article 49 rule was drawn up by a different organ at UEFA: the Congress, the supreme controlling organ of the UEFA consisting of all its Member Associations. Taking into consideration its composition, the Congress is not qualitatively different to the UEFA Executive Committee under para 26 of *ENIC* and so the questions still remain.

Reconciliation between paras 25 and 26 of *ENIC* is offered by acknowledging that para 25 is merely a suggestion to be used whenever the circumstances so require—the words 'can be qualified' do not imply that UEFA necessarily *ought to be* classified as such for every case involving organisation of European competitions. Similarly, in regard to para 26 of *ENIC*, Annex I of the Commission Staff Working Document confirms that rules drawn up unilaterally by sporting associations consisting of undertakings will *usually* (i.e. not always) constitute decisions by an association of undertakings.[37] Therefore, the classification of an entity and its rules will be decided on the basis of the case-by-case approach emphasised on numerous occasions by the Commission, most notably, in the White Paper on Sport. There is no a priori uniform answer but some guidance on the issue is provided by the case law.

In *Meca-Medina*,[38] the Court did not waste its time in classifying the IOC rule enforced by FINA as either a decision of an association or as an agreement between undertakings. In para 45, it simply said that 'even if the anti-doping rules at issue

[35] Cases T-25/95 etc. *Cimenteries CBR SA v. Commission* [2000] ECR II-491, para 1325.

[36] Paragraph 26 [emphasis added].

[37] See Annex I, endnote nr. 27 [emphasis added].

[38] Case T-313/02 *David Meca-Medina and Igor Majcen v Commission* [2004] ECR II-3291 and Case C-519/04 *David Meca-Medina and Igor Majcen v Commission* [2006] ECR I-6991.

are to be regarded as a decision of an association of undertakings limiting the appellants' freedom of action, they do not […] necessarily constitute a restriction of competition incompatible with the common market'. The White Paper assumes that this means that the IOC rule was considered a decision by an association.[39]

In *DLG*, the restriction on membership in a rival cooperative was examined under both Articles 101 and 102 TFEU without specific reference to the status of an entity as an undertaking or an association of undertakings, and the statutes of the cooperative as an agreement or decision. The Court did, however, say that DLG was a 'voluntary association of persons established in order to pursue common commercial objectives' and treated the rules in the statutes simply as restrictions under both competition articles of the Treaty.

In *Wouters*, the Court held the General Council of the Bar of the Netherlands to be an association of undertakings and the regulation prohibiting multidisciplinary partnership of the members of the Bar and the accountants it adopted, to be a decision within the meaning of Article 101 TFEU.[40] The Court did not consider it to be an undertaking for the purpose of the application of Article 102 TFEU since the Bar did not carry out any economic activities, and the Court did not consider it to be a group of undertakings, because the members of the Bar were not sufficiently linked to adopt common conduct on the market.

However, in *Piau*, like in *DLG*, the rule was examinable under both articles. In the context of Article 102 TFEU, FIFA was regarded as an emanation of the clubs acting on their behalf as a second-level association of undertakings formed by the clubs that are so linked on the relevant market that they present themselves as a collective entity.[41] The FIFA rule regulating access to the profession of players' agents was considered to be a decision by an association of undertakings under Article 101 TFEU.[42]

FIFA and the Italian football association were considered as undertakings by the Commission in *FIFA World Cup 1990*.[43] FIFA conferred on the commercial company exclusive rights for the supply of match tickets for the purpose of putting together package tours. The agreement between FIFA and that company was considered as agreement within the meaning of Article 101 TFEU.[44]

The pattern that transpires from the case law is that regulatory rules applicable to the market in which the association is not economically active will constitute decisions of an association of undertakings, whereas the cases in which those associations are economically active on the relevant market will contribute towards the finding of an undertaking.

---

[39] See Annex I, endnote nr. 27 of the White Paper.

[40] Case C-309/99 *Wouters* [2002], para 64.

[41] T-193/02 *Piau*, paras 112 and 116.

[42] T-193/02 *Piau*, para 75.

[43] Commission Decision in Case Cases 33.384 and 33.378—Distribution of package tours during the 1990 World Cup [1992] OJ L 326/31.

[44] Ibid. para 75.

There is much support for the claim that the UEFA Statutes were adopted by UEFA of its own authority and that the Article 49 rule is a unilaterally drawn rule and UEFA its sole author. The cooperation of other entities is not necessarily required for its enforcement on the relevant market, although the enforcement may be substantially aided by concerted efforts with national associations. The Article 49 rule endows the UEFA Executive Committee with the power to decide on any cases of formation of cross-border leagues. The Executive Committee consists of a president and 15 members who each hold an active office (usually the office of the president) within a different Member Association. They are elected by the Congress, a UEFA body composed of all Member Associations. It was this body that adopted the first UEFA Statutes in 1997, including the Article 49 rule, and made all of the subsequent amendments to it.[45] Thus, it could be argued that the Article 49 rule merely reflects the concurrent will of the Member Associations, and that UEFA is acting as an emanation of its members who, through the membership and powers within the bodies of UEFA, represent their own interests. It is indeed in their direct interest to have a rule such as Article 49 included in the Statutes: national associations are the beneficiaries of the solidarity payments resulting from UEFA's collective sales of commercial rights for European competitions organised by it.[46] None of them in isolation can claim the dominion over the organisation of pan-European competitions. This is collectively achieved by using their powers in UEFA organs and via UEFA rules. An emergence of a European rival would terminate UEFA's exclusive organising functions at the European level and would affect, if not completely cease, the financial contributions to Member Associations. The rule was voted in and maintained by all Member Associations via the UEFA Congress, and if needed, will be enforced under Article 49 of the Statutes by the decision of representatives of 15 Member Associations *qua* UEFA Executive Committee. Article 101 TFEU encompasses decisions by associations of undertakings. The idea is to enable those applying Article 101 TFEU 'to hold associations liable for the anti-competitive behaviour of their members'.[47] On the basis of these considerations, the Article 49 rule may be argued to constitute a decision by an association of undertakings.

However, the Member Associations are neither active nor do they constitute undertakings on the relevant market. UEFA on the other hand engages in a wide range of purchasing functions and it clearly can constitute an undertaking. *ENIC* does not help in resolving the puzzle. Paragraph 25 of the case instructs us to conclude that UEFA is an undertaking because it is active on the relevant market for the organisation of European club competitions, but para 26 suggests that the Article 49 rule is likely to be a decision of an association of undertakings because

---

[45] UEFA Statutes, edition 2012, Article 70.

[46] The solidarity payment is made available to Member Associations to develop infrastructure, co-finance some of their statutory tasks, as incentives for good governance, for the clubs licensing project, etc. See UEFA Financial Report 2009/2010, p. 13.

[47] The constitution and rules of trade associations may constitute decisions. Commission Decision in Case IV/27.958—National Sulphuric Acid [1980] OJ L 260/24, para 30.

the rule was drawn by the UEFA Congress. The reference to the activities on the relevant market produces a result different than the reference to the Article 49 rule alone. It is submitted that in this situation, it is the conclusion made by the reference to the relevant market that should prevail because it is the substance and the effects rather than the form that should matter. UEFA could therefore be considered an undertaking and as such outside the scope of Article 101. But this conclusion could also be challenged.

National associations themselves may constitute undertakings to the extent that they carry out economic activities.[48] The General Court ruled in *AC-Treuhand AG* that it is not necessary for an undertaking to itself operate on the market where the restriction takes place to offend against Article 101 TFEU.[49] The General Court rejected the applicant's argument that its firm could not be regarded as a co-perpetrator of an infringement because it did not carry out an economic activity on the relevant market affected by the restriction of competition and because its contribution to the cartel was merely subordinate. The purpose of its conduct, as coordinated with that of other undertakings, was to restrict competition on a specific relevant market. The requisite legal standard to prove participation in a cartel and label an undertaking as a perpetrator is to prove that the undertaking attended meetings at which anti-competitive agreements were concluded without manifesting its opposition to such meetings.

National associations are obliged by Article 59 of the UEFA Statutes to include in their statutes 'a provision whereby it, its leagues, clubs, players and officials agree to respect at all times the Statutes, regulations and decisions of UEFA'. Article 59 of the UEFA Statutes reinforces obligations under the Article 49 rule upon the clubs. Article 7bis(2) of UEFA Statutes provides that

> [l]eagues or any other groups of clubs at Member Association level shall only be permitted with the Association's express consent and shall be subordinate to it. The Association's statutes shall define the powers apportioned to any such group, as well as its rights and obligations. The statutes and regulations of any such group shall be subject to the approval of the Association.

This is the national level equivalent of the Article 49 rule, applicable on the level of national associations whose organisational functions are confined to their respective territories. Together with Article 49 rule it helps build the pyramidal structure with UEFA at the apex. Without some structure and hierarchy at each national level, it would be difficult to secure the best clubs for the European competitions, as the existence of an unsanctioned league could result in some inferior clubs qualifying for the Champions League, which would in turn dilute its commercial value. If there were many unsanctioned competitions in many different European countries, they would not be a subject of national association or UEFA

---

[48] Commission Decision in Cases 33.384 and 33.378—Distribution of package tours during the 1990 World Cup, OJ 1992 L326/31, paras 52 and 53. See also the references in Commission Decision COMP/37.398—Joint Selling of Commercial Rights (UEFA Champions League) [2003] OJ L 291/25, para 106.

[49] T-99/04 *AC-Treuhand AG v Commission* [2008] ECR II-1501.

rule books and they could therefore avoid the application of the Article 49 rule should they decide to organise on a transnational level. The organisational functions of national associations at the national level, therefore can be seen as complementary and facilitating/enabling those of UEFA on transnational level, and their rules implementing Articles 59 and 7bis(2) of UEFA Statutes can be seen as reinforcing the Article 49 rule. In this sense, national associations can constitute undertakings for our purposes even though they are not active on the relevant market but carry out only a subordinate role. Hence, it can be asserted that they are using UEFA as a vehicle to coordinate their conduct to restrict competition on the relevant market, which would make UEFA an association of undertakings rather than an undertaking. The Article 49 rule would then be a decision merely reflecting the will of national associations. Alternatively, UEFA could constitute an undertaking which is engaged in concerted practice with its members.

Having gone through the different options, one must remember that the classification of UEFA as an undertaking or an association of undertakings is important in order to determine which competition article of the Treaty will become applicable to the restrictions emanating from the Article 49 rule. Nevertheless, as the legal test for restrictions is equivalent under both articles, the result will be the same regardless of the precise status of the parties as an association of undertakings or undertakings and the restrictive rules as agreements or decisions. What matters for the applicability of these articles is the existence of an entity engaged in economic activity whose agreements or decisions restrict competition on the relevant market, and in the case of Article 102 TFEU, the existence of a dominant undertaking or a group of undertakings. This is the standpoint that can be traced back to the Court's *DLG* judgment and to the Opinion of Advocate General Lenz in *Bosman*.[50]

7.4.2 Market Power of UEFA on the Relevant Market

Dominance is defined as a position of economic strength which enables an undertaking to prevent effective competition on the relevant market by giving it the power to behave to an appreciable extent independently of its competitors, customers and ultimately its consumers.[51] In addition, the existence of such a dominant position 'derives from a combination of several factors which, taken separately, are not necessarily determinative'.[52] The main feature of a dominant position is the ability of undertaking to act without having to take account of existing or potential competition in its market strategy. Thus, the concept of independence, which has to exist to 'an appreciable extent', is the key factor in finding the existence of a dominant market position.

[50] See his Opinion in C-415/93 *Bosman*, paras 254–259.

[51] Case 27/76 *United Brands v. Commission* [1978] ERC 207, para 65.

[52] Ibid. paras 65–66.

7.4.2.1 Market Shares

On the basis of the market shares indicator, it would be counterintuitive and unrealistic to claim that UEFA is not dominant on the relevant market. Even for a casual observer it does not require much evidence to prove that the UEFA is not just dominant, but holds a monopoly on the market for the provision of organising services for the European club competitions. The Commission Staff Working Document backs up this conclusion in stating that 'sports associations *usually* have practical monopolies in a given sport and may thus *normally* be considered dominant in the market of the organisation of sport events under Article [102 TFEU].'[53] UEFA is the only entity active on the relevant market while the Article 49 rule and organisational structure of European football support that exclusivity.

According to the Court in *Hoffmann-La Roche* 'although the importance of the market shares may vary from one market to another the view may be taken that very large market shares are in themselves, and *save in exceptional circumstances*, evidence of the existence of dominant position'.[54] The size of the UEFA market share raises the presumption that UEFA is the dominant undertaking on the relevant market. This presumption will stand in the absence of 'exceptional circumstances' indicating that the large market shares are deceptive and that, for example a new competitor may easily emerge to disrupt the dominance affects the behaviour of a dominant undertaking. Market shares supply a quantitative value and do not tell us why the undertaking has high market shares, what are its potential competitors, and whether there are any other significant constraints on its behaviour such as countervailing buyer power. According to the Commission '[e]ven firms with very high market shares may not be in a position […] to significantly impede effective competition, in particular by acting to an appreciable extent independently of their customers, if the latter possess countervailing buyer power'.[55]

7.4.2.2 Countervailing Buyer Power

The first indicator of countervailing buyer power is the buyer's market share on the purchase market as it reflects the importance of its demand for possible suppliers.[56] In this context, it is submitted that the elite clubs are collectively dominant undertakings on the connected upstream market for clubs' services and providers of essential input that cannot be duplicated by any other (group of) entities on the relevant market. Links between the elite clubs that support the conclusion on tacit coordination are many. Tightly knit relationships that exist among them due to the nature of their business and the common course of conduct on the relevant market are

[53] Annex I, para 2.1.4.

[54] Case 85/76 *Hoffmann-La Roche* [1979] ECR 461, para 41.

[55] Guidelines on the assessment of horizontal mergers under the Council Regulation on the control of concentrations between undertakings 2004/C 31/03, para 64.

[56] Commission Notice—Guidance on Vertical Restraints, Brussels SEC (2010) 411, para 116.

evidenced by: complete dependence on each other to produce a marketable product; similar cost structures; common marketing and sales of broadcasting rights on the relevant market through UEFA; homogenous product; symmetric growth prospects; no incentive to force other firms out of the market; the interaction of firms in multiple markets; stable demand; transparent or known prices (the media contributes to this); the fact that clubs can effectively impose their agreements on their customers (UEFA on the market for clubs' services); difficulty of defection from the agreed course of action is difficult; use of each other's infrastructure (football stadiums) to play the games; and in general, the structure of the market and nature of the industry being conductive to tacit collusion.[57] From the point of view of UEFA and ultimate consumers, these clubs come as a package deal. Commonality of their interests is predetermined by the high level of interdependency between the clubs to produce a quality product, i.e. the games integrated in championship race. Clubs negotiate terms and conditions of their engagement on the market together and if they were to leave the European football structures, they would do it together. As such, the strategic goals of the clubs as undertakings are sufficiently aligned to give rise to a collectively dominant position, whereas the market provides the perfect conditions for tacit collusion to sustain over long period of time. Therefore, the criteria for a finding of collective dominance under para 62 of *Airtours*[58] as confirmed by *Piau*[59] are easily met, and the required links within the meaning of para 45 of *Compagnie Maritime Belge* case[60] as elaborated in cases such as *Italian Flat Glass*, *Gencor* and *Almelo*,[61] are easily established. This is the type of collective dominance that is superimposed on undertakings by the nature and structure of the market in question. *A fortiori*, it fits the concept of 'superdominance' as elaborated by Advocate General Fennelly in *Compagnie Maritime Belge.*[62]

Further to the analysis of countervailing buyer power, the collectively dominant elite clubs are responsible for stage one of the professional football contest production process and UEFA for stage two.[63] Without the clubs, UEFA's function of organising European club competitions would become obsolete and its role as a regulator able to rely on solidarity payments to fulfil its mandate would be significantly reduced.[64] On the other hand, the clubs would be able to exchange UEFA for another entity capable of performing the league functions, or they could establish a

[57] For more on the list of factors that support a finding of collective dominance see O'Donoghue and Padilla 2006, pp. 137–161.

[58] T-342/99 *Airtours plc. v. Commission* [2002] ECR II-2585, judgment of 6 June 2002.

[59] Case T-193/02 *Laurent Piau v. Commission*, judgment of 26 January 2005, para 111.

[60] C-396/96 P *Compagnie Maritime Belge Transports and Others* v. *Commission* [2000] ECR I-1365.

[61] Cases T-68/89 etc. *Società Italiano Vetro SpA v. Commission* [1992] ECR II-1403; Case T-102/96 *Gencor Ltd. V. Commission* [1999] ECR II-0753; and Case C-393/92 *Almelo v. NV Energiebedriff Ijsselmij* [1994] ECR I-1477.

[62] See Opinion of Advocate General in C-396/96 P *Compagnie Maritime Belge*, para 137.

[63] See Sect. 7.3.1.1.

[64] See Sect. 7.3.3.

jointly owned undertaking entrusted with performing organising functions.[65] The complete dependence on the potential competitor, a sole buyer of organising services who is also the provider of essential input into production of the professional football contest, puts into doubt the presumption of dominance that emerges from the monopolistic market shares. The existence of a monopsony held by the clubs on the demand side in the relevant market, which is not exposed to any present or future challenges, is a powerful counterbalance to any degree of dominance, and may amount to 'exceptional circumstances' under para 41 of *Hoffmann-La Roche*. Countervailing buyer power implies the bargaining strength which a buyer enjoys in relation to its suppliers by virtue of its size, commercial significance to the seller, and its ability to switch to alternative suppliers.[66] According to the Commission '[i] n some circumstances buyer power may prevent the parties from exercising market power and thereby solve a competition problem that would otherwise have existed. This is particularly so when strong customers have the capacity and incentive to bring new sources of supply on to the market [...].'[67] The first sentence of this quote means that, for the conclusion on dominance of an undertaking, the mere *possession* of market power does not count for much without the possibility to *exercise* that power in a corresponding manner by adopting conduct on the market that is characteristic of a dominant undertaking. In regard to the second sentence of the quote, we shall now look at potential competition on the relevant market.

7.4.2.3 Potential Competition: Entry and Expansion

One source of countervailing buyer power is the possibility for the buyer to switch to other suppliers within a reasonable time frame and 'credibly threaten to vertically integrate into the upstream market or to sponsor upstream expansion or entry for instance by persuading a potential entrant to enter by committing to placing large orders with this company'.[68] The existence of this possibility is precisely what made UEFA accommodate the interests of the clubs (to the detriment of other stakeholders including non-elite clubs) when they were set to form a breakaway league, so the credibility of the threat is apparent from the response of the supplier. For a new entry or expansion to be considered as presenting sufficient competitive constraint it has to be likely (sufficiently profitable taking into account the price effects of injecting additional output into the market and the potential responses of the incumbents, and not exposed to very high risks or high barriers to entry), timely (normally considered as a time frame of 2 years, but the characteristics and dynamics of the market may affect this time frame) and sufficient (it cannot be

[65] Ibid.

[66] Guidelines on the assessment of horizontal mergers under the Council Regulation on the control of concentrations between undertakings 2004/C 31/03, para 64.

[67] Commission Notice—Guidance on Vertical Restraints Brussels SEC (2010) 411, para 116.

[68] Guidelines on the assessment of horizontal mergers under the Council Regulation on the control of concentrations between undertakings 2004/C 31/03, para 65.

small scale entry but must be of such magnitude as to constrain the behaviour by the putatively dominant undertaking, for example by deterring price increases).[69] Elements of likelihood, timeliness and sufficiency are all present for a new provider of organising services for elite club competition at the European level.[70] The account of the history of breakaway threats in Chap. 3 and concessions made by UEFA backs up this conclusion. On the other hand, it can also act as a proof of UEFA's ability to fend off the competition by adopting appropriate strategic behaviour in response to the potential new entry to the market which is the feature characteristic of a dominant undertaking. In the case of the 1998 Media Partners proposal such response involved the expansion of the Champions League (which can be taken as analogous to increasing output), whereas in the case of the *Oulmers* affair/release of players rule it meant the creation of a compensation pool (which can be taken as analogous to a decrease in price). In the relevant market as defined above, the fact that these strategic decisions were successful so far does not provide much comfort for UEFA that it will be equally successful in the future under the specific circumstances surrounding an aspiring future entrant. Therefore, the pressure of expansion and entry appears to exist to a sufficient degree to be taken as presenting a competitive constraint on UEFA's behaviour in the relevant market.

7.4.2.4 Industry Specific Aspects of Decision-Making

'Exceptional circumstances' under para 41 of *Hoffmann-La Roche* are presented also by the nature of the industry. UEFA, as a European regulatory body, is neither a typical private undertaking nor a typical private regulatory entity, as it takes its decisions in consultation with various stakeholders, some of which happen to be *both* potential competitors who have the ability to eliminate it from the market for organisation of European club competitions, and powerful customers on the organising market. It has been demonstrated in Chap. 3 that UEFA is therefore taking utmost care of the commercial interests of the elite clubs, as demonstrated by the following matters: (1) their entrenchment on the Executive Board of ECA, their presence at the UEFA Professional Football Strategy Council, and their right to elect five out of nine ordinary members and two out of three vice-chairman at the UEFA Club Competitions Committee, and (2) breakaway threats which they use as a trump card if all else fails. These matters give them the possibility to exercise decisive influence on the strategic decisions of UEFA in its capacity as a regulator of European football and as a provider of organising services. Should the clubs become dissatisfied with the terms and conditions that UEFA offers in its capacity of a provider of organising services, they would likely exert pressure culminating

[69] Ibid. paras 68–75.

[70] The prospect of formation of some other regional alternative league (such as the Balkan league) might not satisfy the requirement of sufficiency, but an elite breakaway on a pan-European level is different in its scope and in the fact that the clubs supply an input that cannot be duplicated in terms of its value for UEFA.

in a threat to break away and cause UEFA to change its envisaged course of action, as has already occurred several times in the past. The market shares alone, even though they point towards a status of monopoly, cannot be taken as an evidence of a dominant position in this case. Far from being independent in making its strategic decisions pertaining to the relevant market, UEFA in fact appears to be highly dependent on the clubs. Thus, any reference to UEFA as having superior market power on the relevant market is highly inappropriate in the light of power struggles and the current governance model. Along with analysis on competitive constraints it becomes apparent that it should not be as easy to establish the dominance of UEFA as had been presumed each time the relevant market under investigation has been mentioned in rare academic writing,[71] by practitioners,[72] and the Commission,[73] all of whom confined their assessment to one sentence merely stating in a matter-of-fact fashion that such dominance exists.

7.4.2.5 Conclusion

The presence of a powerful buyer on the market, the expansion and entry possibilities that UEFA has to account for, and the idiosyncrasies of governance and decision-making, are all factors heavily suggesting that dominance (i.e. appreciable independence) on the market for organisation of European clubs competitions is far from easy to prove. In fact, it might not exist. This is undeniably a surprising result of the UEFA dominance analysis brought about by a closer qualitative examination of the requirements of independence, which revealed a different state of affairs as compared to the overwhelming market shares-based *prima facie* impression that UEFA holds a monopoly on the relevant market. This result is based on a substantive assessment of the concept of independence that is not unlike the concept of 'control' in certain other areas of EU law. For example acquisition of control of an undertaking is a key to establishing the existence of a concentration under Article 3(1)(b) of the Merger Regulation.[74] 'Control', whether joint or sole control, is a qualitative concept defined as 'the *possibility* of exercising decisive influence' (as opposed to *actually* exercising or intending to exercise such decisive influence) on an undertaking and it may be established on the basis of rights, contracts, or 'any other means'

[71] Hornsby 2001, and; Halgreen 2004, p. 155.

[72] Jonathan Taylor and Adam Lewis 'Governing Body Restraint on Breakaways' paper presented at 'Sport and The Law' conference, London, 31 March 2011 and Stephen Hornsby 'Governing Body Restraints on Breakaways. Do They Really Need to Rely on Them or is Dominance Enough?' paper presented at 'Sport and The Law' conference, London, 31 March 2011.

[73] White Paper on Sport (2007), para 2.1.4, and; Professional Sport in the Internal Market, project No. IP/A/IMCO/ST/2005-004, Commissioned by the Committee on the Internal Market and Consumer Protection of the European Parliament (September 2005), para 4.2.6.

[74] Council Regulation (EC) No 139/2004 of 20 January 2004 on the control of concentrations between undertakings. OJ L 24, 29/1/2004, pp. 1–22.

of control.[75] Blocking rights are, for instance, considered as one of the means diminishing the possibility of decisive influence and conferring negative control.[76] In our case, a proven strategy (such as a breakaway threat as well as the institutionalised means of exerting pressure over UEFA in its role of organiser of European club competitions) may amount to such negative control.

Taking the described approach to the assessment of the *United Brands* independence criteria in certain sporting issues may result in practical benefits by presenting a powerful incentive for the sport associations to establish a model of governance which will include the genuine input of all the stakeholders in their decision-making. A governing body should not be held to be dominant on a certain relevant market if its strategic decisions represent a reflection of the will of relevant stakeholders. The restrictions that emerge from this kind of decision-making are likely to constitute agreements between different stakeholders under Article 101, rather than unilateral conduct capable of being reviewed under Article 102 TFEU (though there could be a case for a finding of collective dominance in specific cases). If clubs, players, leagues and others concerned all participate in the adoption (and/or implementation) of a certain rule, and/or in the decisions that pertain to the market which the rule governs, the likelihood of 'internal' challenges within a sport's structure would be brought to a minimum and the autonomy of sport to govern itself would be far more likely to be supported by the European institutions in cases of 'external' legal challenges under Article 101 TFEU by third parties. In this sense, genuine adherence to the principles of good governance is the ultimate course of action for sport governing bodies to make sure their rules are given the maximum chance of surviving legal challenges under EU law.

7.4.3 Article 49 of the UEFA Statutes: Restrictive Effects

Under the Article 49 rule the participation of clubs in alternative cross-border competitions was made subject to prior approval and not to outright prohibition. It is not uncommon for regulatory bodies to take on a function of sanctioning competitions, issuing licenses, and generally making access to a certain market subject to prior authorisation. The issues remain of how the rule is implemented in practice and whether there are clear guidelines based on objective criteria that govern access to the market. In assessing the restrictiveness of the Article 49 rule, therefore distinctions have to be made between the mere existence of prior authorisation as a precondition for access to the market (which in itself is not objectionable), the conditions set for the issuance of approval (which might offend against principle of proportionality), and the actual exercise of the prior authorisation upon application for access to the market.

[75] Commission Consolidated Jurisdictional Notice under Council Regulation (EC) No. 139/2004 on the control of concentrations between undertakings (2008/C 95/01), paras 16–21.

[76] Ibid. para 56.

The Commission in its Staff Working Document considered that rules shielding sports associations from competition, such as in *FIA/Formula One case*,[77] are likely to infringe competition provisions.[78] This concurs with the popular view that the Article 49 rule has a restrictive effect on competition, which is not completely free from being challenged in regard to European elite clubs. The lack of other providers on the market for organising services for elite clubs' competitions on the pan-European level might not be attributable to the Article 49 rule but to the fact that those clubs did not want to leave the UEFA structure so far. As Hornsby noted, UEFA enjoys 'enormous "first mover" advantage'.[79] Apart from the nature of providing the service in question as a high investment operation requiring special know-how and taking of commercial risks while navigating through a demanding legal environment, the lack of will on the part of clubs is probably the biggest reason why there are no large media companies or private investors competing to make the best offer to the European elite clubs to resign from the UEFA and national competitions and form an alternative league. As the Chief Executive of Liverpool FC said, an alternative league did not materialise thus far because the Champions League was so successful and the clubs were broadly happy with it.[80] Nevertheless, he added that a trend of increase in foreign ownership may provoke a change of heart.[81] This is illustrative of the degree to which this Premier League club and one of the founding members of G14 considers the Article 49 rule a restriction on its possible plans to break away. Also, the history of UEFA (and FIFA) concessions in response to breakaway threats by the European elite clubs[82] demonstrates that the rule is not capable of preserving the *status quo* should the clubs be genuinely determined in their intent to separate. From the EU law perspective, it is not objectionable in itself for clubs to resign from traditional structures and form an alternative cross-border league.[83] Therefore, the causal link between the Article 49 rule and the alleged restrictive effect in providing pan-European organising services for the elite competition might not be that strong. The Article 49 rule can be thought to have a restrictive effect for the wealthiest clubs in conjunction with disciplinary measures and fines imposed *post facto*. Namely, if the clubs form an unsanctioned pan-European elite league, they could be collectively boycotted by UEFA and national

---

77 See Sect. 5.6.2 for case analysis. Notice published pursuant to Article 19(3) of Council Regulation No. 17 concerning Cases COMP/35.163—Notification of FIA Regulations, COMP/36.638—Notification by FIA/FOA of agreements relating to the FIA Formula One World Championship, COMP/36.776—GTR/FIA and others (2001/C 169/03).

78 Commission Staff Working Document, Annex I, para 2.2.2.1.

79 Stephen Hornsby 'Governing Body Restraints on Breakaways. Do They Really Need to Rely on Them or is Dominance Enough?' paper presented at 'Sport and The Law' conference, London, 31 March 2011.

80 An interview with Rick Parry, Chief Executive of Liverpool Football Club 1998–2007 and a former head of the Premier League, 2 June 2011.

81 Ibid.

82 See Sect. 3.3.

83 Parrish and Miettinen 2008, p. 213.

associations by, for example cutting all ties with the participating clubs and/or their players. There is not much that can be done to prevent or restrict the elite clubs from forming the alternative pan-European structure in the first place, especially in regard to an alternative structure that would comply with EU law requirements. It is only the possibility of sanctions and legal challenges that may create operational problems for the newly established league. But collective boycotts would likely amount to a breach of the competition provisions, unless they could be justified by the protection of legitimate goals in the public interest.[84]

The view presented here does not apply to the case of smaller regional leagues that cannot afford to disregard the lack of approval by the governing bodies and that cannot use the breakaway threat to their advantage. Whereas a pan-European breakaway would present an alternative to the UEFA Champions League (i.e. the golden goose for the financing of European football) and would commercially destroy it, merely forming a geographically delimited league amongst small market clubs would have a different impact on UEFA's financial goals and the solidarity mechanism, but would nevertheless be perceived as pernicious due to its potential to cause a snowball effect and trigger the erosion of the pyramid structure bringing into question the uniform organisation of sport. The clubs from smaller markets have no ambition to fully break away on their own and their desire so far was only to exploit the benefits that lie outside the structure and outside of the set match calendars. For those clubs, the sanctions based on the Article 49 rule do have a priori restrictive effect, which means that without the necessary approvals from the national governing bodies and UEFA they would not go ahead and form a private league.

There is no doubt that the Article 49 rule would be considered *prima facie* restrictive of the clubs' economic freedoms under the TFEU competition provisions by the Court and the Commission, and this would trigger the application of the *Meca-Medina/Wouters* test. If the Article 49 rule passes the requirements of that test, it would be considered as not having breached the competition provisions in the first place. At the same time, under internal market provisions, the rule would be considered as having infringed the free movement of services, but it could be justified under *Gebhard* objective justification framework[85] which coincides with *Meca-Medina/Wouters* test.

The focus under this limb of analytical framework in our case is to specify which economic freedoms are restricted and what is the nature and designation of restrictions under the EU law. The Court does not take into account the specificity of sport at this level of analysis, as apparent from the case law.[86]

---

[84] Treatment of the players participating in clubs forming breakaway league by the national associations and UEFA is important in this regard due to EU free movement rules. Also, leagues that have no ties with national associations would themselves likely breach competition law because they would, as such, amount to closed leagues. See on this point Parrish and Miettinen 2008, p. 213.

[85] Case C-55/94 *Gebhard* [1995] ECR I-4165 para 37.

[86] For example Case C-325/08 *Olympique Lyonnais SASP v. Olivier Bernard and Newcastle United FC* judgment of grand Chamber of the Court delivered on 16 March 2010. See Sect. 4.8 for detailed analysis.

7.4.3.1 Restrictions Under Article 101 TFEU

On an orthodox application of Article 101 TFEU, any agreement or practice between undertakings or by association of undertakings that has as its object *or* effect the prevention, restriction or distortion of competition will automatically breach Article 101 TFEU, unless a respondent can prove that it satisfies the Article 101(3) TFEU criteria. The question on whether the characterisation of the rule as an 'object rule' may be justified under *Meca-Medina/Wouters* framework, in addition to Article 101(3) TFEU, has not been addressed in either the Court jurisprudence or Commission decision-making and legislative practice. With reference to para 31 *Meca-Medina*, it was submitted in Sect. 6.3.2 that an object rule can survive the Article 101 TFEU scrutiny only by means of exemption under Article 101(3) TFEU and should not be tested under *Meca-Medina/Wouters* as it carries a conclusive presumption that Article 101(1) TFEU has been breached. In determining whether an agreement or a practice may be labelled as restrictive by object, 'close regard must be paid in particular to the objectives which it is intended to attain',[87] 'to its economic and legal context',[88] and to the wording of the contested provision.[89] Evidence of subjective intent to restrict competition is 'a relevant factor but not a necessary condition'.[90] The requirement that the agreement be assessed in its economic and legal context is reminiscent of the *Meca-Medina/Wouters* contextual approach with particular emphasis on the objective of the rule in ascertaining the existence of justification for restriction.[91] Even when the restraint on competition was subjectively intended and not just objectively achieved, should there exist a reasonable support for the view that the restriction was not an end objective but only a means to attain a genuinely pursued legitimate goal, it should be classified as an effect rule to align with the more economic and less form-based approach being promoted by the Commission. This goes in particular for entities such as sport governing bodies in Europe whose commercial and regulatory functions are often so symbiotic that it might be easy to obtain a 'false positive' result on an 'object test' unless the relevant context is taken into account. Typical 'object' agreements would involve one of the hard-core restraints, such as, for example horizontal agreements on price fixing, market sharing, limiting outputs or sales, collective exclusive dealing, and vertical agreements fixing minimum resale price or imposing export bans. Typical restrictions by object are those which *prima facie* do not have any significant beneficial effects but 'have such high potential of negative effects on

---

[87] Case C-8/08 *T-Mobile Netherlands BV and Others v. Raad van bestuur van de Nederlandse Mededingingsautoriteit*, judgment of 4 June 2009, para 27.

[88] Ibid.

[89] Case C-209/07 *Competition Authority v. Beef Industry Development Society Ltd and Barry Brothers (Carrigmore) Meals Ltd* [2008] ECR I-8637, para 21.

[90] Communication from the Commission—Notice—Guidelines on the application of Article 81(3) of the Treaty OJ C 101/97, 27.4.2004, para 22.

[91] The relationship between the two different references to context and objective has not been addressed anywhere, but it can be assumed that there is a great degree of overlap between them.

competition that it is unnecessary for the purposes of applying Article [101(1)] to demonstrate any actual effects on the market'.[92]

On the basis of these legal guidelines, UEFA's Article 49 rule may be categorised as an 'effect' rather than as an 'object' rule.[93] It would be hard to argue that its objective aim in the context in which it applies was to prevent, restrict or distort competition on the relevant market. That might be the side effect of the rule intended to perform certain public interest objectives,[94] as ascertainable from a *prima facie* analysis.

According to *Société La Technique Minière* if an agreement does not have the object of restricting competition

> the consequences of the agreement should then be considered and for it to be caught by the prohibition it is then necessary to find that those factors are present which show that competition has in fact been prevented or restricted or distorted to an *appreciable* extent. The competition in question must be understood within the actual context in which it would occur in the absence of the agreement in dispute.[95]

The Court in *Société La Technique Minière* sets out the necessity to establish a counterfactual by conducting a hypothetical analysis of the market but for the agreement in questions. Its negative effects on competition must be 'appreciable'. It is hard to predict what the relevant market would look like but for the Article 49 rule. UEFA was formed in 1950s and it established a market for pan-European club football. Since then, top national associations' clubs have been competing in various UEFA organised competitions. How would the market for transnational organising services look like today, had the Article 49 rule been non-existent? According to the basic economic theory of competitions

> [the] peculiarity of professional sports production is that, by definition, any championship must possess monopoly status. The validity of a championship rests primarily on such monopoly status. If there are several championships per market area per sport, no consistent ranking of all performers is achieved and, hence, the championship will lose a significant part of its value for consumers.[96]

We can conclude from this that without the Article 49 rule, the most economically viable option for the top clubs would be to organise a single pan-European championship with regulatory and/or organising services correspondingly entrusted to a single entity, be it UEFA or a private promoter. Also, we can assume that some regional competitions would be organised by the clubs that do not perform that well on the pan-European

[92] Guidelines on the application of Article 81(3) of the Treaty, para 21.

[93] For the opposite view which argues that the rule is an object rule, see Hellenthal 2000, Zulässigkeit einer supranationalen Fussball Europaliga nach den Bestimmungen des europäischen Wettbewerbsrechts, Frankfurt am Main, cited in Professional Sport in the Internal Market, project no. IP/A/IMCO/ST/2005-004, Commissioned by the Committee on the Internal Market and Consumer Protection of the European Parliament (September 2005).

[94] For public interest objectives see Sect. 7.6.

[95] Case 56/65 *Société La Technique Minière v. Maschinenbau Ulm GmbH* [1966] ECR 235, at 249–250.

[96] Dietl et al. 2011, p. 3.

level, and by the clubs that do not qualify for the competitions at the pan-European level. Preventing, restricting or distorting formation of such regional cross-border championships can be taken as appreciably restricting the competition within the internal market. Similarly, preventing, restricting or distorting the elite clubs to switch the pan-European organiser restricts competition within the meaning of Article 101(1) TFEU and fulfils the notion of appreciability. It limits the commercial freedoms of the clubs and therefore influences the entry to market of the potential alternative organisers. As such, the Article 49 rule presents a barrier to entry with the effect of limiting production, markets and investment, to use the language of Article 101(1)(b) TFEU.

Putting some familiar labels on the type of restraint in question, it can further be said that via the Article 49 rule (expressly accepted by the ECA in the Memorandum of Understanding) UEFA ties the clubs to their organising services leaving not much room for competitors, comparable to the exclusivity and minimum quantity clauses in vertical agreements which leave the purchaser no spare capacity to stock the competing goods. In the context of single branding agreements (also referred to as exclusive purchasing agreements), the Commission recognised that powerful buyers cannot be easily cut off from the supply of the competing services.[97] It was submitted in Sect. 7.4.2 above that UEFA might not qualitatively qualify as a dominant undertaking on the relevant market due to the existence of, *inter alia*, countervailing buyer power. The role of countervailing buyer power under the dominance test is different than in the context of restraint analysis. The fact that elite clubs may exercise decisive influence on UEFA strategic decisions on the relevant market, thus removing the key element of independence which has to exist to 'an appreciable extent', does not in any way imply that rules which brought about the creation, and subsequently consolidation of UEFA's position on the relevant market, are not liable to restrict competition on that market. More generally, the Commission said that a service supplier may have to compensate its customers for the loss in competition resulting from exclusivity, and where such compensation is given, 'it may be in the individual interest of a customer to enter into a single branding obligation with the supplier'.[98] However, no automatic conclusions should be drawn from this 'that all single branding obligations, taken together, are overall beneficial for customers in that market and for the final consumers'.[99] This is because of cumulative network effects that many equivalent exclusive purchase agreements may produce on the market. There is no need in our case to take the cumulative net effect of all the similar agreements in the market as there are no other such agreements in European transnational football but for the Article 49 rule, and there is no need to analyse the contribution of the Article 49 rule to the foreclosure effect as the Court did in, for example the *Delimitis* case,[100] because UEFA quantitatively holds 100 % of the market share.

---

97 Commission Notice—Guidance on Vertical Restraints, Brussels SEC (2010) 411, para 137.

98 Ibid.

99 Ibid.

100 Case C-234/89 *Stergios Delimitis v Henninger Bräu AG* [1991] ECR I-935.

Exclusive arrangements between all the clubs as customers on the relevant market and UEFA as supplier clearly result in foreclosure of the market for potential suppliers of the organising services.

7.4.3.2 Abuse of a Dominant Market Position Under Article 102 TFEU

Rousseva considered the element of dominance as the only difference between Articles 101 and 102 TFEU when it comes to vertical contractual restraints involving a dominant undertaking.[101] In her view, that makes the current division of labour between Articles 101 and 102 TFEU difficult to sustain from a legal and economic point of view, and suggests discarding Article 102 TFEU and relying exclusively on Article 101 TFEU as a pragmatic solution which would bring many advantages including carrying out a de facto modernisation of Article 102 TFEU without entering into explicit conflict with existing precedents.[102] This approach will be adopted in the current section which proceeds with the assumption that dominant market power does exist.

It must be restated that the existence of a dominant market power is not in itself condemned under Article 102 TFEU, only the abuse of that power. Addressing the concept of abuse of a dominant position, the Court in *DLG* said that 'neither the creation nor the strengthening of a dominant position is in itself contrary to Article [102] of the Treaty'.[103] It is the manner in which a non-dominant undertaking becomes dominant and in which a dominant undertaking behaves that may be deemed abusive. In *Hoffmann-La Roche*, the Court defined exclusionary abuses as an objective concept that pertains to the behaviour of a dominant undertaking which influences the structure of the market so as to hinder the maintenance or growth of competition.[104] As a general designation, the Article 49 rule belongs to the category of exclusionary, non-pricing, abuse. More specifically, it could be seen as an exclusive purchasing arrangement. In its guidance on exclusionary abuses, the Commission reiterated the same approach to these types of restrains as discussed in Sect. 7.4.3.1 above.[105] In the Commission's approach to both vertical restraints and exclusionary abuses, the type of restraint on competition in question was considered as capable of amounting to a restriction under Article 101(1) TFEU and an abuse under Article 102 TFEU, respectively. An organisational rule that restricts competition under Article 101(1) TFEU and that may be attributed to a dominant undertaking, also amounts to abuse under Article 102 TFEU.

---

[101] Rousseva 2005, p. 590.

[102] Ibid. p. 637.

[103] Case C-250/92 *Gøttrup-Klim e.a. Grovvareforeninger v Dansk Landbrugs Grovvareselskab AmbA* [1994] ECR I-5641, para 49.

[104] Case 85/76 *Hoffmann-La Roche v. Commission* [1979] ECR 461, para 91.

[105] Communication from the Commission—Guidance on the Commission's enforcement priorities in applying Article 82 of the EC Treaty to abusive exclusionary conduct by dominant undertakings (2009/C 45/02), para 34.

Depending on the precise facts of the case, *post facto* sanctions by collective boycott of the clubs on the part of UEFA and national association could possibly amount to a refusal to deal with a long-standing client as a punishment for switching suppliers, which is another type of abuse of dominant position. Objective justification would be possible in accordance with the *Meca-Medina/Wouters* test. The exclusion of the players that are affiliated to the clubs participating in the breakaway league from any competitions at national association and UEFA level has primary repercussions for the free movement of workers, but can also amount to an abuse of dominant position in as far as it controls and limits the availability of the factors of production for the non-participating clubs.

7.4.3.3 Market Access Issues Under Article 56 TFEU

Advocate General Kokott in *Murphy* acknowledged that conflicting assessments of the fundamental freedoms and competition law are in principle to be avoided.[106] A finding of restrictive effect under competition law presents cogent and convincing evidence that the breach of the applicable internal market provisions also occurred. Outside the very limited circumstances as explained in Sects. 5.5.5.5 and 6.3.2 above, it is virtually impossible for the measure to escape the designation of restriction also under Article 56 TFEU on freedom to provide services.

For the purposes of the application of the internal market rules, suffice it to say that Article 56 TFEU has horizontal direct effect by virtue of the Court decisions in *Walrave and Koch* and *Laval*, so even though UEFA is not a public authority it could breach that article. It suffices that it is an association exercising exclusive regulatory powers over the provision of services. Furthermore, in *Murphy* the Court reminded us that 'Article 56 TFEU requires the abolition of all restrictions on the freedom to provide services, even if those restrictions apply without distinction[…], when they are liable to prohibit, impede or render less advantageous the activities of a service provider[…]'. This means that not only directly and indirectly discriminatory arrangements but also genuinely non-discriminatory restrictions to provision of services will breach Article 56 TFEU. Advocate General Fennelly argued in *Graf* that '[t]he imposition of conditions regarding entry to the market or the taking up of economic activity is itself sufficient to establish the existence of a restriction, even if the condition can be relatively easily satisfied'. The Article 49 rule is non-discriminatory in its form but it is intrinsically liable to restrict the freedom to provide services. It could however be argued that it is applied in a discriminatory manner. Namely, in September 2012 UEFA approved a cross-border league between the highest ranked Belgian and Dutch women's football teams, the so-called BeNe league.[107] As discrimination involves treating equal cases unequally but also treating unequal cases equally, a counterargument could

[106] Paragraph 249.

[107] 'Cross-Border Women's Soccer League May Lead to Men's Competition' by Tariq Panja, Bloomberg, 4 September 2012.

be made that women's football is not equal to men's football, has no effect on overall financing of the sport, and deserve a more permissive treatment. It is a fact that women's and men's football fall into two distinct markets. In sporting cases so far, all rules, whether discriminatory or not, benefited from the wide range of judicially developed justifications, not just express Treaty-based derogations. So whether classified as discriminatory or non-discriminatory restriction to market access, it will not make a difference for the range of justifications available.

7.5 Applicable Justification Framework

It is clear that the Article 49 rule does not belong to the category I or category II sporting exceptions as classified in Chap. 6. Regarding the category III sporting exception, it must be remembered that the application of 'inherent sporting rules' concept is not identical under free movement and competition law.[108] In free movement law, only non-discriminatory rules that are not related to market access can satisfy the inherent rule test. The same test under competition law articles is not sensitive to the difference between the discriminatory and non-discriminatory rules, and between market access and exercise of economic activity rules. Its scope is therefore broader and more flexible. As the non-discriminatory Article 49 rule relates to market access, the *Gebhard* objective justification framework will apply to it under free movement law. In accordance with the theory on convergence set out in Chap. 6 and portrayed in illustration 6.2, the *Gebhard* framework is transposable and functionally equivalent to the *Meca-Medina/Wouters* test applicable under Articles 101(1) and 102 TFEU.

Furthermore, we are not dealing with the object rule for the conclusive presumption of breach of Article 101(1) TFEU to remove the possibility of convergence on the level of justification and make way for the application of para 31 of *Meca-Medina* as argued at the end of Sect. 6.3.2. None of the initial constitutionally based differences between the articles as discussed above in Sect. 5.5.5.5 applies in our case. Hence, we have the path set for application of a single justification test based on full convergence between its analytical points that will produce a uniform result under competition and internal market provisions.

The discussion that follows belongs to the restriction analysis under competition law. If the *Meca-Medina/Wouters* test is passed the competition articles are considered as not having been infringed in the first place. In other words, no prevention, restriction or distortion of competition under Article 101(1) TFEU or the abuse of a dominant position under Article 102 TFEU was found. On the other hand, in free movement law, the infringement of Articles 49 and 56 TFEU has already been established, but such infringement can be justified if the rule passes scrutiny under the *Gebhard* objective justification framework. Even though the

[108] For more on this discussion see paper by Miettinen S and Parrish R, 'Inherent Rules in EC Sports Law', presented at the Conference on Law and Popular Culture, Onati, Spain (June 2008).

equivalent test can therefore be located in different overall analytical fractions, the end result of the legal analysis is the same. As Parrish and Miettinen put it, 'it is difficult to envisage organisational rules governing access to competitions or breakaway leagues that the Court would accept in the context of only competition law or free movement, but not both'.[109]

7.6 The Existence of Elements of Justification

The considerations in this section rely on factual support more than legal support in assessing the legality of the Article 49 rule. The implicit aspect underpinning the ultimate decision on the fulfilment or non-fulfilment of the justification test pertains to the standard of proof, the 'elusive concept' in the jurisprudence of the EU Courts, which are not bound by any evidentiary thresholds.[110] A closely related aspect concerns the varying proportionality formulas that are chosen by the Court according to the circumstances of each case, as well as varying degrees of intensity in application of the proportionality test ranging from deferential to highly intensive. Some general principles can nevertheless be discerned from the Court's case law. For example there is a perceptible difference between the application of the proportionality test formula to financial burdens and penalties (which is essentially confined to a relatively uncontroversial examination of excessiveness), and the application of the proportionality test to the exercise of discretionary powers (which varies from the rarely applied full proportionality test—suitability, necessity and proportionality—to various combinations of its three subtests depending on specific circumstances of the case). Sometimes the Court uses a completely different formulation and employs a general test of arbitrariness or reasonableness.[111]

In *Meca-Medina*, *Wouters*, and *DLG*, the Court has applied a moderate intensity proportionality test.[112] In *Bernard* the Court referred to Article 165(1) TFEU in the context of the required standard of application of the proportionality test.[113] This reference was omitted at the proportionality stage of analysis in *Murphy* because there were no specificities and social functions of sport involved and the issues considered were strictly commercial. The application of the proportionality test in *Murphy* was therefore markedly stricter than in *Bernard*.[114] In our case, a highly intense review of proportionality can be ruled out, due to (a) the fact that structural and organisational matters are discretionary choices that result from the

109 Parrish and Miettinen 2008, p. 216.

110 As referred to by Gippini-Fournier 2010.

111 For more on principle of proportionality see Harbo 2010.

112 Lavrijssen 2010, pp. 636–659.

113 See para 40 of Case C-325/08 *Bernard*. For discussion see Pijetlovic 2010, pp. 862–867, and Sect. 4.8.

114 See Pijetlovic and Nyman-Metcalf 2013, pp. 88–89, and Sect. 4.10.2.3. See also Kaburakis et al. 2012, p. 313.

autonomy of sport regulatory bodies, as recognised by the EU institutions, (b) the nature of the restriction, objectives of which lie in the social function and specificity of sport and (c) the nature of the affected interests, which are strictly commercial as opposed to interests involving considerations of fundamental rights. On the other hand, the fact that autonomy (i.e. the discretion) is limited by, and conditioned upon, respect for EU law rules out a deferential review of the proportionality of the Article 49 rule. It is therefore submitted that the Article 49 rule would likely be subject to a moderate intensity proportionality review by the Court.

Finally, due to the necessity to facilitate convergence between Articles 101 and 102 TFEU as well as between competition law and internal market law, the burden of proof, as argued in Sect. 6.5, should be on the party seeking to justify its restrictive measures. It was submitted that the Court should re-examine para 55 of *Meca-Medina* in which it implied that the burden to establish that rules were disproportionate under Article 101 TFEU was on appellants.[115]

7.6.1 The Overall Context: Legitimate Aims in Public Interest

The contextual approach to sporting rules and their restrictive effects makes it possible to assess the intended function of those rules with reference to their legitimate objectives. The Commission Staff Working Document specifies that the legitimate objectives of sporting rules will normally relate to the 'organisation and proper conduct of competitive sport'.[116] In a UEFA press release that was published after the Media Partners proposal threat was averted, as discussed in the Sects. 3.3.2 and 3.3.3, UEFA was opposed to 'any concept susceptible of having a negative influence on the existing domestic and European competitions and of endangering the future of national teams'.[117] Justifications put forth in defence of the Article 49 rule include (1) solidarity mechanisms which enable fulfilment of the socio-cultural functions of football and which work to preserve a certain financial and sporting balance between clubs, and (2) effective and proper organisation of sport. These public interest objectives that are contained in a UEFA Statement on club football (2000)[118] have already been accepted as legitimate. At the time of its formation in 1954, UEFA stated that its initial aim was 'to foster and develop

[115] In para 55 of C-519/04 *Meca-Medina* the Court held: '[s]ince the appellants have, moreover, not pleaded that the penalties which were applicable and were imposed in the present case are excessive, it has not been established that the anti-doping rules at issue are disproportionate'.

[116] Commission Staff Working Paper, Annex I, para 2.1.5.

[117] UEFA news item 'European Club Football—National Associations, their leagues and clubs want UEFA to remain in charge' 30 July 1998.

[118] UEFA Statement on club football, 15 December 2000. Available at http://kassiesa.home.xs4all.nl/bert/uefa/news/001215.html.

unity and solidarity among the European football community' and to organise competitions at a European level.[119]

Article 165(1) states that the Union shall take account of the specific nature of sport, its structures based on voluntary activity and its social and educational function in implementation of other Treaty articles. Football performs social functions to the extent that is unmatched by any other sport in Europe, due to its popularity and the sheer number of people involved in football in all capacities.[120] The preservation of essential social benefits of sport is maintained through 'arrangements which provide for a redistribution of financial resources from professional to amateur levels of sport (principle of solidarity)'.[121] In its notification of its joint selling arrangements to the Commission, UEFA advanced as a justification for exemption under Article 101(3) TFEU the issue of financial solidarity. It argued that its financial solidarity model supports the development of European football by ensuring a fairer distribution of revenue. The Commission accepted this argument. Citing the cases *Metro*, *Remia* and *Consten and Grundig*,[122] it said that a solidarity model improves production and stimulates the development of the sport and emphasised that it is in favour of the financial solidarity principle.[123] The Court has accepted solidarity as the grounds for non-application of EU laws or exception from those laws in different contexts, and in *Sodemare v. Regione Lombardia* Advocate General Fennelly defined solidarity as 'an inherently uncommercial act of involuntary subsidisation of one social group by another'.[124] When assessing the status as undertakings of entities involved in social protection, the Court made a distinction between cases where such protection is provided in the market context, and in the context of solidarity. For example in *Poucet* the Court held that regional social security offices administering sickness and maternity insurance schemes for self-employed persons are not acting as undertakings within the meaning of EU competition law as they are intended to provide equal benefits for all the persons to whom they apply.[125] The compulsory nature of the system of contribution from active workers to retired workers, and the manner in which the funds were distributed granted a safe harbour for the entity in question. Furthermore, the Court in *Bosman* accepted as legitimate the aim of

[119] Ducrey et al. 2003, UEFA and Football Governance: A New Model. Adoptions for the Challenges of Modern Football. Centre International D'Etude Du Sport, p. 35. Available at http://www.academia.edu/173028/UEFA_and_Football_Governance_A_New_Model.

[120] For example, there are 23 million registered male and female players, with many more millions playing informally. See the Independent European Sport Review (2006) often referred to as the 'Arnaut Report'. As a matter of comparison, access to motor sport at all levels requires substantial finances and, unlike football, it is not a 'sport for all'—it is first business and then sporting activity. See Cygan 2007, pp. 74 et seq. Other team sports in Europe draw in significantly less people.

[121] Paragraph 3.4.

[122] Case 26/76 *Metro v. Commission* [1977] ECR 1975, Case 42/84; *Remia v. Commission* [1985] ECR 2545 and; Cases 56 and 58/64 *Consten and Grundig v. Commission* [1966] ECR 299.

[123] Paragraphs 164 and 165.

[124] Case C-70/95 [1997] ECR I-3395, para 29.

[125] Paragraph 9.

'maintaining a balance between clubs by preserving a certain degree of equality and uncertainty as to results' and it did so 'in view of the considerable social importance of sporting activities and in particular football in the [Union]'.[126] The argument supporting the acceptance and continuance of horizontal solidarity between clubs is enhanced by the fact that the wealthiest clubs amount to collectively dominant undertakings that have influence in European football governance equivalent to that of UEFA. Much as UEFA and national associations are unavoidable trading partners for the clubs, so are the elite clubs indispensable for UEFA and national associations in fulfilling the terms of their mandate. Thus, the elite clubs have special responsibility under Article 102 TFEU as collectively dominant undertakings, but also, like UEFA, have a social responsibility towards the rest of the football pyramid, the fulfilment of which UEFA ensures by means of the Article 49 rule in conjunction with the central marketing of commercial rights. Due to profound changes in governance, some of the responsibility for the state of affairs in European football would appear to have been shifted onto the elite clubs, not by virtue of their mandate, but by the virtue of their de facto powers in governance and their collective dominant position on the market in which many small clubs are on the verge of bankruptcy. Eliminating a certain number of potential competitors on the market for provision of football clubs' services is not the same as when it happens in ordinary markets (where elimination of some of the competition is tolerated as long as it is not affecting a substantial part of the market in question[127]) due to the social and physical connection that clubs have with their locality and the lack of substitutes. The elite clubs' financial contributions can be seen in this light, while UEFA carries the mandated responsibility to make those financial contributions happen. The Nice Declaration recognised the central role of sports federations in 'ensuring the essential solidarity between the various levels of sporting practice'.[128] It listed numerous social functions which are said to 'entail special responsibilities for federations and provide the basis for the recognition of their competence in organising competitions'.[129] The Nice Declaration also emphasised that 'even though not having any direct powers in this area, the [Union] must, in its action [...] take account of the social, educational and cultural functions inherent in sport and making it special, in order that [...] the solidarity essential to the preservation of its social role may be respected and nurtured'.[130]

---

[126] Case C-415/93 *Union Royale Belge Sociétés de Football Association and others v. Bosman and others* [1995] ECR I-4921, para 106.

[127] This is the final requirement of the Article 101(3). See Commission Notice Guidelines on the application of Article 81(3) of the Treaty, OJ C 101, 27.04.2004, pp. 97–118, paras 105–116 and Communication from the Commission—Guidance on the Commission's enforcement priorities in applying Article 82 of the EC Treaty to abusive exclusionary conduct by dominant undertakings, OJ C 45, 24.2.2009, pp. 7–20, para 30. See also Sect. 5.2.4.

[128] 'Declaration on the Specific Characteristics of Sport and its Social Function in Europe, of which Account Should be Taken in Implementing Common Policies', Presidency Conclusions following the Nice European Council Meeting of 7, 8 and 9 December 2000, para 8.

[129] Ibid. para 9.

[130] Ibid. para 1.

The effective functioning of an agricultural cooperative was the objective justification used in *DLG*[131] to defend restrictions on the participation of its members in alternative cooperative structures. Ensuring proper functioning and proper organisation of competitions was accepted in *Lehtonen* and *Deliège*, respectively.[132] According to the Communication on Sport, the legal concept of specific nature of sport established by the Court and recognised by Article 165 TFEU encompasses characteristics such as the pyramid structure of open competitions.[133] This means that the EU institutions must take such characteristics into account in implementation of other Treaty provisions.

Even though the Article 49 rule pursues legitimate aims, it still needs to satisfy the twin requirements of the proportionality test related to suitability and necessity.

7.6.2 Suitability of the Article 49 Rule: Effectiveness Test

The enquiry in this subsection concerns the suitability of the restrictive Article 49 rule, i.e. its capability to achieve the said objectives. To be suitable, a measure must also contribute to and be targeted at the attainment of those objectives. The Court has not developed any criteria to test the effectiveness of the restrictive rules. From certain cases it can be extracted that the Court does not require complete effectiveness, and instead, a partial contribution to the attainment of legitimate aims will generally be sufficient.[134] However, there exists no specific threshold to indicate the requisite level of effectiveness the rules ought to attain in absolute terms, or in terms of their relative contribution vis-à-vis other measures targeted at pursuing the same objective.

7.6.2.1 Vertical and Horizontal Solidarity

At the outset it is important to look briefly into the operation of the financial solidarity mechanism in European football and set out the figures that make up this concept. According to the UEFA Financial Report, UEFA's total revenue for 2011/12 stands at €2.79 billion (including €1.39 billion from EURO 2012). Solidarity payments

---

[131] C-250/92 *Gøttrup-Klim e.a. Grovvareforeninger v Dansk Landbrugs Grovvareselskab AmbA [1994] ECR I-5641.*

[132] Case C-176/96 *Jyri Lehtonen and Castors Canada Dry Namur-Braine ASBL v. Fédération royale belge des sociétés de basket-ball ASBL (FRBSB)* [2000] ECR I-2681, and Joined Cases C-51/96 and C-191/97 *Christelle Deliège v. Ligue francophone de judo et disciplines associées ASBL, Ligue belge de judo ASBL, Union européenne de judo and François Pacquée* [2000] ECR I-2549.

[133] Communication from the Commission to the European Parliament, the Council, the European Economic and Social Committee, and the Committee of the Regions 'Developing the European Dimension in Sport' COM(2011) 12 final, 18. 1. 2011, para 4.2.

[134] Case C-434/04 *Ahokainen and Leppik* [2006] ECR I-9171, para 39.

represent 22.7 % of overall contributions of this amount, or €642 million.[135] Solidarity contributions are paid out to: national associations to develop infrastructure, to cofinance some of their statutory tasks; and as incentives (participation in other competitions, and for good governance, including club licensing); clubs eliminated in the preliminary stages of the UEFA Champions League and UEFA Europa League; other top-division clubs that do not qualify for UEFA's main competitions, with payments distributed by the leagues or associations for youth development, and; clubs participating in the success of national team football in general and the UEFA EURO in particular through the participation of some of their players.[136] The 2011/2012 is, however, not the most representative year in terms of figures, because 2012 was the year of staging the quadrennial UEFA EURO. In the preceding season UEFA's total income from club competitions was €1.45 billion, over 1 billion of which was distributed back to the participating teams and €238 million (or 16 %) of which covered solidarity payments.[137] Broadcasting rights from central marketing represented 75 %, while other commercial rights represented 19 % of the total income in 2010/2011.[138] The total UEFA Champions League revenue amounted to €1,147.8 million (79 %) of total income, and the UEFA Europa League accounted for €210.4 million (14.5 %).[139] The solidarity payment distribution procedure is delegated from UEFA to the national associations which further transfer the money to their top leagues.[140] The leagues then apportion the revenues among their member clubs that run youth development programmes, according the UEFA-approved national club licensing systems. Clubs that do not run youth academies are not eligible for solidarity payments. National leagues are the entities responsible for determining the criteria and for distributing solidarity payments (except for the Netherlands, where association itself is in charge of specifying the criteria for distribution).[141] There are no uniform criteria for distribution and some leagues distribute the money according to sporting merit, whilst others divide it equally among some or all their affiliated clubs and even sometimes share it with lower divisions. Each UEFA territory is organised differently in this regard, but what they all have in common is that the clubs participating in the Champions League group stages onwards are not eligible to receive solidarity funds.[142]

The figures and system of allocation of solidarity funds presented here are supported by the income that national leagues or associations derive from their domestic competitions. It is indisputable that the redistribution of finances in

---

[135] UEFA Financial Report 2011/12, p. 2.

[136] Ibid. p. 11.

[137] UEFA Financial Report 2010/11, p. 9.

[138] Ibid. p. 6.

[139] Ibid. p. 7.

[140] European Professional Football Leagues, 'Financial Solidarity at Leagues and European Level' (July 2010) p. 18.

[141] Ibid.

[142] Ibid. pp. 19–21.

European football *pursues* the goals of solidarity—it is intrinsic in its very nature. The European Council considers that moves to encourage the mutualisation of part of the revenue from sales of broadcasting rights, at the appropriate levels, are beneficial to the principle of solidarity between all levels and areas of sport.[143] Mutualisation is a generally acceptable and applied principle but it does not tell us much about the details of this arrangement. The question to ask and answer under the effectiveness test relates to the current figures of solidarity contributions, i.e. €642 million (22.7 % of the total revenue) and €238 million (16 % of the total income) in 2011/2012 and 2010/2011, respectively. Are these figures capable of *fulfilling* the goals related to social functions of sport and to which extent? In order to answer this question with certainty, a fully blown study in each UEFA member's territory would be required. In the absence of any such study, there are few viewpoints to consider.

Andreff and Bourg examined the 1998 and 1999 market share of the four top football clubs in England and France in terms of turnover, which stood at 39.4 and 42.3 %, respectively, and which was much bigger than the same concentration ratio for television rights. Because the ratio between the highest and the lowest turnover was significantly higher than the ratio between the highest and the lowest television rights, they considered that 'even though the solidarity mechanism at work through the television rights redistribution does actually narrow the range of television rights revenues across the clubs, it is *not enough to compensate for the uneven distribution of clubs' turnover* due to other sources of finance'.[144]

In this sense, the next question to ask under the effectiveness test is if there is a need to create a completely levelled economic playing field in order to consider solidarity mechanisms effective? Is giving a fair sporting chance to clubs the level of effectiveness that is required? The bar can, however, be located even lower than that. In *Bosman*, UEFA argued that the intention of the rules aimed at maintenance of financial and sporting equilibrium is to ensure the financing, and ultimately the survival, of small- and medium-sized clubs.[145] If so, *the objective should be renamed* and endeavours of maintaining equilibrium substituted with a goal depicting a more realistic intention. *Preserving the social functions of football in general, and ensuring the financial survival of smaller clubs in particular* (rather than referring to 'balance between clubs'), is a more appropriate wording in this regard. It is extremely unlikely that this renamed objective would not be accepted as legitimate by the Court. As Advocate General Lenz pointed out in *Bosman*

> many people in [the EU] are interested in football. The number of spectators in stadiums and in front of television screens emphatically confirms that. In some towns, the local football team is one of the big attractions which contribute decisively to the fame of the

[143] Declaration on the Specific Characteristics of Sport and its Social Function in Europe, of which Account Should be Taken in Implementing Common Policies', Presidency Conclusions following the Nice European Council Meeting of 7, 8 and 9 December 2000, para 15.

[144] Andreff and Bourg, p. 51.

[145] Case C-415/93 *Union Royale Belge Sociétés de Football Association and others v. Bosman and others* [1995] ECR I-4921, para 52.

> place. Thus, in Germany, there are probably only a few interested contemporaries who do not associate the town of Mönchengladbach with football. The big clubs have in addition long since become an important economic factor. It would thus be possible, in my opinion, to regard even the maintenance of a viable professional league as a reason in the general interest which might justify restrictions on freedom of movement.[146]

In the UEFA Champions League, the Commission fully endorsed the European Council's Nice Declaration of 2000, where a redistribution of part of the revenue from the sales of TV rights at the appropriate levels was seen as beneficial to the principle of solidarity between all levels and areas of sport.[147] If a number of small and medium-sized clubs were to become bankrupt, it would deprive many people of supporting their local teams on the stadium, watching them play on TV, and practicing football in local clubs. There would be no football academies in smaller localities and a big number of young people would be deprived of playing youth football. For example in Estonia, Lithuania, Wales and Cyprus, the solidarity system is funding 50–100 % of the youth development budget of the recipient clubs.[148] Vertical and horizontal financial solidarity is therefore a suitable means of preserving the social functions of sport and ensuring the survival and valuable participation in competitions of small- and medium-sized clubs.

On the other side of the argument are the grassroots members who claim that the solidarity system providing them with money earned by the federation does not work properly.[149] The authors of the Arnaut Report recognised that more redistribution modelled upon EURO is needed to finance the grassroots, in particular in the Champions League. Does this imply that the contributions need to be significantly increased to fulfil the suitability criteria? Such an increase should certainly put to rest all doubts as to the suitability of the rule, but it would trigger dissatisfaction and breakaway threats of the wealthy clubs, concessions by UEFA and very likely lead to the withdrawal of any plans to increase solidarity contributions. The Helsinki Report expressed concern at the effects of commercialisation such as the increase in the number of lucrative sporting events, which may undermine sporting principles and the social function of sport and lead big clubs to leave the federation in order to derive maximum profits for themselves alone. This was seen as a threat to financial solidarity and the system of promotion and relegation. The European Council, European Parliament and the Committee of Regions agree on the need to preserve the social function of sport, and therefore to preserve the current structures of the organisation of sport in Europe by a uniform and coordinated approach

---

146 Opinion of AG Lenz in Case C-415/93 *Bosman*, para 219.

147 Commission Decision Relating to a Proceeding Pursuant to Article 81 of the EC Treaty and Article 53 of the EEA Agreement (Comp/C.2-37.398 Joint Selling of the Commercial Rights of the UEFA Champions League) 2003/778/EC, *OJ* 2003 L291/25, para 131.

148 Independent European Sport Review (2006), Annex III, p. 148.

149 Paragraph 3.1.2 of the European Model of Sport.

of the Member States, sporting movement, and the EU.[150] This coordinated and convergent effort would aim at preserving the traditional values of sport, and ensure that organisational aspects of sport assimilate the new economic order.[151]

The Arnaut report further identifies three threats to solidarity: ambush marketing, internet piracy and news access.[152] The effectiveness of solidarity depends on income and there is some validity in seeing ambush marketing and internet piracy as threats to profits, although no specific evidence has been provided. The substitutability of full-length matches with photographs or less-than-a-minute news reports is highly doubtful and, in this sense, the demand market is far less flexible than assumed in the Arnaut Report. What is more important for the effectiveness of solidarity than the threats identified is how the redistribution system is organised from the revenues actually generated. The Arnaut Report pointed out that there is a significant decline in competitive balance in a number of European top-flight football leagues, as supported by statistical analysis, and noted a growing concentration of wealth both within leagues, as only a few teams are capable of winning the national league, and between leagues, as only teams from a few leagues are likely to succeed in international competition.[153] It concluded that concentration of wealth and success 'can only be detrimental to long term interests of football'.[154] This statement is supported by the arguments supplied in Chap. 3 of this volume. However, in the context of suitability of the measures and testing the effectiveness of solidarity as a means of ensuring the preservation of the social functions of sport, including the survival of clubs from small localities, the threats to solidarity of the kind identified by the Arnaut Report are irrelevant because they are external threats that are covered by the relevant Member States' legislation and would pose an equal threat to any alternative financial solidarity measure.

In addition, there are other subcategories of the socio-cultural function of football such as social integration, promotion of health, education and culture that, at least indirectly, benefit from mechanisms of financial redistribution.[155] Unfortunately, some of them suffer from the problem of differing in their intentions and in their reality. For instance, the Nice Declaration describes sport as a 'factor making for integration, involvement in social life, tolerance, acceptance of differences […]'. But the reality is often disturbingly different.[156]

---

150 Report from the Commission to the European Council with a view to safeguarding the current sports structures and maintaining the social function of sport within the Community framework ('The Helsinki Report on Sport') COM(1999) 644 final, para 4.2; Resolution of the European Parliament on the role of the European Union in the field of sport, *OJ C 200*, 30.6.1997, and; Opinion of the Committee of the Regions on "The European model of sport", CdR 37/99, 15.9.99.

151 Ibid.

152 Ibid., Annex 3.

153 Paragraph 3.67 of the Report.

154 Ibid.

155 These social functions are usually directly supported by the local governments.

156 A famous example involved Eric Cantona, a French player in Leeds United in 1993. See Gardiner 1998, pp. 249–64.

> Social encounters through sport most certainly occur and sport has an important social meaning, one has to be aware that social exclusion is also a problem of sport itself (for instance in the form of sexism, racism and homophobia). It should not be forgotten that sport also incites competition, hierarchy, subordination, distinction and rivalry. [...] That is also the reason why sport does not automatically lead to social inclusion, social integration and social cohesion. It might be a tool for fighting any kind of social exclusion and social discrimination, but can also be a field where differences, or even social exclusion and social discrimination are produced or enforced, with respect to gender, social class, race/ethnicity, nationality, physical ability and/or sexual orientation.[157]

This excerpt addresses the issue of the 'internal paradox' of sport, which is according to the French sociologist Gasparini constituted by the fact that sport can easily be seen as integrating, but also as excluding through the existing forms of chauvinism, elitism, nationalism and racism.[158] Health can also be looked at through the same lens of internal paradox: drug abuse sometimes starts because of sports and career-ending injuries occur frequently. Education can also be viewed in a similar way: a glance at the American model of sport[159] should make it clear that European model has not much to do with education and many young people in Europe quit their high schools to dedicate their life to their sporting discipline.

7.6.2.2 Effective and Proper Organisation of Sport

There does not seem to be much controversy surrounding the role of the Article 49 rule in the effective organisation of football. It is generally accepted that the pyramid structure is the supreme way to organise a sport in terms of uniformity of the rules and regulations, institutional hierarchy and clarity of responsibilities. In the European Model of Sport under the 'competition law' heading, the Commission explicitly stated that it does not call the monopolistic role of the federations into question and considers the monopolistic institutional structure as the most efficient way of organising sport and ensuring essential solidarity.[160] The Helsinki Report expressed concern that 'the existence of several federations in one discipline would risk causing major conflicts',[161] while the Commission in its Staff Working Document considered that 'the organisation of national championships and the selection of national athletes and national teams for international competitions often require the existence of one umbrella federation'.[162]

---

[157] Consultation Conference with the European Sport Movement on the Social Function of Sport, Volunteering in Sport and Fight Against Doping, 'The EU and Sport: Matching Expectations', Brussels 14–15 June, 2005.

[158] 'Sport both integrates and excludes', EurActiv, 18 June 2008.

[159] See Sect. 2.2.2.

[160] Paragraph 3.2 of the European Model of Sport.

[161] Paragraph 4.2.3 of the Helsinki Report.

[162] Commission Staff Working Document, para 3.4.

7.6.3 Inherency Requirement

The Article 49 rule will not offend against the economic provisions of the Treaty if it can be demonstrated that its restrictive effects do not go beyond what is inherent in the pursuit of its objectives. Under Article 101(1) TFEU, an inherent rule that is proportionate will amount to 'regulatory ancillarity' or a public policy justification necessary to facilitate the achievement of the legitimate objectives. The process of ascertaining the existence of such justification largely corresponds to the objective justification under Article 102 TFEU as discussed in Sect. 5.2.4, and matches the analysis required under the objective justification framework supplied by the *Gebhard* case[163] under free movement provisions (see Fig. 6.2 in Chap. 6).

The inherency criteria alone demands that, based on their legitimate objectives, the challenged measures derive from the need for, and their restrictive effects are inherent in, the organisation and proper conduct of competitive sport. Without taking these measures, the legitimate objective cannot be achieved. In *Wouters*, a case that involved regulatory ancillarity, the Court left it up to the national court to assess the rules in question against the *Wouters* test.[164] It did not insist on any particular result of its preliminary ruling in the original proceedings, but instead talked of a measure that could '*reasonably be considered to be necessary* in order to ensure proper practice of the legal profession, *as it is organised in the Member State concerned*'.[165] The Court did not require the respondent to comply with a high evidential threshold. According to Whish, this position should be contrasted with Article 101(3) TFEU, where *convincing evidence* of economic efficiencies is required from the respondent.[166] The Court, furthermore, did not require an *absolute necessity* for the challenged rules, and it left untouched a choice of the organisational set-up. In *Meca-Medina* the Court extracted a conclusion on inherency on the basis of an assessment that, in terms of its (lack of) depth, can be compared to a *prima facie* assessment.[167] In *Deliège*, the Court limited its analysis of inherency to a statement that the rules were inherent in the organisation of competition because it 'naturally falls' on the sporting federations to select athletes eligible to participate in competitions.[168] From these cases it appears that inherency is a criterion that is not going to be particularly intensely scrutinised by the Court.

The question important for our analysis is whether the effects of the Article 49 rule and the conditions that restrict the formation of alternative leagues in football

[163] Case C-55/94 *R. Gebhard v. Consiglio dell'Ordine degli Avvocati e Procuratori di Milano* [1995] ECR I-4165.

[164] Case C-309/99 *J.C.J Wouters, J.W. Savelbergh, Price Waterhouse Belastingadviseurs BV v. Algemene Raad van de Nederlandse Orde van Advocaten* [2002] ECR I-1577, paras 97 and 108.

[165] Ibid. para 107.

[166] Whish 2009, p. 127.

[167] Case C-519/04 *David Meca-Medina and Igor Majcen v Commission* [2006] ECR I-6991, para 44.

[168] Joined Cases C-51/96 and C-191/97 *Deliège* [2000] ECR I-2549, para 64.

are inherent in pursuit of the goals related to solidarity and effective organisation of football. It is essentially this question that relates to the necessity of the pyramid as the structural model for the attainment of those goals by UEFA. It is instructive that the Court of Arbitration for Sport (CAS) takes the structure of European football and the mandate of national federations as a rather natural occurrence.[169] CAS also noted that in some countries the mandate of the national federations as promoters and organisers of football at all levels, and as guardians of the interests of all their members, is entrusted upon them by national legislation in the form of delegated governmental powers.[170]

EU institutions, the Court included, will not insist on imposing any particular organisational structure on the sport because selecting the appropriate institutional set-up is in the realm of regulatory autonomy of the sporting bodies. In the Nice Declaration the European Council stressed its support for the 'independence of sports organisations and their right to organise themselves through appropriate associative structures', and noted that 'sports federations have a central role in ensuring the essential solidarity'.[171] Other European policy documents also explicitly support the right to self-govern for sporting organisations, but at the same time condition this support upon respect for certain principles related to good governance in decision-making (such as transparency, democracy, accountability and representation of concerned stakeholders). For instance, the Commission Communication on Developing the European Dimension in Sport states that 'good governance in sport is a condition for the autonomy and self-regulation of sport organisations'.[172] In its White Paper on Sport, the Commission acknowledged the autonomy of sporting organisations and representative structures and considered that 'most challenges can be addressed through self-regulation respectful of good governance principles, provided that EU law is respected'.[173]

Hence, although the Court will not interfere with the choice of organisational structure of a sport, it is the particular arrangements that exist within the structure that will be scrutinised for their compatibility with EU law. In case of the Article 49 rule, however, the very issue to be scrutinised intrinsically relates to the organisational structure. This would make it more difficult for the Court to find that the restrictive effects on the market are not inherent in the pursuit of solidarity goals and the effective organisation of sport, *in particular* due to the remarkable improvements in the standards of governance in European football. Weatherill

---

[169] Court of Arbitration for Sport, 17 July 1998, CAS 98/200.

[170] Ibid. Specifically, CAS cited French Law no. 84-610 of 16 July 1984 as an example.

[171] Declaration on the specific characteristics of sport and its social function in Europe, of which account should be taken in implementing common policies 13948/00, Annex to the Presidency Conclusions, Nice ('Nice Declaration').

[172] Communication from the Commission to the European Parliament, the Council, the European Economic and Social Committee, and the Committee of the Regions 'Developing the European Dimension in Sport' COM(2011) 12 final, 18. 1. 2011, para 4.1.

[173] White Paper on Sport, para 4.

considered that the pyramid represents an exaggerated view of what is necessary for proper organisation of football in Europe.[174] But his objection to the pyramid structure was related to the 'exclusion of the major football clubs from formal participation in taking of decisions that directly affect their commercial interests […]'.[175] This no longer holds true. As explained in Sects. 3.4 and 7.4.2 the governance of football in Europe has undergone radical changes in the recent past. The strategic commercial decisions that affect the clubs are no longer made centrally by UEFA, and clubs have a means of control over such decisions.

It is therefore submitted that the restrictive effects of the Article 49 rule are inherent *in this particular organisational structure*, which, due to the improvements in governance, are not in themselves objectionable from the point of view of EU law and policy. In such a structure, UEFA is the body mandated with promoting, protecting and developing European football at every level of the game, promoting the principles of unity and solidarity, and dealing with all questions relating to European football.[176] It is responsible for

> organisation of competitions for professional, youth, women's and amateur football; increase in access and participation; supporting growth in the grassroots of the game; achieving commercial success and sound finances without distorting the sporting qualities of our competitions; using UEFA's revenues to support reinvestment and redistribution in the game in accordance with the principle of solidarity between all levels and areas of sport; targeting specific aid and assistance to help member associations with the greatest need; promoting positive sporting values (such as fair play, anti-racism and safe and secure match environment); running an anti-doping programme aiming at preserving the ethics of sport, safeguarding the players' health and ensuring equal chances for all competitors; and ensuring that the needs of the different stakeholders are properly reflected in UEFA's thinking.[177]

Restrictions on the formation of an alternative league are merely inherent in pursuing this broad agenda that stems from the need for the proper organisation of sport *in a pyramidal structure* of European football. Properly organising football in this structure means keeping every segment of the pyramid alive and functioning through the mechanisms of financial solidarity enabled by the restrictions on alternative leagues and collective sale of broadcasting rights. Without the Article 49 rule and the conditions imposed on formation of cross-border leagues, the legitimate objectives relied on could not be achieved in such structure, while the organisation of sport would lose on its effectiveness.

The Opinion of the Advocate General in *Deliège* may be used in support of this reasoning. Chiming with the policy statements cited above, he argued that

> [EU] law does not require sport to develop in a particular direction, in the sense that it does not demand that individual sports become fully commercialised or fully professional. On the contrary, in principle, it respects the choices made by the governing bodies of each

---

[174] Weatherill 2007, p. 265.

[175] Ibid. See also Weatherill 2009, p. 100.

[176] UEFA Mission Statement.

[177] UEFA Vision Europe 2005, p. 7.

> sport, who are also the legitimate representatives of its practitioners, its fans and anyone with an interest in it generally. The [EU] legal order merely prohibits the commercialisation or professionalisation of sport in breach of the rules of the Treaty. I take the view, in other words, that the right of self-regulation which sport enjoys and to which I referred above is protected by [EU] law. It ensures that sporting institutions have the power to promote a sport in a manner which they consider to be most consistent with their objectives, provided that their choices do not give rise to discrimination or conceal the pursuit of economic interests. Accordingly, any decision by sporting institutions which has as its exclusive aim or objective the promotion of the social dimension of sport, over and above any intention of an economic nature, is in principle justified, even where it entails a restriction on [EU] freedoms. This is dictated by the need to guarantee sport's right of self-regulation.[178]

In regard to concealing the pursuit of economic interests that this Opinion refers to and that could be thought to constitute a counterargument to the inherency of the Article 49 rule, suffice it to say that the fact that the rule genuinely pursuing the legitimate regulatory objectives *in a proportionate manner* also serves economic purposes, will be irrelevant to the inherency assessment. For instance, the argument of the applicants in *Meca-Medina* that the International Olympic Committee, apart from protecting legitimate objectives, also had in mind protecting its economic interests was, according to the General Court, not sufficient to alter the purely sporting nature of those rules.[179] The General Court judgment was overruled, but this particular point survived in a different form that made no reference to 'purely sporting nature' of rules. Namely, on appeal to the Court, the applicants' argument intended to challenge the inherency of the anti-doping rule failed, as the rule was considered proportionate for safeguarding integrity and ethical values in sport.[180]

What follows next is an examination of proportionality, the key point for the outcome of an analysis on the legality of the UEFA Article 49 rule.

7.6.4 Proportionality

White Paper on Sport specifies that 'the sporting rule must also be proportionate in relation to its objective in order for it not to infringe Articles [101(1) and 102 TFEU] and must be applied in a transparent, objective and non-discriminatory manner'.[181] This is also a valid framework for the examination of sporting rules under internal market provisions. The question at this stage of the analysis is whether there are any other, *less restrictive*, measures that are *capable of achieving* the same objectives. Any proposed alternative measure must therefore comply with the twin principles of suitability and proportionality, and in that sense, it must represent a *viable* less restrictive option, as opposed to merely a possible substitute, in

[178] Opinion of Advocate General in Joined Cases C-51/96 and C-191/97 *Deliège* [2000] ECR I-2549, para 87.

[179] Case T-313/02 *David Meca-Medina and Igor Majcen v Commission* [2004] ECR II-3291, paras 56–57.

[180] Case C-519/04 *Meca-Medina* [2006] ECR I-6991, paras 46–56.

[181] Commission Staff Working Document, Annex I, para 2.1.5.

order for the Article 49 rule to be considered disproportionate in EU law. For the challenged measure to be upheld via an objective justification the Court requires 'an actual showing of fit and proportionality'.[182] This analysis is conducted in an environment where the actual situation on the market is readily available for assessment. On the other hand, a counterfactual analysis of the situation on the market but for the restrictive measure, as well as the analysis of the suitability of alternative measures, is purely hypothetical because the effects of certain regulatory changes can be very difficult to predict with any certainty. Proposed alternatives have to go through essentially the same proportionality test as the challenged measures, but due to the speculative nature of conclusions as to their effects, it is submitted that they should shoulder a de facto higher standard of proof.

The Article 49 rule and possible substitute arrangements, such as the 1998 Media Partners proposal, that are capable of attaining the same goals in a less restrictive manner will be analysed against the requirements of EU law in the final sections of this chapter. First, however, various theories on alternative structures in European football followed by a description of existing alternative leagues in domestic football and in other sports will be set out.

7.6.4.1 Alternative Structures in Theory

Several theories were put forth as regards the possible alternative structures for European football. Parrish and Miettinen merely suggested that the future might bring a deregulated product market based on many supranational, as opposed to national leagues, or a mixed model of a supranational league operating in conjunction with the national leagues, both falling under UEFA regulatory competence.[183]

Hoehn and Szymanski developed a framework to analyse the consequences of the structure of competition in Europe and US, in particular the effects of participation of teams in both domestic and international club competitions as opposed to participation in one hermetic league only.[184] Starting from the premise that the current UEFA Champions League has several major flaws in terms of competitive balance, they argued in favour of creation of a European Superleague detached from domestic competitions. Such a league would be based around four regional conferences of 15 teams, each playing 28 matches against teams from their own league and six matches against teams from each of the other conferences. A play-off system with two top teams at the end of the regular season from each regional league would determine the European champion in club football.[185] However, Hoehn and Szymanski did recognise that the proposed structure would imply clear benefits only for incumbent teams to the detriment of excluded outsiders, consumers and

---

182 McDermott 2010, p. 280.

183 Parrish and Miettinen 2008, p. 215.

184 Hoehn and Szymanski 1999.

185 Ibid. pp. 230–232.

smaller nations and regions.[186] Potential benefits to domestic leagues stripped of the top clubs as participants were portrayed in highly speculative general terms unsupported by any evidence. The article also does not consider the likely possibility of bankruptcies among smaller clubs in the domestic leagues should a truly independent Superleague be established. It was submitted in Sect. 7.6.2.1 above that the legitimate objectives referring to ‘balance between clubs’ should be reformulated to reflect more realistic goals focusing on preserving the social functions of football in general, and *ensuring financial survival of smaller clubs* in particular. Furthermore, the authors identified access, redistributive measures, and the scope of inter-league competition and the role of UEFA, as the most prominent policy issues in endorsing a shift towards a hermetic Superleague.[187] Regarding access, they suggested that the fact that some nations and regions will never qualify to participate in the Superleague, even if the league remains open to promotion and relegation, should not present a problem as the weaker clubs do not enjoy much success in the top European competitions even today and there is nothing to be gained by preserving unbalanced competition. They see redistribution within the clubs in a league as a way of softening competition, reducing incentive to compete, and worsening competitive balance, and acknowledge that the American mechanisms of competitive balance (such as the rookie draft and salary caps) are possible to implement only in a closed league. The greater potential, according to Hoehn and Szymanski, lies in redistribution among leagues, as the big clubs buy and use smaller clubs as farm teams, which can also be successfully implemented only in a closed league system. UEFA is portrayed as facing unsustainable conflict of interests as a regulator of both domestic competitions and a Superleague on the one hand, and as a promoter of a Superleague on the other, which would oblige it to choose between one of these two roles.[188] The standpoint of these authors, both economists, is entirely based on a pro-market approach while not giving much weight to social values, European traditions, consumer welfare, and regional policy issues in their conclusions. EU sports law and policy is specially designed to take all of these aspects into account in the assessment of the compatibility of any sporting rules with the internal market requirements. Access to competitions would certainly become a sensitive issue under EU competition law.

Weatherill proposed not to demolish the pyramid as an organisational paradigm for football but to confine the scope of the pyramid to strictly regulatory matters *or* give clubs more input into decisions that directly and substantially affect their commercial interests.[189] Given that substantial changes in the governance of European football have already taken place[190] since Weatherill’s article on pyramid structure, and that today clubs have a means of control over the decisions that

[186] Ibid. pp. 225–227.

[187] Ibid. pp. 228–230.

[188] Ibid.

[189] Weatherill 2005, para 7.

[190] See Sects. 3.4 and 7.4.2.

affect their commercial interests, it is likely that this author would view the governance in the pyramid as it stands today as being more in line with the requirements of EU law and policy.

Speaking at the Sport&EU 2013 conference in Istanbul, a senior adviser to the UEFA President, William Gaillard, was frank about the fact that cross-border leagues are a taboo in UEFA even though a number of leagues and federations have been talking to one another regarding alternate possibilities, the most visible project at the moment being Russia–Ukraine.[191] He confirmed the rumours of a new Atlantic league and said they reflect the fact that some national leagues are no longer sustainable due to the inability of clubs to pay salaries to their players. Dangers associated with this include match-fixing and corruption, so the lack of sustainability becomes a danger also for the rest of European football.[192] He then suggested, in relatively broad terms, that some leagues have to be set up to allow them to build critical mass and restore the status of those clubs that have no chance to compete in European competitions because of extremely low national TV revenues. In his opinion, UEFA will have to allow some of the alternative leagues to help restore the competitiveness of the leagues and clubs. He further said that it was difficult to get UEFA to agree on a woman's cross-border competition in the Netherlands and Belgium (BeNe League)[193] and that there will be pressure for this model to spread. UEFA will try to resist but eventually will have to let it happen as it is a matter of life and death for all but the top six leagues. Finally, he concluded that European professional football can be made more sustainable by taking some lessons from across Atlantic. What can be read between the lines from the speech of William Gaillard is that UEFA will allow, however reluctantly, the formation of cross-border leagues where it is a matter of survival or restoring competitiveness of the leagues and clubs, but that sanctioning a private league consisting of top European clubs would be a different issue as far as UEFA is concerned.

A study entitled Professional Sport in the Internal Market correctly considered that the European Super League project is essentially a matter of finding common ground in the conflict between the competing interests of top clubs as self-interested entities concerned with financial planning, and of the national umbrella organisations and UEFA motivated by a desire to represent the interest of football as a whole.[194] Views of that study on the Europe-wide cross-border league can be summarised as follows: It is far from clear in which form a European Super League may be expected to be formed. Such a league would not only encounter difficulties in gaining acceptance in different cultures and in facing UEFA

[191] William Gaillard, a personal advisor to the President of UEFA 'Football and the EU in a Wider Historical Perspective' in a speech delivered at Sport&EU annual conference in Istanbul 28 June, 2013.

[192] Ibid.

[193] UEFA news item 'Best of Belgian and Dutch Unite in the BeNe League' 23 January 2013.

[194] Professional Sport in the Internal Market, Project No IP/A/IMCO/ST/2005-004, Commissioned by the Committee on the Internal Market and Consumer Protection of the European Parliament (September 2005), p. 62.

opposition, but the closed circle model would not be permissible under EU competition law. From the legal point of view, an open circle based on the European relegation system that meets the needs of different stakeholders involved in it is therefore a way to go. In practice, however, the open European Super League project might come across issues in regard to its implementation, such as the necessity to be incorporated in the hierarchical league system—the infrastructure exists only in the form of national and international associations occupying monopolistic positions, so the European Super League would have to cooperate with national associations or UEFA—a hard-to-predict process which may take time. The study concludes that the demands of Europe's top clubs and the forces of commercialisation will eventually take over and there will be several interim models before the cross-border league based on an open circle model finally emerges.[195]

These were some thoughts by academics, economists, and practitioners on the topic of European breakaway league. However, the only detailed alternative plan remains the Media Partners proposal from 1998 set out in Sect. 3.3.2.

7.6.4.2 Proportionality Requirement and Nature of Protected Interests in Case Law on Rival Competitions

Apart from the Court's decision in the *DLG* case,[196] there is not much clarity on the application of the proportionality test to the rules and regulations of associations designed to restrict rival competitions in the EU. Carrying out the proportionality test requires a case-by-case approach, and while there are many examples from general EU case law, it would be helpful to have a sample model illustrating what exactly is expected from sport governing bodies in connection with rules restricting rival competitions.

In *Fédération Internationale d'Automobile* (FIA)[197] the Commission required FIA to stick to its regulatory role, so as to prevent any conflict of interests by conflating commercial and regulatory functions.[198] Weatherill saw 'the frequently endemic' conflict of interest as a feature in governance that should be avoided, so that regulatory power is not used to promote *commercial* advantage of the governing body.[199] The Commission position was that the FIA rules might not be used to restrict new competitions *unless* justified on grounds related to the safe, fair or orderly conduct of motor sport, in which case the justifications would relate to

[195] Ibid. pp. 61–62.

[196] Case C-250/92 *Gøttrup-Klim e.a. Grovvareforeninger v Dansk Landbrugs Grovvareselskab AmbA* (*DLG*) [1994] ECR I-5641.

[197] Notice published pursuant to Article 19(3) of Council Regulation No 17 concerning Cases COMP/35.163—Notification of FIA Regulations, COMP/36.638—Notification by FIA/FOA of agreements relating to the FIA Formula One World Championship, COMP/36.776—GTR/FIA and others (2001/C 169/03).

[198] For details and analysis of the case see Sect. 5.6.2.

[199] Weatherill 2008, p. 11.

protecting public interests.[200] When it comes to the issue of restricting breakaway leagues in European football, the justifications relate to solidarity goals and the effective and proper organisation of sport. Importantly, UEFA does not have only a commercial/regulatory role in that its mandate includes the promotion of football at all levels of sport, developing participation in sport, and maximising its health and socio-cultural benefits, among other things.[201] This goes beyond the mere regulation of sport and entails certain other social responsibilities. In order to fulfil this all-encompassing mandate some restrictive rules on participation in rival competitions are deemed necessary by the governing body. Whether acting in its regulatory or commercial capacity, public interests are at the heart of the UEFA mandate as well as its Article 49 rule. FIA by contrast used its regulatory role for the sole purpose of protecting its private interests and solidifying its commercial dominance in a sport that does not have a social and educational dimension, and could not therefore rely on considerations given to sport in EU law that have subsequently been set out in Article 165(1) TFEU. The clauses in agreements with broadcasters according to which severe penalties would be imposed by FIA if broadcasters showed anything deemed as a competitive threat to Formula One, as well as automatic acquisition of television rights for all motor sport events it authorised (even when organised by a different promoter), clearly suggested goals related to private commercial interests, enabled by FIA's dual functionality of regulator and commercial actor. The mere fact that FIA used its dual functionality in the described manner amounted to abuse of a dominant position which could not be justified by reference to any of the sporting (or other) objective justifications, so there was no discussion of proportionality in this case. The *Meca-Medina/Wouters* analytical framework did not apply as this was not a case of regulatory ancillarity, and it was also not the case of commercial ancillarity as the restrictions were not proportionate restrictions on competition that were directly related and objectively necessary for the implementation of the main, non-restrictive transaction. The rule about separating commercial and regulatory functions set out by the Commission in the *FIA/Formula One* case is therefore not appropriate for application to the issue of breakaway leagues in football.

Similarly, in *MOTOE*[202] the issue related to the conflation of regulatory and commercial functions in one body, which ultimately led to blocking of competing organisations.[203] Just like the *FIA/Formula One* case, such conflict of interest was assumedly used to restrict competition for the purpose of protecting *private* commercial interests of the sporting body. In such cases (providing that there is no statutory monopoly and Article 106 TFEU involved as in *MOTOE*), it is only the

[200] Commission Press Release IP/01/1523 'Commission closes its investigation into Formula One and other four-wheel motor sports', Brussels, 30 October 2001.

[201] See Sect. 3.4.2 for details on UEFA mandate.

[202] Case C-49/07 *Motosykletistiki Omospondia Ellados NPID* (*MOTOE*) *v Elliniko Dimosio* [2008] ECR I-4863.

[203] For details and analysis of the case see Sect. 5.6.1.

efficiency defence under Article 102 TFEU and/or Article 101(3) TFEU and the proportionality requirement in those frameworks that could be used, although the exemption is highly unlikely to be granted.

In *DLG*,[204] the interests that the agricultural organisation was safeguarding (by introducing clauses prohibiting membership in any other cooperative organisations or participation in any other forms of organised membership in competition with DLG on the wholesale market) were also of a commercial nature, but DLG acted in the interest of its members, was not a dominant undertaking and the factual analysis revealed that it confined the scope of restrictions only to what was necessary for the attainment of its legitimate objectives. The Court found that the actions of DLG complied with the principle of proportionality because the amendment of DLG's statutes was restricted so as to cover only those farm supplies in respect of which a direct relationship existed between sales volume and price[205]; the option to buy from DLG the whole range of products which it sold on the same terms and at the same prices as members remained open to non-members of the association, including the plaintiffs, except that non-members were not entitled to receive a yearly discount on the amount of the transactions carried out[206]; DLG's statutes authorised its members to buy fertilisers and plant protection products without using DLG as an intermediary, provided that such transactions were carried out otherwise than through an organised consortium[207]; the penalties imposed for infringing DLG's rules did not appear to the Court to be disproportionate, since DLG treated the non-members as if they were members exercising their right to withdraw[208]; the membership period had been reduced from 10 to 5 years, which did not seem unreasonable[209]; and the Court also noted as significant that after their exclusion from DLG the non-members succeeded in creating vigorous competition with DLG through a different organisation and obtained market share similar to DLG.[210] Therefore, its restrictive clauses were held legal and enforceable.

These three cases suggest that the position of the Court and the Commission towards clauses restricting rival competitions was almost exclusively influenced by the nature of the interests being safeguarded (as it was easier for associations to defend restrictions undertaken for the sake of public interests or interests of their members, as opposed to purely commercial private interests) and the proportionality of the restrictions.[211] The *Meca-Medina* analytical framework does not apply

---

[204] C-250/92 *DLG*.

[205] Paragraph 37 of C-49/07 *MOTOE*.

[206] Ibid. para 38.

[207] Ibid. para 39.

[208] Ibid. para 41.

[209] Ibid. para 42.

[210] Ibid. para 43.

[211] In *Wouters* and *Meca-Medina*, both involving regulatory ancillarity, the issue did not relate to preventing breakaway structures but to ethical standards of profession and the Court upheld the legality of the restrictions. Thus, proportionality usually ends up being the main issue in regards to restrictive rules of associations that are designed to protect public interest, ethical standards, or commercial interest that benefit the members.

to the rules of associations adopted for the protection of their private commercial interests, and the exemption would have to be sought under Article 101(3) TFEU and the efficiency defence under Article 102 TFEU.

The treatment in other jurisdictions of the issue of proportionality and restrictions on alternative structures provides a better illustration. In a groundbreaking case before the High Court of Justice of England and Wales (the High Court), *Greig v. Insole*,[212] the International Cricket Council (ICC) governed test cricket and had the exclusive power to regulate the qualification rules for cricketers to play in test matches. At the same time, a private promoter (Kerry Packer's Television Corporation) set up World Series Cricket and engaged 34 of the world's leading test cricketers to play in an autumn and winter series in Australia. The ICC reacted by changing the rules on qualification for test cricketers so that any player who played in a match disapproved of by the ICC was ineligible to play test cricket and was banned indefinitely. The ICC then passed a resolution disapproving of matches organised by the private promoter, and asked its member federations to follow suit in respect of their domestic competitions. The body that regulated county cricket in England complied and proposed to disqualify players who played in World Series Cricket. The private promoter and the players sued these two bodies in the English High Court and relied on the restraint of trade doctrine. The promoter also sued the defendants for unlawful inducement to breach of contract. In *Greig v. Insole* it was held that the public interest required that the game should be properly organised and administered, but that measures taken to this effect must be no more that is reasonably necessary.[213] The High Court recognised that ICC and TCCB had to take measures to protect their objectives as governing bodies and custodians of the public interest because they financed the rest of the game, including the grassroots where future test match players were trained and developed. Breakaway organisers were seen as 'parasitic' because they were creaming off and commercially exploiting the star players from traditional cricket in whose training and preparation for stardom it they had not invested.[214] The High Court considered whether, on the facts of the case, the restraints were reasonably necessary for this public interest objective to be met. Anything that is likely to prejudice the attraction or profitability of the competition that brings finances into the game, according to the judgment, must be of concern to the governing bodies.[215] But the threat posed by World Series Cricket to test match finances was seen as very limited, and presented an immediate threat only to the finances of Australian cricket, because about 20 of its players were under contract with World Series Cricket and the event was going to be staged on its soil.[216] In this respect, indefinite retrospective bans on player participation in breakaway league were seen as disproportionate because players had not breached any rules at that

[212] *Greig v. Insole* [1978] 1 WLR 302 (Ch D 1977).

[213] Ibid. paras 347–348.

[214] Ibid. para 349.

[215] Ibid. para 310.

[216] Ibid. para 351.

point and because the effect of such a ban would be to deprive the public of watching those players in test matches, thus reducing test match revenues. Prospective bans on such participation would likely not be disproportionate and would have been possible to justify as the seriousness of the threat posed to the game by the emergence of the private promoter could change in the long term. The High Court identified three ways that this could happen: 1. other players might join World Series Cricket; 2. the breakaway series could extend its programme beyond the planned 3 years, and; 3. other promoters might join the market and start signing up the players from test cricket. Identified threats could have been adequately averted by 'merely imposing a prospective disqualification from test cricket on all players who should *thereafter* contract with or play for World Series Cricket or other unapproved private promoters'.[217] Had the threat to the sport as a whole been more serious and immediate, it is not inconceivable that the retrospective bans would have been seen as proportionate under the circumstances. The High Court held that (i) the contracts between the promoter and the claimants were to be treated as valid and enforceable and (ii) although the defendants had acted in good faith they had committed a tortious act inducing a breach of contract, and had done so having full knowledge of the contracts.[218]

Given the clarity of the High Court treatment of the proportionality requirement in *Greig v. Insole*, its judgment in *Hendry v. WPBSA*[219] is disappointing. In a very similar factual situation, the High Court acknowledged that the governing body for snooker had a legitimate interest to protect by an already existing rule which provided that players could not participate in events not organised or sanctioned by the governing body, and that the decisive question related to proportionality. The only attempt to differentiate the two cases was the High Court's recognition that WPBSA, unlike cricket authorities, does not have a major investment to protect in the training of players. Nevertheless, protecting its broadcasting and sponsorship agreements was seen as protecting collective benefits of the sport and its players.[220] The judgment followed the reasoning from *Greig v. Insole*, but then the High Court took an unexpected turn and without much explanation decided that the WPBSA refusal to sanction events that clashed with the Main Tour events went further than was necessary to protect the legitimate objectives.[221] Earlier in the judgment, in para 53, the High Court mentioned a meeting that took place between the private promoter and the BBC intended to persuade the BBC to withdraw from a contract with WPBSA making the Main Tour not viable due to the withdrawal of sponsorship that would be certain to follow in that situation. Some commentators on the case asked the right questions and enquired if this sort of behaviour by the private promoter was allowed, why was WPBSA not allowed to defend itself against such behaviour by requiring players to commit to events it organised so as to secure the

---

217 Ibid. para 352.

218 Ibid. para 365.

219 *Hendry and others v. WPBSA* [2001] All ER (D) 71.

220 Ibid. paras 114–115.

221 Ibid. para 116.

revenues that pay their prize money? Similarly, they asked 'if it is legitimate for a governing body to take steps to protect the commercial revenues generated by its events in order to reinvest in all levels of sport, and to prevent outside organisers free-riding on its developmental efforts, how is it supposed to do that if not by requiring players to commit themselves to participate in sanctioned events only?'[222] These questions were not answered anywhere in *Hendry v. WPBSA*. The proportionality requirement was not fulfilled and no reasoned explanation for this conclusion was provided, but this is not to say that the explanation was not available. For example, WPBSA initially agreed to sanction the proposed events as long as they did not clash with the Main Tour that WPBSA organised and their broadcasting schedule did not clash with the BBC's live coverage of the Main Tour events. The decision on proportionality might have been influenced by the fact that the Main Tour events occupied all the dates in the broadcasting calendar that were of interest to broadcasters. Also, the High Court could have referred to the fact that professional snooker lacks many features that sports like cricket and football have, such as the need to establish competitive balance, invest in training and development of young players, the governing body does not need major investments to stage competitions, and there is no strong social and educational element, etc. When the objective justification, as accepted by the High Court in *Hendry v. WPBSA*, is not that forceful and persuasive, then the scrutiny of proportionality of the restrictive rule should be particularly strict and the reasoning set out in more detail.

7.6.4.3 Proportionality Analysis of UEFA Requirements for Setting Up a Cross-Border Competition

According to the proportionality test, the positive effects of the prohibition laid down by the Article 49 rule ought to outweigh the negative effects caused by the restraint placed on clubs and private promoters on entering the market for organisational services in transnational football in Europe. Before analysing the proportionality of UEFA conditions for approval of cross-border competitions, several notes should be made. First, there is a Memorandum of Understanding that governs the relationship between the ECA and UEFA according to which ECA expressly agreed to

> recognise UEFA as the governing body of football at European level in accordance with its Statutes […]; to ensure that none of its member clubs participate in any competition that is not organised or recognised by UEFA/FIFA' and 'to ensure that its member clubs are not members of any other association or grouping involving clubs from more than one country […].[223]

[222] Jonathan Taylor and Adam Lewis 'Governing Body Restraint on Breakaways' paper presented at 'Sport and The Law' conference, London, 31 March 2011.

[223] Memorandum of Understanding between UEFA and ECA (2012), paras D.1, D.3 and D.4.

Second, some of the principles elaborated in *MOTOE*[224] may apply to Article 102 TFEU alone even if the power of the association does stem from an act of public authority. Hence, the criteria and procedures for access to market must be based on transparent, objectively justified and non-discriminatory conditions for selection which are followed faithfully and openly.[225] Third, the proportionality of the rules specified in the 13 UEFA conditions is not a subject of this analysis. The question to ask here is whether the imposition of such rules on alternative competitions goes beyond what is necessary to achieve the legitimate objectives set out in Sect. 7.6.1. Fourth, the conditions are aimed at smaller cross-border competitions, not at organisationally independent leagues, and implicitly exclude the possibility of pan-European structures. However, the analysis will consider the applicability of the conditions of approval to both regionally delimited leagues and pan-European leagues. Finally, both UEFA and (elite) clubs have legitimate but conflicting interests to protect. A conflict involving cross-border leagues is essentially a conflict between private and public interests that culminates in the assessment of proportionality.

In order for a cross-border competition to be approved by UEFA it needs to fulfil 13 conditions *before* putting into effect any alternative league plans. They read as follows:

> 1. The cross-border competition must be approved by the respective UEFA member associations; 2. The cross-border competition must be organised by the respective UEFA member associations; 3. All clubs planning to participate in the cross-border competition must be affiliated to a UEFA member association (or to a league/regional football association subordinated to such association); 4. Geographical aspects should be taken into consideration when a cross-border competition is being assessed; 5. All clubs planning to participate in the cross-border competition must recognise, as a condition of participation, that the ownership of the competition and its core commercial rights belong centrally to the competition organiser—in this case the associations (not the league, clubs, etc.)—not to the individual clubs (same model as the UEFA Champions League); 6. Minimum standards should be fixed with regards to the levels of solidarity distributions from the commercial rights revenues (core commercial rights commercialised centrally) for example: i. Minimum 10 % of commercial rights revenues must be distributed to amateur football in the countries concerned, via the associations involved; ii. Minimum 10 % of commercial rights revenues must be distributed to professional football clubs of the associations concerned but only clubs who are not participating in the cross-border competition concerned (providing that they fulfil, as a minimum, the sporting criteria of the UEFA Club Licensing System); iii. Of the remaining revenues divided amongst the participating clubs, a minimum of 25 % (ideally a minimum of 50 %) must be distributed equally, with the remainder based on on-field performance. 7. The competition regulations must be in compliance with the UEFA statutes/regulations and need to be approved by UEFA; 8. Participating clubs must be licensed in accordance with the UEFA Club Licensing System; 9. The competition regulations must include, among other things, provisions concerning, for example: i. Refereeing; ii. Disciplinary matters; iii. Independence of clubs (integrity of competition); iv. Anti-doping. 10. The cross-border competition must not conflict with the international match calendar; 11. The matches of the cross-border competition may not be played on the same day as UEFA club competitions; 12. The

[224] Case C-49/07 *MOTOE* [2008] ECR I-4863.

[225] Weatherill 2008, p. 8.

cross-border competition must not replace the national championships and must be arranged around the calendar of the national championship; 13. Approval of FIFA.[226]

Conditions 1 and 13 refer to approvals that are required for the cross-border league by both UEFA member associations and FIFA. There are no indications as to what are the conditions for approval by national associations and FIFA, and if these bodies can, without explanation, refuse to sanction competitions that fulfil all of the other conditions. This criterion should be further clarified. Presumably, if the clubs fulfil the rest of the conditions they should be able to obtain such approval automatically, and subsequently automatic approval by UEFA. Even though the power of UEFA does not stem from an act of entrustment by a public authority or statutory duty, it is theoretically possible to test the UEFA approval policy against the stricter requirements laid down by the Court for the exercise of such regulatory functions. In accordance with the principles in *MOTOE*, and elsewhere in the similar case law of the Court,[227] undertakings such as UEFA and national associations possessing both regulatory and commercial powers, must be made subject to restrictions, obligations and review. The fact that a market entry was made subject to prior authorisation is not a problem per se. In freedom of movement cases, the Court has held systems subjecting the marketing of goods and services to a prior authorisation procedure as justified only if they pursue a public interest objective and comply with the principle of proportionality.[228] In *Canal Satélite Digital* the Court specified that in determining whether a system of prior approval complies with the principle of proportionality, it is important to consider[229]:

- *Whether a system is based on objective, non-discriminatory criteria which are known in advance so that the regulatory power is not used arbitrarily*? (UEFA criteria for cross-border competitions are *prima facie* objective and non-discriminatory, however, as will be indicated throughout this section, some of the requirements should be clarified so as to improve certainty for potential applicants when constructing details of their campaign).
- *Whether a system duplicates the control already carried out*? (Considering that concerned national associations and UEFA already carry out a system of prior control, would the approval of FIFA be necessary, or it only duplicates the controls already carried out?)
- *Whether subsequent control system would be too late to be genuinely effective to attain the aim pursued*? (Some of the consequences of the creation of

[226] Cited in Master Thesis by Jaka Lucu, Mico Petcovic, Mihai C. Tudoran and Victor Vasiliev, 'Central European Football League: Dream or Reality' (International Centre for Sports Studies (CIES), Neuchatel, 2007), pp. 42–43.

[227] For e.g., Case C-67/96 *Albany International BV v. Stichting Bedrijfspensioenfonds Textielindustrie* [1999] ECR I-5751.

[228] See for e.g., Case C-432/03 *Commission* v *Portugal* [2005] ECR I-9665, and Case C-390/99 *Canal Satélite Digital SL v. Adminstración General del Estado, and Distribuidora de Televisión Digital SA* (*DTS*) [2002] ECR I-607.

[229] Ibid. para 43.

breakaway league would be that governing bodies would need to review and remodel the format of leagues under their umbrella and adapt their short and long-term business plans to the new situation on the market. They need to make sure that their mandate and the responsibility towards the rest of the sport can be fulfilled. *Ex post* control would not be appropriate to achieve the objectives of solidarity or effective organisation of sport and could challenge the internal balance of national and European football).

- *Whether on account of its duration and the disproportionate cost it deters the operators concerned from pursuing their business plan?* (There are no costs involved for the applicants, while at least the maximum allowed duration for the procedure from the date of application leading up to the formal decision by UEFA should be specified).

Conditions 3 and 7–12 deal with issues pertaining to regulatory competences remaining centralised with the governing bodies. Clubs will likely not succeed in a challenge to this regulatory competence, including the licensing system and centrally designed match calendar. Conditions 3 and 7 provide that all participant clubs must be affiliated to their national associations and cross-border competition regulations must comply with UEFA statutes and regulations. Provisions for some matters such as refereeing, disciplinary matters, independence of clubs and anti-doping must be included in the regulation of cross-border competitions according to condition 9. Not much controversy is involved in any of these three requirements. The Commission acknowledged that consistency of sporting regulations and rules of the game can be achieved only by applicability of uniform, centrally drafted rules.[230] Matters of integrity, such as anti-corruption codes, anti-doping policies, or disciplinary matters are likely to constitute inherent rules in EU sports law much like in the *Meca-Medina* case, and are therefore best left to the competence of governing bodies in charge of their sport (subject to the proportionality principle). They should not be entrusted to clubs and private promoters as undertakings interested in private gain as opposed to safeguarding public interest. Advocate General Kokott similarly saw the uniformity of these rules as enabling participants to compare their performances, which would not be that easy if rules varied greatly from one organiser to another. Without them, in her Opinion, the public's interest and the recognition of the sport might suffer.[231]

Moreover, condition 8 provides that all participant clubs must be licensed by UEFA. In its report on the future of professional football in Europe, the European Parliament firmly supported the UEFA licensing system,[232] whereas the licensing system for clubs in general was listed as an example of a sporting rule unlikely to

---

[230] Communication from the Commission to the European Parliament, the Council, the European Economic and Social Committee, and the Committee of the Regions 'Developing the European Dimension in Sport' COM (2011) 12 final, 18. 1. 2011, para 4.2.

[231] Opinion of AG Kokott in C-49/07 *MOTOE*, para 92.

[232] European Parliament Report on the future of professional football in Europe (2006/2130(INI)), Committee on Culture and Education, final A6-0036/2007, p. 14.

infringe the EU competition provisions in the Commission Staff Working Document.[233] Ensuring the financial stability of sport clubs/teams is seen as one of the objective justifications, as it relates to the organisation and proper conduct of competitive sport.[234] According to the Commission, licensing systems generally aim to ensure that all clubs respect the same basic rules on financial management and transparency, but could also include provisions regarding discrimination, violence, protection of minors and training. The usefulness of robust licensing systems should be acknowledged for professional clubs at European and national levels. Such systems may not go beyond what is necessary for the pursuit of a legitimate objective relating to the proper organisation and conduct of sport.[235] While the applicable licensing system itself must be proportionate, it is a separate question whether the clubs participating in cross-border competitions may be subject to a proportionate licensing system. The Commission Communication on Sport saw club licensing systems as offering a valuable tool to ensure the integrity of competitions and, as discussed above in the section, the regulation of integrity of sport ought to belong to the competence of the governing body. Furthermore, it would be untenable to have different bodies implement different licensing regimes in any open league model based on promotion and relegation. In *Piau*, the General Court accepted that FIFA regulations on a mandatory licensing system for football agents could contribute to economic progress by protecting football players, members of a sporting profession with short playing careers.[236] Similarly, one of many effects of the UEFA Club Licensing and Financial Fair Play Regulations is to protect the interests of football players.

Conditions 10–12 refer to the more controversial centrally controlled match calendar and specify when the clubs participating in a cross-border league are *not* allowed to organise their competitions and schedule their matches. Matters such as the uniform official match calendar are within the regulatory functions of the governing body. In its draft preliminary guidelines on the Application of Competition Rules to Sport of 15 February 1999, the European Commission agreed with the International Rugby Board that control over the official match calendar by a governing body is necessary for the good of the game, ensuring solidarity and development of sport at the grassroots level, matters which individual clubs, if allowed to act in their own self-interest, are unlikely to take into account.[237] Control over the official event calendar is not only necessary to ensure regulatory integrity and a proper balance between different events. It also ensures that certain revenues are generated not

[233] Annex I, para 2.2.1.7 of the Commission Staff Working Document, The EU and Sport: Background and Context, Accompanying Document to the White Paper on Sport, COM(2007) 391 final.

[234] Ibid. Annex I, para 2.1.5.

[235] Paragraph 4.7 of the Commission Staff Working Document.

[236] Case T-193/02 *Laurent Piau v. Commission* [2005] ECR II-209, paras 100–106.

[237] Jonathan Taylor and Adam Lewis 'Governing Body Restraint on Breakaways' paper presented at 'Sport and The Law' conference, London, 31 March 2011.

just for the elite at the top of the pyramid but also for the benefit of football as a whole, as the competitive playing base of the pyramid would shrink without such solidarity.[238] In her opinion on the *MOTOE* case, Advocate General Kokott said that refusing consent to a rival competition may be objectively justified by the need to prevent clashes between competitions.[239] She argued that it is in the interest of the participants in the event as well as spectators and the public in general to have individual competitions in certain sport incorporated into an overreaching framework following a specific timetable. This enables participants and spectators to participate in as many events as possible.[240] It can be argued on the basis of the Advocate General's submission to the Court that preventing clashes between events increases output thus contributing towards the pro-competitive nature of the restriction contained in the Article 49 rule. The requirement to avoid conflict with the uniform international match calendar is closely connected to the obligation on the clubs to release players for the matches of national representative teams. It was argued in Sect. 3.3.6.1 that the compulsory release of players is an inherent and proportionate rule to achieve a set of public interest objectives. Furthermore, preserving viability of national competitions and keeping smaller clubs financially afloat can only be achieved if they are not being ousted in the broadcasting market by the dominant alternative league, which is what condition 12 is aimed at.

Parrish and Miettinen saw the Article 49 rule and UEFA approval policy as escaping the 'restriction' designation under competition provisions if it could be proven that without such a rule national football competitions could be seriously undermined.[241] This could happen, for example, if the cross-border competitions were scheduled at the same time as national competitions, thus replacing them in the broader demand market. Abiding by condition 12 would enable the participating clubs to play in both leagues instead of depleting the national competitions of their best teams and players which in turn affects the interest of both public and broadcasters. The same logic applies to the requirements of condition 11, according to which the matches of an alternative competition may not be played on the same day as UEFA club competitions. In a UEFA press release that was published after the Media Partners International threat was averted, as discussed in Sects. 3.3.2 and 3.3.3, UEFA was opposed to 'any concept susceptible of having a negative influence on the existing domestic and European competitions and of endangering the future of national teams.'[242] Existing football competitions can be harmed, for example, when top teams become dominant players in the sports broadcasting market. This would undermine the ability of the governing bodies to finance the rest of the sport. At the same time, the governing bodies must ensure that the access to the

[238] Ibid.

[239] Opinion of AG Kokott in C-49/07 *MOTOE*, paras 91 and 94.

[240] Ibid. para 94.

[241] Parrish and Miettinen 2008, p. 214.

[242] UEFA Press Release. European Club Football—National Associations, their leagues and clubs want UEFA to remain in charge, 30 July 1998.

broadcasting market remains open for new entrants. Broadcasting time to be allocated to the alternative competitions may become an issue, if a rival is not given any hope of commercial success due to foreclosure in the downstream market. The conditions for approval of cross-border leagues should grant a possibility for healthy economic competition. The Court in *MOTOE* emphasised that '[a] system of undistorted competition, such as that provided for by the Treaty, can be guaranteed only if equality *of opportunity* is secured as between the various economic operators [emphasis added].'[243] The criterion itself providing for the centrally designed calendar does not appear to go further than necessary for the attainment of goals related to effective and proper organisation of sport, as well as solidarity goals. However, it would be important for UEFA to specify the manner of exercise of these regulatory functions in more detail.

The uniformity and uniform application of the regulatory rules mentioned in conditions 7–12 can only be effectively achieved by having all the football clubs in Europe affiliated to the same regulatory structure in accordance with the requirements of condition 3. It is the pyramid structure that helps to ensure that 'the special requirements of sport, such as uniform rules and uniform timetable for competitions, are taken into account'.[244]

According to condition 4, geographical aspects will be taken into consideration and will play a role in the assessment of cross-border competitions by UEFA. This criterion requires further clarification. It appears to indicate that only the clubs from national associations that are in geographical proximity or tied by some other form of geographical logic may fulfil this condition. If so, the pan-European competition prospect would not look promising and only regionally delimited alternative leagues would be considered for approval by UEFA (such as, for example, the Balkan league or Scandinavian league). Moreover, condition 4 indicates the intention of UEFA to support competitions *not* integrated into the promotion and relegation system of European football. In fact, none of the 13 conditions mentions the requirement to integrate the alternative structures with any part of the football pyramid and, together with conditions 10–12, this could imply that participating clubs are expected to treat their cross-border competitions as merely supplementary venture limited by time and space. A refusal to sanction a competition due to the location of the participant clubs is potentially discriminatory and cannot be defended by reference to any of the objective justifications. It should be up to the participant clubs and private promoters how to organise their competitions in Europe in geographical terms and select the option that best suits their commercial goals. Condition 4 should therefore be removed from the list of approval criteria, as the criterion on geographical aspects goes beyond what is necessary to fulfil the objectives related to solidarity and effective and proper organisation of sport.

The most controversial of the 13 UEFA conditions are conditions 2, 5 and 6 as they involve strictly commercial matters. Condition 2 provides that the relevant

[243] Case C-49/07 *MOTOE*, para 51.

[244] Advocate General Kokott in Case C-49/07 *MOTOE*, para 96.

national associations must be the organisers of cross-border competitions and condition 5 places requires the clubs to transfer ownership of those competitions with all commercial rights to national association as organisers. This means essentially transplanting the Champions League model. A truly pan-European applicant league would presumably be asked to transfer the organising functions and commercial rights to UEFA as opposed to national associations, which is in fact the scheme in the current Champions League. Condition 6 further requires that minimum standards should be fixed with regard to the levels of solidarity contributions from the core commercial rights revenues thus acquired.

The purpose of the governing body insisting on organising and commercialising sporting competitions is to control and secure the revenues needed to finance the rest of the sport. Some commentators saw the actions of private promoters and breakaway clubs as undermining the governing body ability to generate funds it needs to invest in the collective, with a consequence that the playing base shrinks, and the quality of the sport at all levels suffers, so reducing popular demand and therefore commercial interest.[245] However, this danger can be averted with a centralisation of the regulatory authority, appropriate solidarity mechanisms, and the instalment of a system of promotion and relegation between the alternative league and the rest of the football pyramid. It is therefore submitted that centralisation of organising and commercial functions with a transfer of ownership is not necessary for solidarity objectives as long as vertical and horisontal solidarity mechanisms exist to effectively ensure financial contributions for the rest of the sport. Should the clubs in an alternative league wish to entrust the commercialising functions to a private promoter or a different agent, this should not, per se, present an obstacle to their project. The objectives related to effective and proper organisation of sport do not necessarily require such centralisation in a governing body either. It has been argued that EU competition law is neutral as regards a choice by a governing body between on the one hand, outsourcing league functions to a separate entity, and on the other hand maintaining the dual functionality of a regulatory and commercial entity.[246] In other words, given that each system of organisation has its own advantages and disadvantages, stakeholders in a specific sport are considered best placed to decide on the structural issues and can choose how to run their discipline in accordance with the requirements of the industry, but within confines of the law. Even though it is generally accepted that the strict pyramidal model is the most efficient way to organise the sport,[247] it is not the only way that can pass the suitability/effectiveness test. Not all sports in Europe, and not all countries in European football, adhere to the pyramidal model and there exist many practical examples of alternative structural arrangements.

For example, in England, the Football Association performs largely regulatory functions while the main concern of the top-level Premier League is profit

---

[245] Jonathan Taylor and Adam Lewis 'Governing Body Restraint on Breakaways' paper presented at 'Sport and The Law' conference, London, 31 March 2011.

[246] Norros 2011, p. 37.

[247] See Sect. 7.6.2.2.

maximising, and organisation and promotion of a top competition between clubs. The Football League consists of three professional leagues below the Premier League and is self-governing. The National League System is below these two leagues and is under the jurisdiction of the Football Association. All of the leagues are hierarchically interconnected via the system of promotion and relegation. In 1992 the Premier League was formed with 20 members of the English First Division breaking away to form their own separate structure. After deduction of specified sums, such as payments to the Professional Footballers Association and Good Causes as approved by shareholders, the Premier League's UK broadcasting money is distributed to clubs as follows: 50 % equally amongst member clubs, 25 % by way of facility fees on live TV appearances; and 25 % depending on the league position at the end of the season, whereby the club finishing 20th receives one share and the club finishing first receives 20 shares. The operating costs of the league are met from overseas broadcasting money and the rest is distributed equally amongst the 20 member clubs. Title sponsorship money is distributed equally amongst all member clubs. Commercial contract and radio contract money is distributed equally amongst the 20 member clubs.[248] Direct financial support from the Premier League to lower league football includes payments to relegated clubs (the so-called 'parachute payments').[249]

Structural reorganisation is relatively common in the Italian football. Currently, Italy has a national regulatory body, the Italian Football Federation (*Federazione Italiana Giuoco Calcio*), that organises national football teams for men and women, the National League of Professionals Serie A (*Lega Nazionale Professionisti Serie A*) governing Serie A, and the National League of Professionals Serie B (*Lega Nazionale Professionisti Serie B*) governing Serie B. Further below in the third and fourth tier are the Prima Divisione and the Seconda Divisione run by the Italian Professional Football League (*Lega Italiana Calcio Professionistico*). Each of the divisions has two subdivisions, which are generally split on the basis of location. Serie D has nine parallel divisions also divided according to geographical location and organised by the *Dipartimento Interregionale* of the National Amateur League (*Lega Nazionale Dilettanti*). Four further levels (Eccellenza, Promozione, Prima Categoria and Seconda Categoria) are organised by regional committees and the last one, Terza Categoria, by provincial committees of the National Amateur League. The system of promotion and relegation ties Italian football leagues. All clubs and leagues, as well as national associations of footballers, referees and trainers are affiliated with the Italian Football Federation.[250] In the National League of Professionals Serie A, 10 % of the revenues are distributed for the purpose of the

---

[248] A study by European Professional Football Leagues 'Financial Solidarity at Leagues and European Level', July 2010.

[249] Seventh Report of Session 2010–2012 'Football Governance'. House of Commons: Culture, Media and Sport Committee, HC 792-I, published on 29 July 2011, p. 50, contains detailed of this arrangement.

[250] For more on the organisation and economics of Italian football see Baroncelli and Caruso 2011, pp. 168–181, and Baroncelli and Caruso 2013, pp. 67–84.

'general solidarity of the system', while the remaining amount is distributed in the following way: 40 % in equal parts among all Serie A clubs based on the so-called market pool, 25 % according to the number of fans in each club, 5 % according to the population of every team city, and 30 % based on sporting results.

In Spain, football is governed by the Royal Spanish Football Federation (*Real Federación Española de Fútbol*). At the insistence of the clubs participating in top flight Spanish competitions, as of the 1984 season this federation delegated powers to the Spanish Professional Football League (*Liga Nacional de Fútbol Profesional*) to organise professional league competitions in Spain in cooperation with the Federation. Each member club of the Spanish Professional Football League sells audiovisual rights of the competitions individually, whereas the sponsorship of the same competitions is exploited by the League collectively. The League enjoys autonomy in its internal organisation and operation. Under Spanish law, clubs are the owners of copyright in their images and of the right to broadcast their matches and can negotiate individual broadcasting contracts to their home matches, which is usually done through an agency. This system created problems of imbalance in the Spanish championship, as FC Real Madrid and FC Barcelona could sell their rights for significantly higher sums than even their next rival FC Valencia. As a consequence, the rest of the clubs in the Spanish top league asked the government to make central negotiations for broadcasting contracts compulsory and give the League more power over the individual clubs.[251] The Spanish government has been considering this proposal since early 2013.[252] Nevertheless, it is to be noted that despite these problems Spanish football is overall one of the most competitive in Europe and the world in both economic and sporting terms.

As an example from other sports, tennis has a global governing body (the International Tennis Federation), a body governing men's professional tennis (the Association of Tennis Professionals), a body governing women's professional tennis (the Women's Tennis Association) and a Grand Slam Committee in charge of the four biggest annual tournaments that are sanctioned by the International Tennis Federation. Developmental professional tours, wheelchair tennis and international circuits for boys and girls under 18 are run by the International Tennis Federation to which all national tennis associations and six regional associations are affiliated. Each pro-tournament owner engages in media and sponsorship deals for the tournaments they organise, while paying certain percentage of the proceeds to the relevant governing bodies.[253]

These examples illustrate that alternatives to conditions 2 and 5, each with their own advantages and disadvantages in relation to European-level football governance, do exist. More specifically, in regard to condition 5 requirement to transfer ownership of commercial rights to a respective governing body, Article 345 TFEU stipulates that

---

[251] For more on the organisation and economics of Spanish football see Gomes et al. 2013, pp. 182–194.

[252] 'La Liga seeks collective TV rights deal to close gap on Premier League' by Andy Hunter, The Guardian, 11 April 2013.

[253] For e.g., all men's professional tournaments (but for Futures that are governed by ITF) pay fees to ATP in accordance with the Chapter III of the ATP World Tour Rulebook 2014.

the system of property ownership is to be determined by the Member States' laws. The issue of who owns the rights in international sporting events (the league, the association or the organiser) may provoke complex legal questions,[254] but it is not an issue that can be dealt with under EU law. However, the allocation of property rights may fall under the scope of EU economic provisions when it conflicts with the Union's goals of economic integration. In its Staff Working Paper, the Commission explained that resolving the ownership question is important as a preliminary point because in cases where the rights are solely owned by the football association (this is the case in France), issues may arise under Article 102 TFEU rather than under Article 101 TFEU, as the sale of rights would be carried out by a single seller and not jointly.[255] In the *UEFA Champions League* decision, the Commission considered that UEFA can 'at best be considered as a co-owner of the rights' to individual matches together with the relevant clubs, but never the sole owner,[256] and therefore Article 101 TFEU was considered applicable. It is, in either case, not a prerequisite that a governing body acting as an organiser and exclusive seller of the broadcasting rights to league matches must possess ownership of those rights. Engaging in commercialisation on behalf of clubs in the agent-like role, or 'at best', as co-owners of the commercial rights, would be a plausible alternative arrangement that would not require the transfer of ownership but would at the same time accomplish the designated objectives.

Condition 6 and arguments for preservation of solidarity mechanisms in European football, regardless of the choice of organisational arrangement, can find a strong support in EU law and policy as discussed in Sect. 7.6.1. The High Court acknowledged in *Greig v. Insole*,[257] that the only competitions likely to generate any substantial profit are top-tier competitions. The teams participating in those competitions buy players that have been developed by less successful and smaller clubs that are dependent on the finances generated at the top level of sport. Taylor and Lewis noted that governing bodies should, at the very least, be able to require those who benefit from the collective to support it and not harm it, and commercial success created by collective must be exploited for the benefit of the whole of the game, and not for the benefit of the few.[258] The professional elite in European football fully utilise the developmental efforts of the governing bodies and they therefore owe some solidarity to the sport. The only matter in question relates to the proportionality of the level of contributions generated from the core commercial rights revenues that UEFA set out as an *example* of an expected solidarity scheme under condition 6. The proper test of proportionality would necessitate detailed calculations to discern the level that would, on the one hand, not make it unattractive and economically unviable for the alternative organisers to enter the

[254] Vollebregt and Brinckman 1998, p. 284.

[255] See Annex I, para 3.1.3.1.2.

[256] Commission Decision in COMP/37.398—Joint Selling of Commercial Rights (UEFA Champions League) [2003] OJ L 291/25, para 122.

[257] [1978] 1 WLR 302, 309.

[258] Jonathan Taylor and Adam Lewis 'Governing Body Restraint on Breakaways' paper presented at 'Sport and The Law' conference, London, 31 March 2011.

market, but that would, on the other hand, offer sufficient financial support for the rest of the sport thus enabling condition 6 to pass the test of suitability/effectiveness under the *Meca-Medina/Wouters* analytical framework. Therefore, it is the level of contributions that might potentially create a problem from the point of view of proportionality, not the solidarity requirement itself.

As long as regulatory authority remains with the federations, alternative leagues are fully integrated into the system of promotion and relegation, and solidarity mechanisms are in place, there is no justified reason for the governing bodies to insist on being a single undertaking in a market for the organisational services of transnational football in Europe or on being the owner of the commercial rights in cross-border competitions. Hence, conditions 2 and 5 appear to go further than necessary for the attainment of the designated objectives, as there are less restrictive means available. Conversely, the solidarity requirement is a restriction that does not go beyond what is required, but the levels of contributions set by the governing body have a potential to offend against the principle of proportionality and should therefore be carefully planned.

7.7 Effect on Intra-Union Trade

It follows from the case law of the Court that

> in order that an agreement between undertakings may affect trade between Member States, it must be possible to foresee with a sufficient degree of probability on the basis of a set of objective factors of law or fact that it may have an influence, direct or indirect, actual or potential, on the pattern of trade between Member States, such as might prejudice the realization of the aim of a single market in all the Member States.[259]

The concept of effect on intra-Union trade serves to establish a jurisdictional threshold between the respective areas of EU and Member States' competence. This analytical point is uncontroversial as regards the Article 49 rule in the UEFA Statutes—the required effect on intra-Union trade exists. Agreements or decisions covering or being implemented in all Member States are by their very nature capable of affecting cross-border economic activity between Member States.[260] UEFA's Article 49 rule is specifically designed to control *cross-border* formations (in the language of the Article 49 rule, 'international competitions') and it applies to all UEFA Member Associations territories. Article 51(1) of the UEFA Statutes, which operates alongside the Article 49 rule prohibits 'combinations or alliances *between* UEFA Member Associations or between leagues or clubs affiliated, directly or indirectly, to *different* UEFA Member Associations [to] be formed without the permission of UEFA'.[261]

---

[259] See, for e.g., Case 42/84 *Remia v Commission* [1985] ECR 2545, para 22.

[260] This follows from the Commission Notice—Guidelines on the effect on trade concept contained in Articles 81 and 82 of the Treaty OJ C 101, 27.4.2004, para 61.

[261] Emphasis added.

7.8 The Conditions of Article 101(3) TEFU

The Commission Guidelines on the application of Article 101(3) TFEU draw a clear distinction between the application of the ancillary restraint concept under the Article 101 prohibition provision and the defence under the exemption provision. Accordingly, balancing of economic benefits produced by restrictive agreements against their anti-competitive effects can take place only in the framework of the exemption provision.[262] The application of the ancillary restraint concept does not involve any weighing of pro-competitive and anti-competitive effects, but is motivated by a somewhat more subjective doctrine that justifies the restriction on competition on the basis of being objectively necessary for the implementation of legitimate goals in the public interest.

Article 101(3) TFEU provides that an agreement found restrictive under Article 101(1) TFEU may be declared applicable if it fulfils four cumulative conditions that include: contributing to improving the production or distribution of goods or to promoting technical or economic progress, allowing consumers a fair share of the resulting benefits, restrictions which are necessary to the attainment of the objectives, and which do not afford undertakings the possibility of eliminating competition in respect of a substantial part of the product or service concerned. An accompanying document to the White Paper makes clear that a justification under Article 101(3) TFEU is most likely to apply where a rule is *not inherent* in the organisation or proper conduct of sport so as to justify the application of the *Meca-Medina/Wouters* test, but where the beneficial effects of a rule outweigh its restrictive effects.[263] Consistency requires that Article 101(3) be interpreted as precluding any application of this exemption to restrictive agreements that constitute an abuse of a dominant position. On the other hand, a company holding a dominant position may benefit from an exemption under Article 101(3) of the Treaty when its conditions are fulfilled.[264] In the *Piau* case, decided in the sporting context, the General Court held that if the conduct of a dominant company satisfies all the conditions of Article 101(3) such conduct should not be classified as an abuse under Article 102 of the Treaty.[265]

However, it is submitted as per the convergence theory set in Chap. 6, that these considerations are only important when competition law alone applies to the case to the exclusion of internal market rules. In *Murphy*, where both sets of provisions were relevant, the Court only referred to its finding that the measure was disproportionate under internal market law to hold that the exemption in Article 101(3)

[262] Commission Guidelines on the application of Article 81(3) of the Treaty OJ C 101/97, para 30. See also Case T-112/99 *Métropole télévision (M6), Suez-Lyonnaise des eaux, France Télécom and Télévision française 1 SA (TF1) v Commission of the European Communities* [2001] ECR II-2459, para 107.

[263] Commission Staff Working Document, Annex I, para 2.1.6.

[264] See Commission Guidelines on the application of Article 81(3) of the Treaty, *OJ C 101*, 27.04.2004, pp. 97–118, para 106.

[265] See Case T-193/02 *Piau*, para 119.

TFEU did not apply in the case.[266] This is a confirmation of the Opinion of the Advocate General in *Murphy*, who argued that the 'conflicting assessments of the fundamental freedoms and competition law are to be avoided in principle [...]'. Consistency between the economic provisions of the Treaty demands that a measure considered disproportionate under the objective justification framework of the internal market provisions and the *Meca-Medina/Wouters* test cannot obtain a justification under Article 101(3). If a measure survives both the objective justification test and the *Meca-Medina/Wouters* test then there is no reason to examine it further under Article 101(3) TFEU. If a measure fails their shared test, it means that it has failed to establish its legality under EU free movement law and to prove that it is worthy of the exception. Even if such a measure produced economic efficiencies which outweigh the negative effects of restraints on competition under Article 101(3) TFEU, that fact still does not legalise the measure under freedom of movement provisions. The measure will be illegal and will have to be abandoned or modified to comply with the requirements of free movement rules. In other words, once the internal market rules apply alongside competition law, as is the case with the Article 49 rule of UEFA Statutes, Article 101(3) TFEU becomes obsolete. This is the opinion shared by Advocate General Lenz in Bosman in whose view

> it would admittedly appear theoretically conceivable that the Commission might grant those rules, which are in breach of Article [45], an exemption from the prohibition in Article [101(1)]. Since such an exemption would, however, make no difference to the breach of Article [45], it would make sense for the Commission to take that factor into account in the exemption procedure. A uniform result ought to be aimed at in any case. That would mean that an exemption under Article [101(3)] would also have to be ruled out.[267]

The result of the analysis of any measure to which the *Meca-Medina/Wouters* framework applies, and which is being examined also from the internal market point of view, will *exclusively* depend on the result of the analysis under the internal market and *Meca-Medina/Wouters* framework.

7.9 Collective Dominance and Collusion by Elite Clubs

Individual elite clubs are undertakings for all purposes[268] and thus the situations originating from contractual relations or concerted practices between these clubs may breach Article 101 TFEU. In the *Bosman* case, Advocate General Lenz

---

[266] Paragraph 145. The Court's selected reference to paras 105–124 also confirms the point made above in Sect. 4.10.2.4, that encouraging public to attend and participate in matches is probably not accepted as objective worthy of protection under EU law, and that the Court was only dealing with the point of proportionality.

[267] Opinion of AG Lenz in C-415/93 *Bosman*, para 278.

[268] Opinion of Advocate General Lenz in C-415/93 *Bosman*, para 255.

considered that football clubs in a professional league could be 'united by such economic links' to be regarded as collectively dominant.[269] This in particular applies to the elite clubs in European football, former members of G14 and the addresses of the Media Partners proposal (as argued in Sect. 7.4.2.2 that spelled out the links between the elite clubs that support the conclusion on tacit coordination). Hence, their behaviour may offend against Articles 102 TFEU and/or 101 TFEU.

Some of the actions of the elite clubs addressed in the Chap. 3, such as the pressure exerted in the context of *Oulmers* litigation/player release rule, or the composition of the Executive Board of the ECA, can be considered as an abuse of dominant position and a concerted practice. In fact, every time that elite group of clubs exerts pressure over a regulatory body to alter the system so as to serve their common commercial interests to the detriment of the smaller clubs and the sport as a whole may constitute a breach of competition law provisions. Van den Brink argued that the top clubs could be found to engage in a concerted practice under Article 101(1) TFEU and an abuse of their (collective) dominant position under Article 102 TFEU in trying to force football's regulatory bodies to adapt the European leagues solely to their benefit.[270] Pursuing commercial goals by breakaway threats, or any other kind of pressure resulting from the position of collective dominance and/or collusion, should not be allowed to negatively affect the competition on the market for provision of clubs' services and competitiveness of other actors on that market, or stand in the way of public interest goals being safeguarded by the governing bodies. The dominance of the elite clubs in Europe as powerful 'buyers' of transnational organisational services[271] fits the concept of 'superdominance' as elaborated by Advocate General Fennelly in *Compagnie Maritime Belge.*[272] It confers onto them a correspondingly high level of special responsibility not to distort competition.[273]

However, taking a hard stand or a legal action in response to the behaviour of elite clubs by UEFA could possibly cause an unsanctioned breakaway of the type envisaged under the Media Partners proposal in 1998. Such a formation would be prone to legal challenges.

First and foremost, many commentators have been of the opinion that a closed European Superleague would not pass the scrutiny under the EU competition law. The Commission could open up an *ex officio* investigation into such closed league, while UEFA and national associations would have recourse to legal action at their disposal. A study on the professional sport in the internal market pointed out that '[q]uite apart from the difficulties that such a league is likely to encounter in gaining acceptance in different cultures, and UEFA's opposition, the closed circle

[269] Ibid. para 285.

[270] Van den Brink 2000, p. 426.

[271] See Sects. 7.4.2 and 7.3.1.

[272] See Opinion of Advocate General in C-396/96 P *Compagnie Maritime Belge,* para 137.

[273] See Sect. 5.7 on the concepts of superdominance and special responsibility.

model for a European League will not work in practice, for the sole reason that it is contrary to the provisions of European competition law.'[274] Van den Brink did not necessarily see a new European Superleague as a bad development, as long as it has a fair system of relegation and qualification and part of the broadcasting revenue is used to the advantage of the smaller clubs, as 'it would clearly be in the interest of fair competition and therefore all participating clubs to ensure that the small and big clubs do not lose touch with each other'.[275] He was of the opinion that Article 101(1) TFEU would preclude the emergence of a football Superleague with discriminative entrance requirements and long-term exclusive participation for the privileged few.[276] Similarly, Parrish and Miettinen argued that in order to comply with Articles 101 and 102 TFEU the closed league as a cartel of undertakings would be expected to adopt fair and non-discriminatory access rules, either by way of promotion or relegation or by way of franchise system. A closed league system without such access conditions would be precluded under those Treaty articles as this could foreclose the market to aspiring entrants and amount to abuse of a dominant market position.[277] Conversely, Hornsby defended the closed league model and saw it as a good candidate for sporting exception.[278] It must be emphasised, however, that the author adopted this line of argument in 2001 when the when the contours of the sporting exception concept in EU law were still far from clear.

Apart from launching a challenge to a closed league model, another option at the disposal of UEFA and national associations would be to impose boycotts on the participating clubs and/or their players, and be ready to defend those boycotts in ensuing legal proceedings. Such boycotts may involve, for example, banning the participating clubs and/or their players from championships organised by national associations and UEFA. There is no doubt that this would trigger the application of the EU law on free movement and competition. Restrictions may be defended by reference to the specificity of sport under Article 165(1), financial solidarity goals, preserving viability of European and national competitions, and the need for proper and effective organisation of sport. As the attack on the functioning of football, future of national and European competitions, and the central regulatory functions of the governing bodies would be particularly severe in case of pan-European elite breakaway, the robust response by UEFA and national associations might be deemed proportionate by the EU institutions if it remains confined to what is necessary for the realisation of the said public interest goals.

Secondly, in *ENIC* ethical considerations on multi-club ownership prevented Commission to find the rule restrictive under competition law, and instead, it was considered 'inherent'. Specifically, the rule stated that no two or more clubs

---

[274] Professional Sport in the Internal Market, Project No IP/A/IMCO/ST/2005-004, Commissioned by the Committee on the Internal Market and Consumer Protection of the European Parliament (September 2005), p. 61.

[275] Van den Brink 2000, p. 426.

[276] Ibid.

[277] Parrish and Miettinen 2008, p. 213.

[278] Hornsby 2001, pp. 162–167.

participating in a UEFA club competition may be directly or indirectly controlled by the same entity or managed by the same person. According to the Commission the rule was designed to 'ensure the uncertainty of the outcome and to guarantee that the consumer has the perception that the games played represent honest sporting competitions […]'.[279] CAS in *ENIC* stated that the crucial element of integrity in football is the public's perception of the authenticity of results and that the most important requirement for football is not honesty in itself or authenticity of results in itself but rather the public perception of such honesty and such authenticity.[280] From a league-wide economic perspective, an increase in competitive balance and the absence of dominant teams brings about the increase in attractiveness of the championship and is therefore economically preferable. The traditional notion of economic competition where undertakings strive to attain monopoly status in order to maximise profits does not apply in a league.[281] In accordance with this classic economic theory, profit maximisation strategies are optimal when teams are relative equals. This might create a concern from the point of view of integrity of competitions in breakaway leagues. Given that match-fixing has plagued European football for long and that effective mechanisms of post control to discover, and prior control to prevent this sporting fraud do not exist, integrity of competitions in the breakaway structure could become an issue if its ownership structures lend themselves to enhanced possibility or incentive to fix the outcome of matches. A prohibition on certain ownership structures in cross-border club competitions with the purpose of ensuring fair sporting competition would therefore be necessary and might still fall under regulatory authority of UEFA. In addition, it is worth mentioning that all EU Member States treat match fixing as criminal offence,[282] thus the possibility of conflict of interests must be avoided by proportionate means at any cost. Consumers must have the *perception* that competition represents an honest game and wagering in the sports betting markets must remain a matter of relative sporting chance. Same ethical considerations as in *ENIC* would apply in the case of breakaway leagues and any conflict of interest that can negatively affect perception of integrity of competition should be avoided. In addition, in the line with Commission reasoning in *ENIC*, public's perception of integrity is an essential precondition to keep the consumer confidence and interest, as well as marketability of sporting competitions. Otherwise, as an inevitable consequence over time, '[c]lubs would be less capable of extracting value from ancillary activities and investment in clubs would lose value'.[283] Without such value, the breakaway competitions would produce less profit and consequently, effectiveness of financial solidarity mechanisms would be affected. UEFA could therefore have a

279 Commission Decision in Case COMP IV/37.806—ENIC/UEFA, para 28.

280 CAS arbitral award dated 20 August 1999 in Case CAS 98/200 *AEK Athens and Slavia Prague v. UEFA*, cited in para 20 of Commission Decision in Case COMP IV/37.806—ENIC/UEFA.

281 Dietl et al. 2011, p. 3.

282 Study on Match-fixing in Sport: A Mapping of the Criminal Law Provisions in EU 27' (2012), pp. 15–16.

283 Commission Decision in Case COMP IV/37.806—ENIC/UEFA, para 32.

legitimate claim of *negatively* regulating ownership structures in a breakaway league to the extent necessary to prevent the conflict of interests.

Finally, certain legal considerations discussed in Sect. 5.5.4 may preclude the joint sales of broadcasting rights by the clubs, as it would amount to price fixing by the league. Clubs could argue for the exemption under Article 101(3) on the basis of improved distribution and economic efficiencies, and rely on other arguments brought up by the UEFA and accepted by the Commission in the *UEFA Champions League* case.[284] However, even though there is no such thing as *per se* violation of Article 101(1) TFEU under the EU competition law, it is highly unlikely that the Commission and the Court would be receptive to such arguments under Article 101(3) in the context of hard-core cartel such as price fixing. Weatherill was also of the opinion that collective selling designed solely a tool of wealth maximisation for the participants alone would not be exempted.[285] There are few options available to clubs to avoid joint selling as a legal hurdle and the most obvious one is for the clubs to engage in individual sales of broadcasting rights. However, this would mean missing the economic efficiencies involved in central marketing, which generates more profits for the clubs in the professional league than individual sales. Another option for the clubs is to create a single economic entity by, for instance, setting up a full-function joint venture.[286] On the basis of annual turnovers of the elite clubs such joint venture will have the 'EU dimension' in accordance with Article 1 of the EU Merger Regulation, and might not be approved by the Commission, or would require commitments (for example, divestitures) which would defeat its profit maximising purpose. Moreover, a joint venture owned by the clubs in a professional league would be possible to implement only in a closed league model and would nevertheless be subject to review under Article 102 TFEU.

The least radical and legally most acceptable set up for any newly formed breakaway league is to remain structurally integrated via the system of promotion and relegation, as well as to remain financially connected by solidarity mechanism with the football pyramid. This could enable the league to obtain recourse to the concept of sporting exception under EU law. Otherwise, such a defence would not be available for exploitation to a purely commercial entity that acts solely to safeguard its private interest. Having said that, 'politics will dictate that there will be a number of interim models before the league finally takes shape, all of which will conform to

---

[284] Commission Decision in Case COMP/37.398—Joint Selling of Commercial Rights (UEFA Champions League) [2003] OJ L 291/25, paras 136–196.

[285] Weatherill 2004, p. 131.

[286] In certain circumstances, a joint venture may be considered full-function even if it does not own the resources that it needs in order to operate on the market, provided it has sufficiently firm access to such resources. In *Celanese/Degussa* (*Case COMP/M.3056, 11 June 2003*), ownership of certain production facilities that were to be used by the joint venture was retained by one of the parents, for technical reasons. Despite this, the Commission confirmed that the joint venture was full-function, as it would have exclusive access to the production capacity of the plant in question. See http://uk.practicallaw.com/1-107-3702.

the open circle model […]'.[287] At the end of this volume, it must be acknowledged that is not inconceivable that the distant future might evolve in the direction that will require a different legal approach to serve football's public interest goals.

7.10 Concluding Remarks

A potential legal conflict brought about by the Article 49 rule in the UEFA Statutes is as much a challenge to EU policy as it is a legal challenge under economic provisions of the Treaty. A decision that would hold this controversial rule illegal and contrary to the free market principles would certainly send a shockwave of new financial arrangements and restructuring in the football industry throughout Europe. However, fully supporting an economic-based approach and demolishing the pyramid structure would be politically embarrassing. As apparent from the discussion in Sect. 3.2.1, EU sports policy is built on socio-cultural considerations that strongly support the preservation of the traditional European model of sports structures and recognise the central role of sports federations in ensuring solidarity between different levels of sport. Even though policy documents are not legally binding they played a role in the Court's sports jurisprudence and were cited in its sports-related judgments of *Deliège* and *Lehtonen*. In para 77 of *Bosman*, the Court accepted that the possible practical consequences of its judicial decisions on the organisation of football as a whole must be carefully weighed, but that this cannot go so far as to diminish the objective character of the law and compromise its application. Thus, it can be expected that a certain degree of political pressure on the Commission and the Court, as well as the pressure of practical consequences on the organisation of European football, will not be ignored.

A decision upholding the legality of the Article 49 rule of UEFA Statutes along with all of its 13 accompanying requirements would make UEFA chiefly responsible for the future structure of European football and, at least for the time being, preserve the structural *status quo*. The most important unintended consequence of such an outcome would be a shift of balance in the power struggles in football governance in favour of UEFA, as breakaway threats by elite clubs would become a matter of the past. However, it is highly unlikely that the Article 49 rule of the UEFA Statutes would find such unconditional support in EU law. As discussed in Sect. 7.6.4.3, some of the 13 requirements placed on the clubs aspiring to create alternative leagues go beyond what is necessary for the attainment of the relevant objectives and, as such, fails to conform to the limits of proportionality principle under the *Meca-Medina/Wouters* test and the internal market objective justification framework.

Finally, one must remember that the EU institutions do not have competence to impose a particular structural model on any sport in Europe, but they may prohibit

[287] Professional Sport in the Internal Market, Project No IP/A/IMCO/ST/2005-004, Commissioned by the Committee on the Internal Market and Consumer Protection of the European Parliament (September 2005), p. 62.

any arrangements within the chosen models that offend against economic provisions of the Treaty. Ultimately and exclusively, it is up to the leading actors in European football to decide on their regulatory and organisational/commercial strategies within the limits of the legal and practical considerations discussed in this volume.

References

Baroncelli A, Caruso R (2011) The organisation and economics of Italian Serie A: a brief overall view. Rivista di Diritto ed Economia Dello Sport 7:67–85

Baroncelli A, Caruso R (2013) The organisation and economics of Italian top football. In: Gammelsater H, Senaux B (eds) Organisation and governance of top football across Europe: an institutional perspective. Routledge, London, pp 168–181

Cygan A (2007) Competition and free movement issues in the regulation of formula one races. In: Bogusz B, Cygan A, Szyszczak E (eds) The regulation of sport in the European Union. Edward Elgar, Cheltenham, pp 74–94

Dietl H et al (2011) Organisational differences between U.S. Major leagues and European leagues: implications for salary cap. International Association of Sports Economists, Working paper series, Paper no 11-05

Ducrey et al (2003) UEFA and football governance: a new model. Adoptions for the challenges of modern football. Centre International D'Etude Du Sport. http://www.academia.edu/173028/UEFA_and_Football_Governance_A_New_Model

Faull J, Nikpay A (2007) The EC law of competition, 2nd edn. Oxford University Press, Oxford

Gardiner S (1998) The law and hate speech: 'Ooh, aah, Cantona' and the demonisation of 'the Other'. In: Brown A (ed) Fanatics! Power, identity and fandom in football. Routledge, London, pp 249–264

Gippini-Fournier E (2010) The elusive standard of proof in EU competition cases. World Compet 33:187–207

Gomes S, Marti C, Bofafull Mollo C (2013) Commercialisation and transformation in Spanish top football. In: Gammelsater H, Senaux B (eds) Organisation and governance of top football across Europe: an institutional perspective. Routledge, London, pp 182–194

Harbo T-I (2010) The function of the proportionality principle in EU law. Eur Law J 16:158–185

Halgreen L (2004) European sports law: a comparative analysis of the European and American models of sport. Forlaget Thomson, Copenhagen

Hoehn T, Szymanski S (1999) European football: the structure of leagues and revenue sharing. Econ Policy 14:204–240

Hornsby S (2001) 'Closed Leagues': a prime candidate for the 'Sporting Exception' in European competition law? Int Sports Law Rev 2:162–167

Kaburakis A, Lindholm J, Rodenberg R (2012) British pubs, decoder cards and the future of intellectual property licensing after Murphy. Columbia J Eur Law 18:307–322

Lavrijssen S (2010) What role for National Competition Authorities in protecting non-competition interests after Lisbon? Eur Law Rev 35:636–659

McDermott J (2010) Direct v. indirect discrimination in European football: the legal differences between UEFA's Homegrown Player Rule and FIFA's '6+5' proposal. Texas Rev Entertain Sports Law 11:267–294

Noll (2003) The organization of sport leagues. Stanford Institute for Economic Policy Research, SIEPR Discussion Paper no 02-43

Norros O (2011) Does the outsourcing of a sports league affect its evaluation under EU competition law? Int Sports Law J 3–4:29–37

O'Donoghue R, Padilla AJ (2006) Law and economics of article 82 EC. Hart Publishing, Oxford

Parrish R, Miettinen S (2008) Sporting exception in European Union law. T.M.C. Asser Press, The Hague

Pijetlovic K (2010) Another classic of EU sports jurisprudence: legal implications of Olympique Lyonnais SASP v. Olivier Bernard and Newcastle UFC (C-325/08). Eur Law Rev 35:858–869

Pijetlovic K, Nyman-Metcalf K (2013) Liberalising the market for satellite transmission: interplay between intellectual property rights, specificity of sport and TFEU economic provisions in Murphy (joined cases C-403/08 and C-429/08). Int Sports Law J 13:82–96

Rousseva E (2005) Modernising by eradicating: how the commission's new approach to Article 81 EC dispenses with the need to apply Article 82 EC to vertical restraints. Common Market Law Rev 42:587–638

Van den Brink JP (2000) EC competition law and the regulation of football: Part 2. Eur Compet Law Rev 21:420–427

Vollebregt E, Brinckman D (1998) The marketing of sport and its relation to E.C. competition law. Eur Compet Law Rev 19:281–288

Weatherill S (2004) Sport as culture in EU law. In: Craufurd SR (ed) Culture in European Union law. Oxford University Press, Oxford, pp 113–146

Weatherill S (2005) Is the pyramid compatible with EC Law? Int Sports Law J (3–4):3–7

Weatherill S (2007) Overlapping legal orders: what is the 'Purely Sporting' rule. In: Bogusz B, Cygan A, Szyszczak E (eds) The regulation of sport in the European Union. Edward Elgar, Cheltenham, pp 48–73

Weatherill S (2008) Article 82 EC and sporting 'Conflict of Interest': the judgment in *MOTOE*. Int Sports Law J 3–4 (special addendum)

Weatherill S (2009) The influence of EU law on sports governance. In: Gardiner S, Parrish R, Siekmann CR (eds) EU, sport, law and policy: regulation, re-regulation and representation. T.M.C Asser Press, The Hague, pp 79–100

Whish R (2009) Competition law, 6th edn. Oxford University Press, Oxford

Table of Cases

EU Courts

Joined Cases 56 and 58/64 *Etablissements Consten SA & Grunding-Verkaufs-GmbH v. Commission* [1966] ECR 299.
Case 56/65 *Société La Technique Minière v. Maschinenbau Ulm GmbH* [1966] ECR 235.
Case 23/67 *Brasserie de Haecht SA v. Wilkin* [1967] ECR 407.
Case 5/69 *Völk v. Vervaecke* [1969] ECR 295.
Case 41/69 *ACF Chemiefarma NV. v. Commission (the Quinine Cartel)* [1970] ECR 661.
Case 48/69 *ICI v. Commission* [1972] ECR 619.
Case 6/72 *Europemballange Corporation and Continental Can Company Inc. v. Commission* [1973] ECR 215.
Case 8/72 *Vereeniging van Cementhandelaren v. Commission* [1972] ERC 977.
Cases 6 and 7/73 *Istituto Chemioterapico Italiano Spa and Commercial Solvents Corp. v. Commission* [1974] ECR 223.
Case 2/74 *Reyners v. Belgian State* [1974] ECR 631.
Case 33/74 *Van Binsbergen v. Bestuur van de Bedrijfsvereniging voor de Metaalnijverheid* [1974] ECR 1299.
Case 36/74 *Walrave and Koch v. Union Cycliste Internationale and others* [1974] ECR 1405.
Case 43/75 *Gabrielle Defrenne v. Société anonyme belge de navigation aérienne Sabena* [1976] ECR 455.
Case 13/76 *Gaetano Donà v. Mario Mantero* [1976] ECR 1333.
Case 26/76 *Metro SB-Großmärkte GmbH & Co. KG (Metro I) v. Commission* [1977] ECR 1875.
Case 27/76 *United Brands v. Commission* [1978] ERC 207.
Case 71/76 *Thieffry v. Conseil de l' Ordre des Avocats à la Cour de Paris* [1977] ECR 765.
Case 85/76 *Hoffmann-La Roche v. Commission* [1979] ECR 461.

K. Pijetlovic, *EU Sports Law and Breakaway Leagues in Football*,
ASSER International Sports Law Series, DOI 10.1007/978-94-6265-048-0

Case 106/77 *Amministrazione delle Finanze dello Stato v. Simmenthal SpA* [1978] ECR 629.

Case 22/78 *Hugin Kassaregister v. Commission* [1979] ECR 1869.

Case 175/78 *Regina v. Saunders* [1979] ECR 1129.

Case 149/79 *Commission v. Belgium* [1982] ECR 1845.

Case 270/80 *Polydor Limited and RSO Records Inc.v. Harlequen Records Shops Limited and Simons Records Limited,* [1982] ECR 329.

Case 15/81 *Gaston Schul Douane Expediteur BV v. Inspecteur der Invoerrechten en Accijnzen, Roosendaal* [1982] ECR 1409.

Case 322/81 *Nederlandsche Banden Industrie Michelin (Michelin I) v. Commission* [1983] ECR 3461.

Case 7/82 *Gesellschaft zur Verwertung von Leistungsschutzrechten mbH (GVL) v Commission* [1983] ECR 483.

Case 96/82 *IAZ International Belgium v. Commission* [1983] ECR 3369.

Case 319/82 *Société de Vente de Ciments et Bétons de l'Est v. Kerpen & Kerpen GmbH & Co KG* [1983] ECR 4173.

Cases 29 and 30/83 *Compagnie Royale Asturienne des Mines SA and Rheinzink GmbH v. Commission* [1984] ECR 1679.

Case 42/84 *Remia BV and Others v. Commission* [1985] ECR 2545.

Case 161/84 *Pronuptia de Paris GmbH v. Pronuptia de Paris Irmgard Schillgallis* [1986] ECR 353.

Case 311/84 *Centre Belge d'Etudes du Marché-Télémarketing (CBEM) v. CLT SA* [1985] ECR 3261.

Joined Cases 89, 104, 114, 116, 117, 125 to 129/85 *Ahlström Osakeyhtiö and others v. Commission of the European Communities(Wood Pulp II)* [1993] ECR I-1307.

Case 62/86 *AKZO v. Commission* [1991] ECR I-3359.

Case 66/86 *Ahmed Saeed Flugreisen and Silver Line Reisebüro GmbH v. Zentrale zur Bekämpfung unlauteren Wettbewerbs e.V.* [1989] ECR 803.

Case 247/86 *Société alsacienne et lorrainne de telecommunications et d'électronique v. SA Novasam* [1988] ERC 5987.

Case 30/87 *Corinne Bodson v. Pompes Funèbres* [1988] ECR 2497, [1989] 4 CMLR 984.

Case C-227/87 *Sandoz Prodotti Farmaceutici Spa. v. Commission* [1990] ECR I-45.

Cases C-69/88 *Krantz v. Ontvanger der Directe Belastingen* [1990] ECR I-583.

Case T-30/89 *Hilti v. Commission* [1991] ECR II-1439.

Case T-51/89 *Tetra Pack Rausing SA v. Commission* [1990] ECR II-309.

Cases T-68/89 etc. *Società Italiano Vetro SpA v. Commission* [1992] ECR II-1403.

Case C-260/89 *Elliniki Radiophonia Tiléorassi AE (ERT) and Panellinia Omospondia Syllogon Prossopikou v. Dimotiki Etairia Pliroforissis and Sotirios Kouvelas and Nicolaos Avdellas and others* [1991] ECR I-2925.

Case C-2/90 *Commission v. Belgium (Walloon Waste)* [1992] ECR I-4431.

Case C-41/90 *Höfner and Elser v. Macrotron [1991] ERC I-1979.*

Cases C-241-242/91 P *RTE & ITP v. Commission* [1995] ECR I-743.

Case C-267 and 268/91 *Criminal Proceedings against Keck and Mithouard* [1993] ECR I-6097.
Case C-320/91 *Criminal Proceedings against Paul Corbeau* [1993] ERC I-2533.
Case C-19/92 *Dieter Kraus v. Land Baden Württemberg* [1993] ECR I-1663.
Case C-93/92 *Motorradcenter v. Pelin Baskiciogullari* [1993] ECR I-5009.
Case C-250/92 *Gøttrup-Klim e.a. Grovvareforeninger v Dansk Landbrugs Grovvareselskab AmbA* [1994] ECR I-5641.
Case C-393/92 *Almelo v. NV Energiebedriff Ijsselmij* [1994] ECR I-1477.
Cases T-24/93, T-25/93, T-26/93 and T-28/93 *Compagnie Maritime Belge v Commission* [1996] ECR II-1201.
Case C-323/93 *Centre d'Insémination de la Crespelle v. Coopérative de la Mayenne* [1994] ECR I-5077.
Case C-415/93 *Union Royale Belge Sociétés de Football Association and others v. Bosman and others* [1995] ECR I-4921.
Case C-55/94 *R. Gebhard v. Consiglio dell'Ordine degli Avvocati e Procuratori di Milano* [1995] ECR I-4165.
Case T-290/94 *Kaysersberg SA v. Commission*, judgment of 27 November 1997.
Case C-333/94 P *Tetra Pak International SA v. Commission* [1996] ECR I-5951.
Joined Cases T-374-5, 384 and 388/94 *European Night Services v. Commission* [1998] ECR II-3141.
Cases T-25/95 etc. *Cimenteries CBR SA v Commission* [2000] ECR II-491.
Cases C-225-227/95 *Kapasakalis, Skiathis and Kougiagakas v. Greece* [1998] ECR I-4329.
Case C-265/95 *Commission v. France (Spanish Strawberries)* [1997] ECR I-6959.
Case C-343/95 *Diego Calì & Figli v. SEPG* [1996] ECR I-1547.
Case C-35/96 *Commission v. Italy* [1998] ECR I-3851.
Joined Cases C-51/96 and C-191/97 *Christelle Deliège v. Ligue francophone de judo et disciplines associées ASBL, Ligue belge de judo ASBL, Union européenne de judo and François Pacquée* [2000] ECR I-2549.
Case C-67/96 *Albany International BV v. Stichting Bedrijfspensioenfonds Textielindustrie* [1999] ECR I-5751.
Case T-102/96 *Gencor Ltd. V. Commission* [1999] ECR II-0753.
Case T-111/96 *ITT Promedia v. Commission* [1998] ECR II-2937.
Case C-176/96 *Jyri Lehtonen and Castors Canada Dry Namur-Braine ASBL v. Fédération royale belge des sociétés de basket-ball ASBL (FRBSB)* [2000] ECR I-2681.
Case C-203/96 *Chemische Afvalstoffen Dusseldorp BV and Others v Minister van Volkshuisvesting, Ruimtelijke Ordening en Milieubeheer* [1998] ECR I-4075.
Joined Cases C-395/96 P and C-396/96 P *Compagnie Maritime Belge Transports SA, Compagnie Maritime Belge SA and Dafra-Lines A/S v Commission* [2000] ECR I-1365.
Case C-7/97 *Oscar Bronner GmbH & Co. KG v. Mediaprint Zeitungs* [1998] ECR I-7791.
Cases C-10-22/97 *Ministero delle Finanze v. IN.CO. GE'90 Srl* [1998] ECR I-6307.

Case C-67/97 *Criminal Proceedings against DitlevBluhme* [1998] ECR I-6717.

Cases C-115, 116 & 117/97 *Brentjens' Handelsonderneming BV v Stichting Bedrijfspensioenfonds voor de Handel in Bouwmaterialen* [1999] ECR I-6025.

Case C-219/97 *Maatschappij Drijvende Bokken BV v. Stichting Pensioenfonds voor de Vervoer- en Havenbedrijven* [1999] ECR I-6121.

Case T-228/97 *Irish Sugar plc v. Commission*, judgment of 7 October 1999.

Case T-65/98 *Van den Bergh Foods v. Commission* [2003] ECR II-4653.

Joined Cases C-180/98 to C-184/98 *Pavlov and Others* [2000] ECR I-6451.

Case C-190/98 *Graf v Filzmozer Maschinebau GmbH* [2000] ECR I-493.

Case T-191/98 *Atlantic Container Line AB v Commission of the European Communities* [2003] ECR II-3275.

Case C-281/98 *Roman Angonese v Cassa di Risparmio di Bolzano SpA* [2000] ECR I-4139.

Case T-112/99 *Métropole télévision (M6) and others* [2001] ECR II-2459.

Case T-144/99 *Institute of Professional Representatives before the European Patent Office v. Commission* [2001] ECR II-1087.

Case T-219/99 *British Airways plc v. Commission* judgment of 17 December 2003.

Case C-309/99 *J.C.J Wouters, J.W. Savelbergh, Price Waterhouse Belastingadviseurs BV v. Algemene Raad van de Nederlandse Orde van Advocaten* [2002] ECR I-1577.

Case T-319/99 *Federación Nacional de Empresas de Instrumentación Cientifica, Médica, Técnica y Dental (FENIN)* v. *Commission* ECR II-351.

Case T-342/99 *Airtours plc. v. Commission* [2002] ECR II-2585, judgment of 6 June 2002.

Case C-438/00 *Deutscher Handballbund v. Kolpak* [2003] ECR I-4135.

Case T-203/01 *Manufacture française des pneumatiques Michelin v Commission (Michelin II)* [2003] ECR II-4071.

Case T-210/01 *General Electric v. Commission* judgment of 14 December 2005.

Joined Cases C-264/01, C-306/01, C-354/01 and C-355/01 *AOK Bundesverband and Others* [2004] ECR I-2493.

Case T-114/02 *BaByliss SA v. Commission*, judgment of 3 April 2003.

Case T-193/02 *Laurent Piau v. Commission* [2005] ECR II-209.

Case T-313/02 *David Meca-Medina and Igor Majcen v Commission* [2004] ECR II-3291.

Case C-265/03 *Igor Simutenkov v. Ministerio de Educación y Cultura, Real Federación Española de Fútbol* [2005] ECR I-2579.

Case C-470/03 *A.G.M.- COS.MET Srl v Suomen Valtio, Tarmo Lahtinen* [2007] ECR I-2749.

Case C-551/03 P *General Motors BV v. Commission* [2006] ECR I-3173.

Case T-99/04 *AC-Treuhand AG v Commission* [2008] ECR II-1501.

Case C-222/04 *Ministero dell'Economia e delle Finanze v.Cassa di Risparmio di Firenze and Others* [2006] ECR I-289.

Cases C-403/04 P and 405/04 P *Sumitomo Metal Industries Ltd. v. Commission*, judgment of 25 January 2007.

Case C-434/04 *Criminal Proceedings against Ahokainen and Leppik* [2006] ECR I-9171.

Case C-519/04 *David Meca-Medina and Igor Majcen v Commission* [2006] ECR I-6991.
Case C-341/05 *Laval un Partneri Ltd. v. Svenska Byggnadsarbetareförbundet and Others* [2007] ECR I-11767.
Case C-438/05 *International Transport Workers' Federation. and. Finnish Seamen's Union. v. Viking Line ABP and OÜ Viking Line Eesti* [2007] ECR I-10779.
Case C-243/06 *SA Sporting du Pays de Charleroi, G14 Groupment des clubs de football européens v Fédération internationale de football association (FIFA),* removed from the Court's registrar.
Case 279/06 *CEPSA Estaciones de Servicio SA v. LV Tobar e Hijos SL,* judgement of 11 September 2008.
Cases C-468-478/06 *Sot. Lelos kai Sia and others EE v. GlaxoSmithKline AEVE Farmakeftikon Proionton* [2008] ECR I-7139.
Joined Cases C-501/06 P, C-513/06 P, C-515/06 P and C-519/06 P *GlaxoSmithKline Services and Others* v *Commission and Others* [2009] ECR I-9291.
Case C-49/07 *Motosykletistiki Omospondia Ellados NPID (MOTOE) v Elliniko Dimosio*, judgment of 1 July 2008.
Case C-209/07 *Competition Authority v. Beef Industry Development Society Ltd and Barry Brothers (Carrigmore) Meals Ltd* [2008] ECR I-8637.
Case T-385/07 *Fédération Internationale de Football Association (FIFA) v. Commission*, judgment of 17 February 2011.
Case C-8/08 *T-Mobile Netherlands BV and Others v. Raad van bestuur van de Nederlandse Mededingingsautoriteit*, judgment of 4 June 2009.
Case T-55/08 *Union des associations européennes de football (UEFA)v.Commission*, judgment of 17 February 2011.
Case T-68/08 *Fédération Internationale de Football Association (FIFA) v. Commission*, judgment of 17 February 2011.
Case C-152/08 *Real Sociedad de Fútbol SAD and Nihat Kahveci v Consejo Superior de Deportes and Real Federación Española de Fútbol* [2008] ECR I-6291.
Case C-325/08 *Olympique Lyonnais SASP v. Olivier Bernard and Newcastle United FC* judgment of Grand Chamber of the Court delivered on 16 March 2010.
Joined Cases C-403/08 and C-429/08 *FAPL and others v. QC Leisure and others; and Karen Murphy v Media Protection Services Ltd.*, judgment of 4 October 2011.
Case C-52/09 *Konkurrensverket v TeliaSonera Sverige AB* [2011] ECR I-000.

Commission Decisions

Case IV/36.888—1998 Football World Cup [2000] OJ L 5/55.
Case M.779—Bertelsmann/CLT [1996] C 364/3.
Case IV/36.539—British Interactive Broadcasting/Open [1999] OJ L 312/1.
Case IV/F 1/36/718—CECED [2000] OJ L 187/47.
Cases IV/33.384 and IV/33.378—Distribution of package tours during the 1990 World Cup [1992] OJ L 326/31, [1994] 5 CMLR 253.

Case IV/37.806—ENIC/UEFA [2002] unpublished decision of 27 June 2002.
COMP/M.2483—Group Canal+/RTL/GJCD/JV [2001] OJ L 2985.
COMP/37.398—Joint Selling of Commercial Rights (UEFA Champions League) [2003] OJ L 291/25.
COMP/C-2/38.173—Joint Selling of Media Rights to the FA Premier League [2006] C 2006/868 final.
COMP/E3/36.85—Lille/UEFA ('the Mouscron case') [1999] unpublished decision of 3 December 1999.
COMP/C-3/37.792—Microsoft [2005] 4 CMLR 965, IP/03/1025.
COMP D3/38.044—NDC Health/IMS Health: Interim measures [2002] OJ L 59/18.
Case IV/27.958—National Sulphuric Acid [1980] OJ L 260/24.
Case IV/30.804—Nuovo Cegam [1984] OJ L 99/29, [1984] 2 CMLR 484.
Case IV/30.373—P&I Clubs [1999] OJ L125/12.
Case IV/31.990—Port of Rødby [1994] OJ L 55/52, [1994] 5 CMLR 457.
Case IV/37/400—'Project Gandalf' [1999] OJ 13, C 70/5.
Case IV/34.174—Sealink/B&I Holyhead: Interim Measures [1992] OJ 378/4, 5 CMLR 255.
Case No. IV/36.237—TPS [1999] OJ L 90/6.
COMP/29.373—Visa International—Multilateral Interchange Fee [2000] OJ L 318/17, [2003] 4 CMLR 283.
Case IV/30.350—Zink Producer Group [1984] OJ L 220/27, [1985] 2 CMLR 108.

Opinions of Advocate Generals

Opinion of AG Trabucchi in Case 7/75 *Mr and Mrs F v Belgian State* [1975] ECR 679, delivered on 10 June 1975.
Opinion of AG Lenz in Case C-66/86 *Ahmed Saeed Flugreisen v Zentrale zur Bekampfung Unlauteren Wettbewerbs* [1989] ECR 803, delivered on 11 January 1994.
Opinion of AG Lenz in Case C-415/93 *Union Royale Belge Sociétés de Football Association and others v. Bosman and others* [1995] ECR I-4921, delivered on 20 September 1995.
Opinion of AG Jacobs in Case C-203/96 *Chemische Afvalstoffen Dusseldorp and others v. Minister van Volkshuisvesting, Ruimtelijke Ordening en Milieubeheer* [1998] ECR I-4075, delivered on 23 October 1997.
Opinion of AG Fennelly in Joined Cases C-395/96 P and C-396/96 P *Compagnie Maritime Belge Transports SA, Compagnie Maritime Belge SA and Dafra-Lines A/S v Commission* [2000] ECR I-1365, delivered on 29 October 1998.
Opinion of AG Alber in Case C-176/96 *Jyri Lehtonen and Castors Canada Dry Namur-Braine ASBL v. Fédération royale belge des sociétés de basket-ball ASBL (FRBSB)* [2000] ECR I-2681, delivered on 22 June 1999.

Opinion of AG Jacobs in Case C-53/03 *Synetairismos Farmakopoion Aitolias & Akarnanias (Syfait) and Others v. GlaxoSmithKline plc and GlaxoSmithKline AEVE, formerly Glaxowellcome AEVE*, delivered on 28 October 2004.

Opinion of AG Kokott in Case C-222/07 *Presidente del Consiglio dei Ministri v Regione Sardegna* [2009] ECR I-1404, delivered on 4 September 2008.

Opinion of AG Sharpston in Case C-325/08 *Olympique Lyonnais SASP v. Olivier Bernard and Newcastle United FC* judgment of Grand Chamber of the Court, delivered on16 July 2009.

Opinion of AG Kokott in Joined Cases C-403/08 and C-429/08 *FAPL and others v. QC Leisure and others; and Karen Murphy v Media Protection Services Ltd.*, delivered on 3 February 2011.

Other Cases

Greig v. Insole [1978] 1 WLR 302 (Ch D 1977).

Olympia Equipment Leasing v Western Union Telegraph 797 F 2d 370 (7th Cir 1986).

Case CAS 98/200 *AEK Athens and Slavia Prague v. UEFA*—CAS arbitral award of 20 August 1999.

Hendry and others v. WPBSA [2001] All ER (D) 71.

Case No. 1001/1/1/01 *Napp Pharmaceutical Holdings Ltd v. Director General of Fair Trading* [2002] CAT 1, [2002] CompAR 13.

Verizon Communications Inc v Law Offices of Curtis V. Trinko 540 US 398 (2004), 124 S.Ct 872.

Murphy v Media Protection Services Ltd [2012] EWHC 466 (Admin).

Table of Legislative Acts

Binding EU Legislation

Regulation 17/62 (EEC), the first regulation implementing Articles 85 and 86 of the Treaty, OJ 013, 21/2/1962, pp. 204–211.

Regulation (EEC) No. 1612/68 of the Council of 15 October 1968 on freedom of movement for workers within the Community (OJ, English special edition, 1968 (II), p. 475).

Council Regulation (EEC) No. 2137/85 of 25 July 1985 on the European Economic Interest Grouping (EEIG) OJ L 199, 31. 7. 1985.

Council Regulation (EC) No. 1/2003 of 16 December 2002 on the implementation of the rules on competition laid down in Articles 81 and 82 of the Treaty OJ L 1, 04/01/2003, pp. 1–25.

Council Regulation (EC) No. 139/2004 of 20 January 2004 on the control of concentrations between undertakings (the Merger Regulation). OJ L 24, 29/01/2004, pp. 1–22.

Regulation (EU) No. 492/2011 of the European Parliament and of the Council of 5 April 2011 on the freedom of movement of workers in the Union OJ L 141, 27/5/2011.

Council Directive of 27 June 1985 on the assessment of the effects of certain public and private projects on the environment 85/337/EEC OJ L 175, 05/07/1985, pp. 40–48, as amended by Council Directive 97/11/EC of 3 March 1997, OJ L 73, 14/3/1997; Directive 2003/35/EC of the European Parliament and of the Council of 26 May 2003, OJ L 156, 25/6/2003; and Directive 2009/31/EC of the European Parliament and of the Council of 23 April 2009, OJ L 140, 5/6/2009.

Council Directive 93/83/EEC of 27 September 1993 on the coordination of certain rules concerning copyright and rights related to copyright applicable to satellite broadcasting and cable retransmission (Satellite Broadcasting Directive) [1993] OJ L 248/15, 06/10/1993.

Council Directive 96/9/EC of 11 March 1996 on the legal protection of databases OJ L 077, 27/3/1996.

K. Pijetlovic, *EU Sports Law and Breakaway Leagues in Football*,
ASSER International Sports Law Series, DOI 10.1007/978-94-6265-048-0

Council Directive 98/84/EC on the legal protection of services based on, or consisting of, conditional access. OJ L 320/54, 28/11/1998.

Commission Decision 98/500/EC on the establishment of Sectoral Dialogue Committees promoting the dialogue between the social partners at European level, OJ L 225/27, 12/8/1998.

Council Directive 2000/78 establishing a general framework for equal treatment in employment and occupation OJ L 303/16, 2/12/2000.

Directive 2004/38/EC of the European Parliament and of the Council of 24 April 2004 on the right of citizens of the Union and their family members to move and reside freely within the territory of the Member States amending Regulation (EEC) No. 1612/68 and repealing Directives 64/221/EEC, 68/360/EEC, 72/194/EEC, 73/148/EEC, 75/34/EEC, 75/35/EEC, 90/364/EEC, 90/365/EEC and 93/96/EEC, OJ L 158, 30/4/2004, pp. 77–128.

Directive 2010/13/EU of the European Parliament and of the Council of 10 March 2010 on the coordination of certain provisions laid down by law, regulation or administrative action in Member States concerning the provision of audiovisual media services (Audiovisual Media Services Directive), OJ L 95, 15/4/2010, pp. 1–24.

Commission Decision 2005/842/EC on the application of Article 86(2) of the EC Treaty to State aid in the form of public service compensation granted to certain undertakings entrusted with the operation of services of general economic interest OJ L 312/67, 29/11/2005.

The Additional Protocol, signed on 23 November 1970 in Brussels and concluded, approved and confirmed on behalf of the Community by Council Regulation (EEC) No. 2760/72 of 19 December 1972 (OJ 1973 C 133, p. 17) ('the Additional Protocol'), annexed to the Agreement establishing an Association between the European Economic Community and Turkey, signed at Ankara on 12 September 1963 by the Republic of Turkey, of the one part, and by the Member States of the EEC and the Community, on the other part, and concluded, approved and confirmed on behalf of the Community by Council Decision 64/732/EEC of 23 December 1963 (OJ 1973 C 113, p. 1) ('the EEC-Turkey Association Agreement').

Europe Agreement establishing an association between the European Communities and their Member States, of the one part, and the Slovak Republic, of the other part, signed in Luxembourg on 4 October 1993 and approved on behalf of the Communities by Decision 94/909/EC, ECSC, Euratom of the Council and the Commission of 19 December 1994 (OJ 1993 L 359, p. 1) ('the Association Agreement with Slovakia').

Agreement on partnership and cooperation establishing a partnership between the European Communities and their Member States, of the one part, and the Russian Federation, of the other part, signed in Corfu on 24 June 1994 and approved on behalf of the Communities by Decision 97/800/EC ECSC, Euratom: Council and Commission Decision of 30 October 1997 (OJ 1994 L 327, p. 1) ('the Communities-Russia Partnership Agreement').

Notices, Guidelines, and Policy Documents from EU Institutions

Treaty of Amsterdam—Presidency Conclusions (2 October 1997) OJ 1997 C 340, 10/11/1999, (No. 29: Declaration on Sport).
Commission Notice on the definition of relevant market for the purposes of Community competition law, OJ C 372, 9.12.1997, pp. 5–13.
Notice on the application of competition rules to access agreements in the telecommunications sector OJ [1998] C 265/2, 5 CMLR 521.
Communication made pursuant to Article 19(3) of Council Regulation No. 17 concerning request for negative clearance or for exemption pursuant to Article 81(3) of the EC Treaty Case No. 37.632—UEFA rule on integrity of the UEFA club competitions: independence of clubs 1999/C 363/02.
Opinion of the Committee of the Regions on 'The European Model of Sport' 1999/C 374/14.
European Commission Discussion Paper at the First European Conference on Sport 'Relations between Sport and Television', Olympia, 21 and 22 May 1999.
Commission White Paper on Modernisation of the rules implementing Articles 81 and 82 of the EC Treaty, Commission Programme No. 99/027 1999/OJ C 132/1.
European Commission, European Model of Sport, Consultation Document of DG X (September 2008).
Report from the Commission to the European Council with a view to safeguarding current sports structures and maintaining the social function of sport within the Community framework 'The Helsinki Report on Sport' Brussels, 10 December 1999 COM(1999) 644 final ('Helsinki Report').
Declaration on the specific characteristics of sport and its social function in Europe, of which account should be taken in implementing common policies 13948/00, Annex to the Presidency Conclusions following the Nice European Council Meeting of 7, 8 and 9 December 2000 ('Nice Declaration').
Notice published pursuant to Article 19(3) of Council Regulation No. 17 concerning Cases COMP/35.163—Notification of FIA Regulations, COMP/36.638—Notification by FIA/FOA of agreements relating to the FIA Formula One World Championship, COMP/36.776—GTR/FIA & others (2001/C 169/03).
Xth European Sports Forum, Conclusions of the working group on the follow up to the Nice Declaration, Brussels 17–18 October 2001.
Commission Notice on agreements of minor importance which do not appreciably restrict competition under Article 81(1) of the Treaty establishing the European Community (de minimis), OJ C 368/07, 22.12. 2001.
Commission Notice—Guidelines on the effect on trade concept contained in Articles 81 and 82 of the Treaty OJ C 101, 27. 4. 2004, pp. 81–96.
Communication from the Commission—Notice—Guidelines on the application of Article 81(3) of the Treaty OJ C 101/97, 27. 4. 2004.

Guidelines on the assessment of horizontal mergers under the Council Regulation on the control of concentrations between undertakings 2004/C 31/03.

Consultation Conference with the European Sport Movement on the Social Function of Sport, Volunteering in Sport and Fight Against Doping, 'The EU and Sport: Matching Expectations', Brussels 14–15 June 2005.

Professional Sport in the Internal Market, project No. IP/A/IMCO/ST/2005-004, Commissioned by the Committee on the Internal Market and Consumer Protection of the European Parliament (September 2005).

European Commission DG Competition Discussion Paper on the application of Article 82 to exclusionary abuses, Brussels (December 2005).

Communication from the Commission to the European Parliament, the Council and the European Economic and Social Committee—Implementing the partnership for growth and jobs: making Europe a pole of excellence on corporate social responsibility, Brussels 22. 3. 2006, COM(2006) 136 final.

European Parliament Report on the future of professional football in Europe (2006/2130(INI)), Committee on Culture and Education, final A6-0036/2007, p. 14.

Commission White Paper on Sport, Brussels 11 July 2007 COM(2007) 391 final, (White Paper on Sport).

Commission Staff Working Document, The EU and Sport: Background and Context, Accompanying Document to the White Paper on Sport, COM (2007) 391 final.

White Paper Consultation by Commissioner Figel with European Sport Federations, Sport Governance in Europe, Brussels 20/09/2006.

Commission Consolidated Jurisdictional Notice under Council Regulation (EC) No. 139/2004 on the control of concentrations between undertakings (2008/C 95/01).

European Parliament resolution of 8 May 2008 on the White Paper on Sport (2007/2261 (INI)).

Communication from the Commission—Guidance on the Commission's enforcement priorities in applying Article 82 of the EC Treaty to abusive exclusionary conduct by dominant undertakings, OJ C 45, 24. 2. 2009.

Commission Notice—Guidance on Vertical Restraints, Brussels SEC (2010) 411.

European Parliament, Directorate-General for Internal Policies, study on the Lisbon Treaty and EU Sports Policy (2010), p. 12.

Communication from the Commission—Guidelines on the applicability of Article 101 of the Treaty on the Functioning of the European Union to horizontal co-operation agreements OJ C 11, 14. 1. 2011, pp. 1–72.

Communication from the Commission to the European Parliament, the Council, the European Economic and Social Committee, and the Committee of the Regions 'Developing the European Dimension in Sport' COM(2011) 12 final, 18. 1. 2011.

European Parliament Resolution of 2 February 2011 on the European Dimension in Sport, 2011/2087(INI).

Other Legislation

UK Copyright, Designs and Patents Act of 1988, as amended.
Liikuntalaki (Sports Law) 18. 12. 1998/1054, as amended.
Spordiseadus (Sports Act) passed on 15. 6. 1998 (RT I 1998, 61, 982), Chap. 1, General Provisions, § 2.
Spordiseadus (Sports Act) passed on 6. 4. 2005 (RT I, 2005, 22, 148), as last amended on 29. 12. 2011.
Physical Activity and Sport Act, passed on 19. 3. 2003, S.C. 2003, c.2, as last amended on 17. 10. 2011.
Resolution adopted by the UN General Assembly [on the report of Sixth Committee (A/64/458)], 22 October 2009.
Recommendation No. R (92) 13 Rev. of the Council of Europe's Committee of Ministers to Member States on the Revised European Sports Law Charter (the European Sports Law Charter) adopted by the Committee of Ministers on 24 September 1992 at the 480th meeting of the Ministers' Deputies and revised at their 752nd meeting on 16 May 2001.

Index

0–9

13 conditions (for approval of cross-border leagues)
  legal analysis of, 292–301
  list of, 73–74, 291–292

A

Abuse
  exclusionary, 160–161, 166, 205, 207, 265, 271
  of a collective dominant position, 68, 166, 173, 239
  of a dominant position, 150, 158, 160–162, 168, 190, 200, 229, 238, 265, 266, 267, 286, 302, 304
  of rights, 137–139
  risk of an, 190–191
Access device
  conditional, 137, 139
  illicit, 136–139
Accountability, 6, 9, 12, 76, 79, 196, 279
Activities
  commercial, 137, 240
  economic, 104, 119, 169, 185, 189, 222, 248, 250, 252
Agreement(s)
  anti-competitive, 232, 252
  commercialisation, 157, 174
  franchising, 152
  horizontal cooperation, 157
  joint selling, 157, 177, *see also* Collective sales
Alternative
  competitions, 51, 54, 71, 291, 295–296
  league(s), 26, 48, 51, 54, 66, 92–93, 238, 240, 257, 260, 278, 280, 282, 284, 291, 295–297, 301, 308, *see also* Breakaway league(s)
  structure, 26, 48, 55, 261, 282, 288, 296
American model of sport, 27, 38, 40–41, 50, 277, *see also* US model of sport
Amsterdam Declaration on Sport, 12, 19, 49, 119, 120
Analytical framework
  for commercial rules, 173–179
  for regulatory rules, 18, 32, 179–187
Anti-doping, 8, 10, 17, 73, 76, 179, 218, 227, 234, 249, 269, 280–281, 291, 293
Arbitration, 10, 179
Arnaut Report, 2, 9, 11, 28, 67, 75, 88, 194–195, 270, 275–276
Article 49 rule, 26, 74, 239–240, 242, 248–249, 251–254, 259–261, 263–269, 271–272, 277–282, 286, 290, 295, 301, 303, 308
Article 165 TFEU, 13, 16, 18, 21–22, 27, 32, 34, 36, 51, 90, 100, 116, 123, 126–127, 134, 140–143, 215, 238, 268, 270, 272, 286, 305, *see also* Sports article
Association
  of undertakings, 25, 151, 169, 174, 182, 233, 234, 238, 248–253, 262
  purchasing, 152, 200, 238
Association Agreement(s), 121–122
Athlete(s)
see also Player(s)
  free movement of, 116
  professionals, 84, 103–104, 106–107, 109, 115, 118, 121, 124, 127–129, 132–134, 230
  selection of, 32, 119, 227
  trainees, 124, 129–131

K. Pijetlovic, *EU Sports Law and Breakaway Leagues in Football*,
ASSER International Sports Law Series, DOI 10.1007/978-94-6265-048-0

Audio Visual Media Services (AVMS)
designated events, 135–136
Directive, 19, 134–136
events of major importance, 135
Authorisation, 25, 54, 74, 137–139, 145–146, 188–189, 191, 240–242, 259, 292

B

Balkan (Super) League, 72, 257, 296
Baltic League, 72
Bans
Prospective, 289
Retrospective, 288–289
Barriers to entry, 159, 205, 256, 259
BeNe League, 72, 266, 284
Betting, 35, 42–43, 306
Blocked hours, 142–144
Blocking competing organisations, 187, 198, 286
Boycott(s), 2, 105, 260–261, 266, 305
Breakaway league(s), 27–29, 44, 48–49, 54, 72–74, 92–94, 237, 239, 240, 256, 261, 266, 268, 285–286, 288, 293, 306–307, *see also* Leagues, alternative
British Sky Broadcasting (BSkyB), 3, 177
Broadcasting rights, *see also* Media rights
collective sale (joint selling) of, 93, 147, 255, 273, 280, 307
sale of, 9, 147, 170, 174, 196, 255, 274, 300, 307
transfer of, 35, 59
unbundling of, 177–178
Bundesliga, 80, 176–178, 110, 144
Burden of proof, 223, 233–234, 269

C

Champions League, *see* UEFA Champions League
Channel One Cup, 71–72
Charter of Fundamental Rights of the EU, 11, 18
Clauses
nationality, 107, 114, 225
policy-linking, 153, 155–156
restrictive, 287
Closed periods, *see* Blocked hours
Club Competitions Committee (CCC), 81, 257
Club Licensing and Financial Fair Play Regulations (CLFFP), 17, 41, 88
Clubs
as undertakings, 25, 168, 255, 297
founder, 56, 58–59
independence of, 74, 230, 249, 291, 293
licensing of, 40, 73–74, 88–89, 240, 246, 273, 291, 294
multiple ownership of, 153, 183, 227
Collective
Bargaining, 82–87
dominance, 158, 162–167, 170, 172–173, 255, 259, 303, 304, *see also* Dominant position
entity, 165, 172, 250
sales, 39, 59, 93, 176, 251, 306, *see also* Agreements, joint selling
Commercial ancillarity, 152, 286
Commercialisation, 3, 24, 27, 50–51, 53, 112, 275, 281, 285, 300
Commonwealth of Independent States Cup, 71
Communication on Developing European
Compensation
pool, 27, 65–68, 132, 257
training, 105, 109–110, 123–125, 127–134
Competition(s)
balanced, 86, 283
cross-border, 73–74, 240, 247, 259, 284, 290–297, 301
domestic, 56, 273, 282–283, 288, 295
fair, 305
international, 54, 56, 59, 60, 63, 67–68, 102, 107, 118–119, 239, 243, 276–277, 301
national, 57, 60, 260, 305
open, 38, 51–52, 94, 238, 272
regularity of, 33, 77, 140, *see also* Matches, regularity of
rival, 244, 285–287, 295
Competitive balance, 33, 35, 37, 41–42, 60, 67, 68, 79, 86, 91–92, 94, 96, 106, 108–110, 112, 115–118, 144, 175, 210, 221, 276, 282–283, 290, 306
Composition of teams, 104
Compulsory player release, 25, 27, 62, 64–68, 111, 221, 304
Dimension in Sport, 20, 33, 51–52, 80, 272, 294
Concerted practice(s), 68, 150–151, 162, 164, 179, 248, 253, 303–304
Conditional Access Directive (CAD), 137
Conflict of interests, 24, 191–192, 196, 198, 283, 285–286, 306–307
Consumer(s)
final, 208, 245–246, 264
Welfare, 67, 155–157, 163, 202, 283

Contract(s)
professional, 40, 124, 127, 129, 132–133
Convergence, 16, 22, 26, 28, 38, 145, 154, 174, 179, 182, 186–187, 211, 215–234, 267, 269, 302
Cooperation Agreement, 122, 157
Copyrights, 137, 140, 145–146, 178, 299
Corporate Social Responsibility (CSR), 26, 28, 74, 76, 208–209
Corruption, 69, 284, 293
Council of Europe, 6, 10, 14
Court of Arbitration for Sport (CAS), 8, 10, 171, 179, 279
Criteria
financial, 38, 88
ownership, 56
selection, 56
Cross-border league, 72–73, 239, 251, 260, 266, 280, 284–285, 291–292, 294, 296
Cross-elasticity, 158, 243, *see also* Substitutability, Interchangeability
Culture, 2, 14, 17–18, 40, 49–50, 155, 180, 276, 284, 304

D

Decisions
by association of undertakings, 150, 154, 169, 193, 248–253
commercial, 243, 280
commitment, 28, 211, 307
Decoder
card, 136, 143, 145–147, 178
foreign, 136–138
De minimis, 151, 186
Democracy, 12, 49, 51, 76, 210, 279
Direct effect, 103, 122, 217, 266
Disciplinary measures, 25, 37, 63, 73, 239, 260
Discriminatory conditions of work, 114, 122–123
Discriminatory measures
directly, 32, 102, 104, 106–107, 111–112, 115, 126, 220–222
indirectly, 101–102, 112, 114–115, 126, 230, 266
Dominant position, 150, 158–168, 173, 190–192, 198, 200, 203, 205–207, 229, 238, 253–255, 258, 265–267, 286, 302, *see also* Collective dominance
Doping, 5, 8, 10, 33, 35, 74, 76, 141, 179, 182, 185, 195, 210, 218, 221, 227, 234, 249, 269, 280–281, 293
Dual functionality, 286, 297
Dual membership, 200, 241

E

Economic
Activity, 14–15, 18, 23, 102–103, 118–119, 150, 169, 173–174, 180–181, 189, 202, 218–221, 223–225, 248, 252–253, 266–267, 301
Arguments, 153, 231
Benefits, 155–156, 229, 302
Constitution, 100
Efficiency, 93, 184, 229
Links, 164–165, 167, 173, 304
Economic Interest Grouping, 27, 61, 75
Educational function of sport, 21, 35, 100, 116, 126–128, 130, 134, 140, 142, 196, 228, 270
Effect(s)
appreciable, 186
disproportionate, 129
on trade, 151, 160, 184, 186–187, 301
Efficiency
Arguments, 184
Defence, 161–162, 184, 229, 233–234, 287–288
Employment, 2, 8, 32, 36, 42, 81, 100, 103, 105–107, 109, 114, 122, 124–126, 154–156, 216, 226
Entrustment, 189, 193–196, 292
Essential facilities, 160–161
Ethical values, 7, 33, 142, 281
Europa League, 70, 81, 111, 116–117, 242, 244–245, 247, 273
European Club Association (ECA), 28, 54, 62, 64–66, 69, 75, 77–81, 83–85, 87, 91–92, 94, 97, 111, 117, 239, 257, 264, 290, 304
European Club Forum (ECF), 75, 77
European Football League (EFL), 55, 59, 78
European Golden Cup, 62
European Parliament, 14, 18, 20–21, 24, 41, 81, 112, 275
European Professional Football Leagues (EPFL), 28, 75, 79, 83–85, 117
European social dialogue, 52, 81, 83–84, 86–87, 111
European sports model, 37, 51–53, 61, 96, 112
EU sports policy, 12, 14, 24, 34, 51, 123, 308
Exceptional circumstances, 157, 161, 205, 254, 256–257

Exclusive rights, 150, 177–178, 189, 190–191, 193, 244–245, 250
Exclusive purchasing agreements, 264
Exclusivity
  territorial, 141–142, 178
Executive Board (in ECA), 28, 78–79, 83, 87, 97, 257, 304

F
Fans, 53, 58, 61, 63, 92, 245–246, 281, 299, *see also* Supporters
FAPL, 136–137, 143–144, 146–147, 176, 178, *see also* Premier League
FIA, 28, 196–199, 260, 285–286
FIFA
  Regulations on the Status and Transfer of Players, 62–63, 109
  Statutes, 69
  World Cup, 3–4, 24, 37, 39, 63–66, 94, 111, 135, 172, 207, 245, 250
FIFPro, 52, 75, 80, 82–85, 87, 117, 130
Financial
  Contributions, 251, 271, 297
  Criteria, 38, 88
  Fair Play Regulation, 17, 44, 52, 86, 88–90, 294
  Instability, 91, 108
  Penalty, 25, 197
  Solidarity, 23–25, 42, 52, 59, 61, 67, 74, 270, 272, 275–276, 280, 305–306
  Stability, 88, 90, 294
  Support, 210, 298, 301
  Survival, 144, 274, 283
Financing of sport, *see also* Sport financing
  macroeconomic aspects, 42–43
  microeconomic aspects, 43–44
Fixtures, 65, 69
Football Association Premier League (FAPL), 136–137, 143–144, 146, 176, 178
Foreign players, 66, 104–105, 108, 112, 116, 119–120, 126
Formula One, 4, 28, 196–199, 260, 286
Franchise, 39, 56–57, 152, 305
Free agent(s), 107, 109, 134
Free movement of services, 18, 25, 102, 119–120, 135, 139, 179–180, 220, 231–232, 240, 261, 266
Freedom of movement for workers, 18, 102, 105–107, 125, 186
Freedom of establishment, 135, 216, 231
Fundamental freedoms, 15, 118, 138, 143, 222, 224, 232, 266, 303
Fundamental rights, 2, 18, 135, 226, 234, 269
Funding, 9, 40, 44, 67, 275

G
G14
  dissolution of, 27–28, 62–66, 78
  formation of, 61–62
Gate receipts, 43, 58, 143–144
Global sports law, 8
Governance
  corporate, 209
  decentralisation of football, 28, 48, 68, 79, 97
  football, 48–49, 68, 87, 92, 96, 271, 299, 308
  good, 11–12, 26, 34, 48, 88, 195, 259, 273, 279
  model, 239, 258
  self, 196
Grassroots, 25–26, 35–36, 40, 75–76, 275, 280, 288, 294

H
Helsinki Report, 19, 49, 275–277
Home and away rule, 172, 183
Home-grown player rule, 28, 36, 111–119

I
Independent European Sports Review, *see* Arnaut Report
Indispensability, 156–157, 161, 224, 231, 242, 271
Inherency requirement/inherent rules, 32–33, 120, 153, 182–184, 202, 210, 224–230, 238, 267, 270–271, 278–280, 293, 295, 302, 305, *see also* Necessity
Integration, 2, 7, 14–15, 100, 155, 157, 159, 171, 276–277, 300
Integrity, 21, 33, 74, 88, 141, 182, 230, 249, 281, 291, 293–294, 306
Intellectual property, 2, 56, 140–141, 152, 160, 178, 244
Interchangeability, 157–158, 171, 245–247, *see also* Substitutability, Cross-elasticity
Interdependence, 34, 51, 165, 166
Interests
  commercial, 5, 14, 25, 27, 48, 60, 67–68, 77–79, 83, 97, 244, 257, 280, 283–284, 286, 288, 304

economic, 24, 144, 189, 194, 208, 281
non-economic, 201, 220
International Cricket Council, 288
International Olympic Committee (IOC), 2, 5, 9, 169, 179, 281

J
Juridification, 3, 5, 8, 10–11

L
League(s)
closed, 27, 51, 95, 111, 261, 283, 304–305, 307
hermetic, 282
open, 38, 51, 86, 96, 294
pan-European, 37, 48, 244, 247, 291
regional, 72, 261, 282
regionally delimited, 291, 296
sanctioned, 54, 72, 290, 299
supranational, 282
top, 28, 83, 95, 273, 299
unsanctioned, 74, 240, 252, 260, 289, 304
Legal certainty, 17, 20, 216
Legitimate aim(s), 28, 101–102, 106, 125, 141, 209–211, 227, 229, 238, 269, 272, *see also* Objectives, legitimate
Lex sportiva, 7–8, 16, 26
Licenses, 17, 38, 40–41, 56, 73–74, 88–89, 120–121, 136, 141–142, 145, 171, 175–176, 178–179, 188, 196–199, 239–240, 242, 244, 246, 251, 259, 273, 291, 293–294
Lisbon Treaty, 17–18, 20–22, 27–28, 34, 36, 51, 100, 123, 140

M
Major League Baseball (MLB), 39–40
Market
Access, 101, 186, 198, 224–228, 230, 266–267
ancillary, 160, 171
broadcasting, 5, 92, 174, 245, 247, 295–296
capital, 44, 170, 171
contest, 170
definition, 243–244
downstream, 5, 161, 174–176, 244, 296
entry, 257, 264, 266, 292
exploitation, 74, 96, 170, 240–245
for gate revenues, 171
for players, 171, 173
for organisation, 241–243, 246, 257–258
foreclosure, 29
geographic, 158–159, 172, 175, 189, 247, 290
labour, 109, 117, 122–123, 170–171, 225, 238, 246
media rights, 171
merchandising, 171
product, 158, 160, 170, 172, 189, 240, 244–245, 282
relevant, 24, 29, 74, 151, 158–159, 163, 165, 168–171, 173–174, 189, 198, 203, 205, 240–243, 247–248, 250–259, 263–265
shares, 204–206, 254, 256, 258
sponsorship, 171
supply, 67, 170
upstream, 175, 208, 240, 246–247, 254, 256
Matches
of national team(s), 25, 27, 220, 221, 295
participation in, 143, 220
regularity of, 77, *see also* Competitions, regularity of
Match calendar, 64, 66, 72, 74, 240, 261, 291, 293–295
Match-fixing, 17, 185, 284, 306
Measures
directly discriminatory, 32, 102, 104, 106–107, 111–112, 115, 126, 220–222
indirectly discriminatory, 101–102, 112, 114–115, 126, 230, 266
restrictive, 18, 116, 125, 137, 141, 269, 282
Media Partners, 27, 54, 55, 59–61, 78, 244, 257, 269, 282, 285, 295, 304
Media rights, 39, 42, 52, 56, 89, 94, 143, 171, 177–178, *see also* Broadcasting rights
Membership
dual, 200, 241
organised, 199, 240, 287
Memorandum of Understanding, 52, 54, 62, 65, 66, 69, 78, 83, 96, 239, 264, 290
Merchandising, 35, 44, 48, 56, 170–171, 244
Model of sport, 36–38, 50, 53, 241, 275–277, 308
Monopoly, 92, 163, 174, 188–189, 191, 193, 195, 203–206, 211, 246, 254, 258, 263, 286, 306

N

National
  Championships, 65, 74, 105, 107, 240, 243, 277, 292
  court(s), 64, 101, 278
  law, 101, 124, 137, 141, 151, 153
  team(s), 2, 10–11, 27, 37, 54, 64–67, 103–104, 107, 109, 111–112, 115, 118, 120, 135, 219–221, 269, 273, 277, 295
National Basketball Association (NBA), 39–41
National Football League (NFL), 39–40, 244
National Hockey League (NHL), 39–40
Nationality clauses, 107, 114, 225
Necessity, 9, 131–132, 194, 224, 268–269, 270, 272, 278–279, 285, *see also* Inherency requirement/inherent rules
Nice Declaration, 11, 19, 32, 49, 80, 174, 210, 271, 275–276, 279
Non-discriminatory
  Criteria, 193, 227, 291–292
  Measures, 101, 126, 186, 230
  rule(s), 104, 106, 219–220, 224–227, 266–267, 305
Non-economic activity(ies), 104, 218

O

Objective justification:
  attendance at stadiums, 35, 143–144
  effective and proper organization of sport, 121, 153, 269, 272, 277, 279–280, 286, 293–294, 296–297, 305
  encouraging recruitment and training, 106, 116, 127
  maintaining the competitive balance, 33, 35, 37, 68, 91, 106, 108, 109–110, 112, 115–118, 144, 175, 210, 221
  preserving uncertainty of results, 33–34, 41, 106, 110, 141, 230, 271, 306
  regularity of competitions, 33, 140
  safeguarding integrity of sport, 182, 230, 249
Objectives
  legitimate, 112, 124–125, 144, 183, 224, 230, 269, 278, 280–281, 283, 287, 289, 291, 294, *see also* Legitimate aims
  non-competition, 153, 183
  non-economic, 161
Obstacle approach, 107, 125
Oulmers affair, 27, 62–64, 66, 257, 304
Ownership, 44, 56, 73, 86, 92, 153, 171, 183, 227, 230, 260, 291, 297, 299–300, 305–307

P

Player(s), *see also* Athletes
  amateur, 119
  as free agents, 107, 109, 134
  assimilated, 105, 112–115
  association-trained, 113
  club-trained, 113
  home-grown, 111–113, 116–118
  locally-trained, 113
  mobility, 14, 108, 123, 170
  non-Community, 121
  out-of-contract, 134
  professional, 84, 103–104, 106–107, 109, 115, 121, 124, 127–129, 132–134, 230
  release, 25, 27, 62, 64–68, 111, 221, 304
Players' agent, 171–174, 250
Premier League, 3–4, 38, 41, 43, 44, 56, 70, 83, 92, 110, 136, 140, 142–145, 176–177, 260, 297–298, *see also* FAPL
Presumption(s), 159, 222–223, 254, 256, 262, 267
Principle(s)
  of good governance, 11–12, 26, 34, 48, 88, 195, 259, 273, 279
  of proportionality, 106, 210, 259, 287, 292, 301
  of supremacy, 101
Private
  Agreements, 114, 145, 198
  bodies, 9, 16, 122, 153, 217
  entities, 216, 243, *see also* Undertakings, private–
  interests, 198, 286-287, 307
  promoter, 240, 246, 263, 288–290, 293, 296–297
Pro Cup, 55, 57
Professional
  Activities, 104, 118
  Contract, 40, 124, 127, 129, 132–133
  Opportunities, 102
Professional Football Strategy Council (PFSC), 28, 52, 78–80, 84–85, 87, 97, 257
Promotion and relegation, 37–40, 48, 52, 60, 70, 74, 88–89, 93–94, 96, 110, 170, 244, 275, 283, 294, 296–298, 301, 307
Property rights, 56, 135, 140–141, 152, 160, 244, 300
Public
  Authority, 9, 16, 23, 90, 103, 125, 153, 189, 194, 196, 198, 216–217, 266, 291–292
  House, 146

interest objectives, 101, 263, 269, 288, 292, 295
original, 146
policy, 43, 140, 155–156, 161–162, 201, 230–231, 278
policy justifications, 161, 278
policy objectives, 155–156
undertakings, 150, 188
Purely sporting
Interests, 103–104, 181, 185, 219, 221
Motives, 181, 221–222
rule(s), 23–24, 181, 218, 228, *see also* Rules of the game
Pyramid, 24, 27, 33, 36–38, 40, 43, 48, 50–53, 55, 66, 74, 76, 80, 86, 96, 238, 252, 261, 271–272, 277, 279–280, 283–284, 295–297, 307–308

Q
Quotas
3+2 rule, 28, 104–105, 107, 112–115, 126, 220
6+5 rule, 111–112

R
Real training costs, 123, 128, 132, 134
Recruitment of young players, 125, 128
Regulatory
ancillarity, 153, 278, 286–287,*see also* Restraints, ancillary
function, 191, 262, 285–286, 292, 294, 296–297, 305
Relevant market, 24, 29, 74, 158, 163, 165, 168–175, 189, 198, 202, 205, 240–243, 247–248, 250–259, 263–265
Representation, 9, 11–12, 28, 48, 51, 59, 68, 79–80, 86–87, 96–97, 279
Required economic effect, 222–223
Restraints
ancillary, 152, 228, 302, *see also* Regulatory ancillarity
horisontal, 157, 176
vertical, 254, 256, 264–265
Restrictions
by effect, 151, 186
by object, 145, 156, 178, 222, 262
hard core, 156
...obligations and review, 191–192, 292
per se, 222, 307
Restrictive rule(s), 25, 41, 122, 128, 153, 210–211, 222, 224, 232, 253, 272, 286–287, 290
(Rookie) draft system, 39, 283
Rule(s)
inherent, 120, 224–229, 267, 278, 293
of reason, 152, 156, 201, 228, 231
of the game, 22–24, 184, 218, 227, 293 *see also* Purely sporting rules
purely sporting, *see* Purely sporting rules
selection, 119–120, 220, 225

S
Salary cap, 39, 41, 86, 283
Self-governance, 12, 196, 279, 298, *see also* Sporting autonomy
Services
clubs', 246–247, 254–255, 271, 304
free movement of, 18, 25, 102, 119–120, 135, 139, 179–180, 220, 231–232, 240, 261, 266
input, 246–247
of general economic interest, 150, 189, 193–195
organisational, 240–243, 246–247, 290, 301, 304
Setanta Cup, 72
Single economic entity, 154, 168, 307
Social
Dialogue, 52, 80–87, 97, 111
function of sport, 6, 135–136, 210, 248, 268–271, 274–276, 283
importance of sport, 3, 106, 119, 125–126, 230, 271
inclusion, 35, 49, 195, 277
objectives, 100
Solidarity
Contributions, 93, 240, 273–275, 297
Mechanism, 33, 35, 39, 42–43, 68, 79, 110, 144, 274, 297, 300–301, 306–307
Payments, 96, 110, 243, 251, 255, 272–273
Principle, 25, 76, 174, 270, 274–275, 280
Special responsibility, 28, 159, 202–209, 211, 271, 304
Special rights, 191
Specific nature of sport, 16, 21, 32–34, 100, 140–141, 173, 270, 272
Specificity of sport, 11, 16, 18, 20–21, 23, 27, 32–34, 36, 51–53, 116, 123, 126–127, 130, 136, 140–141, 183–184, 196, 198, 222, 238, 261, 269, 305
Spectators, 2, 6, 88, 274, 295

Sponsorship, 3–4, 9, 42–44, 56, 65, 95–96, 171, 174–175, 189, 191, 196, 242, 244–245, 247, 289, 298–299
Sport(s)
  article, 13, 22, 27, 115, 123, *see also* Article 165 TFEU
  associations, 52, 119, 170, 238, 254, 260
  definition of, 6–7
  federations, 8–9, 14–15, 23–24, 33, 52, 122, 169, 195, 210, 217, 271, 279, 308
  financing, 42–43, *see also* Financing of sport
  governance, 7, 43
  juridification of, 3, 5, 8, 10–11
  league(s), 34, 38, 186
  organisations, 8, 10–11, 12, 15, 33, 42, 120, 194–196, 279
  teams, 40, 103, 218–219
  Unit, 17
Sporting
  autonomy, 15, 23, 123, 182–184, *see also* Self-governance
  criteria, 60, 73, 88, 291
  events, 4, 9, 94, 140–141, 180, 189, 219–221, 245–246, 275, 300
  industry, 27, 31, 34, 36, 93, 140
Sporting competitions
  integrity of, 182
  regularity of, 33, 140
Sporting exception (exception)
  category I, 185, 218, 223, 227, 267
  category II, 181, 185, 218, 223–224, 226–228, 267
  category III, 224, 267
  category IV, 228, 229
  in EU law, 27, 103, 217, 305
  scope of, 11, 104, 106, 119, 181, 184, 305
SSNIP test, 158, 172, 243, 245
Stakeholder(s), 11–12, 19–20, 23, 27–28, 34, 43, 48–49, 51–53, 68, 74–77, 79–80, 86–87, 96–97, 118, 195, 208–209, 256–257, 259, 279, 280, 285, 297
Standard of proof, 211, 233, 268, 282
Study
  on the Lisbon Treaty, 20–22, 34, 100
  on the UEFA's 'Home grown players rule', 114, 116–117
Stuff Working Paper, 38, 269, 300
Subsidiarity, 14, 53, 114–115, 186–187, 194
Substitutability, 158, 170, 245, 276, *see also* Interchangeability, Cross-elasticity
Suitability, 116, 123, 127–128, 131–132, 144, 210, 224, 268, 272, 275–276, 281–282, 297, 301
Superdominance, 28, 202–206, 255, 304
SuperLeague, 55, 57–58, 62, 69, 72, 91, 95, 282–285, 304–305
Supporters, 12, 53, 56, 60, 75, 77, 244, *see also* Fans
Suspension, 105, 179

T

Television (TV)
  free-to-air, 19, 94
  pay-per-view, 175
Ticketing, 5, 170
Training
  Cost, 123, 128–134
  of young players, 33, 106, 116, 124–125, 127–128, 131–132, 141
Transfer
  of players, 36, 62, 86, 95–96, 104, 109, 132
  rules, 104–107, 109–111, 220–222, 226
  windows, 120–121, 126, 227, 238
Transparency, 12, 20, 76, 88, 96, 163, 164, 209–210, 279, 294

U

UEFA
  11 values, 53
  Approval, 292, 295–296
  Champions League, 27, 37, 41, 55, 59–62, 70, 73, 81, 91–92, 94–95, 110–111, 116–117, 175–177, 242, 244–247, 252, 257, 260–261, 273, 275, 282, 297, 300, 307
  club competitions, 41, 52, 74, 80–81, 230, 249, 291, 295
  Club Competitions Committee (CCC), *see* Club Competitions Committee (CCC)
  Club Licensing System *see* Clubs, licensing of
  Concessions, 38, 53, 59, 60, 62, 64, 93, 257, 260, 275
  Congress, 251–252
  EURO, 65–66, 94, 135, 246, 273
  Executive Committee, 54, 80–81, 90, 169, 239, 249, 251
  Mandate, 25, 54, 68, 74, 76–77, 240, 255, 271, 280, 286
  Member Associations, 54, 73, 94, 239, 291–292, 301
  Mission Statement, 76, 280

Statutes, 10, 15, 25–26, 51, 54–55, 73–74, 77, 142, 239–240, 251–253, 259, 291, 293, 301, 303, 308
Uncertainty of outcome, 33, 41
Undertaking(s)
association of, 25, 151, 169, 174, 182, 233–234, 238, 248–251, 253, 262
entrusted, 150, 189, 191, 193, 195–196, 256, 263, 279, 293
private, 137, 145, 153, 216, 257, *see also* Private entities
public, 150, 188, 216
superdominant, 28, 204–209, 211
US model of sport, 38, 40–41, 50, 277, *see also* American model of sport

W

White Paper on Sport, 11, 19–20, 22, 33–34, 36, 50, 116, 195, 249–250, 279, 281, 294, 302
World Cup, 3–4, 24, 37, 39, 63–66, 94, 111, 135, 169, 172, 207, 245–246, 250
World Series Cricket, 288–289

MIX
Papier aus verantwortungsvollen Quellen
Paper from responsible sources
FSC® C105338

If you have any concerns about our products,
you can contact us on
ProductSafety@springernature.com

In case Publisher is established outside the EU,
the EU authorized representative is:
Springer Nature Customer Service Center GmbH
Europaplatz 3, 69115 Heidelberg, Germany

Printed by Libri Plureos GmbH
in Hamburg, Germany